LIBRARY OF NEW TESTAMENT STUDIES

669

Formerly the Journal for the Study of the New Testament Supplement series

Editor
Chris Keith

Editorial Board
Dale C. Allison, Lynn H. Cohick, R. Alan Culpepper, Craig A. Evans, Jennifer Eyl,
Robert Fowler, Simon J. Gathercole, Juan Hernández Jr., John S. Kloppenborg,
Michael Labahn, Matthew V. Novenson, Love L. Sechrest, Robert Wall,
Catrin H. Williams, Brittany E. Wilson

The Formal Education of the Author of Luke-Acts

Steve Reece

LONDON • NEW YORK • OXFORD • NEW DELHI • SYDNEY

T&T CLARK
Bloomsbury Publishing Plc
50 Bedford Square, London, WC1B 3DP, UK
1385 Broadway, New York, NY 10018, USA
29 Earlsfort Terrace, Dublin 2, Ireland

BLOOMSBURY, T&T CLARK and the T&T Clark logo are trademarks of
Bloomsbury Publishing Plc

First published in Great Britain 2022
Paperback edition published 2024

Copyright © Steve Reece, 2022

Steve Reece has asserted his right under the Copyright, Designs and Patents Act,
1988, to be identified as Author of this work.

All rights reserved. No part of this publication may be reproduced or transmitted
in any form or by any means, electronic or mechanical, including photocopying,
recording, or any information storage or retrieval system, without prior permission
in writing from the publishers.

Bloomsbury Publishing Plc does not have any control over, or responsibility for,
any third-party websites referred to or in this book. All internet addresses given in
this book were correct at the time of going to press. The author and publisher regret
any inconvenience caused if addresses have changed or sites have ceased to exist,
but can accept no responsibility for any such changes.

A catalogue record for this book is available from the British Library.

Library of Congress Cataloging-in-Publication Data

Names: Reece, Steve, 1959– author.
Title: The formal education of the author of Luke-Acts / Steve Reece.
Description: London ; New York : T&T Clark, 2022. | Series: Library of New Testament
studies, 2513-8790 ; 669 | Includes bibliographical references and index. | Summary: "Steve
Reece argues that the author of Luke-Acts was aware of many literary works that formed a
part of basic Hellenistic literate education, and makes his case by proving that many Greek
authors were well known (from papyrological and citational data) at the likely time of Luke's
composition. By focusing solely upon Luke–Acts, Reece is able to explore the evident
Hellenistic education of the author, including the content of the curriculum, and the
papyrological evidence of school exercises, his potential familiarity with Greek authors, and
the influence of each of these major authors upon his work"– Provided by publisher.
Identifiers: LCCN 2022009929 (print) | LCCN 2022009930 (ebook) |
ISBN 9780567705884 (hardback) | ISBN 9780567705921 (paperback) |
ISBN 9780567705891 (pdf) | ISBN 9780567705914 (epub)
Subjects: LCSH: Luke, Saint–Knowledge and learning. | Bible. Luke–Criticism,
interpretation, etc. | Bible. Acts–Criticism, interpretation, etc.
Classification: LCC BS2465 .R44 2022 (print) |
LCC BS2465 (ebook) | DDC 226.4/06—dc23/eng/20220503
LC record available at https://lccn.loc.gov/2022009929
LC ebook record available at https://lccn.loc.gov/2022009930

ISBN: HB: 978-0-5677-0588-4
PB: 978-0-5677-0592-1
ePDF: 978-0-5677-0589-1
ePUB: 978-0-5677-0591-4

Series: Library of New Testament Studies, volume 669
ISSN 2513-8790

Typeset by RefineCatch Limited, Bungay, Suffolk

To find out more about our authors and books visit www.bloomsbury.com
and sign up for our newsletters.

On the day that I placed the finishing touches on my last monograph in the field of Classical studies, Homer's Winged Words, *an investigation of the etymologies of prehistoric words and phrases that appear in early Greek epic, it occurred to me that after having labored daily for almost ten years on that "baby" I might very well suffer some sort of "postpartum blues." But my wife Rhonda wisely advised me that an effective antidote against postpartum blues is to begin thinking about another baby! I immediately began preliminary work on a new project about the Classical and Hellenistic literary influences on the writers of the New Testament, especially the writers of the Pauline epistles and Luke-Acts, a topic that had been percolating in the back of my mind already for some time. For her wise and timely advice, among a host of other gifts, I dedicate this work,* The Formal Education of the Author of Luke-Acts, *to Rhonda Carol Reece, my wife of forty years, with thanks for the assurance that we can continue to have "babies" long after we have become "empty nesters."*

Contents

List of Figures and Table		viii
Preface		x
1	Introduction to the Project	1
2	The Author of Luke-Acts	15
3	The Education of the Author of Luke-Acts	29
4	What Greek Authors would Luke have Known?	51
5	Luke and Homer	87
6	Luke and Aesop	119
7	Luke and Epimenides and Aratus (Acts 17:23, 28a, and 28b)	147
8	Luke and Euripides—Part One: How Did Luke Know the Dramas of Euripides?	171
9	Luke and Euripides—Part Two: Thematic and Verbal Echoes of Euripides' *Bacchae* in the Acts of the Apostles	187
10	Luke and Plato	209
	Appendix I: Earliest Known Manuscript of the Gospel of Luke	231
	Appendix II: Latin Literary Texts Preserved on Documents Contemporary with Luke	233
	Bibliography	237
	Index of Modern Authors	259
	Index of Ancient Passages	265

Figures

1 Colophon appended to an ancient Greek school text (*P.Bouriant* 1 = *P.Sorbonne* inv. 826 leaf 11 recto). Courtesy of the Institut de Papyrologie de la Sorbonne.   xi

2 A school exercise on a wooden writing tablet with an iambic trimeter *sententia* of the comic poet Menander (*T.Louvre* inv. AF 1195). Courtesy of the Musée du Louvre, Département des Antiquités égyptiennes.   35

3 A school exercise on a waxed writing tablet with two verses of the comic poet Menander (British Library Manuscripts accession number Add MS 34186(1)). Courtesy of the British Library Board.   36

4 Multiplication tables written in the hand of a teacher along with five personal names divided into syllables written in the hand of a student (British Library Manuscripts accession number Add MS 34186(2)). Courtesy of the British Library Board.   37

5 Syllabary for primary-level students (O. Guéraud and P. Jouguet, Plate I). Courtesy of the Egyptian Museum in Cairo and the Institut français d'Archéologie orientale du Caire.   38

6 Names of mythic heroes divided into syllables (O. Guéraud and P. Jouguet, Plate III). Courtesy of the Egyptian Museum in Cairo and the Institut français d'Archéologie orientale du Caire.   39

7 A passage of Euripides' *Ino* with the verses divided into syllables by spaces and colons, followed by a passage of Homer's *Odyssey* with no paedagogical devices (O. Guéraud and P. Jouguet, Plate IV). Courtesy of the Egyptian Museum in Cairo and the Institut français d'Archéologie orientale du Caire.   40

8 Mathematical exercises (O. Guéraud and P. Jouguet, Plate X). Courtesy of the Egyptian Museum in Cairo and the Institut français d'Archéologie orientale du Caire.   42

9 Section of *P.Bouriant* 1 (= *P.Sorbonne* inv. 826 leaf 1 recto) listing one-syllable words in alphabetical order. Courtesy of the Institut de Papyrologie de la Sorbonne.   43

10 Section of *P.Bouriant* 1 (= *P.Sorbonne* inv. 826 leaf 7 verso) listing twenty-four *gnomai* in alphabetical order of a type associated with

the comic poet Menander. Courtesy of the Institut de Papyrologie de la
Sorbonne. 44

11 A bilingual Greek-Latin thematic glossary of terms associated with the
sky, stars, and winds (*P.Oxyrhynchus* 78.5162). Courtesy of the Egypt
Exploration Society, London, and the Imaging Papyri Project, University
of Oxford. 48

12 Earliest known manuscript of the Gospel of Luke (P75 = *P.Bodmer*
XIV (Luke)–XV (John) = *Hanna Papyrus* 1). Courtesy of the
Biblioteca Apostolica Vaticana. 231

Table

1 Literary works and school texts on the Egyptian papyri. 61

Preface

The emperor Julian ("the Apostate") once proclaimed sardonically that Christian teachers who do not believe in the Greek gods should cease teaching the Classics—Homer, Hesiod, Demosthenes, Herodotus, Thucydides, Isocrates, and Lysias—and instead go off to their Galilean churches and expound on Matthew and Luke (*Epistulae* 61c in J. Bidez's *Les Belles Lettres* edition). I am a Christian teacher of the Classics who does not believe in the Greek gods, and I intend, even more than sixteen centuries later, to abide by the emperor's proclamation. But, perhaps to the emperor's dismay, I shall be expounding on the New Testament by viewing it against the literary backdrop of these very Classical predecessors.

I was trained as a Classical philologist, with specialization in Greek linguistics and literature, and my research has resided largely in those fields. I have from time to time ventured into the world of New Testament Studies—a monograph on Paul's letter-writing techniques, some articles on textual and philological matters—but I remain fully aware of the perils of wandering too far outside one's comfort zone. I shall no doubt on occasion display my naiveté and even—though hopefully not too often—my ignorance of areas already well trodden by specialists in the New Testament. I am reminded of the cautionary words of the Classicist and ancient historian A. N. Sherwin-White, who once remarked in an introduction to his Sarum Lectures on Roman society and law in the New Testament that scholars attempting to deal with two worlds of the magnitude of Roman History and New Testament Studies need two lives, and even so they risk appearing as amateurs in each other's field. I hope that my deficit in New Testament Studies will be compensated for with the asset of being able to provide the perspective of a Classical philologist and specialist in the very Classical and Hellenistic literature with which I believe some of the writers of the New Testament were more than casually familiar.

Luke was a complicated person living in a complex time. He can be—and should be—viewed from many different angles. Readers of this work may object that I do not offer a balanced view of Luke, inasmuch as I do not counterbalance my claims of Classical and Hellenistic influence with the obviously more powerful influence of his Jewish heritage and cultural background. But it is not my purpose to offer a balanced view of Luke or to present a comprehensive interpretation of Luke within his broad historical and cultural context. Rather it is my purpose to display Luke's acquaintance with certain elements of Classical and Hellenistic literature, an acquaintance that was acquired largely, I believe, by his experience of a typical Greek educational curriculum as a youth but also, surely, by his personal contact with the Hellenistic and Roman world during his adult life. We all tend to understand Luke through a lens that is familiar to us. My lens is the Greco-Roman paganism in which I was trained; someone else's lens will be Hellenistic Judaism—in which case Luke will appear somewhat different.

It has been useful, indeed necessary, in what follows to include many quotations from Greek and Latin texts and documents, but in every case I have provided a very literal English translation. These translations with very few exceptions are my own, and they are offered here for the sake of clarity, not—as any reader will immediately perceive—because I have any literary or poetic aspirations.

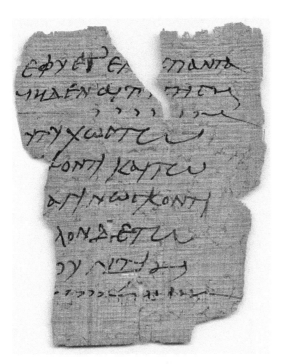

Figure 1 Colophon appended to an ancient Greek school text (*P.Bouriant* 1 = *P.Sorbonne* inv. 826 leaf 11 recto). Courtesy of the Institut de Papyrologie de la Sorbonne.

ɔ ɔ ɔ ɔ ɔ ɔ ɔ

εὐτυχῶς τῷ
ἔχοντι καὶ τῷ
ἀναγινώσκοντι
μᾶλλον δὲ τῷ
νοοῦντι

ɔ ɔ ɔ ɔ ɔ ɔ ɔ ɔ ɔ ɔ ɔ

ɔ ɔ ɔ ɔ ɔ ɔ ɔ

Blessings on the one
holding (this book),
and on the one reading it,
and, especially, on the one
understanding it.

ɔ ɔ ɔ ɔ ɔ ɔ ɔ ɔ ɔ ɔ ɔ

1

Introduction to the Project

"What does Athens have to do with Jerusalem?" asks Tertullian, the second- to third-century Christian apologist from Carthage, "What does the Academy have to do with the Church? What do Heretics have to do with Christians?"[1] Or, as Jerome, picking up on Tertullian's train of thought, asks in a letter toward the end of the fourth century: "What has Horace to do with the Psalter? Vergil with the Gospels? Cicero with the Apostle?"[2]

"Quite a lot," a modern New Testament scholar may very well respond, much to Tertullian and Jerome's surprise. Or at least one could surmise such a response from the titles of several recent monographs and essays on the influence of Classical and Hellenistic Greek literature upon the writers of the New Testament: e.g., *The Gospels and Homer: Imitations of Greek Epic in Mark and Luke-Acts*; *Dialogue and Drama: Elements of Greek Tragedy in the Fourth Gospel*; *What are the Gospels? A Comparison with Graeco-Roman Biography*; *Paul and the Greco-Roman Philosophical Tradition*; *Ancient Letters and the New Testament: A Guide to Context and Exegesis*.[3] Works such as these maintain that the New Testament writers were living in a cultural milieu heavily influenced by Classical and Hellenistic Greek literature: the gospel writers were influenced by the genres of Greek epic, drama, and biography; the author of Acts was trying in his prologue to position his work within the tradition of Greek historiography, while his narrative was drawing readily upon motifs commonly used in the newly popular genre of the Greek novel; the formal structure of Paul's letters can best be recognized through the lens of the ancient Greek and Roman epistolary genre, while his argumentation relies upon the dialectical methods of Greek philosophy and the rhetorical strategies of Greek oratory. In short, the writers of the New Testament appear to have regarded Hellenism as rather more appealing than appalling.

---

[1] Tertullian, *De praescriptione haereticorum* 7: quid ergo Athenis et Hierosolymis? quid academiae et ecclesiae? quid haereticis et Christianis? Further expansion on the topic can be found in *Apologeticus pro Christianis* 47.

[2] Jerome, *Epistulae* 22.29.7: quid facit cum psalterio Horatius? cum evangeliis Maro? cum apostolo Cicero?

[3] D. R. Macdonald, *The Gospels and Homer: Imitations of Greek Epic in Mark and Luke-Acts* (Lanham: Rowman & Littlefield, 2015); J.-A. A. Brant, *Dialogue and Drama: Elements of Greek Tragedy in the Fourth Gospel* (Peabody: Hendrickson, 2004); R. A. Burridge, *What are the Gospels? A Comparison with Graeco-Roman Biography*, 3rd ed. (Waco: Baylor University Press, 2018); J. R. Dodson and A. W. Pitts, eds., *Paul and the Greco-Roman Philosophical Tradition* (London: Bloomsbury T&T Clark, 2017); H.-J. Klauck, *Ancient Letters and the New Testament: A Guide to Context and Exegesis* (Waco: Baylor University Press, 2006).

2   *The Formal Education of the Author of Luke-Acts*

But another modern New Testament scholar may answer Tertullian and Jerome's questions more sympathetically: that the New Testament writers were immersed in Jewish thinking, steeped in the Hebrew Scripture, and antipathetic toward pagan Hellenistic ideas, even if they happened to be accessible. Hence such recent monograph titles as *The Semitic Background of the New Testament*; *Das Alte Testament bei Lukas*; *The Book of Acts in Its Palestinian Setting*; *The Conversion of the Imagination: Paul as Interpreter of Israel's Scripture*; *Paul the Jew: Rereading the Apostle as a Figure of Second Temple Judaism*.[4] Many of these scholars are less eager than their philhellenic colleagues and, incidentally, even than their ancient Rabbinic predecessors, to allow "Japheth to dwell in the tents of Shem" (Gen. 9:27).[5]

The pendulum has swung back and forth for some time, and for many decades the most extreme swings of the pendulum have occurred in scholarship on Paul's letters. About a hundred years ago the pendulum had swung far in the direction of Hellenistic influence, especially among German scholars of the *religionsgeschichtliche Schule*, some of whom had been trained as Classical scholars and were therefore keen to examine early Christianity within its Greco-Roman cultural context.[6] Since that time, however, along with the discovery and publication of the Dead Sea Scrolls and the Nag Hammadi library, the closer attention to apocryphal and pseudepigraphical literature, and the greater appreciation of early Jewish mysticism, Jewish and Christian scholars in particular have focused renewed attention on the Jewishness of Paul, as well as of other New Testament writers.[7] An easy, though not entirely satisfactory or complete, solution to the challenge of dramatic swings in the pendulum is simply to regard first-century Judaism as thoroughly Hellenistic in nature, i.e., to deconstruct the

---

[4] J. A. Fitzmyer, *The Semitic Background of the New Testament* (Grand Rapids: Eerdmans, 1997); D. Rusam, *Das Alte Testament bei Lukas* (Berlin: Walter de Gruyter, 2003); R. Bauckham, ed., *The Book of Acts in Its Palestinian Setting* (Grand Rapids: Eerdmans, 1995); R. B. Hays, *The Conversion of the Imagination: Paul as Interpreter of Israel's Scripture* (Grand Rapids: Eerdmans, 2005); G. Boccaccini and C. A. Segovia, eds., *Paul the Jew: Rereading the Apostle as a Figure of Second Temple Judaism* (Minneapolis: Fortress, 2016).

[5] This passage in Genesis was interpreted in the Rabbinic tradition to mean: "May the words of Japheth [i.e., the Greeks] dwell in the tents of Shem [i.e., the Jews]" (b. Meg. 9b; y. Meg. 1:11, 71b; Gen. Rab. 36:8).

[6] So, for example, J. Weiss, "Beiträge zur Paulinischen Rhetorik," in *Theologische Studien: Festschrift für Bernard Weiss*, eds. C. R. Gregory et al. (Göttingen: Vandenhoeck and Ruprecht, 1897), 165–247; R. Knopf, *Paulus* (Leipzig: Quelle & Meyer, 1909); J. Weiss, *Der erste Korintherbrief* (Göttingen: Vandenhoeck and Ruprecht, 1910); R. Bultmann, *Der Stil der paulinischen Predigt und die kynisch-stoische Diatribe* (Göttingen: E. A. Huth, 1910); A. Bonhöffer, *Epiktet und das Neue Testament* (Giessen: Töpelmann, 1911); P. Wendland, *Die urchristlichen Literaturformen* (Tübingen: Mohr Siebeck, 1912); E. Norden, *Agnostos Theos: Untersuchungen zur Formengeschichte religiöser Rede* (Leipzig: Teubner, 1913); H. Böhlig, *Die Geisteskultur von Tarsos im augusteischen Zeitalter mit Berücksichtigung der paulinischen Schriften* (Göttingen: Vandenhoeck and Ruprecht, 1913). For a synopsis of the trends in this movement, see R. Knopf, "Paul and Hellenism," *American Journal of Theology* 18 (1914): 497–520.

[7] So, for example, K. Stendahl, *Paul Among Jews and Gentiles* (Philadelphia: Fortress, 1976); E. P. Sanders, *Paul and Palestinian Judaism: A Comparison of Patterns of Religion* (Philadelphia: Fortress, 1977). The scholars of the so-called "new perspective" on Paul and Judaism (e.g., E. P. Sanders, H. Räisänen, J. D. G. Dunn, F. Thielman, N. T. Wright) are representative of this group. For a synopsis of the trends in this movement, see C. J. Roetzel, "Paul and the Law: Whence and Whither?" *Currents in Research: Biblical Studies* 3 (1995): 249–75.

dichotomy.[8] But this can be taken too far: obviously there remained a distinction between Jew and gentile, from the perspectives of both groups; and just as real was the tension between the more conservative and traditional Palestinian Judaism and the more Hellenized Judaism of the Diaspora.

The truth, as usual, probably lies somewhere in between the extreme swings of this pendulum. On the one hand, the New Testament writers were immersed in their Jewish way of thinking—the gospel writers in the long tradition of Jewish salvation history as preserved in the Hebrew Scripture, and Paul in the Rabbinic tradition in which he was trained. On the other hand, they were also immersed in Hellenistic Greek culture, and their lands were administered by Roman authorities. Greco-Roman agoras, theaters, stadiums, and baths were within a short walking distance of even the most provincial Jewish towns. The town of Gadara, for example, just south of the Sea of Galilee, where Jesus is said to have healed two demoniacs (Mt. 8:28-34), had already produced four distinguished Greek literary figures: the satirist Menippus, the anthologist Meleager, the philosopher Philodemus, and the rhetorician Theodorus (so Strabo 16.2.29). The Jewish historian Flavius Josephus—a contemporary of Luke, with whom he had much in common—mentions many Classical and Hellenistic Greek authors by name and even quotes several at length, among them: the epic poets Homer, Hesiod, and Choerilus; the philosophers Thales, Pythagoras, Anaxagoras, Zeno of Elea, Socrates, Plato, Aristotle, Theophrastus, Demetrius of Phaleron, Cleanthes, and Posidonius; and the historians Herodotus, Thucydides, Ephorus, Theopompus, Polybius, and Strabo. It does not seem beyond the pale to imagine the author of Luke-Acts—who was perhaps the only gentile among the writers of the books of the New Testament—browsing the texts of Classical and Hellenistic Greek authors in the libraries or bookshops of Philippi, Antioch, and even Jerusalem; nor does it seem beyond the pale to imagine Paul—who apparently enjoyed at least some level of formal Greek education—witnessing the performances of Classical or Hellenistic Greek dramas in the theaters of Corinth, Isthmia, and Caesarea. One can easily visualize Paul's entire entourage pausing to listen in on teachers of Greek philosophy or rhetoric lecturing to their students in the markets, gymnasia, and stoas of the many Hellenistic cities through which they passed.

Nonetheless, not a single Classical or Hellenistic Greek author is mentioned by name in the New Testament, and identifying Classical and Hellenistic Greek influence on a single passage, or in a specific episode, or even in the overall narrative structure of a New Testament work can be an elusive goal. Most arguments for Classical or Hellenistic Greek influence are posed in a manner such as this: "the claim of a rigorous historiographical method in the prologues to Luke and Acts appears to be influenced by Thucydides' description of historiographical method in the prologue to his *Peloponnesian Wars*"; "the narrative of Paul's departure from Miletus in Acts 20 is reminiscent of Hector's departure from Troy in *Iliad* 6"; "the description of Peter's

---

[8] So, for example, M. Smith, "Palestinian Judaism in the First Century," in *Israel: Its Role in Civilization*, ed. M. Davis (New York: Jewish Theological Seminary, 1956), 67–81; M. Hengel, *Judaism and Hellenism: Studies in their Encounter in Palestine during the Early Hellenistic Period Volume I* (Minneapolis: Fortress, 1974); J. J. Collins, *Between Athens and Jerusalem: Jewish Identity in the Hellenistic Diaspora* (New York: Crossroad, 1983).

4 *The Formal Education of the Author of Luke-Acts*

deliverance from prison in Acts 12 contains echoes of the account of the liberation of the women in Euripides' *Bacchae*." There are at least three inherent weaknesses in this approach. First, parallels of shared typological elements associated with a genre, or of shared narrative motifs and plot structures, are very impressionistic and subjective. Rarely do two scholars agree on the particulars of the presumed influences. Nor is there any consensus among scholars regarding the procedures that should be applied or the standards that need to be met to establish a genetic relationship in such comparisons. Second, many of the features in the New Testament that have been attributed to Classical or Hellenistic Greek influence can more readily, and often more convincingly, be attributed to Jewish sources, and to the Septuagint in particular. Third, the vast majority of Classical and Hellenistic literature, as well as of Jewish literature, that may have been available to the writers of the New Testament has not survived to our time. We need humbly to keep in mind that any parallels that we propose are based on a very small fraction of what was once a much larger corpus of available material. In short, while I sympathize with the general assumptions of those who see the New Testament writers drawing from the deep and nourishing well of Classical and Hellenistic Greek culture, I am not so sympathetic with their theoretical approaches or convinced by their particular arguments. I would like to see something more tangible than the iteration of generic features or of common motifs and plot structures—ideally some signs of clear and direct verbal dependence on specific Classical or Hellenistic Greek authors. If a New Testament writer were to allude clearly and directly to a passage from a Greek novelist or biographer or to lift a phrase from a Greek historian or philosopher or to quote a snippet of a dialogue from a Greek dramatist or epic poet, then an argument for Classical or Hellenistic Greek influence, at least at some level, would become undeniable. It has been in search of such quotations and close verbal allusions that I have devoted a good deal of time and effort over the past several years. In short, I have combed through the entire New Testament for verbatim quotations, looser verbal allusions in word combinations, and even metrical patterns that may go back directly or indirectly to Classical and Hellenistic literature. I have done this in the hope of adding to the small corpus of New Testament material clearly attributable to Classical and Hellenistic Greek sources and also in the hope of asking, and perhaps answering, questions about what purpose the New Testament writers had in drawing from this deep well and what reaction they may have elicited from their audiences.

I first had the pleasure of studying the Acts of the Apostles in Greek as a nineteen-year-old Classics major in college. When I came to Paul's speech to the Athenians on the Areopagus, I was surprised to discover him quoting a verse from the *Phaenomena* by the third-century BCE Cilician astronomer and poet Aratus. But there it was, in black and white, the first half of a dactylic hexameter verse embedded in Paul's speech (Acts 17:28): Τοῦ γὰρ καὶ γένος ἐσμέν (- - / - ‿ ‿ / - ‿) "For we too are his offspring." The only difference was that Paul had substituted the metrically equivalent prosaic form ἐσμέν "we are" for Aratus's epic form εἰμέν. I was very pleased by this discovery, as it bridged my academic and religious worlds: a Classics major studying ancient Greek literature who has been steeped in a church tradition that resounded with the Hebrew and Christian Scripture. I found it utterly intriguing that in introducing the Jewish and Christian god to the Athenians Paul would choose to draw upon a pagan hymn to

Introduction to the Project 5

Zeus. It did not occur to me at the time to consider whether Paul himself had actually quoted Aratus or whether the author of Acts had placed the quotation in the mouth of his hero.[9] Before long I discovered that there were more and that the early Church Fathers had been aware all along of Paul's practice of quoting Classical and Hellenistic poets.[10] In his first letter to the Corinthians Paul warns his audience against false beliefs about the afterlife by quoting a full iambic trimeter verse attributed by the Church Fathers both to the fifth-century BCE Athenian tragedian Euripides and also to the fourth-century BCE Athenian comedian Menander (1 Cor. 15:33): Φθείρουσιν ἤθη χρηστὰ ὁμιλίαι κακαί (- - ᴗ - / - - - ᴗ - / ᴗ - ᴗ -) "Evil communications corrupt good manners." The metrical pattern of the verse had been slightly effaced when either Paul himself or his amanuensis—or the scribes who later copied the text—chose not to observe a minor euphonic nicety required by the poetic meter: the elision of the final vowel of χρηστὰ and the consequent aspiration of its final consonant, i.e., χρήσθ'.[11]

---

[9] I was to learn later that many modern commentators had attributed Paul's quotation in Acts 17:28 to the Stoic philosopher Cleanthes, who composed a *Hymn to Zeus* whose fourth verse apparently began with a similar phrase. But Cleanthes' hymn has survived only as a quotation in a single manuscript (Codex Farnesinus III D 15) of the fifth-century CE *Anthology* of Stobaeus (1.1.12), where the verse does not scan properly, and where the meaning is unclear. The original form of the fourth verse of Cleanthes' hymn remains indeterminable—ἐκ σοῦ γὰρ γένος ἐσμέν? ἐκ σοῦ γὰρ γένος εἶσ? ἐκ σοῦ γὰρ γενόμεσθα/γενόμεσθ'?—but, whatever it was, it was not identical to Paul's quotation in Acts 17:28, which is clearly drawn from the fifth verse of Aratus's *Phaenomena*, with which it is identical (save for the substitution of ἐσμέν for Aratus's εἰμέν). Ancient commentators on Acts from as early as Clement and Origen are unanimous in attributing the quotation to Aratus, while no one in antiquity ever suggested any connection with Cleanthes.

[10] Clement of Alexandria (second century CE), *Stromata* 1.14.59 and 1.19.91, attributes Titus 1:12 to Epimenides, 1 Corinthians 15:33 to Euripides, presumably (ἰαμβείῳ συγκέχρηται τραγικῷ "he has used a tragic iambic verse"), and Acts 17:28 to Aratus's *Phaenomena*. Jerome (fourth century CE), *Epistulae* 70.2, attributes Titus 1:12 to Epimenides (but notes that the verse is later quoted by Callimachus), 1 Corinthians 15:33 to Menander, and Acts 17:28 to Aratus. The church historian Socrates Scholasticus (fourth to fifth century CE), *Historia ecclesiastica* 3.16.24–6, attributes Titus 1:12 to Epimenides, 1 Corinthians 15:33 to Euripides, and Acts 17:28 to Aratus's *Phaenomena*.

[11] I was surprised at the time to observe how confidently my United Bible Societies' *Greek New Testament* ascribed this verse to Menander's lost comedy *Thais*, and I learned later that many New Testament editors and commentators followed suit, apparently not realizing that the verse very likely appeared earlier in a Euripidean tragedy: the beginning of the verse can be found among some extracts of Euripidean verses on the very fragmentary late third-century BCE papyrus *P.Hib.* 1.7 (see B. P. Grenfell and A. S. Hunt, *The Hibeh Papyri: Part I* (London: Egypt Exploration Society, 1906), 35–9). Of course this does not exclude the possibility that Menander, who drew upon Euripidean verses regularly, incorporated this tragic verse into a comedy, though not necessarily the *Thais*. In fact the evidence for attributing the verse specifically to Menander's *Thais* is rather slim. The practice seems to have arisen from a single comment by the 16th-century French scholar H. Estienne that he recalled once seeing in a New Testament manuscript that his father R. Estienne was collating a note in the margin of the text of 1 Corinthians 15:33 reading Μενάνδρου τοῦ κωμικοῦ γνώμη ἐν Θαδία "a proverb in the *Thadia* of the comic poet Menander," which he assumed should be emended as Θαΐδι "*Thais*" (so H. Estienne, *Comicorum Graecorum Sententiae* (Geneva: Henricus Stephanus, 1569), 351–2). Yet this purported marginal note in Estienne's Greek New Testament manuscript, which has since been lost, does not appear to have been an utter eccentricity: J. G. Cook has recently called attention to a marginal note in another Greek New Testament manuscript from the 11th century (Vat. gr. 1650), as well as to some marginalia in three Syriac versions of the so-called "Euthalian Apparatus" (noted earlier in the old *Wettstein*), that also ascribe the verse to Menander's *Thais*: J. G. Cook, "1 Cor 15:33: The Status Quaestionis," *Novum Testamentum* 62 (2020): 375–91.

6   *The Formal Education of the Author of Luke-Acts*

Again, in his letter to Titus Paul warns his addressee about the bad character of his fellow Cretans by quoting a full dactylic hexameter verse that the Church Fathers attributed both to the seventh- to sixth-century BCE Cretan prophet and poet Epimenides and also to the third-century BCE Alexandrian scholar and poet Callimachus (Tit. 1:12): Κρῆτες ἀεὶ ψεῦσται, κακὰ θηρία, γαστέρες ἀργαί (- ˘ ˘ / - - / - ˘ ˘ / - ˘ ˘ / - ˘ ˘ / - ˵) "The Cretans are always liars, evil beasts, lazy bellies." Paul himself clearly regarded Epimenides as the original source of the verse, as he refers to the author as "one of their own prophets." The first part of Epimenides' verse was later quoted by Callimachus in his famous hymn to Zeus. When I considered together Paul's quotes from Aratus in Acts and from Epimenides/Callimachus in Titus, it struck me that Paul must have had a penchant for Hellenistic hymns to Zeus. I was not aware at the time of any controversy over the Pauline authorship of Titus.

Another feature that struck me about the three Pauline passages in which these ancient verses are embedded was that in no case was the poetic source actually named: Acts 17:28 is attributed to "some of their poets"; Titus 1:12 is attributed to "one of their own prophets"; 1 Corinthians 15:33 is simply stitched into the text and is not attributed to anyone. I was to discover later that this is no different from the attribution practices of many ancient writers, but it struck me at the time, as an aspiring academic, as a rather cavalier attitude toward attribution, and it occurred to me that there might be other quotations from Classical and Hellenistic Greek literature residing inconspicuously in the New Testament narrative, stitched seamlessly into the text, without attribution, in fact without any external cue that something is being quoted. I listed these three quotations dutifully on the blank pages at the back of my United Bible Societies' *Greek New Testament* and made a note to myself to look further into the matter someday.

A BA, MA, and PhD in Classics later, as well as a thirty-year career as a professor and researcher of ancient Greek literature, I returned one day to that note that I had jotted down as a teenager in the back of my Greek New Testament. Since that time I had taught almost every genre of Greek literature, including the New Testament, I had published three books and three dozen articles on various aspects of Greek literature and philology, and I had familiarized myself with at least the fundamentals of the discipline of New Testament Studies. How was I to proceed? I decided first of all that I should read through the entire New Testament very carefully in Greek, marking down those passages that struck me as possibly drawn from Classical and Hellenist Greek sources. In some cases a sentence or phrase reminded me of a particular passage from Classical or Hellenistic Greek literature with which I was familiar. In some cases a sentence or phrase appeared to strike an aphoristic tone and at the same time seemed ancient in its content and sentiment. In some cases a sentence or phrase, again aphoristic in tone, appeared to retain a metrical shape that was commonly used among ancient poets: mostly iambic, trochaic, or dactylic.

I also had several rich resources and sharp tools at my disposal that I had not had forty years earlier. First, the earliest reconstructible form of the text of the New Testament had become increasingly clear, owing to the work of several generations of textual critics—so clear, in fact, that the editors of the rival scholarly editions of the New Testament had finally agreed on a single text: the third (and later) edition of the

Introduction to the Project 7

United Bible Societies' *Greek New Testament* had become the same as the twenty-sixth (and later) edition of Nestle-Aland's *Novum Testamentum Graece*. It goes without saying that for the project I proposed it was of paramount importance to work with as early a text as could be reconstructed and not with later additions to, and reformations of, that text, interesting though they might be.

Second, ancient Greek literary texts had continued to be discovered, edited, and made available to the public both as published texts and in digital repositories. In the early 1990s, for example, a papyrus roll was discovered in the wrappings of an Egyptian mummy dating to about 180 BCE containing 112 poems of the Hellenistic poet Posidippus, only two of which had been previously known.[12] New texts of such well-known poets as Sappho, Simonides, and Menander, among many others less well-known, had also been discovered in recent years. Some legible texts from the dusty basements of European libraries, though discovered long ago, had only recently become accessible, such as the 839 unpublished Oxyrhynchus papyri of Homer that had been lying in storage in the Ashmolean Museum in Oxford for the previous century. Some papyrological texts that had until recently been illegible were, for the first time, able to be read with the help of new technologies such as the multispectral imaging techniques developed by NASA; these included new texts of Hesiod, Archilochus, Sophocles, Euripides, Parthenius, and Lucian, the most remarkable recent discovery being a substantial portion of a previously unknown epic poem of the archaic poet Archilochus. Some previously inaccessible and illegible texts on papyrus rolls from Herculaneum that had been carbonized by the eruption of Mt. Vesuvius in 79 CE had recently been rendered readable by means of thermal imaging technologies and CT scans; these turned out to be mostly Epicurean philosophical treatises, the writings of Philodemus being especially well represented. About 500 of these carbonized papyrus rolls from Herculaneum had never been opened, but computer-assisted tomography, developed to view the interior of the human body, began to "unwind" these rolls virtually, thus avoiding the destruction caused by earlier techniques. Scholars close to these projects have estimated that over the next several years the surviving corpus of Classical and Hellenistic Greek literature may grow by as much as 20 percent. It does not seem implausible, then, that as the 400,000 papyrus fragments from Oxyrhynchus and the 1,000 carbonized rolls from the Villa of the Papyri in Herculaneum (as well as the many more rolls that are likely to be discovered should the excavation of the villa ever be allowed to continue), not to speak of the roughly one million additional papyrus fragments in over 1,400 collections throughout the world, continue to be read, studied, and published (and papyri continue to be unearthed in the sands of Egypt at a faster rate than previously discovered papyri are being published), it will be found that they contain some Classical and Hellenistic Greek literature that turns out to be the source of previously unrecognized quotations by New Testament writers.

---

[12] The poems were first published in G. Bastianini, C. Gallazzi, and C. Austin, eds., *Posidippo di Pella Epigrammi (P. Mil. Vogl. VIII 309)* (Milan: Edizioni Universitarie di Lettere Economia Diritto, 2001); they are more readily accessible in C. Austin and G. Bastianini, *Posidippi Pellaei quae supersunt omnia* (Milan: Edizioni Universitarie di Lettere Economia Diritto, 2002).

8 *The Formal Education of the Author of Luke-Acts*

Third, almost all surviving Greek literature had become easily accessible and searchable through electronic means. The richest database is the Thesaurus Linguae Graecae (TLG), housed at the University of California, Irvine, which contains virtually all Greek texts surviving from the period between Homer (eighth century BCE) and 600 CE—including, of course, all of the New Testament and other early Christian writings—and the majority of surviving works up to the fall of Byzantium in 1453 CE. The database currently contains 4,000 authors and 10,000 works, adding up to approximately 110 million words. The entire database can be searched electronically in a few seconds for strings of individual letters, for full words, or for combinations of words or word fragments. The TLG is complemented by quickly searchable databases of epigraphical and papyrological collections, such as the Packard Humanities Institute's (PHI) Searchable Greek Inscriptions, the Diccionario Griego-Español's (DGE) Concordance of Greek Inscriptions (CLAROS), the Heidelberger Gesamtverzeichnis der griechischen Papyrusurkunden Ägyptens (HGV), the Duke Data Bank of Documentary Papyri (DDBDP), the Advanced Papyrological Information System (APIS), the Mertens-Pack Online Database, known as Mertens-Pack³ (M-P³), created by the Centre de Documentation de Papyrologie Littéraire (CEDOPAL), the Leuven Database of Ancient Books (LDAB), the Catalogue of Paraliterary Papyri (CPP), the PapyrusPortal, designed to connect all German collections of papyri, and Oxyrhynchus Online (POxy). Many of these epigraphical and papyrological resources are linked on Trismegistos, an interdisciplinary portal of papyrological and epigraphical resources primarily dealing with Egypt and the Nile valley between 800 BCE and 800 CE (www.trismegistos.org). These resources are also linked by a customized search engine called the Papyrological Navigator (PN) (https://papyri.info). It is now possible to conduct comprehensive searches of words and phrases that appear throughout the entire history of Greek writing in a few minutes—searches that forty years ago would have taken many months to complete.

With the development of such large electronic databases and powerful search engines, parallels between the New Testament and other Greek literature have become increasingly easy to identify. This has led to some very ambitious projects such as the *Corpus Hellenisticum Novi Testamenti* and the *Neuer Wettstein*. The international research project *Corpus Hellenisticum Novi Testamenti*, conceived in 1910 for the purpose of collating and arranging material from Greek and Latin texts that could be useful for interpreting and understanding the New Testament, has produced many papers, articles, and monographs as a series of intermediary steps intended to lead eventually to a complete *Neuer Wettstein*, an updated and expanded version of Johan Jakob Wettstein's 1751–1752 critical edition of the New Testament, with its commentary of 30,000 parallel passages from ancient Hebrew, Greek, and Latin texts.[13] This *Neuer*

---

[13] J. J. Wettstein, *Η ΚΑΙΝΗ ΔΙΑΘΗΚΗ, Novum Testamentum Graecum editionis receptae cum lectionibus variantibus codicum MSS., editionum aliarum, versionum et Patrum, nec non commentario pleniore ex scriptoribus veteribus Hebraeis, Graecis et Latinis Historiam et vim verborum illustrante opera et studio Joannis Jacobi Wetstenii,* vols. 1–2 (Amsterdam: Dommeriana, 1751–1752).

Introduction to the Project 9

Wettstein is now almost complete, though it still lacks the very volumes most pertinent to the present topic on the Gospel of Luke and the Acts of the Apostles.[14] Therefore, using both my intuition and my familiarity with Classical and Hellenistic Greek literary texts, I first read carefully through the entire New Testament in Greek, taking note of all the manuscript variants catalogued in the *apparatus critici* of the most recent editions of the United Bible Societies and Nestle-Aland and collecting those passages that struck me as possibly drawn from Classical and Hellenist Greek sources. Then I subjected this collection, which amounted to several hundred passages, to further scrutiny, using the various new tools at my disposal. Did the passage occur in any of the thousands of texts from the archaic to the Byzantine periods with which I was not intimately familiar but which were now easily searchable through electronic means? Did the passage occur in any of the newly discovered, and largely unpublished, ancient texts, including those that have survived only among the papyri? Did the passage occur in a different form, perhaps one closer to an ancient comparand, either as a textual variant or in a quotation of a later Church Father?

The result was that in some cases a phrase or sentence in the New Testament proved to be identical, or nearly identical, to one in a Classical or Hellenistic Greek text that has been preserved in the manuscript tradition. In some cases a phrase or sentence in the New Testament proved to be identical, or nearly identical, to an ancient passage preserved not through the manuscript tradition but rather in a later Byzantine commentary or lexicographical work. And in some cases a phrase or sentence in the New Testament, usually aphoristic in tone, appeared to retain the metrical shape, word order, or style of an ancient poetic passage but one that I could not find in the surviving corpus of Greek texts of any kind. But given that most Greek texts from antiquity have not survived (probably over 90 percent), it seemed reasonable at least to take note of such New Testament passages as possibly drawn from Classical or Hellenistic Greek sources. I offer an example from each of these categories.

---

[14] G. Strecker, U. Schnelle, and G. Seelig, eds., *Neuer Wettstein: Texte zum Neuen Testament aus Griechentum und Hellenismus* (II/1–2: *Texte zur Briefliteratur und zur Johannesapokalypse*) (Berlin: Walter de Gruyter, 1996); U. Schnelle, M. Labahn, and M. Lang, eds., *Neuer Wettstein: Texte zum Neuen Testament aus Griechentum und Hellenismus* (I/2: *Texte zum Johannesevangelium*) (Berlin: Walter de Gruyter, 2001); U. Schnelle, M. Lang, and M. Labahn, eds., *Neuer Wettstein: Texte zum Neuen Testament aus Griechentum und Hellenismus* (I/1.1: *Texte zum Markusevangelium*) (Berlin: Walter de Gruyter, 2008); U. Schnelle and M. Lang, eds., *Neuer Wettstein: Texte zum Neuen Testament aus Griechentum und Hellenismus* (I/1.2 (1): *Texte zum Matthäusevangelium: Matthäus 1–10*) (Berlin: Walter de Gruyter, 2013). I have not benefited from the *Corpus Hellenisticum Novi Testamenti* and the *Neuer Wettstein* in my own research as much as one might expect. Primarily, of course, this is because the volumes on Luke-Acts have not been published yet, and they are not expected to be published for at least two more years. But more fundamentally this is because the thousands of so-called parallels in vocabulary, phrases, sentiments, customs, institutions, or *realia* that have been marshaled from Greek and Roman texts from before, during, and after the period of the composition of the New Testament do not usually arise from any genetic relationship between any two texts, only from a shared language, shared practices and experiences, shared values, and a shared way of thinking—in sum, a shared *Zeitgeist*.

10   *The Formal Education of the Author of Luke-Acts*

1. Waxing eloquent in his final words of exhortation to the Galatians, Paul strings together several aphorisms (Gal. 6:1-10), including at 6:3:

εἰ γὰρ δοκεῖ τις εἶναί τι μηδὲν ὤν

"for if someone thinks that he is something, being nothing"

This is very close verbally to Plato's account of Socrates' famous last words at his trial to his accusers summarizing his wishes for his own sons (*Apol.* 41e):

καὶ ἐὰν δοκῶσί τι εἶναι μηδὲν ὄντες

"and if they think that they are something, being nothing"

The word choice and word order are nearly identical, the differences being the use of the singular rather than the plural and the use of εἰ plus indicative rather than ἐάν plus subjunctive in the protasis of the condition. Plato's *Apology*, and particularly this memorable passage from the end of Socrates' final speech, would of course have been well known even in the far reaches of the eastern Mediterranean.

2. An impassioned exhortation by Paul in his second letter to Timothy includes the claim (4:6):

Ἐγὼ γὰρ ἤδη σπένδομαι, καὶ ὁ καιρὸς τῆς ἀναλύσεώς μου ἐφέστηκεν.

"For I have already been poured out as a libation, and the time of my departure has come upon me."

When this verse first came to my attention, I noticed that the first half was metrical, composed of iambic feet. That, combined with its poetic tone, led me to suspect that it might be a quotation of dramatic verse. There came to mind Euripides' *Bacchae* 284, where the god Dionysus (as god of wine) is said "to be poured out as a libation to the gods, though a god himself" οὗτος θεοῖσι σπένδεται θεὸς γεγώς and where the verb σπένδεται occurs in the same metrical position in the iambic verse as σπένδομαι does in 2 Timothy 4:6. Next, from the Koine Greek prosaic form of the New Testament, I reconstructed a possible Attic Greek poetic model, with crasis and assimilation of the combination καί and ὁ, which is very common in dramatic verse, and with a possessive adjective instead of a genitive pronoun, and I was pleased to see that it could be scanned, with the exception of a flaw in the third foot, as a longer string of iambic feet, possibly even as an iambic tetrameter: Ἐγὼ γὰρ ἤδη σπένδομαι, χὠ καιρὸς τῆς ἐμῆς . . . (˘ – ˘ – / – – ˘ – / – – – – / ˘ – . . .).

My curiosity was further aroused when I discovered that Eusebius, John Chrysostom, and some other Church Fathers quoted the verse slightly differently from the way it appeared in the manuscripts of the New Testament—in fact in a way closer to my own reconstruction: Ἐγὼ γὰρ ἤδη σπένδομαι, καὶ ὁ καιρὸς τῆς ἐμῆς ἀναλύσεως ἐφέστηκεν. And, indeed, when I subjected my reconstructed form to an exhaustive search in the electronic databases of ancient Greek literature I discovered the fragmentary verse Ἐγὼ

Introduction to the Project

γὰρ ἤδη σπένδομαι, χὢ καιρὸς τῆς ἐμ ... listed as fragment 768 in the collection of *Fragmenta Incertorum Poetarum* in T. Kock's edition of *Comicorum Atticorum Fragmenta*.[15] Kock asserts that the words are clearly an iambic tetrameter verse drawn from either an old or a new comedy, but he observes that, in order for the verse to scan properly, a vowel must have followed καιρὸς.[16] Kock discovered this fragmentary verse in an eleventh-century codex from Oxford that contains several lexicographical works including an alphabetically arranged word list called ἘΠΙΜΕΡΙΣΜΟΙ ΚΑΤΑ ΣΤΟΙΧΕΙΟΝ ΓΡΑΦΙΚΑ.[17] Within the definitions of the words on the list are many quotations from Homer and from ancient drama, some identifiable, some not, including this one, under the heading Σφενδόνη. The lexicographer has wrongly associated the word σπένδομαι "I libate" with σφενδόνη "a sling," as though the phrase should mean "for I have already been slung." But in spite of this mistake the manuscript has apparently preserved a snatch of ancient poetry that seems to have been the source of the expression in 2 Timothy 4:6. The first four words of the iambic verse—ἐγὼ γὰρ ἤδη σπένδομαι—are also quoted in the ancient etymological dictionaries, the Etymologicum Gudianum (eleventh century) and the Etymologicum Magnum (twelfth century), under their entries for Σφενδόνη "sling."

3. Finally, I mention an aphorism attributed to Paul by the author of the Acts of the Apostles that appears to have been inspired by an earlier poetic source. According to Acts 27:34, after fourteen storm-tossed days at sea, Paul attempts to deliver an encouraging speech to the weary and hungry sailors:

οὐδενὸς γὰρ ὑμῶν θρὶξ ἀπὸ τῆς κεφαλῆς ἀπολεῖται

"for the hair of not one of you will be lost from your head"

This is clearly an aphoristic expression—we can compare καὶ θρὶξ ἐκ τῆς κεφαλῆς ὑμῶν οὐ μὴ ἀπόληται in Luke's gospel (21:18), which is uniquely Lucan among the synoptics— and it is well placed rhetorically at the end of Paul's exhortation. It is remarkable that if γάρ, a conjunction that simply connects this phrase syntactically to the previous clause in this particular context, is omitted, the line scans perfectly as a dactylic hexameter, even with a proper third-foot caesura and a regular dactylic fifth foot (- ⏑ ⏑ / - - / - ‖ - ⏑ / - ⏑ ⏑ / - ⏑ ⏑ / - ⏒). While I have found no extant source for this verse in its entirety, all the words that compose it occur individually in ancient dactylic hexameter poetry, and the four main words of the verse—οὐδενός, θρίξ, κεφαλῆς, and ἀπόλεῖται—are placed here in metrical positions in which they also appear in those extant verses. So while we cannot attribute this aphorism to a specific poetic source, I think we can say

---

[15] T. Kock, *Comicorum Atticorum Fragmenta* (Leipzig: Teubner, 1888), 3:543.

[16] The updated version of Kock's work by J. M. Edmonds, *The Fragments of Attic Comedy after Meineke, Bergk, and Kock* (Leiden: Brill, 1961), 3:467 (fr. 768K), simply refers the fragment to 2 Timothy 4:6, but simply observing a New Testament parallel that Kock apparently failed to notice does not prove that 2 Timothy 4:6 was the original source of the verse rather than being itself a quotation of a more ancient verse of poetry.

[17] This manuscript is published in J. A. Cramer, *Anecdota Graeca e Codd. Manuscriptis Bibliothecarum Oxoniensium* (Oxford: Typographeus Academicus, 1835), 2:331–426, where the verse appears on 408–9, with the text reading Ἐγὼ γὰρ ἤδη σπένδομαι, καὶ ὁ καιρὸς τῆς ἐμ' * *.

12   *The Formal Education of the Author of Luke-Acts*

with some measure of confidence that it has been inspired in some way by epic verse. It is entirely to be expected that the metrical shape of quotations of poetry would have become corrupted, effaced, even unrecognizable, during the manuscript transmission of the New Testament text, for Koine Greek did not differentiate accurately in pronunciation between long and short syllables (as attested in inscriptions and papyri from this period). Nor did the scribes of New Testament manuscripts regularly observe such poetic features as elision and crasis. Moreover, when metrical verses embedded in a prosaic text failed to be recognized as such, they were incorporated into the grammar and syntax of the prose, making them even less recognizable as quotations.

When I began my search for quotations of Classical and Hellenistic literature in the New Testament my first inclination was to concentrate on Paul, for I had first become interested in this topic when I encountered Paul's quotation of Aratus's *Phaenomena* in his speech to the Athenians in Acts 17, and then his quotation of Euripides and/or Menander in his first letter to the Corinthians, and finally his quotation of Epimenides and/or Callimachus in his letter to Titus. Further, I was discovering a number of other possible quotations in the corpus of letters in the New Testament that have traditionally been ascribed to Paul and also in Paul's speeches recorded in the Acts of the Apostles. Naturally, I began to search for everything that we know, or think we know, about Paul's youth, upbringing, and education in order to gauge his level of familiarity with Classical and Hellenistic Greek literature.

This was trickier than I anticipated since there are only a few details recorded in the New Testament about Paul's early life, and even about these few details there is an absence of clarity: whether, for example, Paul grew up in Tarsus or Jerusalem. The testimony of the Church Fathers was no help, as it is drawn for the most part simply from the text of the New Testament. Further, it became fairly clear to me that the letter to Titus, with its concentration on the proper conduct of the officers of the established church (πρεσβύτεροι, ἐπίσκοποι), was too late in the development of Christianity to have been written by Paul himself. Hence, it was someone other than Paul who saw fit to quote a verse of Epimenides and/or Callimachus in the letter to Titus. Most consequentially, I began to realize that Paul's speeches in Acts were probably largely Luke's creations rather than Paul's own words. That is to say, in his record of the speeches of Paul, Luke, who was absent from many if not all of them, was following the normal practice of ancient historians—Herodotus, Thucydides, Xenophon, Polybius, Dionysius of Halicarnassus, the authors of Maccabees, Josephus, Caesar, Sallust, Tacitus, and Livy—in giving only a general sense of what was said phrased in a way that seemed to him most appropriate for the speaker and for the occasion. In short, the quotation of Aratus in Acts 17, for example, is better attributed to Luke than to Paul.[18]

---

[18] On the Lucan origin of Paul's speeches in Acts, see the influential work of M. Dibelius, *Studies in the Acts of the Apostles* (New York: Charles Scribner's Sons, 1956), 26–77, 138–85. Dibelius argues that since the Lucan style of the narrative of Acts extends to the speeches, they are largely Luke's inventions, and he compares the common practice of inventing speeches among ancient historians. This view was already expressed in seminal form two centuries ago by J. G. Eichhorn, *Einleitung in das Neue Testament* (Leipzig: Weidmann, 1810), 33–43, and it has had strong scholarly support now for over a century. For a survey of scholarship on the issue, see M. L. Soards, *The Speeches in Acts: Their Content, Context, and Concerns* (Louisville: Westminster/John Knox Press, 1994), 1–17.

Introduction to the Project   13

Meanwhile, as I continued to peruse the New Testament slowly and carefully, syllable by syllable, marking and investigating combinations of words that appeared to me, a Classicist, as Classical or Hellenistic in nature, either in their meaning and sentiment, or in their verbal structure (meter, alliteration, clausulae, etc.), one thing was becoming increasingly clear, even as dozens of possibilities presented themselves: Paul's genuine letters were not as rich a repository of Classical and Hellenistic quotations as I had expected; nor were the gospels of Matthew, Mark, and John, where I found almost nothing; nor were the non-Pauline letters, where I found but a few possibilities; nor was Revelation. But the disappointment in my failure to detect a significant number of possible Classical and Hellenistic Greek quotations in these works was offset by the pleasure of discovering many excellent possibilities in the Gospel of Luke and the Acts of the Apostles. My further examination and consideration of these possibilities have resulted in the following study on the Classical and Hellenistic literary influences upon the author of the Gospel of Luke and the Acts of the Apostles—a literary heritage to which he gained access, I conclude, largely through the traditional Greek education that he enjoyed.

Now, a seasoned New Testament scholar will probably condescend: "that should have been no surprise"; "you could have saved yourself a lot of time and trouble by focusing on Luke-Acts to begin with"; "Luke, being the sole gentile author of the New Testament, would obviously be the most likely repository of Classical and Hellenistic literary quotations and allusions"; "after all, it has been recognized since the time of Jerome that 'among all the Evangelists Luke was most skilled in the Greek language' and that 'his language is very elegant in both of his volumes (the Gospel and Acts) and smacks of secular eloquence.'"[19] This may all be true, but I was gratified to have gone through the exercise and discovered it on my own. Sometimes the most convincing conclusions are those that you did not anticipate when you began your quest, in fact those whose very opposite you expected, for you can then be assured that the ever-present specter of prejudice and confirmation bias has played a lesser role in the process. In any case, I have come to the conclusion, already obvious to some, that of all the writers of the New Testament, the one most familiar with and most influenced by Classical and Hellenistic literary texts was the author of Luke-Acts.

---

[19] Jerome, *Epistula ad Damasum* (20.4): inter omnes euangelistas Graeci sermonis eruditissimus fuit; *Commentarium ad Esaiam* 3.6.9: sermo eius ... in utroque volumine comtior est, et saecularem redolet eloquentiam ...

2

The Author of Luke-Acts

In what follows, I shall be treating the author of the Gospel of Luke and the Acts of the Apostles as a historical person—and an interesting one at that—who lived in the eastern Mediterranean during the first and perhaps second centuries of our era.[1] I shall assume that this author was influenced by the unique political and cultural milieu of the time: he was familiar with the scriptures, religion, and theology of Judaism but had embraced a new religious movement called Christianity; he was well versed in the intricacies of Roman politics and government; and, most importantly for our purposes, he was a fluent Greek speaker and a proficient Greek writer, and like most writers of this period he likely attained these skills in his encounter as a youth with the traditional Greek educational system. None of this should be too controversial, but since the understanding of the author of these two works as a historical person is so critical to what follows I feel obligated as a preliminary step to lay out on the table what I shall assume concerning the authorship of these two works and what biographical details I believe can be reconstructed about that author.

Some Traditions about the Author
of Luke-Acts

The two works that we refer to today as the Gospel of Luke and the Acts of the Apostles are anonymous: there are references in neither work to the name of the

---

[1] For the sake of efficiency I shall use the name "Luke" to refer both to the title of the third gospel and to the author of the third gospel and the Acts of the Apostles. This does not necessarily indicate a commitment to the tradition that identifies this author with the Luke mentioned as a companion of Paul in Colossians 4:14, 2 Timothy 4:11, and Philemon 24.

16   *The Formal Education of the Author of Luke-Acts*

author.[2] Nor do we know the original titles of these works or even if they had titles.[3]

References elsewhere in the New Testament to someone named Luke, the name traditionally attached to the two works by at least as early as the mid-second century CE (see below), are few and brief. In the subscription to his letter to Philemon (23-5) the apostle Paul includes a simple greeting from his coworkers Epaphras, Mark, Aristarchus, Demas, and Luke. Toward the close of the second letter to Timothy (4:9-12) the sender states that his other comrades—Demas, Crescens, Titus, Mark, Tychicus—have gone elsewhere and that Luke alone remains with him. The final greetings at the end of the letter to the Colossians (4:10-14) offer somewhat more information. The sender seems to separate the greetings of Aristarchus, Mark, and Justus, who are "of the circumcision," from the greetings of Epaphras, Luke, and Demas, who, presumably, are not. More specifically, Luke is here called "the beloved physician." Hence arose the tradition that Luke was a gentile physician who served as a coworker of Paul.

If, along with many commentators since as early as the second century, we were to venture to identify this Luke with one of the "we" in the "we-passages" of Acts—those passages where the author shifts from third- to first-person narration (16:10-17; 20:5-15; 21:1-18; 27:1-28:16)—Luke would have been a companion of Paul at least from Troas to Philippi during the second missionary journey, from Philippi to Jerusalem during the third missionary journey, and from Caesarea to Rome during Paul's voyage as a prisoner to Rome.[4] If Philemon, as well as Colossians and 2 Timothy, all three of

---

[2]   An Armenian version of St. Ephraem's fourth-century Syriac commentary on Acts, which is based on an Old Syriac text of Acts, which, in turn, is based on a Greek version of the Western text of Acts that is almost identical with the text of the Codex Bezae, includes in the second "we" section in Acts 20:13 the phrase (in Armenian) "I, Luke, and those with me" (i.e., embarked on a ship and set out for Assos). That the Armenian translator found this phrase in Ephraem's Syriac commentary is almost certain; that Ephraem found this phrase in the actual Old Syriac text (rather than in a gloss) is less certain; that the Old Syriac text, if it contained the phrase, drew it from a Greek version of the Western text (as J. R. Harris proposed over a century ago in the April, 1913 issue of *The British Friend*) is very uncertain; that the Western text, if it contained the phrase, reflected the original reading of Acts here (as the unnamed editor of *The Expository Times* 24 (1913): 530-1 suggested soon after Harris's proposal) seems most unlikely. The Armenian version of Ephraem's commentary is translated into Latin by F. C. Conybeare, "The Commentary of Ephrem on Acts," in *The Beginnings of Christianity: The Acts of the Apostles*, eds. F. J. Foakes Jackson and K. Lake (London: MacMillan, 1926), 3:373-453 (see 442-5 for the passage under consideration here).

[3]   Papyrus 75 (= Papyrus Bodmer XIV-XV = *Hanna Papyrus* 1), possibly written as early as the late second or early third century, is one of the oldest surviving manuscripts of the third gospel. It does include at the end of its text of the gospel the title ΕΥΑΓΓΕΛΙΟΝ ΚΑΤΑ ΛΟΥΚΑΝ "Gospel according to Luke." The beginning of the Gospel of Luke is missing from this papyrus, but since the title of the Gospel of John, ΕΥΑΓΓΕΛΙΟΝ ΚΑΤΑ ΙΩΑΝΗΝ, which immediately follows on the papyrus, is included at its beginning, the same must have held true for the Gospel of Luke. For an illustration of this section of the papyrus, see Appendix I.

[4]   If we were to accept at face value the reading of Acts 11:28 preserved in codex Bezae, we would have another "we-passage," this one indicating that Luke was in Antioch, along with Barnabas and Paul, even before the first missionary journey. But this is probably a later addition to the text motivated by a very early tradition that already connected Luke with Antioch. Also, a Latin version quoted by Irenaeus (*Haer.* 3.14.1) apparently began the first "we-passage" slightly earlier, at 16:8 rather than 16:10, reading *nos venimus in Troadem* "we came to Troas" (all Greek manuscripts have a third-person verb here).

which mention Luke as accompanying the sender of the letter, was written from Rome, where Paul was imprisoned, then Luke apparently remained with Paul in Rome for some time after traveling with him from Caesarea. In short, if we were to identify Luke with the "we-passages" of Acts, we would have a Luke, author of the Gospel of Luke and the Acts of the Apostles, who knew Paul personally, traveled with him, and shared in his many travails. We would also have a Luke who spent quite a lot of time in Jerusalem and its environs, where he would have had the opportunity to gather material for his gospel—even from eyewitnesses of the events narrated in that gospel. Rome too could have provided a venue for the writing or completing of his two works. John Mark, to whom is traditionally ascribed the authorship of the Gospel of Mark, upon which the Gospel of Luke is clearly reliant, was in Rome at the same time as Luke according to the greetings in Philemon 24 and Colossians 4:10, 14, and, according to early tradition, Peter, with whom John Mark was traditionally associated, ended his life there along with Paul. In sum, the witness of the Epistles, combined with the evidence of the "we-passages" in Acts, harmonizes well with the author's claim in the prologue to his gospel (Lk. 1:1-4) that, while he is a secondary witness, he has had access to the accounts of eyewitnesses and followers of Jesus.

The earliest traditions about the authorship of the Gospel of Luke and the Acts of the Apostles are in general agreement that the author was a follower and traveling companion of Paul and was named Luke. Among the texts that have survived of the early Church Fathers (second and third centuries CE) those of Irenaeus are the earliest to mention Lucan authorship of the gospel and Acts: *Adversus haereses* 3.1.1 refers to the gospel writer as Luke the companion of Paul; 3.14.1-4 invokes the "we-passages" of Acts as evidence that Acts was written by Paul's constant companion and fellow traveler Luke. Clement of Alexandria refers to Luke as the author of the Acts of the Apostles (*Strom.* 5.12.82.4) and of the gospel (*Strom.* 1.21.145.2). Tertullian attributes the gospel to Luke (*Marc.* 4.2). Origen attributes the gospel and Acts to Luke (according to Eusebius, *Hist. eccl.* 6.25.6, 14).[5] It seems unlikely that the early Church Fathers would have attributed the third gospel and Acts, the two longest books of the New Testament, together composing more than a quarter of the whole, to so obscure a figure as Luke unless the attribution had been based on a very early tradition. The Patristic tradition ascribes all other anonymous works in the New Testament to prominent figures: Jesus's apostles Matthew and John, the apostle Paul, Barnabas's cousin and Paul's (and Peter's?) companion John Mark.

The no-longer-surviving Greek original of the Muratorian Canon, dated by some to as early as 170 CE, attributes the third gospel to Luke, a well-known physician, who was not an eyewitness to the events narrated but rather learned of them as a traveling companion of Paul. On the other hand, the Muratorian Canon continues, this same Luke compiled the narrative of the Acts of the Apostles from his own experiences. The so-called "Anti-Marcionite Prologues" to the Gospel of Luke, which may date in their

---

[5] A full collection of references to Luke and the other gospel writers by the Church Fathers, from Papias to Augustine, can be found in K. Aland, *Synopsis Quattuor Evangeliorum*, 15th ed. (Stuttgart: Deutsche Bibelgesellschaft, 1996), 547–64, where all the passages are presented in their original languages.

18   *The Formal Education of the Author of Luke-Acts*

original Greek form to as early as the late second century but survive primarily in several dozen later Latin (one Greek) Biblical manuscripts, add the further details that Luke was Syrian by race, from Antioch, a physician by profession, a disciple of the apostles, who later accompanied Paul until his martyrdom. He was unmarried and childless. He wrote his gospel in Achaea, and he died in Boeotia at the age of eighty-four (or eighty-nine or seventy-four). This same Luke also wrote the Acts of the Apostles.

Most of these biographical details are mentioned as accepted truths by the later Church Fathers—e.g., Eusebius, Epiphanius, Jerome[6]—who also record further details about Luke's old age, death, burial, and relics: he composed his gospel in Achaia and Boeotia;[7] he became bishop of Thebes, and he died and was buried there;[8] in the twentieth year of Constantius, his bones were transferred to Constantinople and reburied there.[9] Procopius the sixth-century historian states that Constantine's son Constantius had built a Church of the Holy Apostles in Constantinople in the fourth century that housed the remains of Luke, among other apostles, and that Luke's remains, which had become lost to view, were discovered and reinstalled during the rebuilding of the church by Justinian in the sixth century (*De aedificiis* 1.4.9–24). The body identified as Luke's was later removed from Constantinople, perhaps during the iconoclastic movement in the eighth or ninth century, eventually ending up, at least by the early twelfth century in the Benedictine Basilica of St. Justina in Padua, Italy, where it currently resides.[10] However, the Roman emperor and king of Bohemia

---

[6] Eusebius, *Historia ecclesiastica* 3.4; Epiphanius, *Index apostolorum* (116–17 in T. Schermann's edition); Jerome, *De viris illustribus* 7, *Commentariorum in evangelium Matthaei prologus*.

[7] So Jerome, *Commentariorum in evangelium Matthaei prologus*. Gregory of Nazianzus, *Orationes* 33 (Migne 36.228) also mentions Achaea as the focus of Luke's later ministry.

[8] So Epiphanius, *Index apostolorum* (116–17 in T. Schermann's edition).

[9] So Jerome, *De viris illustribus* 7; also the early fifth-century church historian Philostorgius fr. 3.2. Later church histories, biblical commentaries, and hagiographies record additional traditions about Luke: that he was one of the seventy (or seventy-two) apostles sent out by Jesus in Luke 10:1; that he was the unnamed companion of Cleopas in the story of Jesus's appearance on the road to Emmaus in Luke 24; that he was the anonymous brother whom Paul sends to the Corinthians in 2 Corinthians 8:18; that he was the Lucius from whom Paul sends greetings in Romans 16:21; that he was attended later in life by the couple Priscila and Aquila mentioned in Acts 18; that he preached in Italy, Gaul, Dalmatia, and Macedonia; that his authority spread all the way to Byzantium, where he built a church and wrote ordinances for ministry in the priesthood; that he was a painter and was the first to depict the Madonna and child; that he was martyred in Achaea by being crucified on an olive tree.

[10] According to a Paduan tradition, fleshed out in a lawsuit in Venice in 1463 concerning the identification of the "true" body of Luke, Luke's relics were transferred to Padua from Constantinople already in the fourth century, during the reign of the emperor Julian. See C. Bellinati, "Peregrinazioni del corpo di San Luca nel primo millennio," in *San Luca evangelista testimone della fede che unisce. Atti del Congresso internazionale, Padova, 16–21 ottobre 2000*, eds. V. T. W. Marin and F. G. B. Trolese (Padua: Istituto per la storia ecclesiastica Padovana, 2003), 2:173–99. The discovery in "Luke's" leaden coffin at Padua of twenty-four skeletons of snakes (*coluber viridiflavus*), dating to the fifth to sixth century, and native to Europe, not the Middle East, is consistent with an early date for the coffin's removal from Constantinople to Padua. See B. Sala, "I resti di microvertebrati della tomba di San Luca Evangelista," in *San Luca evangelista testimone della fede che unisce. Atti del Congresso internazionale, Padova, 16–21 ottobre 2000*, eds. V. T. W. Marin and F. G. B. Trolese (Padua: Istituto per la storia ecclesiastica Padovana, 2003), 2:373–88.

The Author of Luke-Acts 19

Charles IV had the skull removed from the skeleton in 1354 and taken to the Cathedral of St. Vitus in Prague, where it can be seen to this day.[11] There is now a further addendum to this tradition, for the sarcophagus of Luke in Padua was reopened in 1998 for examination. The leaden coffin within the sarcophagus, which, at 180 centimeters × 48 centimeters × 40 centimeters, happens to fit perfectly into the empty marble sarcophagus at the orthodox church in Thebes that claims to be the site of Luke's original burial, contains an intact male skeleton (minus the skull) that appears to have decomposed in this very coffin. The skeleton in Padua has now been compared to the skull in Prague, and they fit precisely at the conjunction of the first cervical vertebra of the spine and the occipital condyles of the skull; also, a tooth found on the floor of the coffin fits into the right socket of the skull's jawbone. The skeleton and skull, then, belonged to the same man, who was 163 to 165 centimeters tall (about average for the late Roman period), with good posture and healthy physique, right side dominance, with narrow head and face, narrow shoulders, and very narrow pelvis, who endured periods of heavy work as a youth and some nutritional deficiency during growth, suffered general osteoporosis, arthrosis of the lumbar spinal column, and pulmonary emphysema, and who died between the ages of seventy and eighty-five.[12] Radiocarbon dating of the femur, carried out in two different laboratories, has offered very broad parameters for the date of death: between the second half of the first century

---

[11] A contemporary account of the removal of the skull by Charles IV to Prague in 1354 is recorded on two parchments in the metropolitan archives of Prague, and a short version of the account is also inscribed on the interior of the skull itself. See E. Vlček, "Studio antropologico del cranio attribuito a San Luca della Cattedrale di San Vito di Praga," in *San Luca evangelista testimone della fede che unisce. Atti del Congresso internazionale, Padova, 16–21 ottobre 2000*, eds. V. T. W. Marin and F. G. B. Trolese (Padua: Istituto per la storia ecclesiastica Padovana, 2003), 2:206; also J. Matějka, "La donazione del capo di San Luca all'Imperatore Carlo IV di Lussemburgo nel 1354," in *San Luca evangelista testimone della fede che unisce. Atti del Congresso internazionale, Padova, 16–21 ottobre 2000*, ed. F. G. B. Trolese (Padua: Istituto per la storia ecclesiastica Padovana, 2004), 3:331–51.

[12] The palaeoanthropological examination was directed by Vito Terribile Wiel Marin, Professor of Anatomy and Histology at the University of Padua, and published in the second volume of V. T. W. Marin and F. G. B. Trolese, eds., *San Luca evangelista testimone della fede che unisce. Atti del Congresso internazionale, Padova, 16–21 ottobre 2000* (Padua: Istituto per la storia ecclesiastica Padovana, 2003). This is part of a three-volume work documenting the international congress in Padua in 2000 on the topic of Luke the evangelist, including his relics. See 201–54 (on the palaeoanthropological examination of the skull), 255–312 (on the palaeoanthropological examination of the skeleton), 313–36 (on evidence for the decomposition of the skeleton in the lead coffin, and on C^{14} evidence for the date of death), 337–53 (on mitochondrial DNA evidence for the body's origin in Syria or Anatolia), 355–72 (on a moderately low mineral density of the bones consistent with old age at the time of death), 373–88 (on the twenty-four skeletons of snakes [*coluber viridiflavus*] found in the coffin that indicate that the coffin may have been in Padua already by the fifth or sixth century), 389–466 (on the pollen and needles of the Grecian Fir [*abies cephalonica*] found in the coffin that indicate that the coffin once lay open in Greece), 467–81 (on the composition of the lead of the coffin, but not of the lid, as similar to many Roman artifacts), 483–509 (on the chemical and mineralogical evidence that the lead coffin, but not the lid, was buried and remained below the water level for some time in the area of Padua), 732–4 (on the observation that the lead coffin from Padua fits perfectly into the cavity of the late second-century CE marble sarcophagus of the Greek Orthodox church in Thebes that claims to be the site of Luke's original burial).

20   *The Formal Education of the Author of Luke-Acts*

CE and the first quarter of the fifth century CE.[13] Genetic testing of two teeth indicates a high likelihood of Syrian origin, although Anatolian origin is also possible—but not Greek.[14] In 2000, as an ecumenical gesture by the Catholic Church, one rib from the body—the one closest to the heart—was donated to the Greek Orthodox church in Thebes that claims to be the site of Luke's original burial. The chain of connections has thus come full circle.

What the Text of Luke-Acts Itself Tells Us about Its Author

Each one of the dozen or so details about the author of Luke-Acts preserved and transmitted through these later traditions, rich and weighty though they be, has at some time since been called into question, and often for good reason. While only a few have denied the tradition of the common authorship of the gospel and Acts, many have doubted the various traditions about the author's later life and death: that he was unmarried and childless, that he wrote his gospel in Achaea, that he became bishop of Thebes, that he died in Boeotia at an advanced age, that his bones were transferred to Constantinople and reburied there, and that his bones eventually ended up in the Benedictine Basilica of St. Justina in Padua. The earlier traditions have been met by mixed responses as well: that the author's name was Luke, that he was a gentile, that he was a physician, that he was from Antioch, and that he was a companion of Paul.

For our purposes, however, this is of little consequence, for in our investigation we shall set aside these external traditions, both the earlier and the later ones, so far as we are able. Yes, if these traditions were true, they would offer some context for our examination of Luke's educational background and reliance on Classical and Hellenistic literature. It would be illuminating if we could assume, for example, that the author really had the common Roman praenomen *Lucius* or the cognomen *Lucanus*, that he was a gentile rather than a Jew, that he was a physician, that he traveled extensively throughout the Greco-Roman world, and that he lived, worked, died, and was buried in Greece. But in our quest for reliable evidence about the author's educational and literary background, we may disregard these external traditions and focus instead on

---

[13] So G. Molin, G. Salviulo, and P. Guerriero, "Indagini sulle reliquie attribuite a 'San Luca Evangelista,' Basilica di Santa Giustina in Padova: Studi cristallochimici, isotopici e datazione mediante ^{14}C dei reperti ossei," in *San Luca evangelista testimone della fede che unisce. Atti del Congresso internazionale, Padova, 16–21 ottobre 2000*, eds. V. T. W. Marin and F. G. B. Trolese (Padua: Istituto per la storia ecclesiastica Padovana, 2003), 2:173–99.

[14] Professor Guido Barbujani, a population geneticist at the University of Ferrara, extracted the DNA from the two teeth and identified it as compatible with someone living near the region of Antioch in Syria. See C. Vernesi et al., "Caratterizzazione genetica del corpo attribuito a San Luca," in *San Luca evangelista testimone della fede che unisce. Atti del Congresso internazionale, Padova, 16–21 ottobre 2000*, eds. V. T. W. Marin and F. G. B. Trolese (Padua: Istituto per la storia ecclesiastica Padovana, 2003), 2:337–53; the results are also summarized in C. Vernesi et al., "Genetic Characterization of the Body Attributed to the Evangelist Luke," *Proceedings of the National Academy of Sciences* 98, no. 23 (2001): 13,460–3.

the internal evidence—what the texts themselves reveal about their author—for we can elicit quite a lot of information about the author from the contents and characteristics of the two texts.

We have already mentioned the internal evidence of the "we-passages" in the Acts of the Apostles, where the author seems to insert himself into the narrative, and their possible relationship to the three references in the "Pauline" epistles to a traveling companion of Paul named Luke. Indeed, the "we-passages," with their vividness, immediacy, and great attention to detail, do appear to be composed by an eyewitness of the events narrated in them. Their author includes descriptions of the islands, towns, directions of winds (windward and leeward sides of islands), and so forth, in his accounts of the second and third missionary journeys and the voyage to Rome that are lacking in his accounts of other journeys: Paul's journey from Beroea to Athens, for example, where we are not even told whether he traveled by land or by sea. Paul's brief visit to Philippi (16:12-40), which is part of a "we-passage," receives more attention than his eighteen-month stay in Corinth (18:1-17), which is not part of a "we-passage." Paul's itinerary from Caesarea to Rome, which is part of a "we-passage," is laid out in minute detail (27:1–28:16), while his very significant travels through the inland areas of Asia Minor, which are not part of a "we-passage," are passed over in a most cursory fashion (16:6-8; 18:23; 19:1). If it could be determined that the author of Acts was himself the eyewitness of the "we-passages," they would be important items of evidence about the author from the texts themselves. However, for various reasons their evidentiary value has not been universally acknowledged. Other conceivable explanations have been proposed for the "we-passages": that the author has inserted material wholesale from a source, who was the eyewitness of the events narrated; that the author has fictitiously inserted himself into the narrative for dramatic purposes; that the author has used a conventional literary device characteristic of the historiographical or novelistic genres of the period.[15]

Much less contestable is the internal evidence of the "I-passages" in the prefaces to the Gospel of Luke and to the Acts of the Apostles. The preface to the gospel refers to a single author ("me") and specifies by the masculine gender of the participle used in this self-reference that the author is a man: Luke 1:3—ἔδοξε κἀμοὶ παρηκολουθηκότι "it seemed good also to me, having given close attention …" The singular verbal form

---

[15] The first to question the traditional view, articulated already in the second century by Irenaeus (*Haer.* 3.14.1), that the author of Acts was himself the eyewitness of the "we-passages" was perhaps B. L. Königsmann, who in a seminar program in 1798 titled "*De fontibus commentariorum sacrorum, qui Lucae nomen praeferunt deque eorum consilio et aetate*," in *Sylloge Commentationum Theologicarum*, ed. D. J. Pott (Helmstadt: Fleckeisen, [1798] 1802), 3:215–39, proposed, based on Luke's statements about his sources in the prologue to his gospel, that Luke was also not an eyewitness of the events narrated in Acts. For a survey of scholarship on this issue from the early nineteenth to the mid-twentieth centuries, see J. Dupont, *The Sources of the Acts* (New York: Herder and Herder, 1964), 75–112. For a more recent survey of the status of the question, see S. E. Porter, "The 'We' Passages," in *The Book of Acts in its Graeco-Roman Setting*, eds. D. W. J. Gill and C. Gempf (Grand Rapids: Eerdmans, 1994), 545–74.

22   *The Formal Education of the Author of Luke-Acts*

ἐποιησάμην "I made" in the preface to Acts (1:1), as well as another reference to "me" in Acts 1:4, confirms the single authorship for that work as well. This may not seem like much, but it is more than can be said about the other synoptic gospels, whose authors do not insert themselves even obliquely into their texts.[16]

We can also elicit from the preface to Acts that the author is the same as the author of the third gospel since he dedicates the work to the same Theophilus to whom he had dedicated his gospel and since he explicitly refers to his earlier work (πρῶτος λόγος "the first account"). Unsurprisingly, the end of the Gospel of Luke dovetails nicely with the beginning of the Acts of the Apostles, as though they were intended as two volumes of a single work. Common authorship is also indicated implicitly by the close similarities in language (e.g., a shared "Lucan" vocabulary), grammar (e.g., a comparatively refined usage of the subjunctive and optative moods), syntax (e.g., a preference for hypotactic over paratactic constructions), and style (e.g., parallelism and triptychs).[17] Further, both works share an interest in, and familiarity with, the larger Hellenistic and Roman world (e.g., geography, political institutions, rulers and officials), and they exhibit sympathy toward the gentiles and, in fact, work apologetically to present the Christian movement in the best light before a gentile audience, stressing in particular that it poses no threat to Roman law or custom. Also, both works rely extensively on the Greek Septuagint rather than the Hebrew Bible, and they share

---

[16] The authors of the Gospels of Matthew and Mark do bring their audiences, but not themselves, into the narrative implicitly by translating Semitic words into Greek, for example, and at least once quite explicitly by addressing their readers directly: "let the reader understand" (Mt. 24:15 and Mk 13:14). The author of the Gospel of John explicitly addresses his audience in an epilogue (20:30-31): "These things have been written in order that you may believe . . ." He inserts himself explicitly into the text only in a second epilogue in the last two verses of his work (21:24-5): "This is the disciple who is testifying about these things, and who wrote them down, and we know that his testimony is true. And there are many other things that Jesus did, which if written down one by one, not even the world itself, I suppose, would hold the books that would be written." This second epilogue has all the internal characteristics of a later addition to the gospel. There is some external evidence as well that this is a later addition: the final verse was for some reason missing in the original text of Codex Sinaiticus, but it was added later, apparently by the same scribe who wrote what preceded (so H. J. M. Milne, D. Cockerell, and T. C. Skeat, *Scribes and Correctors of the Codex Sinaiticus* (London: British Museum, 1938), 12-13); Theodore, the fourth- to fifth-century bishop of Mopsuestia, asserts in his commentary on John at verse 21:25 that "these are not the words of the Evangelist but were inserted by some functionary" (fr. 140 column 2 in R. Devreesse's edition); a fourth-century Coptic translation of John omits the entirety of the twenty-first chapter.

[17] Still useful on vocabulary, grammar, and syntax in Luke-Acts are H. J. Cadbury, *The Style and Literary Method of Luke* (Cambridge: Harvard University Press, 1919), and J. De Zwaan, "The Use of the Greek Language in Acts," in *The Beginnings of Christianity: The Acts of the Apostles*, eds. F. J. Foakes Jackson and K. Lake (London: Macmillan, 1922), 2:30-65. On some stylistic features shared by Luke and Acts, see C. H. Talbert, *Literary Patterns, Theological Themes, and the Genre of Luke-Acts* (Missoula: Scholars Press, 1974). J. José Alviar, "Recent Advances in Computational Linguistics and their Application to Biblical Studies," *New Testament Studies* 54 (2008): 139–59, offers an update on advances in computer-based techniques for comparing stylistic features of the books of the New Testament; in all the recent studies that he cites the stylistic similarity between Luke and Acts has been confirmed.

The Author of Luke-Acts 23

similar theological concerns: Jesus as risen Lord and Messiah promised by the ancient Hebrews, a suffering Christ, muted interest in eschatology, etc.[18]

And what do the contents and characteristics of the texts of Luke-Acts tell us about this masculine, singular author who composed both works? On the one hand, he appears to have been well versed in Judaism and familiar with its sacred scriptures. Substantial portions of his gospel, as well as the early chapters of Acts, though written in Greek, are expressed with Semitic phrases and grammatical and syntactical constructions that resound with echoes from the Hebrew Scripture. These Semitisms probably arise, of course, from Hebrew and Aramaic source materials rather than from the author's own lexicon and grammar, but the author's reliance on Hebrew and Aramaic sources itself indicates a certain level of Jewish acculturation. Indeed, the author of Luke-Acts appears knowledgeable of Jewish theology, such as the doctrinal differences between Pharisees and Sadducees, and of Jewish worship practices both in the synagogues and in the temple in Jerusalem, with the layout of which he is intimately familiar. He also appears familiar with some details of Palestinian geography, especially the roads from Jerusalem to the Mediterranean coast, and the ports, towns, and cities of the coastal plain.[19] Moreover, theologically, he portrays Jesus as the Messiah anticipated in the Hebrew Scripture. While the author of the third gospel has commonly been labeled the sole gentile writer of the New Testament, there is no compelling evidence against him being a Jew or having had a Jewish upbringing.[20] The possibility that Luke was a Jew or, perhaps, a proselyte, or at the very least, a so-called "God-

---

[18] Marcion presumably denied that the Gospel of Luke and the Acts of the Apostles were by the same author since he does not include Acts in his canon. And some have from time to time over the last century and a half challenged, unpersuasively, the common authorship of Luke and Acts. F. C. Baur, *Paulus, der Apostel Jesu Christi: sein Leben und Wirken, seine Briefe und seine Lehre* (Stuttgart: Becher & Müller, 1845), 1–14, and J. H. Scholten, *Das Paulinische Evangelium: kritische Untersuchung des Evangeliums nach Lucas und seines Verhältnisses zu Marcus, Matthäus und der Apostelgeschichte* (Elberfeld: R. L. Friderichs, 1881), 254–316, challenged single authorship on historical and theological grounds. A. C. Clark, *The Acts of the Apostles: A Critical Edition with Introduction and Notes on Selected Passages* (Oxford: Clarendon, 1933), 393–408, challenged single authorship on literary and linguistic grounds. A. W. Argyle, "The Greek of Luke and Acts," *New Testament Studies* 20 (1974): 441–5, challenged single authorship on linguistic grounds. P. Walters, *The Assumed Authorial Unity of Luke and Acts: A Reassessment of the Evidence* (Cambridge: Cambridge University Press, 2009), challenged common authorship based on stylistic considerations: hiatus, long and short syllables, sentence structure, etc. But many of the differences in language, style, and even theology between the two works can be attributed to their different sources and to the differences in the context and genre of the two works. In spite of its provocative title, M. C. Parsons and R. I. Pervo, *Rethinking the Unity of Luke and Acts* (Minneapolis: Fortress, 1993), does not challenge the authorial unity of Luke-Acts but rather focuses on the generic, narrative, and theological differences in order to highlight the individuality of the two works. Parsons and Pervo conclude that Luke-Acts is not a single volume that was later split up for canonical purposes and that we should therefore get back into the habit of saying "Luke and Acts" rather than "Luke-Acts."

[19] His knowledge of the Galilee, Samaria, the Jordan valley, and the hinterland of Judaea, on the other hand, is inexact, as though he had never visited these areas. So M. Hengel, *Between Jesus and Paul* (London: SCM Press, 1983), 97–128, 190–210.

[20] As noted above, in the final greetings at the end of the letter to the Colossians (4:10-14), the sender appears to separate the greetings of Aristarchus, Mark, and Justus, who are "of the circumcision" from the greetings of Epaphras, Luke, and Demas, who, presumably, are not. This need not mean that the latter three are so-called "God-fearing gentiles" rather than proselytes or Jews from birth. The phrase may simply indicate that there were two subgroups of Jewish Christians who regarded the law somewhat differently.

24   *The Formal Education of the Author of Luke-Acts*

fearing" gentile who had great respect for Judaism, has been gaining traction among New Testament scholars in recent years.[21] In any case, a matter that has become increasingly clear over the last few decades is that in the first century CE, "Jewish" and "Hellenistic" were not mutually exclusive categories.[22]

On the other hand, the author of Luke-Acts was a product of Hellenistic Greek and Roman culture. He is familiar with many facets of Greco-Roman religion: e.g., sacrificial customs, oracular procedures, imperial cult, magic, mythology (Zeus, Hermes, Artemis, the Dioskouroi), the cult of the unknown god.[23] He is aware of Greek philosophical traditions: Epicureanism and Stoicism. He is knowledgeable of the workings of Roman government: the names and proper titles of rulers and magistrates, the nature and functions of civic offices, the intricacies of judicial procedures, the requirements of citizenship.[24] The

---

[21] So M. Wilcox, *The Semitisms of Acts* (Oxford: Clarendon, 1965); J. Jervell, *Luke and the People of God: A New Look at Luke-Acts* (Minneapolis: Augsburg, 1984); R. L. Brawley, *Luke-Acts and the Jews: Conflict, Apology, and Conciliation* (Atlanta: Scholars Press, 1987); M. Klinghardt, *Das lukanische Verstandnis des Gesetzes nach Herkunft, Funktion und seinem Ort in der Geschichte der Urchristentums* (Tübingen: Mohr Siebeck, 1988); G. Leonardi, *Comunità Destinatarie dell' Opera di Luca e Identità dell' Autore*, in *San Luca evangelista testimone della fede che unisce. Atti del Congresso internazionale, Padova, 16–21 ottobre 2000*, eds. G. Leonardi and F. G. B. Trolese (Padua: Istituto per la storia ecclesiastica Padovana, 2002), 1:187–215; M. L. Rigato "Luca originario giudeo, forse di stirpe levitica, seguace dei 'testimoni oculari' (Lc 1.2-3)," in *San Luca evangelista testimone della fede che unisce. Atti del Congresso internazionale, Padova, 16–21 ottobre 2000*, eds. G. Leonardi and F. G. B. Trolese (Padua: Istituto per la storia ecclesiastica Padovana, 2002), 1:391–422.

[22] On the Hellenization of Jews, even in Palestine, see R. Meyer, *Hellenistisches in der rabbinischen Anthropologie* (Stuttgart: W. Kohlhammer, 1937); E. R. Goodenough, *Jewish Symbols in the Greco-Roman Periods*, vols. 1–13 (New York: Pantheon Books, 1953–1968); S. Lieberman, *Greek in Jewish Palestine* (New York: Jewish Theological Seminary, 1942); S. Lieberman, *Greek in Jewish Palestine*, 2nd ed. (New York: Jewish Theological Seminary, 1962); S. Lieberman, *Hellenism in Jewish Palestine* (New York: Jewish Theological Seminary, 1962); V. Tcherikover, *Hellenistic Civilization and the Jews* (Philadelphia: Jewish Publication Society of America, 1959); H. A. Fischel, *Rabbinic Literature and Greco-Roman Philosophy* (Leiden: Brill, 1973); M. Hengel, *Judaism and Hellenism*; M. Hengel, *Jews, Greeks, and Barbarians: Aspects of Hellenization of Judaism in the Pre-Christian Period* (Philadelphia: Fortress: 1980); M. Hengel, *The Hellenization of Judaea in the First Century after Christ* (London: SCM Press, 1989); A. Kasher, *Jews and Hellenistic Cities in Eretz Israel* (Tübingen: Mohr Siebeck, 1990); J. J. Collins and G. E. Sterling, eds., *Hellenism in the Land of Israel* (Notre Dame: University of Notre Dame Press, 2001).

[23] See L. A. Kauppi, *Foreign but Familiar Gods: Greco-Romans Read Religion in Acts* (London: T&T Clark, 2006). Based on the narrative of Acts, Kauppi proposes that Luke had a working knowledge of many elements of Greco-Roman religion: oracular procedures (Acts 1:15-26); magic (8:4-25; 13:4-12; 19:17-20); manticism (16:16-18); imperial cult and its rituals (12:20-3); sacrificial procedures and terminology (14:8-18); mythology and its literary expression (17:16-34); votive offerings (19:23-8); cultic use of aniconic objects (19:35); cults of personified abstractions (28:4); mythological traditions about divine justice (28:4); the cults of Zeus, Hermes, Artemis, and the Dioskouroi (14:11-13; 19:23-41; 28:11); the cult of the unknown god (17:23). Kauppi infers that Luke would have expected at least some of his audience to have sufficient knowledge of Greco-Roman religion, myth, and literature to comprehend these details of his narrative.

[24] On Luke's knowledge of Roman legal and judicial procedures and of the intricacies of Roman citizenship rights, see A. N. Sherwin-White, *Roman Society and Roman Law in the New Testament* (Oxford: Clarendon, 1963), who stresses that Luke accurately reflects the conditions of the Julio-Claudian period. On Luke's knowledge of ancient geography, politics, and the military, see M. L. Soards, "The Historical and Cultural Setting of Luke and Acts," in *New Views on Luke-Acts*, ed. E. Richard (Collegeville: The Liturgical Press, 1990), 33–47. On Luke's awareness of the geography, political situation, and society of the larger Mediterranean world, and the implications of this awareness for identifying Luke's own social class, see V. K. Robbins, "The Social Location of the Implied Author of Luke-Acts," in *The Social World of Luke-Acts*, ed. J. Neyrey (Peabody: Hendrickson, 1991), 305–32.

prologues to his gospel (1:1-4) and, less so, to Acts (1:1-2) are characteristic of someone versed in the ancient historiographical tradition: e.g., his promise to provide for his readers an account that is superior to those of his predecessors; his claim to be relying on sources that are ultimately eyewitnesses (αὐτόπται).[25] His narrative includes dating mechanisms that attempt to synchronize the various secular and religious rulers of the time in a manner reminiscent of earlier Greek historians. He places speeches at critical points in the narrative, reflecting what the speaker ideally would have said, given the situation, rather than what the speaker actually said verbatim, in the manner of someone familiar with both ancient historiography and ancient rhetoric.

Most pertinent for our goal of reconstructing the educational level of the author of Luke-Acts based on Classical and Hellenistic literary influences on his works is the fact that he was proficient and, in fact, quite at home in the Greek language. Jerome was right when he claimed that among all the evangelists Luke was the "most skilled" (*eruditissimus*) in Greek and that his language "smacked of secular eloquence" (*saecularem redolet eloquentiam*).[26] Luke knew the Hebrew Scripture through its Greek translation in the Septuagint, which he uses extensively, even in subtle and sophisticated ways.[27] But his proficiency in the Greek language went well beyond Septuagintal Greek. His vocabulary, grammar, syntax, and style are those of someone proficient in idiomatic,

---

[25] While Luke is not quoting verbatim any extant predecessor in the prologue to his gospel, there are some verbal, contextual, and methodological similarities between Luke's prologue and those of Herodotus, Thucydides, and Polybius. The hypotactic syntax—one long periodic sentence, with a main clause framed by four subordinate clauses—would be comfortable in Classical and Hellenistic Greek of a fairly high style. Some of the vocabulary is much more common in Classical and Hellenistic Greek than in Septuagintal (LXX) and New Testament (NT) Greek (ἐπιχειρέω, διήγησις): notably, the first word of Luke's treatise, the stately compound ἐπειδήπερ, which occurs hundreds of times in Classical and Hellenistic Greek, is found only here in the LXX and NT; also Luke's reliance on sources that are ultimately eyewitnesses (αὐτόπται), again a word that occurs only here in the LXX and NT, hearkens back to the historical methodology developed by Herodotus, who uses the term several times, as do other major historians, such as Xenophon, Polybius, and Diodorus Siculus. For H. J. Cadbury's classic statement that Luke's prologues reveal him to be a historian in the Classical and Hellenistic tradition, see his "Commentary on the Preface of Luke," in *The Beginnings of Christianity*, eds. F. J. Foakes Jackson and K. Lake, 2:489–510. But L. C. A. Alexander has recently challenged Cadbury's influential assertion and proposes instead that Luke's prologues were modeled on those of ancient technical handbooks: *The Preface to Luke's Gospel* (Cambridge: Cambridge University Press, 1993), and "The Preface to Acts and the Historians," in *History, Literature and Society*, ed. B. Witherington III (Cambridge: Cambridge University Press, 1999), 73–103.

[26] Jerome, *Epistula ad Damasum* 20.4; *Commentarium ad Esaiam* 3.6.9.

[27] On Luke's use of the Septuagint in his underlying vocabulary, grammar, and style, as well as in his direct quotations of the Hebrew Scripture, see W. K. L. Clarke, "The Use of the Septuagint in Acts," in *The Beginnings of Christianity*, eds. F. J. Foakes Jackson and K. Lake, 2:66–105; J. H. Moulton and W. F. Howard, *A Grammar of New Testament Greek*, vol. 2 (Edinburgh, T&T Clark, 1929) 411–85; A. Wifstrand, "Lukas och Septuaginta," *Svensk Teologisk Kvartalskrift* 16 (1940): 243–62; H. F. D. Sparks, "The Semitisms of St. Luke's Gospel," *The Journal of Theological Studies* 44 (1943): 129–38; H. F. D. Sparks, "The Semitisms of the Acts," *The Journal of Theological Studies*, n.s. 1 (1950), 16–28; M. Wilcox, *The Semitisms of Acts*; E. Plümacher, *Lukas als hellenistischer Schriftsteller: Studien zur Apostelgeschichte* (Göttingen: Vandenhoeck & Ruprecht, 1972), 38–72; A. Hogeterp and A. Denaux, *Semitisms in Luke's Greek: A Descriptive Analysis of Lexical and Syntactical Domains of Semitic Language Influence in Luke's Gospel* (Tübingen: Mohr Siebeck, 2018) 25–61, 477–515.

26   *The Formal Education of the Author of Luke-Acts*

sometimes even literary, Hellenistic Greek.[28] In those passages in which he draws from the Gospel of Mark he tends to make improvements to Mark's sometimes inelegant style, paratactic syntax, and common, sometimes awkward, diction.[29] He avoids many of Mark's Semitisms.[30] He also possesses fairly well polished literary skills: as we shall see, he was familiar with some earlier Greek literary works, and he even used these as inspiration for components of his own work.

In short, Luke had been properly educated in the traditional Hellenistic Greek school curriculum. It was in school that he learned how to read and write, using Classical and Hellenistic Greek literature, both at a primary and secondary level, in his school texts. It was in school that he learned how to compose speeches and letters, which were common paedagogical exercises. And it was in school that he developed his penchant for etymological wordplay, again a common paedagogical exercise of the school curriculum. Moreover, Luke's exposure to Classical and Hellenistic Greek literature would not have ceased when he completed his formal education. In addition to the ancient Greek texts to which he was exposed in school, he would, no doubt, have come to know Greek texts from his general experience of reading, hearing, and otherwise witnessing (i.e., dramatic productions) them as a well-educated, Greek-speaking adult traveling through the major cities of the Mediterranean.

In what follows, I wish to concentrate primarily on what I perceive to be Luke's conscious and intentional allusions and references to, and quotations of, ancient Classical and Hellenistic Greek authors, such as Homer, Aesop, Epimenides, Euripides, Plato, and Aratus—allusions, references, and quotations that indicate that Luke was familiar with actual Greek literary texts, most likely from his formal school training.

---

[28] On the character of the language and style of Acts (vocabulary, grammar, syntax, style, use of Semitisms and Latinisms, and reliance on the Septuagint), see the full treatment of E. Jacquier, *Les Actes des apôtres* (Paris: J. Gabalda, 1926), clxiv-cc; also, L. Rydbeck, *Fachprosa, vermeintliche Volkssprache und Neues Testament* (Stockholm: Almquist & Wiksell, 1967), who compares the Greek of Luke-Acts to that of popular philosophical literature and of technical treatises of the period and concludes that Luke's language and style is literate but not literary; and L. C. A. Alexander, "Septuaginta, Fachprosa, Imitatio: Albert Wifstrand and the Language of Luke-Acts," in *Die Apostelgeschichte und die hellenistische Geschichtsschreibung: Festschrift fur Eckhard Plümacher zu seinem 65. Geburtstag*, eds. C. Breytenbach and J. Schroter (Leiden: Brill, 2004), 1–26, who examines Luke's varied language and style, from Septuagintal to almost Classical, and concludes that it is a form of standard Hellenistic prose that appears also among the writers of technical treatises.

[29] For the details of Luke's improvements on Mark's language, from a Classical or "Atticizing" standpoint, especially in his diction, see E. Norden, *Die antike Kunstprosa vom VI. Jahrhundert v. Chr. bis in die Zeit der Renaissance* (Leipzig: Teubner, 1898), 2:480–92. Norden's work is expanded by H. J. Cadbury, *The Style and Literary Method of Luke*, 1–72, and also by M.-J. Lagrange, *Évangile selon Saint Luc* (Paris: J. Gabalda, 1921), xlviii–lxviii. Some caution should be taken in our use of categories here, for Luke was not adopting the affected "classicizing" or "atticizing" language of some second-century writers; he was simply using a higher "register" of standard Hellenistic Greek prose than Mark. A. Wifstrand, "Lukas och den grekiska klassicismen," *Svensk Exegetisk Årsbok* 5 (1940): 139–51, warns against using the term "Atticism" or even "Classicism" to describe Luke's style: the difference between the other gospel writers and Luke is the difference between vulgar and literary Koine, not between Koine and Atticism or Classicism.

[30] The most obvious examples are those passages in which Luke omits—or translates into Greek—a Hebrew or Aramaic word left untranslated in Mark (e.g., *Amen, Hosanna, Rabbi/Rabbouni, Golgotha*).

For whether Luke was a Jew or gentile, or something in between, from Antioch or Philippi, or somewhere in between, writing in the 60s or the 120s, or sometime in between, he would still have experienced as a youth the very homogeneous Hellenistic educational curriculum (ἐγκύκλιος παιδεία/*enkyklios paideia*) that had been, and would continue to be, used for centuries throughout the eastern Mediterranean.

3

The Education of the Author of Luke-Acts

One possible approach in our search for Classical and Hellenistic Greek quotations in Luke-Acts is to ascertain what level of Greek literacy we should expect from its author, a thoroughly Hellenized, Greek-speaking man living in the eastern Mediterranean during the first century of our era. This approach requires us to begin our search broadly, comparatively, from the outside in—that is, from the context to the text. But someone may justly object that this approach requires considerable effort to achieve what will inevitably be an uncertain answer. Hence one's effort will be more efficiently expended by searching for and identifying actual Classical and Hellenistic Greek quotations within the text of Luke-Acts. In contrast to the first approach, this one requires us to begin our search narrowly, particularly, from the inside out—that is, from the text to the context.

On the one hand, even the most thorough analysis of the broader question of Luke's Greek literacy can result only in possibilities or, at best, probabilities: that Luke may have been raised and educated in a cultural context in which he may have become familiar with Classical and Hellenistic Greek literature (i.e., the first approach will result in a hypothesis). On the other hand, the identification of actual quotations of Classical or Hellenistic Greek literature in Luke-Acts, in which the author is clearly aware of the contexts of the original passages—he is not simply quoting popular, free-floating aphorisms or recalling from his youth isolated verses that he had recited or written repeatedly as school exercise—will prove, in and of itself, that the author of Luke-Acts had achieved a certain level of literacy in the Classics (i.e., the second approach will result in a verification of our hypothesis). My view is that both approaches are essential, that they should be conducted simultaneously, and that they will ultimately complement each other. The former will present the *probabilities* (the hypothesis); the latter will posit the *proofs* (verification of the hypothesis). The former will provide the *context* for the latter; the latter will provide the *text* for the former. The former will shed light on Luke as a *whole* person; the latter will illuminate some of his *specific* inclinations.

There are other practical reasons for including an outside-in approach. 1) Not all passages that I identify through the inside-out approach will be obvious cases of quotations of Classical and Hellenistic texts, agreed to without objection by all. Valid objections could be raised, for example, to the identification of a Lucan passage as a poetic verse if it has lost its original metrical shape, whether by misquotation by Luke

30   *The Formal Education of the Author of Luke-Acts*

himself or by effacement in the course of textual transmission. Where there is such ambiguity, the outside-in approach will offer the support of probability. 2) Some passages that I identify as quotations of Classical and Hellenistic texts may be categorized by others as popular maxims and aphorisms housed in anthologies that Luke quotes without any knowledge of their original literary contexts: in epics, hymns, fables, dramas, philosophical dialogues, and so forth. Often commentators seem to fall back on this solution simply because they assume that Luke could not have been familiar with these genres of literature. An outside-in approach will provide a broad context in which one can weigh the likelihood of Luke being familiar with these original works of literature, a familiarity that will then have to be supported, and perhaps even proven, by comparing the texts and contexts of Luke's passage with those of the original works: Homer's *Odyssey*, Euripides' *Bacchae*, Plato's *Apology*, etc. 3) Some scholars have identified literary devices in Luke-Acts that appear to be based on progymnastic exercises of the sort that a student typically learned in school: maxims (*gnomai*), anecdotes (*khreiai*), fables (*mythoi*), etc. Some have seen evidence of even higher levels of rhetorical training in Luke's use of encomium (*enkomion*), invective (*psogos*), comparison (*synkrisis*), ecphrasis (*ekphrasis*), and speech in character (*ethopoiia* or *prosopopoiia*), as well as in his use of certain rhetorical devices, such as *captatio benevolentiae*, paradigm, parallelism, paronomasia, and litotes. We would do well to ask whether Luke could ever have achieved the level of educational training— the most advanced level of the educational system—required to master some of these artifices. That is to say, if we were to deem such a high level of education improbable based on an outside-in approach, then we can take precautions to avoid mistakenly identifying advanced rhetorical devices in the text of Luke or Acts based exclusively on an inside-out approach.

The following two chapters, then, will use an outside-in approach, while all subsequent chapters will use an inside-out approach. In this chapter, we shall try to answer the following questions: What level of Greek literacy can we reasonably expect of someone like Luke, a Hellenized, Greek-speaking man who lived somewhere in the eastern Mediterranean during the first century CE? What level of formal education was he likely to have attained? What was the structure, methodology, and content of the traditional school curriculum available to him? Is it likely that he continued to read, hear, and witness performances of Classical and Hellenistic Greek literature in his adult life, and if so, what works would have been most popular and accessible? And what about Latin? Would someone like Luke have learned the Latin language in school, and would he have become familiar with Roman literature as well as Greek?

Ancient Education

I propose that Luke was a πεπαιδευμένος/*pepaideumenos* "educated man" who had completed at least the first two stages of the ἐγκύκλιος παιδεία/*enkyklios paideia* "curricular education" regularly experienced by children of the upper social classes throughout the eastern Mediterranean cities during the Hellenistic and early Roman periods.[1] Some may object to placing Luke in the upper classes, both socially and culturally, but by this I mean simply that Luke was among the 15 percent or so of the population that was literate.[2] Moreover, as someone who could compose large treatises that included historical prefaces, rhetorical speeches, dramatic stories, detailed travelogues, formal letters, and so forth, he was on the high end of even this 15 percent, at least so far as his education was concerned.

Luke would have become familiar with Classical and Hellenistic Greek literature simply by virtue of studying the Greek language as a youth in school. The advice of ancient rhetoricians and grammarians about what authors should be read in the educational curriculum, the evidence of actual school texts from Egypt, and the many ancient depictions on vase paintings of school children learning their letters by reading the ancient poets all combine to present a picture of an educational curriculum in the eastern Mediterranean during the Hellenistic and Roman Imperial periods that revolved primarily around the ancient poets but that also included some prose authors. In other words, the process of learning to read and write the Greek language at the primary and secondary school levels involved close contact with the ancient epic poets, tragedians, and comedians, as well as with some of the historians, orators, philosophers, and fabulists at a very early stage in Luke's life. This is not unique to Hellenistic and Roman culture, of course: until fairly recently this was the manner in which many primary and secondary students in America learned to read, honing their linguistic skills in the English language by reading aloud, copying, memorizing, and studying passages from American and British poets, such as Henry Wadsworth Longfellow, Alfred Lord Tennyson, and William Shakespeare and American and British prose writers, such as Washington Irving, Louisa May Alcott, and Christopher North. The ever-popular 1611 version of the King James Bible provided models of both poetry and prose for many young American students.

Athletics, music, poetry, and mathematics (which included arithmetic, geometry, astronomy, and musical theory) had always played important roles in Classical Greek education, but Hellenistic and Roman Imperial-era education was focused more narrowly on the correct understanding and usage of language and literature. The curriculum was structured around three more or less distinct levels:

---

[1] I use the term πεπαιδευμένος/*pepaideumenos* here in a general sense, as the ancients did, to describe someone who has received some formal education or training (e.g., Xenophon, *Mem.* 4.7.2; Plato, *Leg.* 654d; Aristotle, *Eth. nic.* 1128a), not exclusively, as some modern scholars do, to refer only to someone who has completed the advanced level of rhetorical education. The roots of the ἐγκύκλιος παιδεία/*enkyklios paideia* "curricular education" can be traced back at least to Isocrates (most extensively in his *Antidosis*), but Diodorus Siculus (first century BCE) provides the earliest surviving usage of the term itself (33.7.7). Others from the first century BCE and thereafter use the term regularly: Dionysius of Halicarnassus, Philo, Strabo, Plutarch, Athenaeus, Clement of Alexandria, Diogenes Laertius, etc. There is little reason to believe that Luke continued his formal education into the third stage of advanced grammar, rhetoric, and philosophy; perhaps after the second stage he chose instead to pursue the study of medicine through an apprenticeship (cf. the tradition of Luke as the "beloved physician" of Col. 4:14).

[2] W. V. Harris, *Ancient Literacy* (Cambridge: Harvard University Press, 1989), 323–32, offers this widely accepted calculation of literacy rates in antiquity.

32   *The Formal Education of the Author of Luke-Acts*

1. The first level involved seven- to eleven-year-old children, mostly boys but some girls, at a formal "school of letters" (γραμματεῖον or διδάσκαλεῖον or γραμματοδιδασκαλεῖον) or, perhaps just as commonly, on a portico, under an awning, or simply in a makeshift structure on the side of a street or other public place, under the tutelage of a "teacher of letters" (γραμματιστής or διδάσκαλος or γραμματοδιδάσκαλος or γραμμάτων διδάσκαλος). This level is now commonly termed "primary" education, during which period the material for learning the basics of reading and writing (letters, syllables, then complete words) was introduced, along with basic arithmetic. The curriculum included the reading (always aloud), writing, and studying of simple compositions, such as maxims and fables. Students also practiced articulating and copying passages of even very difficult ancient poetry, from the epics of Homer and the dramas of Euripides and Menander, even though they probably had little understanding of the meaning of these passages.

2. The second level involved twelve- to fifteen-year-old children, almost all boys at this stage, at a formal "grammar school" (διδασκαλεῖον) or, like primary instruction, on a portico, under an awning, or in a makeshift structure in some public place, or at the home of the teacher (ἐν διδασκάλων or εἰς διδασκάλων—*scil.* οἶκος), under the tutelage of a "grammarian" (γραμματικός or sometimes, simply διδάσκαλος or παιδευτής, or, rarely, σχολαστικός). This level is now commonly termed "secondary" education, during which period the main exercises entailed reading (again, always aloud), copying, memorizing, and construing a fairly wide range of poetry, along with some prose, and by the beginning of the first century CE, instruction in formal grammar. Instruction in more advanced mathematics, geometry, music, and astronomy sometimes complemented this core study of the literary arts. It was apparently at this stage that the carefully graded series of exercises called *progymnasmata*/προγυμνάσματα was introduced.[3] These exercises began with the study of maxims, anecdotes, fables, and short stories about famous historical and mythical figures and then proceeded, initially at the secondary level and then more fully at the tertiary level, with more sophisticated rhetorical training in refutation, affirmation, commonplace, encomium,

---

[3] Recently some New Testament scholars—e.g., M. C. Parsons, "Luke and the *Progymnasmata*: A Preliminary Investigation into the Preliminary Exercises," in *Contextualizing Acts: Lukan Narrative and Greco-Roman Discourse*, eds. T. Penner and C. Vander Stichele (Atlanta: Society of Biblical Literature, 2003), 43–63; M. W. Martin, "Progymnastic Topic Lists: A Compositional Template for Luke and other *Bioi?*" *New Testament Studies* 54 (2008): 18–41—have placed the *progymnasmata* exclusively in the advanced level of education in rhetoric, or possibly in the "transition" between the study of grammar and the study of rhetoric (it is difficult to decipher what this would mean in practice). But ancient rhetorical treatises envision these exercises beginning at a much earlier stage of education (hence the term *progymnasmata*): Quintilian lists several progymnastic exercises that he believes ought to be taught to students still too young for rhetoric (*Inst.* 1.9; 2.1, 4); Suetonius implies that all the progymnastic exercises were at one time relegated to the grammarian rather than the orator (*Rhet.* 1); Theon has very young students in mind—ones who had just learned to read and write—in his exercises that require recasting a maxim in various grammatical inflections, e.g., switching from singular to plural number or from active to passive voice (*Progymnasmata* 101–5). The duties of the grammarian must have differed from place to place throughout the Mediterranean world, depending partly, of course, on whether a professional orator was available.

The Education of the Author of Luke-Acts

invective, comparison, characterization, description, proposition, and finally, the introduction of hypothetical laws. Examples of *progymnasmata* from various periods have survived in remarkably homogeneous form in the treatises of Theon (first century CE?), "Hermogenes" (second century CE?), Aphthonius (fourth century CE), Nicolaus (fifth century CE), and "Libanius" (fourth to sixth century CE).[4]

3. The third level involved a number of years of instruction, until the age of at least eighteen, and in many cases well beyond, in a public place such as a temple, bath, "gymnasium" (γυμνάσιον), or other civic center, or in a private place such as a rented room or the teacher's own home (again, διδασκαλεῖον), under the tutelage of a resident "orator" or "sophist" (ῥήτωρ or σοφιστής), complemented on occasion by traveling scholars. This level is now commonly termed "tertiary" or "higher" education, during which period formal grammar, rhetoric, and philosophy were practiced. The curriculum entailed the completion of the higher-level exercises of the *progymnasmata* as well as direct study of the Classics: primarily Homer, Euripides, and Menander from among the poets but also many prose authors, including the Attic orators, especially Demosthenes and Isocrates, the historians Herodotus, Thucydides, Xenophon, and Theopompus, and the philosopher Plato. These two components of the curriculum complemented each other, for a student could not fulfill the basic requirements of the *progymnasmata*—e.g., to craft an encomium or invective about a Homeric hero, to compose a comparison of the lives of two mythological figures, to deliver a speech in the *persona* of a mythic or historical figure from the hoary past, to describe a scene from an ancient drama—without having read and studied the Greek Classics.

This is, with some minor refinements, the tripartite system of education—primary, secondary, tertiary—canonized by H.-I. Marrou, S. F. Bonner, and M. L. Clarke, reconstructed largely on the evidence of the many references to education by ancient rhetoricians and grammarians such as Dionysius of Halicarnassus, Dio Chrysostom, and especially Quintilian.[5] A similar reconstruction, though viewed from a different perspective, has since been envisioned by R. Cribiore and T. Morgan, who have documented the multitude of papyri, ostraca, and waxed and bleached wooden tablets from Greco-Roman Egypt that offer the witness of actual school texts and anthologies to the activities of primary and secondary level students specifically and that also offer the witness of copies of literary works to the activities of those involved in higher

---

[4] For a translation, along with some commentary, of all the treatises save "Libanius," see G. A. Kennedy, *Progymnasmata: Greek Textbook of Prose Composition and Rhetoric* (Atlanta: Society of Biblical Literature, 2003). For a translation and commentary on "Libanius," see C. A. Gibson, *Libanius's Progymnasmata: Model Exercises in Greek Prose Composition and Rhetoric* (Atlanta: Society of Biblical Literature, 2008).

[5] H.-I. Marrou, *Histoire de l'éducation dans l'antiquité* (Paris: Éditions du Seuil, 1948), H.-I. Marrou, *A History of Education in Antiquity* (London and New York: Sheed and Ward, 1956), S. F. Bonner, *Education in Ancient Rome: From the Elder Cato to the Younger Pliny* (Berkeley: University of California Press, 1977), esp. 35–75, 165–276, and M. L. Clarke, *Higher Education in the Ancient World* (London: Routledge & K. Paul: 1971).

34 *The Formal Education of the Author of Luke-Acts*

education as well as of the general reading public.[6] Cribiore points to the great emphasis placed on the skills of writing and copying, in addition to reading, especially at a primary stage of education. Morgan cautions that the educational curriculum may not have been quite as ambitious as the literary references to education, such as those of Quintilian, portray and that most students attained only a simple core of skills, not real reading knowledge of the Classics. The material from Egypt marshaled by Cribiore and Morgan is most important, since, given the uniformity of the educational curriculum throughout the Mediterranean world, the evidence from Greco-Roman Egypt can be extended by analogy to such Hellenized cities as Tarsus and Antioch and even Jerusalem.[7] Further modifications to the traditional view of the tripartite educational structure have been proposed by A. D. Booth and R. A. Kaster, who question the overly generalized description of this system, show how the distinction between the primary and secondary levels was sometimes effaced, especially among the aristocrats, and propose an alternate two-track system, one to provide rudimentary education for the poor and the slaves, the other to provide a liberal education for the aristocrats.[8] In any case, we can assume with some confidence that any student who had completed the primary and secondary levels of education in a typical Hellenized city of the East would have become familiar with a fairly wide array of Classical and Hellenistic Greek authors.

---

[6] R. Cribiore, *Writing, Teachers, and Students in Graeco-Roman Egypt* (Atlanta: Scholars Press, 1996), R. Cribiore, *Gymnastics of the Mind: Greek Education in Hellenistic and Roman Egypt* (Princeton: Princeton University Press, 2001), and T. Morgan, *Literate Education in the Hellenistic and Roman Worlds* (Cambridge: Cambridge University, 1998), draw on much new evidence, but they are also reliant on earlier collections of evidence on papyri, tablets, and ostraca. Significant earlier works include J. G. Milne, "Relics of Graeco-Egyptian Schools," *Journal of Hellenic Studies* 28 (1908): 121–32; F. G. Kenyon, "Two Greek School-Tablets," *Journal of Hellenic Studies* 29 (1909): 29–40; E. Ziebarth, *Aus der antiken Schule: Sammlung griechischer Texte auf Papyrus, Holtztafeln, Ostraka* (Bonn: A. Marcus & E. Weber, 1910); P. Beudel, *Qua ratione Graeci liberos docuerint, papyris, ostracis, tabulis in Aegypto inventis illustratur* (Monasterii Guestfalorum: Aschendorffiana, 1911); J. G. Milne, "More Relics of Graeco-Egyptian Schools," *Journal of Hellenic Studies* 43 (1923): 40–3; P. Collart, *Les Papyrus Bouriant* (Paris: H. Champion, 1926); P. Collart, "A l'école avec les petits Grecs d'Égypte," *Chronique d'Égypte* 11 (1936): 489–507; P. Collart, "Les papyrus scolaires," in *Mélanges offerts à A.M. Desrousseaux,* eds. "*par ses amis et ses élèves*" (Paris: Hachette, 1937), 69–80; O. Guéraud and P. Jouguet, *Un livre d'écolier du IIIe siècle avant J.-C.* (Cairo: Institut français d'Archéologie orientale, 1938); R. A. Pack, *The Greek and Latin Literary Texts from Greco-Roman Egypt,* 2nd ed. (Ann Arbor: University of Michigan Press, 1965), 137–40; J. M. Galé, *Las escuelas del antiguo Egipto a través de los papiros griegos* (Madrid: Publicaciones de la Fondación Universitaria Española, 1961); G. Zalateo, "Papiri scolastici," *Aegyptus* 41 (1961): 160–235; W. Clarysse and A. Wouters, "A Schoolboy's Exercise in the Chester Beatty Library," *Ancient Society* 1 (1970): 201–35; J. Kramer, *Glossaria Bilinguia in Papyris et Membranis Reperta* (*C. Gloss. Biling.* I) (Bonn: R. Habelt, 1983); J. Debut, "Les documents scolaires," *Zeitschrift für Papyrologie und Epigraphik* 63 (1986): 251–78.

[7] On the homogeneity of Greco-Roman education in the Mediterranean world during the Hellenistic and Roman Imperial periods, see H.-I. Marrou, *A History of Education,* 95–6, 265–6; P. E. Easterling and B. M. W. Knox, eds., *The Cambridge History of Classical Literature,* vol. 1 (Cambridge: Cambridge University Press, 1985), 22–9; T. Morgan, *Literate Education,* 3–4, 21–5, 44–7; K. Vössing, "Augustins Schullaufbahn und das sog. dreistufige Bildungssystem," in *L'Africa Romana,* vol. 2, ed. A. Mastino, (Sassari: Gallizzi, 1992), 881–900; R. Cribiore, *Gymnastics of the Mind,* 5–9.

[8] A. D. Booth, "Elementary and Secondary Education in the Roman Empire," *Florilegium* 1 (1979): 1–14, and R. A. Kaster, "Notes on 'Primary' and 'Secondary' Schools in Late Antiquity," *Transactions of the American Philological Association* 113 (1983): 323–46.

Illustrations of Ancient School Exercises

Two Primary-Level School Exercises

Actual teachers' manuals and students' school texts from Greco-Roman Egypt, written on papyri, ostraca, and waxed and bleached wooden tablets, offer a treasure trove of information on the ancient school curriculum. Our first illustration is a fifth-century CE (?) wooden tablet from Antinoopolis in Egypt (*T.Louvre* inv. AF 1195 = SB 20 14654) upon which a teacher models a didactic iambic trimeter verse in a large and proficient hand that a student then tries to copy three times, with many mistakes, in a painfully rudimentary hand.[9] Underneath the model the teacher signs his name: Flavius Collouthos son of Isakios. The verse—which is included among Menander's *sententiae* and also appears in several other school texts—runs: ἀρχὴ μεγίστη τοῦ φρονεῖν τὰ γράμματα "letters (*grammata*) are the greatest beginning of understanding."

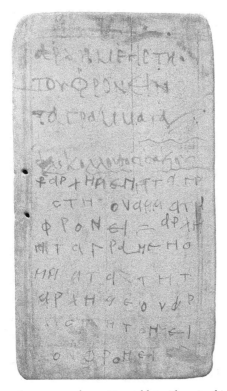

Figure 2 A school exercise on a wooden writing tablet with an iambic trimeter *sententia* of the comic poet Menander (*T.Louvre* inv. AF 1195). Courtesy of the Musée du Louvre, Département des Antiquités égyptiennes.

---

[9] The *editio princeps* of this tablet is P. Cauderlier, "Cinq tablettes en bois au Musée du Louvre," *Revue archéologique* 2 (1983): 276–9. The tablet is also considered by R. Cribiore, *Gymnastics of the Mind*, 39–40.

Our second illustration is a second-century CE (?) waxed writing tablet, of unknown provenance in Egypt, of a school text containing two iambic trimeter verses from the comic poet Menander (British Library Manuscripts accession number Add MS 34186(1) = Mertens-Pack³ 2713).¹⁰ The first two lines of the tablet, written neatly in the large, formal hand of a teacher, serve as a model for a student, who copies them twice in a hesitant and rudimentary hand:

σοφοῦ παρ' ἀνδρὸς προσδέχου συμβουλίαν
μὴ πᾶσιν εἰκῆ τοῖς φίλοις πιστεύεται [sic]

Accept counsel from a wise man
Don't vainly trust all your friends

The teacher has misspelled πιστεύετε as πιστεύεται at the end of the second verse (owing to the phonetic similarity of the two words at the time). The student, who apparently did not understand the meaning of the verses, has mangled them further, omitting the first letter of the first word σοφοῦ in the first verse, thereby creating a meaningless word ὀφοῦ, and has further mutilated the teacher's misspelling πιστεύεται with the nonexistent ending πιστεύετλι and then with the equally meaningless πιστεύθται.

Figure 3 A school exercise on a waxed writing tablet with two verses of the comic poet Menander (British Library Manuscripts accession number Add MS 34186(1)). Courtesy of the British Library Board.

---

¹⁰ The *editio princeps* of this tablet is F. G. Kenyon, "Two Greek School-Tablets," 29–40.

Figure 4 Multiplication tables written in the hand of a teacher along with five personal names divided into syllables written in the hand of a student (British Library Manuscripts accession number Add MS 34186(2)). Courtesy of the British Library Board.

The two holes at the top of the tablet could be used to bind it to other tablets to create a schoolbook of sorts. In fact, on a second tablet that was once bound to this one can be found some multiplication tables, arranged consecutively from 1 × 1 to 3 × 10, written in the hand of (the same?) teacher and five two-syllable personal names divided into syllables written in the hand of the same student.[11]

Two Primary- and Secondary-Level School Texts

Our first illustration is a late third-century BCE papyrus roll, reportedly from Arsinoites in the Fayum, currently housed in the Egyptian Museum in Cairo (*Journal d'entrée* no. 65445), that contains an extensive series of school exercises.[12] The clear and skillful hand suggests that the roll is a teacher's manual rather than a student's schoolwork. Two large fragments survive, both from the lower half of the papyrus roll. The first fragment is 66 centimeters long and is from near the beginning of the original roll. The second fragment is 176 centimeters long and includes the end of the roll. The space between the two fragments (i.e., the missing section in the middle of the roll) is very small, and one can assume with some confidence that the lower half of almost the entire roll, which would originally have been about 285 centimeters long, has survived.

---

[11] On this second tablet see W. Brashear, "A Trifle," *Zeitschrift für Papyrologie und Epigraphik* 86 (1991): 231–2.

[12] The entire papyrus was edited and well illustrated in its first publication: O. Guéraud and P. Jouguet, *Un livre d'écolier*.

The roll contains exercises that served students at various levels of literacy. The (missing) beginning of the roll probably included an alphabet. The first fragment begins with a list of short syllables: e.g., ΨΑ, ΨΕ, ΨΗ, ΨΙ, ΨΟ, ΨΥ, ΨΩ. This is followed by a long list of three- and four-letter syllables that work their way through the alphabet: e.g., ΒΙΝ, ΓΙΝ, ΔΙΝ, ΖΙΝ, ΘΙΝ ... It does not seem to matter that some of the combinations of letters do not actually exist in the Greek language: e.g., ΖΡΑΣ, ΖΡΕΣ, ΖΡΗΣ, ΖΡΙΣ, ΖΡΟΣ, ΖΡΥΣ, ΖΡΩΣ.

The syllabary is followed by a list of Macedonian months, a sequence of numbers from one to at least twenty-five, and a series of hard-to-pronounce, monosyllabic words (ΣΤΡΑΓΞ, ΚΝΑΞ, ΚΛΑΓΞ), mostly nouns of the third declension (ΘΗΡ, ΠΥΡ, ΚΗΡ), many of which are names of animals (ΛΥΓΞ, ΧΗΝ, ΑΙΞ) and of various parts of the human body (ΣΑΡΞ, ΠΟΥΣ, ΧΕΙΡ).

Next in order is a list of the names of the Olympian gods, some of them arranged in natural pairs: Ares and Athena (gods of war); Hephaestus and Aphrodite (husband and wife); Apollo and Artemis (siblings). A list of the world's rivers, most from Greece, Thrace, and Asia Minor, many of which are mentioned in Homer, Hesiod, and Herodotus, bridges the small gap between the two fragments of the papyrus roll. The second fragment continues with a long list of two-, three-, four-, and then five-syllable

Figure 5 Syllabary for primary-level students (O. Guéraud and P. Jouguet, Plate I). Courtesy of the Egyptian Museum in Cairo and the Institut français d'Archéologie orientale du Caire.

The Education of the Author of Luke-Acts   39

Figure 6 Names of mythic heroes divided into syllables (O. Guéraud and P. Jouguet, Plate III). Courtesy of the Egyptian Museum in Cairo and the Institut français d'Archéologie orientale du Caire.

names of mythic heroes (along with the names of a few famous historical figures): Orpheus, Telephos, Eteokles, Anaxagoras. More than a third of the names appear in the Homeric epics: Kastor, Hektor, Arktos, Thoas, Gouneus, Zethos, Aias, Teukros, Odysseus, Iason, Achilles, Amphimachos, Askalaphos, Elpenor, Polyneikes, Antilochos, Arkesilaos. Because of the scarcity of five-syllable names in Greek, the teacher has had to resort in two instances to occupational names: ΟΡΓΑΝΟΠΟΙΟΣ "instrument-maker," ΑΡΜΑΤΟΠΗΓΟΣ "chariot-builder." These lists of names are primarily intended as exercises in syllabification: each name is divided properly into syllables, separated by a space and a colon: e.g., ΙΠ : ΠΟ : ΜΕ : ΔΩΝ. Also, the choice of both divine and mortal names on the two lists appears to be determined to some extent by the selection of literary passages that follow, where, for example, we again meet Eteokles and Polyneikes in the Euripidean passage and Artemis and Demeter in the Homeric passage.

Then—surely to the surprise of a modern educator—the series of school exercises transitions abruptly into an anthology of ancient Greek poetry with selections illustrating various genres of verse. Placed first is a selection of two tragedies of Euripides in iambic trimeter: the extremely popular *Phoenissae* (529–34) and the much less frequently attested *Ino* (fr. 420 Nauck).[13] These passages were selected not for

[13] On the high frequency of representations of the *Phoenissae* during this period in both literary and school papyri, see J. M. Bremer, "The Popularity of Euripides' *Phoenissae* in Late Antiquity," in *Actes du VIIe Congrès de la Fédération Internationale des Associations d'Études classiques*, vol. 1, ed. J. Harmatta (Budapest: Akadémiai Kiadó, 1984), 281–8, and R. Cribiore, "The Grammarian's Choice: The Popularity of Euripides' *Phoenissae* in Hellenistic and Roman Education," in *Education in Greek and Roman Antiquity*, ed. Y. L. Too (Leiden: Brill, 2001), 241–59.

reading pleasure but for their gnomic value. The passage from the *Phoenissae* is a moralizing speech by Jocasta to her son Eteocles warning him not to be overly ambitious and advising him that the experience of old age has something to teach the young. The passage from the *Ino* contains a warning that power and wealth are fleeting. The passages are laid out instructively: like the preceding list of names of mythic heroes, the iambic trimeter verses are divided into syllables by spaces and colons in order to illustrate both syllabification and versification. In the passage from the *Phoenissae*, each verse occupies two lines in the school text, with the first line-end demarcating the caesura of the second metron of each verse. This paedagogical device is dispensed with in the passage from the *Ino*, where each iambic trimeter verse occupies a full line in the text.

The selection of iambic trimeters of Euripides is followed by a selection of dactylic hexameters from Homer's *Odyssey* (5.116–24). This is a memorable passage in which Hermes delivers a message from Zeus to Calypso that she must give Odysseus up and allow him to return home to Ithaca. Hermes' message causes Calypso to lament the misfortune that inevitably comes upon goddesses who fall in love with humans. In the presentation of this passage the paedagogical devices that illustrated the syllabification and versification of the Euripidean passages have been dispensed with altogether, and

Figure 7 A passage of Euripides' *Ino* with the verses divided into syllables by spaces and colons, followed by a passage of Homer's *Odyssey* with no paedagogical devices (O. Guéraud and P. Jouguet, Plate IV). Courtesy of the Egyptian Museum in Cairo and the Institut français d'Archéologie orientale du Caire.

The Education of the Author of Luke-Acts   41

the text is similar to that of a typical manuscript of Homer from this period. It is written line by line in full verses, with no punctuation or diacritical marks, without any indication of syllabic or even word divisions (i.e., *scriptio continua*), and with the scansion superficially obfuscated by the nonobservance of elision (i.e., *scriptio plena*). In other words, this selection poses increasingly difficult challenges for the student, who would have needed a significant amount of formal training simply to read it and, of course, even more actually to understand it.[14]

There follow some selections from poets closer in time to the composition of the papyrus. The first is an epigram in elegiac couplets (i.e., dactylic hexameters alternating with dactylic pentameters), perhaps by Posidippus, the Macedonian poet who had moved to the court of Ptolemy I Soter and later Ptolemy II Philadelphus in Alexandria in the mid-third century BCE. The epigram is an example of ecphrasis, celebrating a marble fountain built by Ptolemy II that is apparently decorated with a statue of Ptolemy, his wife Arsinoe, and a group of nymphs. Like the preceding Homeric passage, the paedagogical devices that illustrated the syllabification and versification of the Euripidean passages have been dispensed with: the text is written line by line in full verses, with no punctuation or diacritical marks and without any indication of syllabic or even word divisions (i.e., *scriptio continua*). However, unlike the Homeric passage, the scansion is not obfuscated by the nonobservance of elision (i.e., it is not written in *scriptio plena*). The second selection, also an epigram in elegiac couplets, by a poet later in the third century BCE, possibly Eratosthenes, celebrates a monument dedicated to Homer apparently by Ptolemy IV Philopator.

The remaining literary texts on the papyrus are from new comedy. The first two fragments, possibly from the same play, contain monologues, spoken in iambic trimeter, by a cook. In the first fragment, a cook is complaining that while he has completed all the preparations for a banquet and/or sacrifice the guests continue to dillydally outside the door. In the second fragment, a cook is describing how he has pilfered many of the food items on the menu: meat, tripe, cheese, suet, olive oil, honey, laserwort, acid juice, cumin, mustard. Cooks serve as stock characters in new comedy, but this particular passage may have been selected to introduce students to the specialized vocabulary of the kitchen.

The third and fourth fragments contain a passage from a late fourth-century BCE comedy, the *Phoenicides*, by the new comic poet Strato—Athenaeus quotes the same passage in his *Deipnosophist* 9.29 and identifies the author. The passage records a cook and his master having a conversation about an upcoming feast. The pompous cook interjects numerous Homeric words and phrases into his speech, much to the annoyance of his master. This passage may have been selected precisely because of this interplay of Homeric diction and the vernacular.

Finally, some mathematical exercises are appended to the end of the roll: first the squares of 1–10, 20–90, and 100–800—e.g., $5 \times 5 = 25, 6 \times 6 = 36, 7 \times 7 = 49 \ldots$ $20 \times 20 = 400, 30 \times 30 = 900, 40 \times 40 = 1{,}600 \ldots 600 \times 600 = 360{,}000, 700 \times 700 = 490{,}000,$

---

[14] Any reader in the ancient world would have had to overcome these challenges, including Luke himself, who wrote the autographs of his gospel and Acts—or had them written by an amanuensis—in a similar style and format (see Appendix I).

42 The Formal Education of the Author of Luke-Acts

Figure 8 Mathematical exercises (O. Guéraud and P. Jouguet, Plate X). Courtesy of the Egyptian Museum in Cairo and the Institut français d'Archéologie orientale du Caire.

800 × 800 = 640,000; then a list of acronyms representing sub-multiples of the drachma (i.e., exercises in counting money)—e.g., 1/6 of a drachma is 1 obol; 1/3 of a drachma is 2 obols; 1/2 of a drachma is 3 obols.

This teacher's manual offers just a glimpse, of course, of the ancient Greek educational curriculum. The contents of other school texts from this period indicate that the teacher would have supplemented these exercises and readings with many others, both written and oral. So far as other genres of literature are concerned (i.e., in addition to the epic, tragedy, comedy, and elegy in this manual), the teacher would have included many maxims in poetic form, some attributable to Euripides and Menander, as well as some prose readings: sayings of a gnomic nature, fables, summaries of myths, and paraphrases of famous passages of literature (i.e., primitive forms of what would later become the secondary-level *progymnasmata*). School texts from later periods illustrate students being subjected also to a formidable array of grammatical exercises: conjugating verbs, declining nouns and pronouns, arranging verbs according to what cases they governed, classifying substantives into nouns, adjectives, and pronouns, and declining entire sentences using complex syntax that tested case usage.[15] For our purpose of reconstructing Luke's educational reading list, a few features stand out: the

---

[15] Illustrations of these exercises can be found in the many third-century CE wooden school tablets from Egypt: e.g., British Museum Add. MS. 37516 and 37533, first published by F. G. Kenyon, "Two Greek School-Tablets," 29–40; *T.Bodl.Gk.Inscr.* 3019, first published by P. J. Parsons, "A School-Book from the Sayce Collection," *Zeitschrift für Papyrologie und Epigraphik* 6 (1970): 133–49.

speed with which students advanced from elementary writing and pronunciation exercises to fairly difficult literature; the centrality of poetry in teaching students to read and write; the exposure of students to most of the common genres of poetry (the iambic trimeters of tragedy and comedy, the dactylic hexameters of epic, the elegiac couplets of epigrams). In short, ancient students throughout the Mediterranean world learned to read and write by being exposed to Classical and Hellenistic Greek literature. This would have applied as much to a young Luke doing his lessons in Antioch or Ephesus or Troas, or, really, anywhere in the eastern Mediterranean, as it does to our anonymous students in the far reaches of inland Egypt.

One may object that a third-century BCE school text from inland Egypt is of little value in trying to reconstruct the education of a first-century CE student like Luke, who probably grew up in Syria or somewhere in Asia Minor, but this is to fail to appreciate the temporal and geographical homogeneity of ancient Greek education. It may be useful, for example, to compare a school exercise on the other end of the spectrum: hence, our second illustration, an excellent example for the sake of comparison, *P.Bouriant* 1 (= *P.Sorbonne* inv. 826), a fourth-century CE school text on

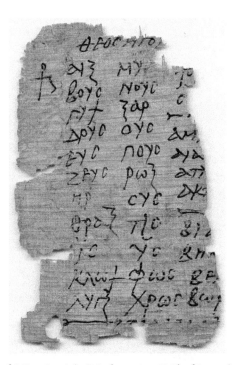

Figure 9 A section of *P.Bouriant* 1 (= *P.Sorbonne* inv. 826 leaf 1 recto) listing one-syllable words in alphabetical order: αἴξ "goat," βοῦς "cow," γύψ "vulture," δρῦς "oak," εὔς "noble," Ζεύς "Zeus," etc. The manuscript begins with the word θεός "god," and a Christogram has been drawn in the top left corner. Courtesy of the Institut de Papyrologie de la Sorbonne.

papyrus from somewhere in Egypt (provenance unknown).[16] The text is apparently written in the hand of a student at the secondary level, the surviving portion of which begins with lists of increasingly long words, beginning with one-syllable words and ending with four-syllable words, all arranged in alphabetical order, many of them proper names from Homer, Hesiod, Attic drama, Menander, and Apollonius of Rhodes (presumably to prepare the student for reading these works).

There follow five *khreiai* (prose sayings) of the philosopher Diogenes; twenty-four *gnomai* (one-line iambic trimeter aphorisms), in alphabetical order, of a type associated with the comic poet Menander; eleven iambic trimeter verses from a prologue to the fables of Babrius; and an imitation of a colophon of a literary papyrus.

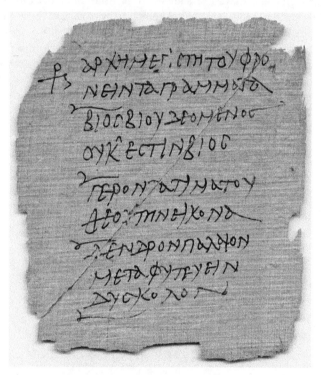

Figure 10 Section of *P.Bouriant* 1 (= *P.Sorbonne* inv. 826 leaf 7 verso) listing twenty-four *gnomai* (one-line iambic trimeter aphorisms), in alphabetical order, of a type associated with the comic poet Menander. Each trimeter occupies two or three lines in this manuscript. The first trimeter is identical to the one on the wooden tablet treated above (*T.Louvre* inv. AF 1195): ἀρχὴ μεγίστη τοῦ φρονεῖν τὰ γράμματα "letters (*grammata*) are the greatest beginning of understanding." A Christogram has been drawn in the top left corner. Courtesy of the Institut de Papyrologie de la Sorbonne.

---

[16] First edited by P. Jouguet and P. Perdrizet, "Le Papyrus Bouriant no. 1: Un cahier d'écolier grec d'Egypte," *Studien zur Palaeographie und Papyruskunde* 6 (1906): 148–61.

The Education of the Author of Luke-Acts   45

A comparison of this fourth-century CE school text with the late third-century BCE school text treated above illustrates how little educational methodology and content changed during the interim.[17] *P.Bouriant* 1 is additionally interesting because it shows that the education of the student who writes this text, who is apparently a Christian—a Christogram is drawn at the top of each section—was no different in methodology or content from that of his pagan counterparts.

Did Luke Know Latin?

What about Latin? Can we assume that someone who lived in the eastern Mediterranean during the time of Luke and who underwent the typical education available there at that time would have learned Latin as well as Greek and would have become familiar with Roman as well as Greek literary works? Some have thought so and have even proposed that Luke drew inspiration from works of Roman literature.[18] But the simple answer is "no." In Luke's era the populace of the eastern Mediterranean, though living in Roman provinces ruled by Roman laws, did not normally learn Latin except for very practical purposes: if they intended to move westward or wanted to advance themselves in the areas of business, civil administration, law, politics, or in the military. There is no

---

[17] There are many other examples of school texts, spanning a several-hundred-year period, that illustrate the same homogeneity in education. A particularly interesting example can be found in the remains of a fourth-century CE Greek school building, discovered in 2006 in upper Egypt, with three rooms, benches along the walls, and copious writing on the walls: individual letters and words; mythological names; exhortations in elegiac couplets that employ diction from Homer, Apollonius of Rhodes, and some later epic verse; three lines of Homer's *Odyssey* (4.221–3); a line of Euripides' *Hypsipyle*; and what appears to be a reworking of a passage from Plutarch's *Moralia*. There is heavy use of accentuation and other lectional signs. The school is probably a grammarian's (i.e., secondary level), but there is evidence of various levels of education being conducted in the space. See R. Cribiore, P. Davoli, and D. M. Ratzan, "A Teacher's Dipinto from Trimithis (Dakhleh Oasis)," *Journal of Roman Archaeology* 21 (2008): 170–91, and R. Cribiore and P. Davoli, "New Literary Texts from Amheida, Ancient Trimithis (Dakhla Oasis, Egypt)," *Zeitschrift für Papyrologie und Epigraphik* 187 (2013): 1–14. Cribiore and Ratzan identify the teacher as an orator and a poet, based largely on the evidence of the elegiac couplets, but this seems to me an overly generous estimation of the quality of the poetry.

[18] So M. Bonz, *The Past as Legacy: Luke-Acts and Ancient Epic* (Minneapolis: Fortress, 2000), who proposes that Luke was profoundly influenced by Vergil and that Luke-Acts imitates Vergil's *Aeneid* inasmuch as its appropriation of the account of Israel's history in the Septuagint is analogous to the *Aeneid*'s appropriation of various accounts in the Homeric epics. Similarly, D. R. MacDonald, *Luke and Vergil: Imitations of Classical Greek Literature* (Lanham: Rowman & Littlefield, 2015), and D. R. MacDonald, *Luke and the Politics of Homeric Imitation: Luke-Acts as Rival to the* Aeneid (Lanham: Lexington Books/Fortress Academic, 2019), assumes Luke's familiarity with Vergil's *Aeneid* and proposes that Luke shaped his two-volume work to rival it. Both Bonz's and MacDonald's proposals are implausible, as there are no—even faint—allusions to Vergil's *Aeneid* in Luke-Acts and since the likelihood of Luke even knowing Latin, much less to a degree that he could read Vergil's *Aeneid* and then attempt to rival it, is very slim. The same objection applies to some recent attempts to position other works of the New Testament as responses to Vergil's *Aeneid*: e.g., D. R. Wallace, *The Gospel of God: Romans as Paul's* Aeneid (Eugene: Pickwick, 2008), who proposes that Paul's strategy in writing his letter to the Romans was to reject and counterbalance the nationalistic agenda espoused by Vergil's *Aeneid*; F. E. Schneider, *Mark Challenges the* Aeneid (Eugene: Wipf & Stock, 2019), who proposes that Mark wrote his gospel as a deliberate and intertextual challenge to Vergil's *Aeneid*.

46   The Formal Education of the Author of Luke-Acts

reason to suppose that the author of Luke-Acts, despite his Roman name—if Luke was his name—knew Latin beyond a rudimentary level: i.e., a level at which he could communicate in simple terms with a Roman soldier or official. Indeed, like the other gospel writers, Luke sometimes uses Latin loan words, transliterating them into Greek and adding Greek suffixes: πραιτώριον, κολωνία, σικάριος, ἀσσάριον, δηνάριον, σιμικίνθιον, σουδάριον. But this is no indication of his familiarity with the Latin language, for this was a common practice among writers of Koine Greek generally when addressing Roman military, political, and commercial matters. Moreover, Luke is the least predisposed among the gospel writers to resort to Latin loanwords, and he sometimes even eschews Latin terms where his sources embrace them: e.g., he substitutes Greek ἑκατοντάρχης for Latin κεντυρίων, φόρος for κῆνσος, σκεῦος for μόδιος.[19]

Greek authors of the eastern Mediterranean contemporary with Luke, such as Plutarch, Philo, and Josephus, illustrate a general lack of interest in Latin literature. For as often as they quote and cite Greek literary figures, their works are almost entirely lacking in references to the works of Latin literary figures. Plutarch, a first-century CE philosopher and biographer from Chaeronea in Greece, as highly educated and well read as he was, as prodigious an amount of writing as he produced, and despite the fact that he lived much closer than Luke to the Roman sphere of influence, even teaching in Rome for some time, cites only four Latin authors in his entire *Moralia* (excepting the *Quaestiones Romanae*): Livy at 326a, Cicero at 797d, Valerius Antias at 323c, and Sulla at 786e. This is a stark contrast to his many thousands of citations of Greek authors. It is therefore not surprising to learn that Plutarch did not even attempt to learn the Latin language until he was old, as he himself admits, and even then was not able to devote much time or energy to mastering it (*Demosthenes* 2.2–3). Philo, a Jewish philosopher from Alexandria, who, like Luke, lived in the first century CE in a large city in a Roman province of the eastern Mediterranean and was familiar with, and even well educated in, Greek literature and philosophy, quotes and refers to Greek writers hundreds of times in his considerable works, most frequently Homer, Heraclitus, Euripides, Plato, and Aristotle, but he does not mention a single Latin author. The Jewish historian Josephus, whose lifetime coincides almost exactly with that of Luke, was utterly steeped in Judaism, and Aramaic was his native tongue, but he mentions and quotes an astounding number of Classical and Hellenistic Greek authors, showing the most interest in the genres of epic, philosophy, and history, both in his own history *Antiquities* and in his treatise *Against Apion*. Of authors of Latin literature, however, Josephus mentions only Livy by name, referring to him in a single passage as a writer of Roman history.

The more mundane documentary manuscripts from the eastern Mediterranean too indicate a general lack of familiarity with Latin language and literature. Of the many thousands of published papyrological texts from Egypt that were written during the three centuries surrounding Luke's lifetime, only 1 percent have any Latin written on

---

[19] F. Blass, A. Debrunner, and R. W. Funk, *A Greek Grammar of the New Testament and Other Early Christian Literature* (Chicago: University of Chicago Press, 1961), 4–6 (paragraph 5), offers a brief treatment of Latin loan words in the New Testament that is sufficient for our purposes.

The Education of the Author of Luke-Acts   47

them, and these are largely from Roman military contexts.[20] Of the documentary papyri that appear from the style and content of their writing to be school texts, less than 3.5 percent have any Latin written on them, and the few that do were probably used in the education of children in Roman military camps.[21] The situation in the Roman province of Egypt illustrates what must have been the situation in the other Roman provinces of the eastern Mediterranean as well.

It appears, then, both from literary works and from documentary texts of the period that Latin played little or no part in the formal education of children or in the literary sensibilities of adults in the Hellenistic and Roman Imperial-era East—except in the context of Roman military camps. Vergil's *Aeneid*, which was always popular among Roman soldiers, is the most commonly quoted Latin text on these documents; in fact we now have quotations of Vergil on documents from several different Roman military camps located throughout the Roman world: the Roman garrison of Vindolanda along Hadrian's Wall in Britain, the Roman garrison built on top of Masada in Judaea, and several of the military camps in Egypt.[22] Clearly Vergil was on the minds of Roman soldiers as far apart as Britain, Judaea, and Egypt during the first century CE; this is completely understandable, given that parts of his *Aeneid* served as a "mission statement" for the expansion of Roman power abroad. These documents do not suggest, however, that Vergil was known among the general populace of the far western and eastern Mediterranean at this early date. In fact, with the exception of these texts found in a Roman military context, it is not until after the fourth century CE that Latin texts begin to show up in the East in any significant numbers, first on papyrus and then on parchment, and this is also about the time that a few writers of Latin actually begin to originate in the East: e.g., the court poet Claudian of Alexandria and the historian Ammianus Marcellinus of Antioch.

There is an interesting category of "Latin" documents from the first century and thereafter that may illustrate how someone like Luke would have engaged with the Latin language. Some papyri from this period contain bilingual Greek-Latin glossaries, with both the Greek and Latin words written in the Greek alphabet: names of various animals, fish, insects, vegetables, household furniture and other items, zodiac signs, winds, Roman and Egyptian months, and the Greek divinities and their Roman

---

[20] The numbers of published Greek, Demotic, and Latin documentary papyri are readily calculable through the interdisciplinary portal Trismegistos (www.trismegistos.org). From between 800 BCE and 800 CE Trismegistos lists 50,707 Greek, 4,019 Demotic, and 684 Latin documentary papyri. From the Hellenistic Greek and Roman Imperial periods, between 300 BCE and 300 CE, Trismegistos lists 38,089 Greek, 4,180 Demotic, and 471 Latin documentary papyri. From the period that we are most concerned with in our examination of Luke's education, between 100 BCE and 200 CE, Trismegistos lists 24,454 Greek, 2,316 Demotic, and 289 Latin documentary papyri.

[21] From between 800 BCE and 800 CE Trismegistos lists 852 in Greek, 70 in Demotic, and 31 in Latin. From the Hellenistic Greek and Roman Imperial periods, between 300 BCE and 300 CE, Trismegistos lists 517 in Greek, 58 in Demotic, and 20 in Latin. From the period that we are most concerned with in our examination of Luke's education, between 100 BCE and 200 CE, Trismegistos lists 373 in Greek, 53 in Demotic, and 15 in Latin.

[22] See Appendix II for a comprehensive list of Latin literary texts that have been found on documents dated between 100 BCE and 200 CE—on papyrus rolls, parchment codices, ostraca, and leaf tablets—most of which are identifiable as from a Roman military context.

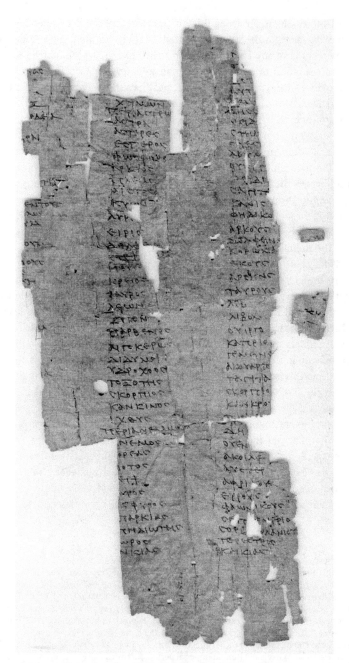

Figure 11 A bilingual Greek-Latin thematic glossary of terms associated with the sky, stars, and winds (*P.Oxyrhynchus* 78.5162). This illustration is from the section on constellations: περὶ ἄστρων – δη σε[ιδεριβους] (= *de sideribus* "concerning the stars"). Courtesy of the Egypt Exploration Society, London, and the Imaging Papyri Project, University of Oxford.

The Education of the Author of Luke-Acts

counterparts. Such glossaries became commonplace in the later *Hermeneumata* (below), but with the Latin words increasingly written in the Latin alphabet. In lieu of learning the Latin language formally, Luke may have carried around with him a bilingual list of such useful words and phrases—a sort of "Berlitz Latin" for foreign travelers. A good example of this genre is *P.Oxyrhynchus* 78.5162, which dates precisely to the time of Luke (50–150 CE) and contains a bilingual Greek-Latin thematic glossary of terms associated with the sky, stars, and winds. The owner of the glossary need not have even known the Latin alphabet, for the Latin words are written in Greek letters. A document of this sort would have served Luke well during his travels by ship from Caesarea to Rome, as narrated in Acts 27–28.

In the following transcription, I have left the several misspellings as they appear on the papyrus:

ἵππο[ς] – εκους (= *equus* "horse")
κρειός – αρειηνς (= *aries* "ram")
ταῦρος – ταυρους (= *taurus* "bull")
λέων – λεο (= *leo* "lion")
ζυγόν – λιβολ (= *libra* "scales")
παρθένος – ουιργο (= *virgo* "virgin")
αἰγόκερως – καπριοκ[ορνους] (= *capricornus* "goat-horned")
δίδυμοι – γεμεινει (= *gemini* "twins")
ὑδροχόος – ακουαριου[ς] (= *aquarius* "water-pourer")
τοξότης – ταγιταρ[ιους] (= *sagittarius* "archer")
σκορπίος – σκορπιο (= *scorpio* "scorpion")
κανκίνος – κανκρου[ς] (= *cancer* "crab")
ἰχθῦς – πισκε[ι]ς (= *piscis* "fish")

The later *Hermeneumata*—bilingual (Greek and Latin) lists of alphabets, conjugated verbs, prepositional phrases, maxims, anecdotes, models of letters (i.e., epistles), fables of Aesop and Babrius, summaries of Greek myths, and short dialogues and narratives that reproduced scenes of everyday life—while mostly intended for Latin speakers who wished to learn Greek, were also clearly intended for Greek speakers who wished to learn some Latin. These *Hermeneumata* are found in their most systematic form in about fifty medieval manuscripts and early printed books, much of the material of which was originally composed between the second and fourth centuries CE, but elements of the *Hermeneumata* appear more piecemeal also in earlier papyri, some of which go back to as early as the first century BCE (especially bilingual alphabets and glossaries).[23]

---

[23] For a critical edition, with commentary, of the *Hermeneumata* in the medieval manuscripts, see E. Dickey, *The Colloquia of the Hermeneumata Pseudodositheana, Vol. I: Colloquia Monacensia-Einsidlensia, Leidense-Stephani, and Stephani* (Cambridge: Cambridge University Press, 2012); E. Dickey, *The Colloquia of the Hermeneumata Pseudodositheana, Vol. II: Colloquium Harleianum, Colloquium Montepessulanum, Colloquium Celtis, and Fragments* (Cambridge: Cambridge University Press, 2015). On the papyri, see J. Kramer, *Glossaria Bilinguia in Papyris*; J. Kramer, *Glossaria Bilinguia Altera* (*C. Gloss. Biling.* II) (Munich: K. G. Saur, 2001); E. Dickey, "Teaching Latin to Greek Speakers in Antiquity," in *Learning Latin and Greek from Antiquity to the Present*, eds. E. P. Archibald, W. Brockliss, and J. Gnoza (Cambridge: Cambridge University Press, 2015), 30–51.

50 *The Formal Education of the Author of Luke-Acts*

These bilingual lists of the *Hermeneumata* were intended for older students and adults who wanted to learn some Latin for practical reasons: in order to advance themselves in business, the military, civil administration, law, or politics.[24]

In sum, while Greek was regularly taught to young children in the schools of the Latin-speaking western Roman Empire, Latin never became part of the school curriculum of Greek speakers in the East. And while Latin students read Greek literature as a core element in their school curriculum, Greek speakers in the East showed little interest in Latin literature until the medieval period.

---

[24] So B. Rochette, *Le Latin dans le Monde Grec: Recherches sur la Diffusion de la Langue et des Lettres Latines dans les Provinces Hellénophones de l'Empire Romain* (Brussels: Latomus, 1997), who has examined the role of Latin in the Greek-speaking East and concludes that knowledge of Latin in the East became fairly widespread no earlier than the third century CE and peaked in the fourth century CE.

4

What Greek Authors would Luke have Known?

We can be fairly certain that Luke was familiar with a wide array of Classical and Hellenistic Greek authors. In what follows, I have crafted several lists of authors in an attempt to reconstruct what we might call Luke's "core reading list." That is to say, I am striving to reconstruct Luke's library, be it a mental library, based on Luke's recollection of texts that he had read, studied, and even memorized, or a literal library of material texts that he could access or that he actually owned.[1]

I base Luke's core reading list firstly on the readings prescribed for students, and especially for aspiring orators, advocated by such ancient rhetoricians and grammarians as Dionysius of Halicarnassus, Dio Chrysostom, and Quintilian. While these reading lists tend to be idealistic and aimed at the most well-educated and upper-class members of Hellenistic and Roman society, they can be useful when counterbalanced by the evidence of other types of reading lists in reconstructing the real-life, educational experiences of typical students of the period.

I base Luke's core reading list secondly on the remains of literary papyri from Hellenistic and Roman Egypt, for these offer clear evidence of the interests of the general reading public in the Hellenized East. I use the Egyptian materials simply because, given climatic conditions, Egypt is almost the only place in the Mediterranean world where such texts have survived in significant numbers. Moreover, Egypt should not be regarded as peculiar or exotic in any way in its accommodation of Greek literary texts but rather representative of the eastern Mediterranean generally. Greek remained the official language for administration and education in Egypt through the Hellenistic, Roman, and even into the Byzantine periods.

I base Luke's core reading list thirdly on the remains of actual school texts on papyrus, parchment, pottery, wood, and stone from Hellenistic and Roman Egypt. Given the homogeneity of the school curriculum throughout the eastern Mediterranean,

---

[1] I am reminded of the efforts of the Library of Congress to reconstruct the personal library of Thomas Jefferson, which he sold to the Library of Congress in 1815, but which was largely destroyed in a fire on Christmas Eve of 1851. The aim of these efforts is to reassemble the exact editions that Jefferson owned and to arrange them in the manner in which Jefferson himself cataloged them. In a similar manner Saint Olaf College has for many years been striving to acquire all the books that Sören Kierkegaard possessed in his personal library, in the same editions, and to reassemble them on the bookshelves of a reconstruction of Kierkegaard's private office. In both cases the goal is for scholars to be able to experience, in a very tangible way, the intellectual influences on these two figures. The reconstruction of Luke's "personal library" is, of course, a much more nebulous prospect.

52   *The Formal Education of the Author of Luke-Acts*

these texts illustrate the material typically studied by students in cities like Jerusalem, Antioch, Tarsus, Ephesus, Troas, and Philippi as well. There is of course considerable overlap in these last two categories: the contents of school texts used in the educational curriculum are a reflection of the interests of the general reading public (and *vice versa*). Passages used repeatedly in composition exercises were commonly drawn from literary texts that were already popular among the general populace; in fact these passages were selected for these school texts in order to prepare students for eventually reading the literary texts from which they were drawn.

I base Luke's core reading list fourthly on the relative frequencies of quotations and citations of ancient literary works by Luke's near-contemporaries Plutarch of Chaeronia, Philo of Alexandria, Josephus of Jerusalem, and Chariton of Aphrodisias, since they had educational backgrounds and cultural orbits similar in some ways to those of Luke.

Reading Lists for Students Advocated by Ancient Rhetoricians and Grammarians

Hellenistic and Roman Imperial-era historians, philosophers, rhetoricians, and grammarians attributed to their earlier counterparts—particularly to the third- to second-century BCE Alexandrian scholars and head librarians Aristophanes and Aristarchus—the idea of compiling lists of the best writers in selected genres: four epic poets (Homer, Hesiod, Panyassis, and Antimachus), three tragedians (Aeschylus, Sophocles, and Euripides), three old comedians (Aristophanes, Eupolis, Cratinus), and so forth.[2] The term κανών "canon," popularly bandied about today, was not used in antiquity to refer to these lists but rather a variety of loose designations: ποιηταὶ κράτισται "the greatest poets" (Dionysius of Halicarnassus, Proclus, Photius), ἀξιολογώτατοι "the most worthy of mention" (Dionysius of Halicarnassus, scholia to Aristophanes), ἐπισημότατοι "the most distinguished" (Diodorus Siculus), and οἱ (ἐγ) κριθέντες "those that have been included" (the anonymous Byzantine encyclopedia *Suda* under the entries Δείναρχος, Λυκοῦργος, and Νικόστρατος).[3] The works of the authors on these lists by and large constituted the core of the readings used in the Greek educational system. As time passed, new authors were of course added to the list: e.g., Apollonius of Rhodes, Aratus, and Theocritus to the list of epic poets. This later "canon," which included many Hellenistic as well as Classical authors, can be reconstructed from two medieval manuscripts that appear to have preserved ancient

---

[2] On the "canons" of Aristophanes and Aristarchus, see G. Steffen, *De canone qui dicitur Aristophanis et Aristarchi* (Leipzig: Typis Reuschi, 1876); J. E. Sandys, *History of Classical Scholarship: From the Sixth Century B.C. to the End of the Middle Ages* (Cambridge: Cambridge University Press, 1903), 129–30; R. Pfeiffer, *History of Classical Scholarship from the Beginnings to the End of the Hellenistic Age* (Oxford: Clarendon, 1968), 203–8; P. M. Fraser, *Ptolemaic Alexandria* (Oxford: Clarendon, 1972), 1:456; 2:659.

[3] In Latin the designations used were *classici* "belonging to the highest class" (Aulus Gellius 19.8.15), *summi auctores* "the best authors" (Quintilian), and those of a certain *ordo* "rank" (Quintilian).

What Greek Authors Would Luke Have Known?　　53

lists of recommended authors: first, a tenth-century manuscript from Mt. Athos (Codex Coislinianus 387) that includes a list of the most highly venerated ancient poets, orators, and historians;[4] second, a nearly identical list in a later manuscript in the Bodleian Library (Codex Bodleianus Auct. T. II. 11; once called Codex Meermannus).[5] The following is a collation of the two lists arranged, as in the two codices, by genre and, roughly, by chronology.[6]

Epic Poets (5): Homer, Hesiod, Peisander, Panyassis (not included in Codex Bodleianus), Antimachus.
Iambic Poets (3): Semonides (listed incorrectly as Simonides in both Codex Coislinianus and Codex Bodleianus), Archilochus, Hipponax.
Tragic Poets (5): Aeschylus, Sophocles, Euripides, Ion, Achaeus.
Comic Poets, Old (7): Epicharmus, Cratinus, Eupolis, Aristophanes, Pherecrates, Crates (not included in Codex Coislinianus), Plato.
Comic Poets, Middle (2): Antiphanes, Alexis (listed as Alexithourius in both Codex Coislinianus and Codex Bodleianus).
Comic Poets, New (5): Menander, Philippides, Diphilus, Philemon, Apollodorus (not included in Codex Bodleianus).
Elegiac Poets (4): Callinus, Mimnermus, Philetas, Callimachus.
Lyric Poets (9): Alcman, Alcaeus, Sappho, Stesichorus, Pindar, Bacchylides, Ibycus, Anacreon, Simonides (listed incorrectly as Semonides in Codex Coislinianus).
Orators (10): Demosthenes, Lysias, Hyperides, Isocrates, Aeschines, Lycurgus, Isaeus, Antiphon, Andocides, Dinarchus (not included in Codex Coislinianus).
Historians (10): Thucydides, Herodotus, Xenophon, Philistus (listed incorrectly as Philippus in both Codex Coislinianus and Codex Bodleianus), Theopompus, Ephorus, Anaximenes, Callisthenes, Hellanicus, Polybius.

Oddly, a list of ancient philosophers is not included in either manuscript.

That this practice of arranging recommended authors according to genre goes well back into antiquity is indicated by the similar reading lists for schools advocated by various Hellenistic and Roman Imperial-era historians, philosophers, rhetoricians, and grammarians.

Dionysius, the first-century BCE historian and rhetorician from Halicarnassus in Asia Minor, broaches the topic of a "canon" of authors in two of his many works on rhetoric. First, in some fragments of his short treatise Περὶ Μιμήσεως *"On Imitation,"* Dionysius renders judgment on the value of individual authors as models for the

---

[4]　This manuscript was first published by B. de Montfaucon, *Bibliotheca Coisliniana Olim Segueriana* (Paris: Ludovicum Guérin et Carolum Robustel, 1715), where the list can be found on pages 596–7.
[5]　This manuscript was first published by J. A. Cramer, *Anecdota Graeca e Codd. Manuscriptis Bibliothecae Regiae Parisiensis*, vol. 4 (Oxford: Typographeus Academicus, 1891), where the list can be found on pages 196–7.
[6]　Slight variations on these lists are offered by H. Usener, *Dionysii Halicarnassensis Librorum de Imitatione Reliquiae Epistulaeque Criticae Duae* (Bonn: M. Cohen, 1889), 129–31, and W. Peterson, *M. Fabi Quintiliani Institutionis Oratoriae Liber Decimus* (Oxford: Clarendon, 1891), xxxvi–xxxvii.

54 The Formal Education of the Author of Luke-Acts

aspiring orator, much as Dio Chrysostom and Quintilian (who was particularly indebted to Dionysius) would do later. Dionysius mentions in particular: the epic poets Homer, Hesiod, Panyassis, and Antimachus; the lyric poets Pindar, Simonides, Stesichorus, and Alcaeus; the tragedians Aeschylus, Sophocles, and Euripides; all the comic poets (but he does not mention them by name), including, later, Menander; the historians Herodotus, Thucydides, Philistus, Xenophon, and Theopompus; the Pythagorean philosophers, along with Xenophon, Plato, and Aristotle; and the orators Lysias, Isocrates, Lycurgus, Demosthenes, Aeschines, Hyperides, and Gorgias. Second, in his treatise Περὶ Συνθέσεως Ὀνομάτων "On Arrangement of Words," which is directed at all students of practical oratory, of whatever age, but especially the young beginners, Dionysius divides composition into three categories of style. He claims that the most distinguished practitioners of the "austere" style are: Antimachus of Colophon and Empedocles for epic; Pindar for lyric; Aeschylus for tragedy; Thucydides for history; and Antiphon for oratory. The most distinguished practitioners of the "smooth" style are: Hesiod for epic; Sappho, Anacreon, and Simonides for lyric; Euripides for tragedy; perhaps Ephorus and Theopompus for history; and Isocrates for oratory. The most distinguished practitioners of the "mixed" style—the one Dionysius considers the best, since it is the mean between the two extremes—are: Homer for epic; Stesichorus and Alcaeus for lyric; Sophocles for tragedy; Herodotus for history; Demosthenes for oratory; and, of the philosophers, Democritus, Plato, and Aristotle.

Dio Chrysostom, the first-century CE (c. 40s–c. 120) philosopher and rhetorician from Bithynia in Asia Minor, raises the topic of a "canon" of authors in his 18th Oration: Περὶ Λόγου Ἀσκησέως "On Training for Public Speaking." In this oration Dio prescribes a reading list, not for a typical young student training to be an orator in the courts, but for a wealthy man in the prime of life who has failed to get a proper education as a youth and now wants to assume a larger role in public life as a statesman (perhaps an influential Greek official in one of the larger cities of Asia Minor that was under Roman control). In Orationes 18.6–17 Dio advises that the man read first the poets, then the historians, and finally the orators, and thereafter he recommends the reading of the followers of Socrates. More specifically, of the poets he recommends that the man have someone skilled in reading recite to him aloud the plays of Menander and Euripides. As much as possible of Homer should be read throughout anyone's life, by boys, adults, and old men. Lyric and elegiac poetry, as well as iambics and dithyrambs, are valuable for someone with leisure, but there is no time for the aspiring statesman to enjoy them. The historians should be read attentively: Herodotus is enjoyable, but Thucydides is the best of the historians; Theopompus is second-rate; Ephorus is third-rate and not well suited for a statesman's training. Of the orators Demosthenes is highly recommended for his style, thought, and copious vocabulary, Lysias for his brevity, simplicity, and cleverness, but Hyperides, Aeschines, and Lycurgus should also be read, and acquaintance with more recent orators is also recommended (Dio mentions Antipater, Theodorus, Plution, and Conon). Finally, the writings of the Socratics (i.e., Plato and Xenophon) are indispensable; Xenophon is particularly praised as the only one of the ancients who can satisfy all the requirements of the statesman.

Quintilian, the first-century CE (c. 35–c. 90s) teacher and rhetorician from Calagurris in Spain, brings up the topic of a "canon" of authors frequently in his

Institutio Oratoria "Training in Oratory." This twelve-volume textbook prescribes the proper training for an aspiring orator from infancy onward. In two short sections (1.4.4; 1.8.5–12) and one long section (10.1.20–131), Quintilian recommends an extensive reading list of both Greek and Latin authors—since he is living in the western Mediterranean—as part of the aspiring orator's formal education. His list of Greek authors is indebted to Dionysius of Halicarnassus's Περὶ Μιμήσεως—the lists are very similar, except that Quintilian adds several Hellenistic authors.

Epic Poets: Homer, Hesiod, Panyassis, Antimachus, Apollonius of Rhodes, Aratus, Theocritus.
Elegiac Poets: Callimachus, Philetas.
Iambic Poets: Archilochus.
Lyric Poets: Pindar, Stesichorus, Alcaeus, Simonides.
Comic Poets, Old: Aristophanes, Eupolis, Cratinus.
Tragic Poets: Aeschylus, Sophocles, Euripides.
Comic Poets, New: Menander, Philemon.
Historians: Thucydides, Herodotus, (Xenophon is included under the philosophers), Theopompus, Philistus.
Orators: Demosthenes, Aeschines, Hyperides, Lysias, Isocrates.
Philosophers: Plato, Xenophon, Aristotle, Theophrastus.

Quintilian especially recommends Homer, Euripides, Old Comedy generally, Menander, Demosthenes, and Plato. Within the Homeric epics he is particularly enthusiastic about the proems of both the *Iliad* and *Odyssey*, the disputes between the chiefs in *Iliad* 1, the speeches in *Iliad* 2, the embassy to Achilles in *Iliad* 9, the announcement of Patroclus's death in *Iliad* 18, and Priam's speech to Achilles in *Iliad* 24.

The "canons" of authors recommended by Dionysius of Halicarnassus, Dio Chrysostom, and Quintilian are constructed primarily for the training of aspiring orators, and several of the authors on their lists were introduced to students only at the highest levels of education—during their formal instruction in rhetoric. A broader view of the authors studied throughout the entire course of education, including at the lower levels, can be attained by examining the recommendations of the several surviving treatises on *progymnasmata*, the graded series of exercises for teaching prose composition and elementary rhetoric in the schools.

Aelius Theon, the first-century CE (?) rhetorician from Alexandria in Egypt, offers the earliest surviving specimen of this genre. At the end of his *Progymnasmata*, in a section which survives only in an Armenian translation, Theon advises that so far as the prose writers are concerned young men should begin with the easiest and progress to the hardest: [Lysias[7]], Isocrates, Hyperides, Aeschines, and finally Demosthenes. Theon also recommends the speeches of the historians, starting with the most simple stylistically, Herodotus, and then the more demanding, Theopompus, Xenophon,

---

[7] Lysias's name does not actually appear in this section of the corrupt text, but since he is mentioned later in the text as the polar opposite of Demosthenes, we can assume that his name has dropped out by mistake.

56   *The Formal Education of the Author of Luke-Acts*

Philistus, Ephorus, and finally Thucydides. Elsewhere in his treatise Theon cites and quotes several of the poets, especially Homer, as models of oratory as well.

In the earlier sections of his *Progymnasmata*, which survive in Greek, Theon mentions, quotes, and refers to the works of many ancient authors, some poets, but mostly prose authors, since he is providing models for exercises in prose composition. In what follows I use Quintilian's list as a basic template for comparing and contrasting the reading list proposed or assumed in Theon's *Progymnasmata*. The numbers to the right of each author indicate how many times that author is mentioned, quoted, or referred to in Theon's work.[8]

Epic Poets: Homer 21 (*Iliad* 10, *Odyssey* 5, Generic 6), Hesiod 3.
Lyric Poets: Archilochus 2, Alcaeus 1, Simonides 1.
Tragic Poets: Sophocles 1, Euripides 2.
Comic Poets, Old: Aristophanes 1.
Comic Poets, New: Menander 5.
Historians: Thucydides 23, Herodotus 17, Xenophon 7, Theopompus 8, Philistus 7.
Orators: Demosthenes 31, Aeschines 7, Hyperides 4, Lysias 7, Isocrates 8 (not
    counting incidences of his name as a character in the progymnastic exercises).
Philosophers: Plato 18, Aristotle 5, Theophrastus 1.
Others (i.e., not on Quintilian's list): Sappho (poet) 1, Aesop (fabulist) 6, Connis
    (fabulist) 1, Thyris (fabulist) 1, Cybissus (fabulist) 1, Ephorus (historian) 8, Ctesias
    (historian) 1, Lycurgus (orator) 2, Isaeus (orator) 1, Hegesias (orator) 1, Heraclitus
    (philosopher) 1, Phaedo (the Socratic) 2, Epicurus (philosopher) 2, Zeno of Citium
    (philosopher) 1, Palaephatus (mythographer) 1.

Further examples of progymnastic exercises can be found in the later treatises of "Hermogenes" (second century CE?), Aphthonius (fourth century CE), Nicolaus (fifth century CE), and "Libanius" (fourth to sixth century CE). Though late in date, these progymnastic exercises are similar to those of Theon, are very homogeneous amongst themselves, and are therefore clearly drawn from a common source from a much earlier period. Here I offer the results of simple searches of these four works of *progymnasmata*, conducted on the *Thesaurus Linguae Graecae*, for the names of the ancient authors mentioned by Quintilian and Theon. This is admittedly a rather blunt tool, but, as mentioned above, it yields results that are roughly similar in absolute numbers, and very similar in the ratios of frequencies among ancient authors, to my more fully tabulated results of Theon's *Progymnasmata*.

---

[8] These are my tabulations of mentions, quotations, and references to the works of ancient authors in the Greek portion of Theon's *Progymnasmata* (not the Armenian translation of the end portion). A simple search of the authors' names in the *Thesaurus Linguae Graecae* yields results whose ratios are very similar, but my numbers are more accurate and refined since I omit redundant mentions and since I include quotations that are not explicitly attributed to anyone by Theon.

Epic Poets: Homer 45 (*Iliad* 6, *Odyssey* 1, Generic 38), Hesiod 12.
Lyric Poets: Archilochus 1, Pindar 3, Simonides 4.
Tragic Poets: Euripides 2.
Comic Poets, Old: Eupolis 1.
Comic Poets, New: Menander 2.
Historians: Thucydides 16, Herodotus 4, Xenophon 1.
Orators: Demosthenes 49, Aeschines 20, Lysias 9, Isocrates 15 (not counting
    incidences of his name as a character in the progymnastic exercises).
Philosophers: Plato 6, Aristotle 3, Theophrastus 5.
Others (i.e., not on Quintilian's list): Aesop (fabulist) 7, Lycurgus (orator) 1,
    Isaeus (orator) 1.

When one compares the authors mentioned in the *progymnasmata* to those on
Quintilian's list, it is noticeable that the number of authors canonized under each genre
of poetry has been reduced: e.g., of the seven epic poets, only Homer and Hesiod are
now being recommended; of the three tragedians, Aeschylus has dropped out, and only
Sophocles and, more so, Euripides are being recommended; of the new comedians,
only Menander is being recommended, and he has become very popular. On the other
hand, several new prose writers have been introduced in the genres of history, oratory,
and philosophy. Some new recommendations have also been introduced in the prose
category of the fable—notably Aesop.

The Material Remains of Literary Papyri, Generally, and of School Texts, Specifically, in Hellenistic and Roman Egypt

One may reasonably object that reading lists prescribed for aspiring orators by highly
educated Hellenistic historians, philosophers, rhetoricians, and grammarians are too
idealistic and that they do not reflect accurately the educational experiences of typical
students of the period. Fortunately, the prescriptions of these scholars can be weighed
against the actual papyrological remains of literary works and school texts from the
period, and, as it turns out, these material remains indicate that the prescribed reading
lists of the scholars are not so far divorced from the texts actually consumed by the
reading public and incorporated into the school curriculum of the period.

The relative numbers of the actual literary works of ancient authors that have
survived on papyrus fragments from Hellenistic and Roman Egypt are a good
indication of the literary interests of the reading public—interests that shaped and in
turn were shaped by the texts that were encountered in the schools. Consequently, the
contents of the literary papyri and the school texts overlap, the passages of authors
used repeatedly in composition exercises having been drawn from literary texts that
were also popular among the reading public. The material remains of school texts from
Hellenistic and Roman Egypt offer clear evidence of which authors were included in
the educational curriculum. But because of the fragmentary nature of most of this
material, it is sometimes difficult to differentiate school texts from literary works. The
telltale signs that a document was used in the schools include: larger than normal

58 *The Formal Education of the Author of Luke-Acts*

letters; numerous mistakes, erasures, and corrections; horizontal and vertical rulings; accents, breathing marks, and marks of vowel quantity; and spaces, dots, and strokes to mark the division of syllables and words normally written *scriptio continua*.[9] But these telltale signs become less prominent as students work their way through the educational curriculum and their handwriting becomes more skillful. Many school texts from a higher level of education probably remain unidentified as school texts owing to the more experienced hands of their writers. An analysis of the papyri must take into account the fact that ancient authors that were used in school texts at an earlier level of education (e.g., Homer, Euripides, Menander) may in some cases appear more numerous than others (e.g., Hesiod, Aristophanes, Pindar, Callimachus) simply because the school texts that used these authors are more readily identifiable as school texts owing to the rudimentary level of writing.

The following chart offers figures for both literary papyri and school texts from Hellenistic and Roman Egypt that contain passages from ancient Greek authors, with the literary passages that appear in school texts (right column) treated as a subcategory of the larger corpus of literary papyri generally (left column). I have chosen to concentrate on the three centuries between 100 BCE and 200 CE simply because these centuries frame the lifetime of the author of the Gospel of Luke and the Acts of the Apostles. I have chosen to concentrate on the Egyptian papyri simply because Egypt, owing to climatic conditions, is the source of almost all surviving papyri that have to this point been discovered.[10] These figures are drawn primarily from the Leuven Database of Ancient Books (LDAB), a database of information on ancient copies of Greek and Latin literary texts.[11] The Centre de Documentation de Papyrologie Littéraire (CEDOPAL), which includes the most recent avatar of R. A. Pack's catalogue of Greek

---

[9] On these and other distinguishing characteristics of the hands witnessed in school exercises, see R. Cribiore, *Writing, Teachers, and Students*, 75–118.

[10] There are very few Greek literary papyri from this period outside of Egypt: only 252, in fact, with 215 of these being from Herculaneum in Italy (from the library that was buried by the eruption of Vesuvius in 79 CE), 10 from Dura-Europos in Mesopotamia, 6 from Murabba'at in Palestine, 11 from Qumran in Palestine (all from the Septuagint), and a handful from elsewhere (along with most papyrologists I include ostraca, as well as waxed and bleached wooden tablets, in the category of "papyri"). And of these 252 literary papyri, only four are possibly school texts: two first-century CE ostraca from Masada, Palestine, containing the Greek alphabet; one second-century CE papyrus from Murabba'at, Palestine, containing Greek writing exercises; and, by far the most interesting for our purposes, a collection of seven third-century CE waxed tablets, the so-called *Tabulae ceratae graecae Assendeftianae*, acquired at Palmyra in Syria in 1881 and now in the library at Leiden University, which contain fourteen fables of Babrius, most in meter but some in prose, along with verse 347 of Hesiod's *Works and Days* written on the verso of the first and seventh tablets. The tablets are clearly a young student's copy book, as the handwriting is very poor and the text marred by many errors, additions, and omissions. These tablets were first published by D. C. Hesseling, "On Waxen Tablets with Fables of Babrius (Tabulae Ceratae Assendelftianae)," *Journal of Hellenic Studies* 13 (1893): 293–314.

[11] LDAB has collected the basic information on copies of ancient Greek and Latin literary texts dating from the fourth century BCE to the ninth century CE. The database can be accessed through the interdisciplinary portal Trismegistos (www.trismegistos.org).

What Greek Authors Would Luke Have Known? 59

and Latin literary papyri, Mertens-Pack[3] (M-P[3]), offers similar results.[12] To anticipate: most of the authors are the very ones recommended by the historians, philosophers, rhetoricians, and grammarians, including Quintilian (above). There is only one author, the epic poet Panyassis, who is canonized by Quintilian (and others) but does not appear in the literary papyri and school texts of this period. There are several authors, however, left unmentioned by Quintilian (and others) who appear fairly frequently in the literary papyri and school texts of this period: e.g., Alcman, Bacchylides, and Hipponax, among the lyric poets.

There have been several attempts to identify and catalog the school texts on the Egyptian papyri. J. Debut has constructed a useful catalog of 395 school texts on papyri dating from the third century BCE to around the eighth century CE that are concerned with the study of the Greek language: exercises on the alphabet, the construction of syllables, lists of words of various lengths, lists of aphorisms, etc., as well as quotations of ancient Greek literature.[13] R. Cribiore has added a few more to total 412 school texts from Egypt from the Hellenistic, Roman, and Byzantine periods.[14] T. Morgan counts 419 total papyri of school texts from Egypt, but within these papyri she counts 713 examples of 10 types of exercises in Greek; i.e., there are more quotations and citations of ancient authors than there are school texts since some school texts have multiple quotations and citations.[15] LDAB also uses this last method of counting and calculates a total of 834 quotations of ancient Greek works in the school texts on the Egyptian papyri.

---

[12] The first edition of R. A. Pack's *The Greek and Latin Literary Texts from Greco-Roman Egypt* (Ann Arbor: University of Michigan Press, 1952) contained 2,369 entries; the second edition of 1965 contained 3,026 entries; the regularly updated digital database, CEDOPAL, *Catalogue des papyrus littéraires grecs et latins* (Mertens-Pack[3] Database Project, 1999–) (web.philo.ulg.ac.be/cedopal) currently contains some 7,000 entries. This most recent database is indebted to many important collections and treatments of literary and school papyri from Egypt that have been published in print since the publication of the second edition of Pack (in chronological order): W. H. Willis, "A Census of the Literary Papyri from Egypt," *Greek, Roman, and Byzantine Studies* 9 (1968): 205–41; P. Mertens, "Vingt années de papyrologie odysséenne," *Chronique d'Égypte* 60 (1985): 191–203; J. Lenaerts and P. Mertens, "Les papyrus d'Isocrate," *Chronique d'Égypte* 64 (1989): 216–30; D. Marcotte and P. Mertens, "Les papyrus de Callimaque," *Papyrologica Florentina* 19 (1990): 409–27; O. Bouquiaux-Simon and P. Mertens, "Les papyrus de Thucydide," *Chronique d'Égypte* 66 (1991): 198–210; P. Mertens, "Les témoins papyrologiques de Ménandre: Essai de classement rationnel et esquisse d' étude bibliologique," in *Serta Leodiensia secunda: mélanges publiés par les Classiques de Liège à l'occasion du 175 anniversaire de l'université*, eds. A. Bodson, P. Wathelet, and M. Dubuisson (Liège: Université de Liège, 1992), 331–56; O. Bouquiaux-Simon and P. Mertens, "Les témoignages papyrologiques d' Euripide: Liste sommaire arrêtée au 1/6/1990," in *Papiri letterari greci e latini*, ed. M. Capasso (Lecce: Congredo, 1992), 97–107; P. Mertens and J. A. Straus, "Les papyrus d'Hérodote," *Annali della Scuola Normale Superiore di Pisa, Classe di Lettere e Filosofia* 3, no. 22 (1992): 969–78; D. Marcotte and P. Mertens, "Catalogue des Femmes et Grandes Éoées d' Hésiode," in *Storia, poesia e pensiero nel mondo antico: studi in onore di Marcello Gigante*, ed. F. del Franco (Naples, Bibliopolis, 1994), 407–23; P. Mertens, "Les papyrus d'Aristophane. Actualisation des données bibliologiques et bibliographiques," in *Hodoi Dizesios: studi in onore di Francesco Adorno*, ed. M. S. Funghi (Firenze: Olschki, 1996), 335–43; R. Cribiore, *Writing, Teachers, and Students*, 173–284; T. Morgan, *Literate Education*, 308–13 (esp. tables 11–15); R. Cribiore, "The Grammarian's Choice," 241–59.

[13] J. Debut, "Les documents scolaires," 251–78.

[14] R. Cribiore, *Writing, Teachers, and Students*, 173–284.

[15] T. Morgan, *Literate Education*, 308–13 (tables 11–15), 320–2 (tables 20–3).

The absolute numbers of school texts on the Egyptian papyri presented here are somewhat different from the calculations of others. My own numbers, both for the literary papyri and for the school texts on papyri that contain ancient Greek literature, are in the case of some ancient authors higher than those of other scholars because they are updated by the recent cataloging of the Leuven database and by new discoveries and publications, because I include in the total for each author not just those papyri in which that author is the primary text but also those in which the author is quoted secondarily or simply mentioned by name, and because I include all papyri that have any indication of having been used as a school text (i.e., perhaps a more liberal definition than that of R. Cribiore and T. Morgan). On the other hand, my numbers are in the case of some ancient authors lower than those of other scholars because I am concerned here not with the entire corpus of papyri from the early Hellenistic to the Byzantine era but only with those from around the time of Luke (100 BCE–200 CE). Including the late Roman and Byzantine papyri would have distorted the picture for our purpose, which is to determine what was generally read in schools in the time of Luke. For example, the fact that Aristophanes replaced Menander as the primary representative of comedy in school texts during the later Roman and Byzantine periods—interesting though it be—has no bearing on our objective. That said, while my absolute numbers of 3,315 literary papyri and 175 school texts are different from those of others, the relative numbers remain for the most part remarkably similar (e.g., the ratio of Homeric to Hesiodic texts, Sophoclean to Euripidean texts, Herodotean to Thucydidean texts, Platonic to Aristotelian texts, and so forth).

There are two matters that should be kept in mind while considering the figures in this chart. First, a very small matter: in the enumeration of references to, and quotations of, specific works of authors—as of the works of Homer, Hesiod, Callimachus, Pindar, Aeschylus, Sophocles, Euripides, Aristophanes, and Menander—the sum total does not add up to the total of references to, and quotations of, the author as a whole. This is because some references and quotations cannot be associated or identified with specific works of those authors. Second, a matter of considerable importance already mentioned briefly above: ancient authors that were a mainstay in school texts used at an earlier level of education, such as Homer, Euripides, and Menander, may in some cases appear more heavily represented in this chart than other authors, such as Hesiod, Aristophanes, Pindar, and Callimachus, simply because the school texts that used the former authors—Homer, for example—are, owing to the rudimentary level of the handwriting of the students, more readily recognizable as school texts. Many school texts from a higher level of education that used the latter authors—Hesiod, for example—probably remain unidentified as school texts owing to the more experienced hands of the students by this stage. I shall return to this matter again in more detail below.

In the following chart authors have been marked off by brackets who appear in the literary papyri and school texts but are not specifically recommended by the Hellenistic and Roman Imperial-era rhetoricians such as Dionysius of Halicarnassus, Dio Chrysostom, and, especially, Quintilian, and by Theon and the later *progymasmata*. Some of the names of authors and works, especially ones that have not survived to our time, may appear inconsistently Romanized or Anglicized, but these are the forms that are now conventionally used in the field of Classical philology.

What Greek Authors Would Luke Have Known? 61

Table 1 Literary works and school texts on the Egyptian papyri.

Author	Literary Papyri Generally (100 BCE–200 CE)	School Texts Specifically (100 BCE–200 CE)
Epic:		
Homer	1,624	96
	Iliad 1,332	*Iliad* 73
	Odyssey 223	*Odyssey* 18
	H.Dionysus 3	*H.Dionysus* 1
	H.Hermes 2	
	H.Demeter 1	
Hesiod	130	3
	Theogony 31	*Works and Days* 1
	Works and Days 27	*Shield* 1
	Catalogue of Women 54	
	Shield 9	
	Megalae Eoeae 3	
Panyassis	0	0
Antimachus	12 (mostly *Thebaid*)	0
Apollonius of Rhodes	42	0
Aratus	11 (almost all *Phaenomena*)	0
Theocritus	18 (almost all *Idylls*)	0
Callimachus	79	1
	Aetia 31	*Hymns* 1
	Hymns 11	
	Hecale 8	
	Iambics 8	
	Elegy 3	
Philetas	2	0
[Peisander]	1	0
Lyric:		
Archilochus	23	1
Pindar	55	1
	Olympian Odes 5	
	Pythian Odes 3	
	Isthmian Odes 2	
	Nemean Odes 1	
Stesichorus	12	0
Alcaeus	34	0
Simonides	21	0
Sappho	27	0
Anacreon	10	0
[Mimnermus]	4	0
[Alcman]	26	0
[Bacchylides]	25	1
[Hipponax]	10	0
[Euphorion]	13	0

(continued)

62   *The Formal Education of the Author of Luke-Acts*

Table 1 (continued)

Author	Literary Papyri Generally (100 BCE–200 CE)	School Texts Specifically (100 BCE–200 CE)
[Ibycus]	6	0
[Theognis]	4	2
[Timotheus]	4	0
[Cercidas]	1	0
Tragedy:		
Aeschylus	42	2
	Agamemnon 2	*Psychagogoi* 1
	Aetnaeae 2	*Niobe* or *Phorcides* 1
	Glaucus Potnieus 2	
	Hydrophoroi 2	
	Isthmiastae 2	
	Myrmidones 2	
	Niobe 2	
	Philoctetes 2	
	Prometheus Pyrcaeus 2	
	Prometheus Pyrphoros 3	
	Semele 3	
	Septem contra Thebas 3	
	Theoroi 2	
	17 other plays once each	
Sophocles	34	2
	Ajax 3	*Niobe* or *Tantalus* 1
	Antigone 2	
	Inachus 2	
	Niobe 4	
	Trachiniae 2	
	Some Satyr plays	
	17 other plays once each	
Euripides	141	17
	Alcestis 3	*Autolycus* 1
	Andromache 7	*Bacchae* 1
	Andromeda 2	*Electra* 1
	Archelaus 2	*Hecuba* 2
	Autolycus 2	*Hippolytus* 2
	Bacchae 6	*Phoenissae* 5
	Cresphontes 5	*Temenidae* 1
	Cretes 3	*Troades* 1
	Electra 3	
	Hecuba 8	
	Helen 3	
	Hercules Furens 2	

What Greek Authors Would Luke Have Known?

	Hippolytus 5	
	Hypsipyle 5	
	Iphigenia in Aulide 2	
	Iphigenia in Tauris 4	
	Medea 7	
	Melanippe Sophe 2	
	Orestes 15	
	Peliades 2	
	Phoenissae 23	
	Phoenix 2	
	Phrixus 5	
	Rhesus 2	
	Stheneboea 2	
	Telephus 5	
	Temenidae 2	
	Theseus 2	
	Troades 3	
	24 other plays once each	
[Lycophron]	9	0
Old Comedy:		
Aristophanes	27	0
	Acharnians 2	
	Clouds 2	
	Knights 3	
	Plutus 3	
	Thesmophoriazusae 3	
	Wasps 2	
	7 other plays once each	
Eupolis	10	0
Cratinus	7	0
[Epicharmus]	8	0
[Pherecrates]	1	0
[Plato Comicus]	2	0
[Apollodorus]	1	0
Middle Comedy:		
[Antiphanes]	7	1
[Alexis]	3	0
New Comedy:		
Menander	125	17
	Apistos 2	*Hiereia* 1
	Aspis 3	*Imbrioi* 1
	Daktylios 2	*Kitharistes* 4
	Dis Exapaton 4	*Misoumenos* 1

(continued)

The Formal Education of the Author of Luke-Acts

Table 1 (continued)

Author	Literary Papyri Generally (100 BCE–200 CE)	School Texts Specifically (100 BCE–200 CE)
	Dyskolos 4	*Oneiros* 1
	Epitrepontes 10	*Progamoi* 1
	Heauton Timoroumenos 2	Collections of *sententiae* 8
	Karchedonios 3	
	Kekryphalos 2	
	Kitharistes 8	
	Kolax 3	
	Leukadia 2	
	Misoumenos 10	
	Perikeiromene 7	
	Phasma 2	
	Samia 4	
	Sikyonioi 3	
	Synaristosai 3	
	Thais 2	
	Theophoroumene 2	
	14 other plays once each	
Philemon	8	3
[Diphilus]	1	1
History:		
Thucydides	83	0
Herodotus	47	2
Xenophon	38	1
Theopompus	7	0
Philistus	2	0
Ephorus	5	0
[Hellanicus]	1	0
[Polybius]	3	0
Oratory:		
Demosthenes	173	5
Aeschines	52	0
Hyperides	12	1
Lysias	12	0
Isocrates	92	5
Lycurgus	3	0
Isaeus	5	0
Antiphon	7	0
[Andocides]	2	0
[Dinarchus]	5	0
Philosophy:		
Democritus	2	0
Plato	74	0
Aristotle	25	2
Zeno of Citium	1	0

Epicurus	6	0
Theophrastus	7	1
[Thales]	1	0
[Antisthenes]	2	1
[Diogenes the Cynic]	6	5
[Cleanthes]	1	0
[Chrysippus]	6	0
[Metrodorus]	1	0
[Hermarchus]	2	0
Fable:		
Aesop	9	2
[Babrius][16]	3	2

As we have already observed, it appears that the ancient Greek authors recommended in the treatises of the historians, philosophers, rhetoricians, and grammarians are the very ones enjoyed by the reading public in Hellenistic Egypt between 100 BCE and 200 CE. There is only one author, the epic poet Panyassis, who is canonized by Quintilian, and by others, but who does not appear in the literary papyri of this period. There are several authors, however, left unmentioned by Quintilian, and by others, who appear fairly frequently in the literary papyri: Alcman, Bacchylides, Hipponax, Euphorion, and Ibycus, of the lyric poets; Lycophron, of the tragedians; Epicharmus and Antiphanes, of the comedians; Dinarchus, of the orators; and Diogenes and Chrysippus, of the philosophers.

Homer is by far the most cited and referenced author of any genre, with the *Iliad* vastly more popular than the *Odyssey*. Of the other epic poets, Hesiod has remained remarkably popular, and the two Hellenistic epic poets, Apollonius of Rhodes and Callimachus, have made their way into the ranks; the relatively high frequency of passages from these two epic poets, along with those from Theocritus, is perhaps attributable to their connections to Egypt. It is somewhat surprising that, of the lyric poets, two of the most difficult are also the most popular: Pindar, who writes in a Doric dialect, and Alcaeus, who writes in an Aeolic dialect. The "big three" of the tragedians— Aeschylus, Sophocles, and Euripides—are all well attested, and Euripides, in particular, is broadly popular. His most cited tragedies are *Phoenissae* and *Orestes*, but several others are popular as well: *Andromache, Bacchae, Cresphontes, Hecuba, Hippolytus,* and *Medea*. New comedy is preferred to old comedy, with Menander by far the most popular representative of the genre. His most cited comedies are *Epitrepontes, Misoumenos,* and *Perikeiromene*. The "big three" of the historians—Thucydides, Herodotus, and Xenophon—are all well attested, but it is surprising to find Thucydides, with his narrow regional interests, austere style, and tortured syntax, more popular than Herodotus, with his broad international interests (including Egypt) and his flowing, enjoyable narrative. All ten of the canonized orators are represented, with Demosthenes, Isocrates, and Aeschines particularly popular. Plato's philosophical works, with their literary flourish, are predictably preferred to Aristotle's crabby lecture

---

[16] While it is just outside the specific parameters of our timeframe, and therefore not included in the chart, I should perhaps mention again the third-century CE waxed tablets that contain school exercises on fourteen Babrian fables (see above).

66 *The Formal Education of the Author of Luke-Acts*

notes. Finally, there occurs more interest—a recent development—in the fabulist traditions. *In toto*, we witness interest among the reading public in a broad array of ancient authors and genres, both poetry and prose.[17]

Many fewer ancient Greek authors, however, appear to have been incorporated into the formal curriculum of the schools during this period. The most notable feature of the school curriculum, at least at the primary and secondary levels, is the prominence of poetry over prose. The epics of Homer are by far the most popular works, with the *Iliad* much more heavily represented than the *Odyssey*. The tragedies of Euripides and the comedies and *sententiae* of Menander place a distant second. Of the prose writers, some fables of Aesop and some gnomic sayings of Isocrates and Diogenes the Cynic are included in primary- and secondary-level instruction.[18]

Within these selections, several features are notable. Of Homer's epics, the first two books of the *Iliad* are the most heavily represented, including the catalog of ships, then books 1–6 generally; also, the first few verses of individual books tend to be disproportionately represented.[19] Of Euripides' tragedies, the *Phoenissae* is notably popular.[20]

---

[17] It is instructive to compare the more targeted data of J. Krüger, *Oxyrhynchos in der Kaiserzeit: Studien zur Topographie und Literaturrezeption* (Frankfurt: Peter Lang, 1990), 214–46, who has listed all the literary papyri discovered exclusively at the site of Oxyrhynchus and noted the frequency of mentions and citations of the various authors. He comes up with an unsurprising list of the following top ten authors: Homer, Hesiod, Callimachus, Plato, Euripides, Menander, Demosthenes, Thucydides, Herodotus, and Pindar.

[18] R. Cribiore, *Gymnastics of the Mind*, 138–43, 192–201, whose analysis stretches over a much longer historical period, emphasizes the popularity in the primary and secondary schools of the poets Homer, Hesiod, Euripides, and Menander. She claims that no prose was read except for fables, such as those of Aesop and Babrius, and gnomic works of Isocrates, such as *Ad Demonicum* and *Ad Nicoclem*. On the prominence of Isocrates, among the prose authors, and especially of these two orations, perhaps owing to their moralistic content, see P. Pruneti, "L'*Ad Demonicum* nella scuola antica: esempi di utilizzazione," in *Munus Amicitiae: Scritti in memoria di Alessandro Ronconi*, ed. G. Pasquali (Firenze: Le Monnier, 1986), 211–19, and F. Maltomini and C. Römer, "Noch einmal 'Ad Demonicum' auf einer Schultafel," *Zeitschrift für Papyrologie und Epigraphik* 75 (1988): 297–300.

[19] R. Cribiore, *Gymnastics of the Mind*, 194–7, remarking on the use of Homer in school texts throughout antiquity, observes that *Iliad* books 1 and 2 are strongly favored, then books 1–6 generally and 1–12 generally, and finally 1–24 for advanced students, including the "unpopular" books 14, 19, 20, and 21. The *Odyssey* is represented in much fewer school texts than the *Iliad*. T. Morgan, *Literate Education*, 100–19, 308–13 (tables 11–15), 320–2 (tables 20–3), who counts 86 quotations and citations from the *Iliad* and 11 from the *Odyssey* in school texts, notes that the first few verses of the individual books are disproportionately cited (25/97 are from the first 20 lines of the book, 17/97 are from the very first line). For the manner in which the study of Homer may have been divided among the three levels of the ancient educational curriculum, see R. F. Hock, "Homer in Greco-Roman Education," in *Mimesis and Intertextuality in Antiquity and Christianity*, ed. D. R. MacDonald (Harrisburg, Trinity Press International, 2001), 56–77.

[20] On the high frequency of representations of the *Phoenissae* in both literary and school papyri, see J. M. Bremer, "The Popularity of Euripides' *Phoenissae*," 281–8, and R. Cribiore, "The Grammarian's Choice," 241–59. Cribiore notes the frequent representations of the drama in the school papyri of Hellenistic Egypt, the 30 representations of the drama in the literary papyri between the third century BCE and the seventh century CE, as well as the disproportionately high frequency of quotations of the drama by ancient writers such as Plutarch, Lucian, and Athenaeus. Cribiore attributes the popularity of this play to its accessible language, its comprehensive treatment of the popular myth of the royal house of Thebes, and its abundant gnomic material, which was useful for paedagogical purposes. She observes that the drama was used at all three levels of education and then maintained its popularity among those for whom formal schooling was long over.

What Greek Authors Would Luke Have Known?　　　67

Regarding Menander, it is sometimes difficult to determine if the school text is quoting from a comedy or from a collection of *sententiae*.[21]

As mentioned earlier, we need to exercise caution when drawing conclusions from the data marshaled in this chart. For while it appears from the figures that some authors were quite popular among the reading public but were not incorporated in any significant way into the school curriculum, it is possible that the data are misleading. Hesiod's works, for example, may have been studied only at the upper levels of the curriculum, the educational texts of which are almost impossible to distinguish—based on the materials upon which they were written, the quality and size of the handwriting, and the absence or presence of certain reading aids (accents, breathings, word division, etc.)—from normal manuscripts, mostly papyrus rolls at this time, of Hesiod's works intended for the reading public.[22] Of the other epic poets, Apollonius of Rhodes and Callimachus may have been used in advanced education, but they too have left scarcely a trace in identifiable school texts. The same could be surmised about the dramatists Aeschylus, Sophocles, and Aristophanes and the lyric poets Archilochus, Pindar, Alcaeus, Simonides, Alcman, Sappho, and Bacchylides. And this may be especially true of the prose authors: the historians Herodotus, Thucydides, and Xenophon, the orators Demosthenes, Isocrates, and Aeschines, and the philosophers Plato and Aristotle.

Some observations need to be included here about the status of libraries and book collections throughout the ancient Mediterranean world. Because of the circumstances of survival of the Greek literary papyri in Egypt—the fact that so many have been

---

[21] The remains of school texts on papyri, if considered in isolation, might suggest the latter, since *sententiae* are commonly used as exercises in school texts. T. Morgan, *Literate Education*, 120–5, notes that the popularity of *sententiae* continues unabated in school texts from the earliest Hellenistic to the latest Byzantine period, i.e., well into the Christian era. She counts 7 Menandrian quotations and citations in school texts that are clearly not *sententiae*, and she assumes that all the rest are. Yet Quintilian (*Inst.* 10.1.69) advocates for the reading of full dramas in his recommendations, for he praises Menander's style, characterization, and representation of real life. Likewise, Plutarch (*Comp. Arist. Men. Compend.* 854a–b) claims that Menander's poetry provides reading, study, and entertainment for a wider public than any other Greek masterpiece, in the theater, in the lecture room, and at the dinner party. Both Quintilian and Plutarch are thinking of full plays of Menander, not of collections of his *sententiae*. Based on remarks by Dionysius of Halicarnassus (*De imit.* II fr. 6.2), Quintilian (*Inst.* 1.11.4–13; 10.1.69, 71), and Dio Chrysostom (*Or.* 18.6, 7) about the use of Menander in literary training, S. Nervegna, *Menander in Antiquity: The Contexts of Reception* (Cambridge: Cambridge University Press, 2013), 201–51, argues for the use of full dramas of Menander in the school system, at least at an advanced level, with students not just copying and studying them but also using them as models for the progymnastic exercises of "speeches in character" (*ethopoiia* or *prosopopoiia*), as well as even reciting and performing them (as "reading marks" on some Menandrian papyri suggest: e.g., *P.Oxy.* 50.3533, 53.3705). It appears, then, that the distillation of Menander's rich array of dramas into anthologies of one-line *sententiae* was completed long after the New Testament period. The misfortune that not a single one of Menander's 100-plus comedies has survived through normal manuscript transmission is owed to a lack of interest during the Medieval and Byzantine periods, not during the Hellenistic and Roman Imperial periods. All this is pertinent, of course, to any conjecture about how Paul became familiar with the aphorism that he quotes in 1 Corinthians 15:33, which is possibly from Menander's comedy *Thais* (though ultimately, I think, is of Euripidean origin).

[22] R. Cribiore, *Gymnastics of the Mind*, 138, 192–204, and R. Cribiore, "Education in the Papyri," in *The Oxford Handbook of Papyrology*, ed. R. S. Bagnall (Oxford: Oxford University Press, 2009), 328–32, makes this point.

68 *The Formal Education of the Author of Luke-Acts*

excavated from rubbish heaps, divorced from any meaningful archaeological context—it is usually impossible to determine where these literary texts were originally housed. We do not generally know whether any particular fragment of a literary text originated in a public library, a private book collection, a bookseller's inventory, or a school's stock of textbooks.

We do, of course, have an idea of what was housed in the famous library of Alexandria because of our knowledge of the work of several of the scholarly head librarians there. Also, the third-century BCE poet and scholar Callimachus, who, though never a head librarian in Alexandria, was very engaged with the library's collection, is said to have compiled a 120-volume catalogue of the contents of the library that included all the authors and all their known works. This work, the *Pinakes* "Writing-Tablets," has not survived, but two dozen or so references to it, as well as a handful of actual quotations of it, by later authors such as Athenaeus, Dionysius of Halicarnassus, and Diogenes Laertius allow us to glimpse its basic structure: a fundamental division between poetry and prose; further subsections based on genre; an alphabetically arranged list of authors within each subsection, along with a list of all known works by each author.

Owing to the ravages of time, no physical remains of the contents of this great library have survived; nor have the contents of any of the other dozens of libraries that would have been features of every metropolitan area of the Mediterranean world—with one exception. A fairly extensive library in the Villa of the Papyri at Herculaneum in Italy survived, ironically, because the entire building was engulfed by the pyroclastic flow from the eruption of Mt. Vesuvius in 79 CE. This collection of at least several hundred rolls is composed almost entirely of philosophical texts of interest primarily to its Epicurean owner. It is possible, though, that a more extensive library collection of broader interest will be discovered in the future, if excavations on the villa are ever allowed to resume.

In the absence of direct evidence anywhere else in the ancient Mediterranean world, the search for information on the nature of collections of literary texts involves an indirect pathway through the Egyptian papyri. I wish to conclude this section on the Egyptian papyri by drawing attention to a few large concentrations of extracts of literary texts that have been discovered at single sites. Most notably, excavators have discovered in some mounds of ancient rubbish in Oxyrhynchus some concentrations of literary texts that may have had their origins in the holdings of public libraries or private book collections, the inventories of texts on hand at booksellers, or even the stock of textbooks used in schools.

The surviving evidence for libraries and book collections in Egypt includes three substantial deposits discovered by B. P. Grenfell and A. S. Hunt in Oxyrhynchus in January of 1906, the fragments of which date from the first to third centuries CE. The first deposit contained a basketful of literary papyrus rolls (sixteen manuscripts in all) that included Pindar's *Paeans*, Euripides' *Hypsipyle*, Thucydides' *History*, Plato's *Phaedrus* and *Symposium*, Aeschines Socraticus's *Alcibiades*, Antiphon's *On Truth*, speeches of the orators Lysias, Isocrates, and Demosthenes, two other unidentified speeches, a *Hellenica* by the historian Theopompus (or Cratippus), a treatise on literary composition, and a commentary on the second book of Thucydides' history. The second deposit contained numerous small fragments of what appear to have been roughly thirty-five manuscripts that included works by the poets Hesiod, Sappho, Alcaeus, Pindar, Bacchylides, Ibycus, Sophocles, Euripides, Menander, Callimachus, Theocritus, and Cercidas, and the prose writers Herodotus, Plato, Demosthenes, and Ephorus. The third deposit contained fewer but larger fragments of around twenty-five manuscripts that included the epic poets Homer and Hesiod, the lyric poets Pindar and Sappho, the tragedians Sophocles and Euripides, the historians Herodotus, Thucydides, and Xenophon, the philosopher Plato, and two Hellenistic poets Callimachus and Lycophron.[23] A fourth substantial deposit of literary texts was discovered by Evaristo Breccia in 1932 in the same mound that had produced Grenfell and Hunt's second and third deposits. Breccia was allowed by local officials to remove the tomb of Sheikh Ali el Gamman located at the top of the mound and thereby exposed underneath the tomb an area that had been inaccessible to Grenfell and Hunt. There he discovered a deposit containing fifty-two manuscripts that included numerous ancient authors: among the poets, the epic poets Homer and Hesiod, the tragedians Aeschylus, Sophocles, and Euripides, the comedians Aristophanes, Cratinus, and Eupolis, and the Hellenistic poets Callimachus and Euphorion; among the prose writers, the historians Thucydides and Xenophon, the philosopher Plato, and the orators Demosthenes, Isocrates, and Lysias. Some contemporary writers were also included: Philo, perhaps Arrian, two novels, and a contemporary speech.[24]

In addition to these concentrations of actual literary texts, we also find on occasion in the Egyptian documentary papyri lists of names of literary works that shed further light on the accessibility and contents of collections of ancient literary texts in the eastern Mediterranean around Luke's lifetime. R. Otranto has collected and analyzed nineteen papyri from Egypt containing such lists of texts, of which three are especially informative for our purposes:[25]

1. *P.Vindob.Gr.* inv. 39966, Arsinoites, first century CE, contains two lists of literary texts. One list includes almost all the works of the poets Homer, Hesiod, and Callimachus, followed by some selections of the orators Aeschines and Demosthenes, as well as several otherwise unknown prose works. The other list includes works of the poets Homer, Hesiod, Pindar, Sappho, and Callimachus. Each collection must have comprised between fifty and one-hundred papyrus rolls.

---

[23] For a fascinating first-person account of the discovery of these three deposits, see B. P. Grenfell and A. S. Hunt, "Excavations at Oxyrhynchus," in *Archaeological Report of the Egypt Exploration Fund*, ed. F. Griffith (London: Gilbert and Rivington, 1905–1906), 8–16. Unfortunately, Grenfell and Hunt's notes, here and elsewhere, do not differentiate clearly between the contents of the finds from the second and third deposits.

[24] G. Houston has weighed the evidentiary value of these four deposits for identifying some of the physical qualities and organizational features of ancient libraries and book collections: G. Houston, "Grenfell, Hunt, Breccia, and the Book Collections of Oxyrhynchus," *Greek, Roman, and Byzantine Studies* 47 (2007): 327–59, and G. Houston, *Inside Roman Libraries: Book Collections and Their Management in Antiquity* (Chapel Hill: University of North Carolina Press, 2014), 130–79.

[25] R. Otranto, *Antiche liste di libri su papiro* (Rome: Edizioni di Storia e Letteratura, 2000). G. Houston, *Inside Roman Libraries*, 39–86, has used these lists to illustrate how book collections were inventoried in antiquity.

70 *The Formal Education of the Author of Luke-Acts*

2. *P.Oxy.* 33.2659, Oxyrhynchus, second century CE, is part of an alphabetic list of comic poets and their plays that includes the works of eleven poets of old comedy. The poets range from Amipsias to Epicharmus, so the surviving portion of the papyrus is just a small part of what was once a much more comprehensive list of comedies. A total of sixty-three titles of comedies are listed, twenty-four of which are from Aristophanes and eighteen from Epicharmus. This alphabetic list appears to be a catalogue of the collection of a provincial library in Oxyrhynchus. If the holdings of this collection were as substantial in other genres of literature, the library must have held several thousand rolls of literary works.

3. *PSI Laur.* inv. 19662 verso, Oxyrhynchus, third century CE, is a catalogue of texts probably belonging to a library or large book collection. After a list of twenty (mostly) Platonic dialogues and a list of five works of Xenophon, the poets Homer, Menander, Euripides, Aristophanes, and, possibly, Cratinus are listed, along with the phrase ὅσα εὑρίσκ(εται) "as much as is found," which appears to mean "all known works." This was clearly a very large collection of papyrus rolls. It is notable that the collection contains three copies of Plato's *Alcibiades*, two of his *Protagoras*, and two of his *Philebus*—so this is more likely a catalogue of a collection than, as some have suggested, a required reading list for a school or a scholar's bibliography, for in the latter cases there would be no reason to list multiple copies of the same texts.

What is most remarkable for our purposes is that these three catalogues of literary texts, one from Arsinoites and two from Oxyrhynchus, along with the four deposits of actual extracts of literary texts from Oxyrhynchus mentioned earlier, whether they are evidence of collections of texts from public or private libraries, of texts owned by scribes or booksellers, or of texts originally housed in schools, are all composed of corpora of literary texts very similar to those found all over Egypt, which in turn, as we have seen, mirror the canons of texts recommended by Hellenistic and Roman Imperial-era historians, philosophers, rhetoricians, and grammarians from all over the Mediterranean world. We get a clear picture here that these canonical literary works were as accessible in the provincial towns on the periphery of the Roman Empire as they were in the major coastal cities of the eastern Mediterranean—or in Greece itself. Thus these texts would have been knowable and accessible to the author of Luke-Acts and to his audience, regardless of where they lived. It is not unreasonable to suppose that Luke himself possessed a collection of texts of ancient Greek literature, perhaps composed of a core of the texts that he had used in school as a youth, and thereafter enhanced by the acquisition in his adult life of texts that were of particular interest to him.

Quotations and Citations of Ancient Literary Works by Luke's Contemporaries

There survive substantial works written in Greek by many authors of the eastern Mediterranean roughly contemporary with Luke: the historians Josephus of Jerusalem, Arrian of Nicomedia, Appian of Alexandria, and Cassius Dio of Nicaea; the novelists Chariton of Aphrodisias, Xenophon of Ephesus, Achilles Tatius of Alexandria, and Longus of Lesbos (?); the orators Dionysius of Halicarnassus, Dio Chrysostom of

Prusa, Aelius Aristides of Smyrna, Maximus of Tyre, and Hermogenes of Tarsus; the geographers Strabo of Amaseia and Pausanias of Magnesia ad Sipylum (?); the biographer Plutarch of Chaeronea; the philosopher Philo of Alexandria; the satirist Lucian of Samosata; and the physician Galen of Pergamum. If we were to formulate a substantial and reliable database of the works cited and quoted by these authors, we could reasonably extrapolate from it a list of works that Luke himself might have known, all the more so if these contemporaries happened to be within Luke's cultural, as well as his temporal and spatial, orbit. This makes all the more pressing, of course, the question of the nature of Luke's cultural orbit, for we would want to select for examination from this long list those authors that have the most in common with Luke.

As we observed in an earlier chapter, what we know with certainty about the personal life of the author of the Gospel of Luke and the Acts of the Apostles is quite limited, but we can be fairly confident of the following: the author was a man; he was alive during the latter half of the first century CE; he was an inhabitant of the eastern Mediterranean, probably of one of the major cities of Asia Minor or the Levant. On the one hand, he was a product of Hellenistic Greek and Roman culture, familiar with the larger Hellenistic and Roman world: its geography, political and governmental institutions, religion and myth, and philosophy. On the other hand, if he was not a Jew himself, he was a "God-fearing" gentile, well versed in Judaism, familiar with its sacred scriptures through the Greek Septuagint, knowledgeable of its theology, doctrines, and worship practices both in the synagogues and in the temple in Jerusalem. And fundamentally, of course, he was a convert to the new Messianic sect of Judaism called within his lifetime, at least in some places, Christianity. He was at home and, in fact, quite proficient in the Greek language, adopting an idiomatic, sometimes even literary, style of Hellenistic Greek, and on occasion displaying fairly well-polished literary skills. This means that he was not only among the 15 percent or so of the population that was literate but that, moreover, as someone who could compose such large and detailed treatises, he was on the high end of even this 15 percent. Like almost all literate people in the eastern Mediterranean, he probably received his education through the traditional Hellenistic Greek school curriculum: the *enkyklios paideia*. Using his educational skills, he composed at least two long works that can best be classified, with respect to genre, as a biography of Jesus and a history of early Christianity, both heavily reliant on earlier sources. It is possible that he was a Roman citizen. It is possible that he had a Roman name: the common praenomen *Lucius* or the cognomen *Lucanus*. It is possible that he was trained as a physician. And it is possible that, as a companion of Paul, he traveled extensively in the eastern Mediterranean, and eventually as far west as Rome.

In what follows, I shall attempt to reconstruct the mental and literal libraries of four authors from the eastern Mediterranean who wrote works in Greek and who were rough contemporaries of Luke: Plutarch, who illustrates the potential breadth of familiarity with ancient Greek literature by those who had achieved the highest level of education available at the time; Philo and Josephus, two Jews who had attained a high degree of familiarity with ancient Greek literature, probably, like Luke, through the experiences of their formal educations; and the novelist Chariton, who with respect to his genre, his language and writing style, and his audience shares with Luke several elements of his cultural orbit.

72   *The Formal Education of the Author of Luke-Acts*

Plutarch

Lucius Mestrius Plutarch (*c.* 45–*c.* 120 CE) was a philosopher and biographer from Chaeronea in Greece who was intimately familiar with Athens, traveled to Egypt and Italy, taught in Rome, and then spent the last thirty years of his life as a priest in Delphi. Some 78 of the miscellaneous works (*Moralia*) and 50 of the parallel lives (*Vitae*) of this prolific writer survive to our time. It may seem preposterous to compare Luke with so highly educated and productive a scholar as Plutarch, but the two have several things in common. They were both, of course, Greek-speaking writers—biographers of sorts—of the eastern Mediterranean whose lives overlapped during the second half of the first century CE. Both traveled broadly along the same routes, by sea and by land. Both were Roman citizens (Luke apparently) and in fact shared the Roman praenomen *Lucius* (Luke apparently). Their social classes and educational levels were probably quite different: Plutarch was much more highly educated than Luke, even studying philosophy at the Academy in Athens, and he clearly had formal training in rhetoric. Yet Plutarch, like Luke, writes in the Greek of his time, not, like the conceited writers of the Second Sophistic, in imitation of fifth- and fourth-century BCE Attic Greek; his language and style, like the most polished passages of Luke's work, can be categorized as a form of literary Hellenistic Greek. So, in spite of their differences, an examination of Plutarch's familiarity with ancient Greek literature can, I propose, shed at least some light on Luke's.

The figures in the list below represent the sum total of quotations and paraphrases of ancient Greek literature in Plutarch's entire surviving corpus.[26] In other words, the list is a reflection of the contents of Plutarch's mental and literal library of ancient Greek literature, whether he experienced this literature by attending performances, by reading and studying entire texts or substantial passages of texts, or by consulting abstractions of these texts in handbooks and collections of aphorisms. I have used as a template the list of authors used above in my calculation of the number of references to ancient Greek authors in the Egyptian papyri, which, in turn, was based on the lists of suggested readings by Hellenistic and Roman Imperial-era rhetoricians and grammarians. Again, bracketed ([ ]) authors are those that appear in the papyri that are in addition to the rhetoricians' and grammarians' lists. I have then added in braces ({ }) additional authors that are cited frequently (more than six times) in Plutarch.

Epic Poets: Homer 889 (*Iliad* 580, *Odyssey* 300, *H.Demeter* 1, *H.Apollo* 1, *H.Hermes* 1, *Hymn* 18 (to Hermes) 1, *Hymn* 27 (to Artemis) 1, *Cypria* 4); Hesiod 207 (*Theogony* 21, *Works and Days* 177, *Shield* 1, Other 8); Antimachus 7; Aratus 17 (all *Phaenomena*); Theocritus 2; Callimachus 15.

Lyric Poets: Archilochus 42; Pindar 148 (*Olympian Odes* 7, *Pythian Odes* 12, *Isthmian Odes* 8, *Nemean Odes* 3, fragments 118); Stesichorus 8; Alcaeus 9; Simonides 64; Sappho 17; Anacreon 6; [Mimnermus] 4; [Alcman] 17; [Bacchylides] 6; [Hipponax] 9; [Euphorion] 4; [Ibycus] 4; [Theognis] 19; [Timotheus] 14.

---

[26] The numbers are drawn from lists of citations of ancient Greek literature collected by W. C. Helmbold and E. N. O'Neil, *Plutarch's Quotations* (Baltimore: American Philological Association, 1959).

Tragic Poets: Aeschylus 63 (*Agamemnon* 2, *Choephori* 2, *Persae* 1, *Septem contra Thebas* 7, *Supplices* 9, fragments 42); Sophocles 140 (*Ajax* 2, *Antigone* 13, *Electra* 3, *Oedipus Coloneus* 6, *Oedipus Tyrannus* 16, *Philoctetes* 1, *Trachiniae* 6, fragments 93); Euripides 367 (*Alcestis* 3, *Andromache* 8, *Bacchae* 20, *Cyclops* 1, *Electra* 4, *Hecuba* 1, *Helen* 2, *Heraclidae* 1, *Hercules Furens* 10, *Hippolytus* 16, *Ion* 4, *Iphigenia in Aulide* 7, *Iphigenia in Tauris* 7, *Medea* 12, *Orestes* 21, *Phoenissae* 35, *Supplices* 5, *Troades* 8, fragments 202).

Comic Poets, Old: Aristophanes 64 (*Acharnians* 7, *Birds* 8, *Knights* 16, *Lysistrata* 2, *Clouds* 6, *Peace* 5, *Plutus* 2, *Frogs* 6, *Thesmophoriazusae* 1, *Wasps* 2, fragments 9); Eupolis 12; Cratinus 18; [Epicharmus] 14; [Pherecrates] 1; [Plato Comicus] 8.

Comic Poets, Middle: [Antiphanes] 4; [Alexis] 6.

Comic Poets, New: Menander 73; Philemon 9; [Diphilus] 1.

Historians: Thucydides 156; Herodotus 304; Xenophon 122; Theopompus 33; Philistus 17; Ephorus 23; [Hellanicus] 10; [Polybius] 54.

Orators: Demosthenes 91; Aeschines 27; Hyperides 21; Lysias 14; Isocrates 34; Lycurgus 16; Isaeus 6; Antiphon 4; [Andocides] 5; [Dinarchus] 4.

Philosophers: Democritus 66; Plato 915; Aristotle 515; Zeno of Citium 62; Epicurus 279; Theophrastus 129; [Thales] 30; [Antisthenes] 20; [Cleanthes] 22; [Chrysippus] 388; [Metrodorus] 40.

Fabulists: Aesop 50.

Others (cited at least six times (arranged alphabetically)): {Agathon-tragedian} 12; {Alcmaeon-philosopher} 9; {Anaxagoras-philosopher} 63; {Anaxarchus-philosopher} 15; {Anaximander-philosopher} 19; {Anaximenes-philosopher} 14; {Antipater-philosopher} 15; {Aristippus-philosopher} 14; {Aristobulus-historian} 16; {Ariston of Chios-philosopher} 17; {Aristoxenus-philosopher} 19; {Callisthenes-historian} 22; {Crantor-philosopher} 10; {Crates-philosopher} 17; {Critias-tragedian} 13; {Ctesias-historian} 14; {Demades-orator} 44; {Demetrius of Phaleron-philosopher} 26; {Dicaearchus-philosopher} 13; {Diogenes of Apollonia-philosopher} 14; {Dionysius of Halicarnassus-historian} 125; {Duris-historian} 17; {Empedocles-philosopher} 142; {Epimenides-philosopher/poet} 8; {Eratosthenes-librarian, etc.} 16; {Eudoxus-mathematician} 19; {Gorgias-philosopher} 18; {Heraclides Ponticus-philosopher} 24; {Heraclitus-philosopher} 76; {Hippocrates-physician} 17; {Idomeneus-biographer} 12; {Ion-tragedian} 20; {Leucippus-philosopher} 8; {Metrodorus of Chios-philosopher} 19; {Nearchus-historian} 8; {Nicander of Colophon-poet} 6; {Onesicritus-historian} 11; {Panaetius-philosopher} 10; {Parmenides-philosopher} 24; {Philochorus-historian} 14; {Philolaus-philosopher} 9; {Philoxenus-poet} 11; {Phylarchus-historian} 13; {Posidonius-philosopher} 22; {Solon-poet} 34; {Speusippus-philosopher} 12; {Stesimbrotus-biographer} 12; {Straton-philosopher} 15; {Terpander-poet} 18; {Timaeus-historian} 25; {Tyrtaeus-poet} 8; {Xenocrates-philosopher} 61; {Xenophanes-philosopher} 24; {Zeno of Elea-philosopher} 7; {plus many comica, tragica, and lyrica adespota, anthologia palatina, orphica, oracula, etc.}.

On the one hand, this list, as full as it is, does not include every ancient Greek author with whom Plutarch was familiar; he surely had access to other works that he simply

74   *The Formal Education of the Author of Luke-Acts*

chose not to cite or quote. On the other hand, it is likely that he had not read the entire texts of every author whom he cites and, moreover, that he may have gained familiarity with some of these works indirectly, through quotations in other authors or through collections of aphorisms or anthologies of passages from various works. Plutarch's method of citing and quoting ancient Greek texts suggests that he did not read them for pleasure and did not particularly relish their aesthetic features; rather, he used them primarily for his own moralizing purposes.

There are several notable features of this list: in comparison with other lists (above), the prose authors, and especially the historians, philosophers, and orators, are much more heavily represented in Plutarch, given his interests in these fields. As elsewhere, among the poets, Homer, Euripides, and Menander are very well represented. Hesiod (especially *Works and Days*) and Pindar are more highly represented than elsewhere, perhaps because of their connection to Plutarch's homeland in Boeotia. Likewise, drama having to do with Thebes, near Plutarch's hometown of Chaeronea, is highly represented (*Bacchae, Antigone, Septem contra Thebas, Oedipus Tyrannus*). Euripides' *Phoenissae* is very well represented, as elsewhere. The lyric poets Simonides and Archilochus are more well represented than elsewhere. Of the philosophers Chrysippus and Epicurus are very highly represented, as is Empedocles; Diogenes the Cynic does not appear at all. The Hellenistic poet Apollonius of Rhodes is never cited.

Plutarch's *modus operandi* for citation and quotation is especially worthy of note for our purposes, for it is sometimes similar to that of Luke and of other writers of the New Testament. Some quotations he pulls out of thin air, without any attribution, and weaves them seamlessly into his text, especially Homeric quotations but also some from Hesiod, Euripides, Heraclitus, Plato, Epicurus, and tragic and comic adespota. Sometimes he attributes a quotation generically to "the poets": Homer, Hesiod, and Euripides. But often he cites the poet's name: Homer, Hesiod, Archilochus, Pindar, Simonides, Theognis, Bacchylides, Thespis, Aeschylus, Sophocles, Euripides, Aristophanes, Timotheus, Alexis, Menander, and Philemon. Similarly he quotes several of the philosophers by name: Xenophanes, Empedocles, Gorgias, Plato, Cleanthes, Zeno of Citium, Epicurus, and Diogenes. In four cases he cites both the name of the author and the title of the work: Plato's *Gorgias* and *Republic*; Timotheus's *Persians*; and Menander's *Thais*. As we have already mentioned, and as we shall see in the following chapters, Luke embraces Plutarch's first two methods of citing and quoting ancient Greek writers: without any attribution; with attribution generically to "the poets."

In the following chapters, I shall propose that the author of Luke-Acts consciously and intentionally alludes to, references, and even quotes several ancient Classical and Hellenistic Greek authors: Homer, Aesop, Epimenides, Euripides (specifically the *Bacchae*), Plato (specifically the *Apology*), and Aratus (specifically the *Phaenomena*). It is worth noting for the sake of comparison, then, that Luke's contemporary Plutarch cites all of these authors and works on numerous occasions: Homer's *Iliad* and *Odyssey* 880 times; Aesop 50 times; Epimenides 8 times; Aratus's *Phaenomena* 17 times; Euripides 367 times, including the *Bacchae* 20 times; Plato 915 times, including the *Apology* 10 times.

Philo

Philo, the Hellenistic Jewish philosopher from Alexandria, can in several respects serve as an analogue to Luke: he lived in the first century CE in a large city in a Roman province of the eastern Mediterranean; he was a Greek-speaking Jew of the Diaspora, who was steeped in the Hebrew Scripture, which he knew chiefly through the Greek Septuagint, but he was familiar with, and even well educated in, Greek literature and philosophy; he traveled extensively throughout the Mediterranean world, and he even composed accounts of journeys from Alexandria to Rome and to Jerusalem; he dealt with issues of strife between Jewish and gentile communities, even participating in an embassy to the emperor Gaius in Rome to address the strife in Alexandria; he was granted Roman citizenship and given the Latin praenomen *Julius*. There were, of course, probably important differences between Philo and Luke as well, especially with respect to their social, economic, and political classes, their levels of education, and their connection and devotion to Judaism, but we have to admit that we really know very little for certain about these matters in Luke's case.

In his *De congressu eruditionis gratiae* "Concerning Meeting for the Sake of Instruction" (71–80) Philo describes the trajectory of his own education, using the very term ἐγκύκλιος παιδεία/*enkyklios paideia* "curricular education" (73). He relates how he became interested in pursuing philosophy but that he first had to master the preliminaries: first grammar, including reading, writing, and study of the poets and historians, second geometry, third music, and finally philosophy, which is the goal of everything previous. Philo uses as an allegory the story of Abraham, who, failing at first to have a child with his legitimate wife Sarah (= Philosophy), took in her place Sarah's handmaid Hagar (= the preliminary curricular disciplines). This is not the only occurrence in antiquity of the use of this metaphor of a handmaid to describe the curricular education. In a treatise on liberal education attributed in antiquity to Plutarch (*De liberis educandis* = *Moralia* 1a–14c) the same metaphor is used to demonstrate that the *enkyklios paideia* is incidental to the higher goal of philosophy (*Moralia* 7c). The treatise invokes the third-century BCE philosopher Bion who reportedly said that just as the suitors in Homer's *Odyssey*, not being able to approach Penelope, instead consorted with her handmaids, so also do those who are not able to attain philosophy wear themselves out with the other disciplines that have no worth.

Though he may have regarded the *enkyklios paideia* as preliminary (and inferior) to philosophy, Philo nonetheless values this preparation. In *De somniis* "Concerning Dreams" (1.205) he describes the "lover of wisdom" (σοφίας ἐραστής) as someone who has followed a progression from primary education in grammar (writing and reading), followed by exposure to the ancient poets and historians, then training in arithmetic and geometry, music (rhythm, meter, harmony, chromatics, diatonics, and melodies), rhetoric (invention, expression, order, arrangement, memory, and delivery), and, finally, philosophy (everything else of which human life consists).

Philo is especially illuminating for our purposes because he comments specifically on the nature of the education of Jews in a Hellenistic city of the eastern Mediterranean. In *De specialibus legibus* "Special Laws" (2.229–30), his commentary on the fifth commandment, "Thou Shalt Honor Thy Father and Thy Mother," Philo acknowledges

76 *The Formal Education of the Author of Luke-Acts*

the enormous debt that children owe their parents for their education. He praises (Jewish) parents in Alexandria who attend to the education of their children so that they may not only live but also live well. Philo's description of an ideal education, including for Jewish boys, is basically that of typical Hellenistic Greek boys: training their bodies through gymnastics and athletics to achieve a healthy and vigorous physical state; training their souls through grammar, arithmetic, geometry, music, and every kind of philosophy. Philo believed that their exemplar, Moses, had, after all, been led by Greek teachers through the *enkyklios paideia* (*Vit. Mos.* 1.23–4).

Philo illustrates the fruits of his own Greek education throughout his works. The figures in the list below represent the sum total of both explicit quotations and looser paraphrases of ancient Greek literature in Philo's entire surviving corpus.[27] In other words, this list, like the list of Plutarch's quotations and paraphrases (above), is a reflection of the contents of Philo's mental and literal library of ancient Greek literature, whether he experienced this literature by attending performances, by reading and studying entire texts or substantial passages of texts, or by consulting abstractions of these texts in handbooks and collections of aphorisms. Again, I have used as a template the list of authors used earlier in my calculation of the number of references to ancient Greek authors in the Egyptian papyri, which, in turn, was based on the lists of suggested readings by Hellenistic and Roman Imperial-era rhetoricians and grammarians. And, again, bracketed ([ ]) authors are those that appear in the papyri that are in addition to the rhetoricians' and grammarians' lists. I have then added in braces ({ }) additional authors that are cited in Philo.

Epic Poets: Homer 73 (*Iliad* 44, *Odyssey* 29); Hesiod 11 (*Theogony* 6, *Works and Days* 5); Theocritus 2: Callimachus 2.

Lyric Poets: Pindar 6 (*Pythian Odes* 1, *Nemean Odes* 1, fragments 4); Simonides 1; [Theognis] 1.

Tragic Poets: Aeschylus 15 (*Eumenides* 1, *Prometheus Vinctus* 1, fragments 15 (including fragments of *Argo*, *Myrmidones*, and *Niobe*)); Sophocles 8 (*Oedipus Coloneus* 1, fragments 7); Euripides 25 (*Hecuba* 1, *Hippolytus* 2, *Iphigenia in Aulide* 2, *Phoenissae* 1, fragments 19 (including fragments of *Antiope*, *Auge*, *Ino*, *Melanippe*, *Syleus*, and *Chrysippus*)).

Comic Poets, Old: Aristophanes 2; [Epicharmus] 3.

Comic Poets, New: Menander 4.

Historians: Thucydides 3; Herodotus 7; Xenophon 7.

Orators: Demosthenes 6.

Philosophers: Democritus 1; Plato 333 (131 from the *Timaeus*); Aristotle 36; Zeno of Citium 6; Theophrastus 2; [Antisthenes] 3; [Diogenes the Cynic] 2; [Cleanthes] 1; [Chrysippus] 4.

---

[27] The numbers are drawn largely from lists of citations of ancient Greek literature collected by D. Lincicum, "A Preliminary Index to Philo's Non-Biblical Citations and Allusions," *The Studia Philonica Annual* 25 (2013): 139–67, and D. Lincicum, "Philo's Library," *The Studia Philonica Annual* 26 (2014): 99–114, which include allusions and echoes in addition to direct quotations. Philo's citations of Greek authors can also be elicited from the indices of J. W. Earp, "Indices to Volumes I–X," in *Philo*, ed. F. H. Colson (Cambridge: Harvard University Press, 1962), 10:269–486.

What Greek Authors Would Luke Have Known? 77

Others (arranged alphabetically): {Anaxagoras-philosopher} 5; {Anaxarchus-philosopher} 1; {Anaximander-philosopher} 1; {Bias-philosopher} 1; {Critolaus-philosopher} 2; {Diodorus Siculus-historian} 3; {Empedocles-philosopher} 6; {Eratosthenes-librarian, etc.} 1; {Heraclitus-philosopher} 46; {Hippocrates-physician} 4; {Ion-tragedian} 1; {Ocellus-philosopher} 1; {Philolaus-philosopher} 1; {Posidonius-philosopher} 6; {Protagoras-philosopher} 1; {Pythagoras-philosopher} 2; {Solon-poet} 1; {Theodorus-philosopher} 1; {Xenophanes-philosopher} 2; {Zeno of Elea-philosopher} 1.

Greek authors who are mentioned by name in Philo, and whose works are quoted or alluded to explicitly, are the poets Homer, Hesiod, Solon, and Pindar, the tragedians Aeschylus, Sophocles, Euripides, and Ion, the physician Hippocrates, the historian Xenophon, and the philosophers Heraclitus, Democritus, Philolaus, Ocellus, Plato, Aristotle, Theophrastus, Anaxarchus, Diogenes, Zeno of Citium, Cleanthes, and Chrysippus. Of these, Homer, Heraclitus, Euripides, Plato, and Aristotle are the authors most often quoted or alluded to, making up over three-fourths of the total. Philo quotes or alludes to passages from many other Greek authors without mentioning them by name: e.g., Theocritus and Callimachus, among the epic poets; Simonides and Theognis, among the lyric poets; Aristophanes, Epicharmus, and Menander, among the comedians; Thucydides, Herodotus, and Diodorus Siculus, among the historians; Demosthenes the orator; and many philosophers from the Archaic to the Hellenistic period.

Philo calls Homer the "greatest and most respected of the poets" (*Conf. Ling.* 2.4) and clearly regards the *Iliad* and *Odyssey* as central to a good education: he knows the texts of the *Iliad* and *Odyssey* well, drawing from passages throughout the span of the two epics, and not, as among some other authors, just from a few specific books (he references passages from sixteen of the Iliadic books and twelve of the Odyssean books). He uses Homeric expressions frequently, quotes entire verses and passages occasionally, and is aware of the context of the Homeric passages that he quotes. He had a positive view of Homeric epic, in spite of its paganism, and appears to have used the same allegorical methodology in his interpretation of Homer as he did in his interpretation of Hebrew Scripture. Like other texts from this period of antiquity, including the literary works and school texts on papyrus, Philo favors the *Iliad* over the *Odyssey*, citing the two epics at a ratio of about 3:2.

Plato, whom Philo admires greatly and refers to as "the great Plato" (*Aet. Mund.* 52), is by far the most frequently attested author in Philo's works, his philosophical dialogues being the source of almost exactly half of Philo's quotations of, and allusions to, Greek literature. The *Timaeus* is by far the most often cited dialogue, followed by the *Phaedrus* and *Theaetetus*.[28] Philo clearly knows the actual texts of many of the Platonic dialogues. The philosopher Heraclitus is vastly overrepresented in Philo, partly because their philosophical interests overlapped, but also perhaps because Philo believed that

---

[28] On the centrality of the *Timaeus* in Philo's works see D. T. Runia, *Philo of Alexandria and the* Timaeus *of Plato* (Leiden: Brill, 1986).

Heraclitus received some of his learning from Moses. It appears that Philo had in his possession an actual copy of Heraclitus's Περὶ φύσεως *"On Nature,"* which he mentions by name.[29] On the other hand, while Philo mentions Aristotle by name and alludes to his philosophical tenets many times, he does not provide any actual quotations from Aristotle's writings; it thus appears that Philo may have known Aristotle's work secondhand, perhaps through commentaries rather than from the primary texts.

In sum, Philo, though steeped in the Torah and in the traditions of Judaism, was a πεπαιδευμένος/*pepaideumenos* who knew Classical and Hellenistic Greek literature as well as many secular Greek writers of his day. He quotes passages of Greek epic, lyric, drama, history, and philosophy purposefully and aptly, even in those treatises that are intended primarily for a Jewish audience. Like some other highly educated and upper-class citizens of the eastern cities of the Mediterranean, Philo must have possessed a substantial private library that he could consult and refer to in his own writings.[30]

Philo embraced secular Hellenistic culture in other ways too. In addition to his study of Greek literature and philosophy, he acculturated himself by attending athletic games in Alexandria (*Omn. Prob. Lib.* 26; *Prov.* 2.58). More pertinent to the question of Philo's education and familiarity with Greek literature is the fact that he attended and seemed to enjoy theatrical productions in Alexandria (*Ebr.* 177; also *Op. Mund.* 78; *Agr.* 35; *Abr.* 103; *Leg. Gai.* 78–9; *Spec. Leg.* 4.185; *Gig.* 31; *Flacc.* (generally)). Philo even quotes some verses from Euripides' *Auge* that he recalls having heard recited at the theater (*Omn. Prob. Lib.* 141). Thus, it is possible that in some instances in which Philo is quoting or paraphrasing a passage from the tragedians Aeschylus, Sophocles, and Euripides, or the comedian Menander, he is quoting from a production that he witnessed at a theater rather than from a text that he had in his possession. In a later chapter, we shall want to consider theatrical production as a possible source of inspiration for the author of Luke-Acts too, who appears to have been familiar with the tragedies of Euripides.

---

[29] On Philo's close familiarity with the text of Heraclitus, see L. Saudelli, *Eraclito ad Alessandria: studi e ricerche intorno alla testimonianza di Filone* (Turnhout: Brepols, 2012).

[30] On Philo's secular education generally, see I. Heinemann, *Philons griechische und jüdische Bildung* (Breslau: Marcus, 1932); M. Alexandre, "La culture profane chez Philon," in *Philon d'Alexandrie, Lyon Colloque*, eds. R. Arnaldez, C. Mondésert, and J. Poillous (Paris: Cerf, 1967), 105–29; A. Mendelson, *Secular Education in Philo of Alexandria* (Cincinnati: Hebrew Union College Press, 1982), 25–46; K. O. Sandnes, *The Challenge of Homer: School, Pagan Poets and Early Christianity* (London: Bloomsbury T&T Clark, 2009), 68–78; M. Alexandre, Jr., "Philo of Alexandria and Hellenic *Paideia,"* *Euphrosyne* 37 (2009): 121–30; C. J. P. Friesen, "Hannah's 'Hard Day' and Hesiod's 'Two Roads': Poetic Wisdom in Philo's *De ebrietate,"* *Journal for the Study of Judaism* 46 (2015): 44–64; E. Koskenniemi, *Greek Writers and Philosophers in Philo and Josephus: A Study of their Secular Education and Educational Ideals* (Leiden: Brill, 2019), 21–151, who summarizes and extends here his previous research on the topic: e.g., E. Koskenniemi, "Philo and Classical Drama," in *Ancient Israel, Judaism and Christianity in Contemporary Perspective: Essays in Memory of Karl-Johan Illman*, eds. J. Neusner et al. (Lanham: University Press of America, 2006), 137–52; E. Koskenniemi, "Philo and Greek Poets," *Journal for the Study of Judaism* 41 (2010): 301–22; E. Koskenniemi, "Philo and Classical Education," in *Reading Philo: A Handbook to Philo of Alexandria*, ed. T. Seland (Grand Rapids: Eerdmans, 2014), 93–113.

Josephus

Titus Flavius Josephus was born Yosef ben Mattityahu in Jerusalem in 37 CE to a wealthy and aristocratic Jewish priestly family, and he was raised and educated also in Jerusalem. As a Jewish historian he is best known for his *Jewish War*, about the first Jewish war of 66–70 CE against the Roman occupiers, and *Antiquities of the Jews*, about the history of the world from a Jewish perspective from creation to Josephus's own time. He initially fought against the Romans as a general in the Jewish military in the Galilee but then accepted the inevitability of Roman rule and ingratiated himself to the future emperor Vespasian, later becoming a Roman citizen and serving as an advisor of the emperor Titus.

His lifetime (37–*c*. 100 CE) overlaps with the lifetime of Luke. The two apparently lived and traveled in the same geographical areas: Judaea, including Jerusalem, and the Hellenistic cities of the eastern Mediterranean. They both traveled abroad to Puteoli and then Rome, enduring many hazards by sea, in order to consult the emperor Nero—at around the same time. Both were familiar with Jewish, Greek, and Roman religions, customs, administrative systems, and so forth. Both attempted to explain Jewish/Christian matters to a gentile audience in their written works, striving to achieve a rapprochement between Jews/Christians and Greeks/Romans; they did this partly by presenting their religious movements as philosophical schools rather than as religious cults, thereby making them more palatable to their audiences. They were probably both Roman citizens, and they adopted Roman names, but they wrote in the Koine Greek widely spoken in the eastern Mediterranean in the first century CE. Surely, to some degree, we can extrapolate from Josephus's familiarity with ancient Greek literature the degree to which Luke was likely familiar with these same texts.[31]

---

[31] New Testament scholars have from time to time even proposed that Luke was familiar with the texts of Josephus's *Jewish War* and *Antiquities* and used them as a source for some of the historical details in his own composition of Luke-Acts. This proposal was presented very fully in the late nineteenth century by M. Krenkel, *Josephus und Lucas: Der schriftstellerische Einfluss des jüdischen Geschichtschreibers auf den christlichen nachgewiesen* (Leipzig: H. Haessel, 1894), a 300-page monograph that argues that Luke depended on Josephus in 92 passages in Luke-Acts. Krenkel's methodology is suspect, however, since it is based simply on commonly used words and phrases, accounts of similar events, and other such parallels that would inevitably occur between any two contemporary authors writing in the same language about the events of the same historical period. Krenkel's proposal lay dormant for some time but has reemerged over the past thirty years or so, its most notable advocates being S. Mason, *Josephus and the New Testament* (Peabody: Hendrickson, 1992), 185–229, and R. I. Pervo, *Dating Acts: Between the Evangelists and the Apologists* (Santa Rosa: Polebridge Press, 2006), 149–201. I remain unconvinced by the proposal in all of its forms: it imagines a scenario whereby the author of the Gospel of Luke and Acts of the Apostles, very late in the first century or early in the second, hunts and pecks for historical information through early drafts, or perhaps more widely distributed versions, of the texts of Josephus's *Jewish War* and *Antiquities*, very casually lifting details out of their historical contexts—most importantly for the proposal the census of the Syrian governor Quirinius, the rule of Lysanias the Tetrarch of Abilene, the rebellions of Judas the Galilean, Theudas, and "the Egyptian," and the role of the *sicarii*—and then hopelessly distorting these details as he tries to incorporate them into his own narrative, and, finally, deliberately deceiving his readers in the preface to his work regarding the sources of his historical information (Lk. 1:1-4). This is a very dim view of the author of Luke-Acts as a historian, as a writer, and, indeed, as a person, and it does not comport with what we witness in his work generally.

80   *The Formal Education of the Author of Luke-Acts*

Somehow or other Josephus learned how to read and write Greek with some fluency, but we know almost nothing about his formal Greek education, just as we know almost nothing about the status and availability of Greek education generally in Judaea during his lifetime.[32] Even though Josephus writes an autobiography (*Life*), he remains silent about the period of his childhood when he would have been attending primary- and secondary-level schools. Several times throughout his works (*War* 1.3; *Ant.* 1.7, 20.263–4; *Apion* 1.50) Josephus issues a formal apology for the deficiencies of his Greek, not out of modesty, to be sure, in which he was notoriously lacking, perhaps as a literary and rhetorical convention ("unaccustomed to public speaking as I am"), but probably simply because it was, to some degree, true. Yet we can see clearly the results of some sort of Greek education in the quality of the Greek prose of Josephus's works, as well as in his references to other, even Classical, works of Greek literature of the type that constituted the traditional Greek educational curriculum.

While Josephus was utterly steeped in Judaism, and although Aramaic was his native tongue, he mentions and quotes an astounding number of Classical and Hellenistic Greek authors both in his history of the Jews *Antiquities* and in his treatise *Against Apion*, an apologetic work in which he defends Judaism as an ancient religion against the relatively new traditions of the Greeks. Of ancient Greek literature Josephus shows the most interest in the genres of epic, philosophy, and history.[33]

Like so many of his contemporaries, Josephus is familiar with the Homeric epics. He mentions Homer by name four times in *Against Apion* and once in *Antiquities*. He is far ahead of his time in advocating the theory that Homer passed his songs down orally and that they were not written down until later, which, he claims, explains the many discrepancies that are to be found in the poems (*Apion* 1.12). Josephus appears to have consulted the actual texts of both the *Iliad* and *Odyssey*: for example, he claims that Homer never uses the term νόμος "law" in all his poems (*Apion* 2.155)—which is in fact true; he reports the view that Homer is referring to Jerusalem when he mentions Solyma (in some mss. of *Ant.* 7.67)—surely a reference to the Homeric Solymoi in *Iliad* 6.184, 204 and *Odyssey* 5.283; and he even places a slightly adapted verse of the

---

[32] The evidence from later Rabbinic literature is anachronistic (e.g., b. B. Qam. 82b-83a; b. B. Bat. 2a; y. Ketub. 8:11, 32c). The existence of a gymnasium at the foot of the Temple Mount in Jerusalem during the second century BCE (e.g., 2 Macc. 4:7-17) presupposes the existence of primary and secondary preparatory schools at that time (so M. Hengel, *The Hellenization of Judaea*, 22), but it is not clear that the gymnasium still existed in the first century CE. C. Hezser, *Jewish Literacy in Roman Palestine* (Tübingen: Mohr Siebeck, 2001), 90–4, supposes the existence of Greek schools in Judea in the first century CE and suggests that Josephus reached the competency level of a student in the grammar school (i.e., secondary level), either through private instruction or through attendance at a Greek school, which would have been open to native Jewish as well as non-Jewish students. This may be a correct conclusion, but the lack of evidence renders it highly speculative.

[33] Possible references to Classical and Hellenistic Greek authors in Josephus can be elicited from the general index of L. H. Feldman, *Josephus: Jewish Antiquities Book XX and General Index* (Cambridge: Harvard University Press, 1965), 159–383. Feldman perceives many subtle allusions in the *Antiquities* to ancient Greek (and Latin) authors and collects them in his *Josephus's Interpretation of the Bible* (Berkeley: University of California Press, 1998), and *Studies in Josephus' Rewritten Bible* (Leiden: Brill, 1998), but I have limited myself here to explicit mentions and actual quotations of ancient Greek authors, as in those analyzed by E. Koskenniemi, *Greek Writers and Philosophers*, 152–293.

Iliad (14.90) in the mouth of a Roman senator (*Ant.* 19.92). Josephus mentions Hesiod twice, once in *Against Apion* (1.16), where he observes that the mythographer Acusilaus corrected Hesiod on details of his genealogies, once in *Antiquities* (1.108), where he cites Hesiod in support of his assertion that men of old, like Noah, lived an extraordinarily long life—presumably a reference to the "ages of humankind" section of Hesiod's *Works and Days*. Josephus also mentions the much less well-known fifth-century BCE epic poet from Samos, Choerilus, whose epic *Persica* survives in just a few fragments. In *Against Apion* (2.172–5) Josephus quotes five dactylic hexameter verses from a section of the epic cataloguing the various tribes that crossed the Hellespont with the Persians, and he claims that Choerilus included the Jews in Xerxes' expedition. This is the longest fragment of Choerilus to survive from antiquity, and it survives only in Josephus's quotation. Of other Greek poets—epic, lyric, dramatic—the only one mentioned by Josephus explicitly, in passing, is a fourth-century BCE tragic poet named Theodectes (*Ant.* 12.113).

Josephus suggests that Greek philosophers acquired their concept of God from acquaintance with the Books of Moses (*Apion* 1.162; 2.168, 257, 280–4). Of the pre-Socratics, Josephus mentions by name Thales, Pythagoras, Pherecydes, and Anaxagoras, but he does not show himself familiar with any real or supposed texts of these philosophers. Josephus shows great admiration for Plato, claiming that Plato, among other Greek philosophers, had the notion, like the Jews, that god was unbegotten and unchangeable through all time, different from every mortal form in his beauty, and while known to humans in his power yet unknown in his essence (*Apion* 2.167–169). From Josephus's description of Socrates it appears that he was familiar with Plato's Socratic dialogues: in *Against Apion* (2.263–4) Josephus blames the Athenians for putting Socrates to death, references his reliance on a *daimonion*, asserts that he was accused of corrupting the youth, and reports that he was tried and drank the hemlock. The similarity of the vocabulary and phrases, as well as the content, of Josephus's description suggests that he has actually read the dialogues of Plato pertaining to Socrates' trial and death. He was familiar with other dialogues of Plato as well, showing, in particular, familiarity with Plato's strictures regarding his ideal city-state in the *Republic*: that Homer and the other poets should be banished from the ideal city-state lest they destroy with their myths the true notion of god; that the populace should pay due attention to the laws of the city-state; that the populace of the city-state should not intermarry with foreigners (*Apion* 2.256–8). Josephus implies elsewhere that he has carefully perused Plato's writings on law and politics (*Apion* 2.224). Of the remaining philosophers mentioned by Josephus he seems to have but a casual acquaintance derived from secondhand sources and common stereotypes rather than from his own study of their actual texts. Of other Platonists, Josephus briefly mentions Philo of Larissa, head of the Academy in the late second century BCE. Josephus also makes passing reference to Aristotle and his school, quoting passages from Aristotle's students Clearchus and Theophrastus and mentioning Demetrius of Phaleron. Of the Stoic philosophers, Josephus mentions Zeno, Cleanthes, and Posidonius, and he observes more generally the compatibility of Stoic philosophy with Pharisaic beliefs (*Life* 12). He criticizes the Epicurean view that God exercises no providence over human affairs (*Ant.* 10.277–80), but he does not mention any Epicurean philosophers by name.

82   *The Formal Education of the Author of Luke-Acts*

As a historian himself, and as someone who fancied himself placing his own stamp on the Greek historiographical tradition, Josephus was especially well versed in Classical, Hellenistic, and Roman Imperial-era historical works. In particular, he seems to have perused the works of many Greek histories for references to the Jews. He lists a number in *Against Apion*, but then he admits that he "has not chanced upon all the Greek books" (1.216). Not all his references are correctly attributed, and not all are to authentic sources, but since some of his sources are still extant we can see how Josephus used them; we can see where Josephus changed from one source to the next, as his knowledge gets more or less detailed; and we can see that Josephus saw that it was important on occasion to quote actual passages from these sources. Josephus mentions and quotes several of the Classical, Hellenistic, and Roman Imperial-era historians who wrote in Greek and who because of their importance and popularity have survived to our time through the manuscript tradition: Herodotus he mentions by name nine times, and he quotes several lines from him almost verbatim concerning the history of circumcision, though with some differences in dialect and vocabulary (Herodotus 2.104); Thucydides, whose standard of accuracy he admires, he mentions by name twice; Theopompus, who was immensely popular during the Hellenistic and Roman Imperial periods, he mentions by name twice; Polybius he mentions by name five times and quotes two short passages from what he claims was the sixteenth book of Polybius's *Histories* (*Ant*. 12.135–7); Strabo, whose life almost overlapped with that of Josephus, he mentions by name sixteen times, and he quotes many passages from Strabo's *Histories*, a massive work that survives in only nineteen fragments, ten of which are found only in Josephus. Josephus also mentions dozens of Classical (e.g., Hellanicus, Philistus, Ephorus), Hellenistic (e.g., Timaeus, Manetho, Berossus), and Roman Imperial-era (e.g., Chaeremon, Nicolaus of Damascus, Apion) historians, writing in Greek, from various parts of the Mediterranean world, whose works have not survived. We would not even know of the existence of some of the historians Josephus mentions but for the fact that he cites their works: e.g., Dio's history of Phoenicia; Cleodemus/ Malchus's history of the Jews; Philostratus's histories of India and Phoenicia. Of historians who wrote in Latin Josephus mentions only Livy, referring to him as a writer of Roman history (*Ant*. 14.68).

One lesson to be learned from this survey of Josephus's use of Greek sources is that as many authors as Josephus cites, and as often as he quotes from these authors, if it had not been for Josephus himself we would be unfamiliar with the many of them. Complete works of only nine of the seventy-one authors that Josephus mentions, cites, and quotes in *Antiquities* and *Against Apion* have survived to our time. Moreover, of Josephus's twenty-one direct quotations of the texts of these authors, only one is independently attested in a surviving text: Herodotus's musings concerning the history of circumcision in 2.104 (*Apion* 1.169–71). This should cause us to consider whether there may not be some quotations embedded in the texts of the Gospel of Luke and the Acts of the Apostles that we simply fail to recognize because the sources of the quotations are no longer extant. In such cases we can identify quotations only internally, by meter, style, aphoristic tone, and so forth, and ultimately, any conclusions about the nature of these quotations and their sources will entail a good deal of guesswork rather than proof.

Chariton

The genre of the "Romance" or "Novel" arose and became popular around the time of the composition of Luke-Acts. Some have observed the similarities between several of the narrative motifs in Acts, in particular, and those in the early novels and have even proposed a certain level of novelistic influence upon the narrative of Acts.[34] Shared motifs include voyages by sea, storms, and shipwrecks; trials, imprisonments, and miraculous rescues; plots and conspiracies; mobs and riots; dreams and visions; and magicians and miracle workers.

The novelist Chariton, from Aphrodisias in Asia Minor, was probably a contemporary of Luke. He composed his novel *Callirhoe* in a type of literary Hellenistic Greek not dissimilar to that of Luke-Acts: i.e., the novel is not a scholarly Atticizing work of the Second Sophistic intended for a highly cultured audience; rather, it was probably written for a "popular" audience with a level of education similar to that of the audience of Luke-Acts. Notably, Chariton is familiar with the ancient Greek Classics, and he expects a certain level of familiarity among his audience as well. In *Callirhoe* Chariton twice explicitly mentions Homer's name (1.5.2; 2.3.7), and dozens of Homeric quotations are interspersed throughout the text of the novel. Chariton's knowledge of the Homeric texts was more than incidental: he includes quotations from fourteen different books of the *Iliad* and from fourteen different books of the *Odyssey*. He also quotes verses of New Comedy (1.3.7, etc.), including Menander (4.7.7, etc.), and he makes several specific verbal allusions to passages in the histories of Herodotus (6.7.7, etc.) and Thucydides (7.5.11, etc.) and in Xenophon's *Cyropaedia* (2.5.7, etc.). There are also direct quotations or at least very close verbal allusions to Demosthenes' *De corona* (1.3.1) and *Olynthiacs* 3 (3.9.3), and Aeschines' *In Ctesiphontem* (2.3.6; 4.2.4), and there appear to be some looser imitations of some of the rhetorical devices of Isocrates.[35]

Based partly on these quotations, allusions, and imitations, B. P. Reardon has concluded that Chariton "certainly had a decent secondary education, perhaps more."[36] R. F. Hock goes further and proposes that Chariton completed all three levels of education: he attributes Chariton's quotations of ancient Greek literature specifically to his exposure to maxims in school at the primary level, to his reading of the Homeric epics at the secondary level, and to his study of the historians and orators, as well as his practice of progymnastic exercises, at the tertiary level.[37] I am not certain that Chariton's

---

[34] M. J. Schierling and S. Schierling, "The Influence of the Ancient Romances on the Acts of the Apostles," *The Classical Bulletin* 54 (1978): 81–8; R. I. Pervo, *Profit with Delight: The Literary Genre of the Acts of the Apostles* (Philadelphia: Fortress, 1987), 131–8.

[35] These are my own calculations, which, because of the subtlety and ambiguity of some of Chariton's allusions and imitations, differ somewhat from those of others: e.g., K. Plepelits, *Chariton von Aphrodisias: Kallirhoe* (Stuttgart: Hiersemann, 1976), 9–20 and indices; G. Molinié, *Chariton: Le roman de Chairéas et Callirhoë* (Paris: Budé, 1979), indices; R. F. Hock, "The Educational Curriculum in Chariton's *Callirhoe*," in *Ancient Fiction: The Matrix of Early Christian and Jewish Narrative*, eds. J.-A. A. Brant, C. W. Hedrick, and C. Shea (Atlanta: Society of Biblical Literature, 2005), 15–36.

[36] B. P. Reardon, "Chariton," in *The Novel in the Ancient World*, ed. G. Schmeling (Leiden: Brill, 1996), 323.

[37] R. F. Hock, "The Educational Curriculum in Chariton's *Callirhoe*," 15–36.

84 *The Formal Education of the Author of Luke-Acts*

education can be so tidily reconstructed, and that his relative indebtedness to each level of education can be so specifically quantified, but I agree with Hock's main point that Chariton may have received the full cycle of education, including formal rhetoric.

Our examination of Chariton's novel *Callirhoe* is instructive for our analysis of citations and quotations of ancient Greek authors in Luke-Acts in several respects. First, it reminds us that just as there no doubt remain quotations and allusions in the novel to many other ancient works that we fail to recognize because they have been lost to us, so too may unidentified quotations and allusions still reside in the text of Luke-Acts. Second, it cautions us that it is not necessary to assume that all readers of the novel detected every allusion to ancient Greek literature any more than it is necessary to assume that all readers of Luke-Acts detected its literary allusions to Homer, Aesop, Epimenides, Euripides, Plato, and Aratus, as we shall see. Third, it impresses upon us that Chariton acknowledges his sources in what is by modern standards a very cavalier manner but is by ancient standards quite normal. Twice he refers to Homer by name (1.5.2; 2.3.7), and once he refers to his source as "the divine poet" (5.5.9); elsewhere he simply inserts the Homeric passage seamlessly into his text. His quotations of Herodotus, Thucydides, Xenophon, Demosthenes, Aeschines, and Menander are also woven seamlessly into his text, always without any reference to the source. As we shall see, this is similar to the procedure of the author of Luke-Acts: on one occasion he attributes a quotation to "some of your poets" (Acts 17:28), but elsewhere he simply weaves the quotations seamlessly and without attribution into his text.

Conclusion

In these last two chapters, we have tried to determine what level of Greek literacy we can reasonably expect from the author of the Gospel of Luke and the Acts of the Apostles, who was a thoroughly Hellenized, Greek-speaking man living in the eastern Mediterranean during the first century of our era. We have proposed some answers to the following questions. What was the structure, methodology, and content of the traditional Greek school curriculum that was available to Luke? What level of formal education was he likely to have attained? Is it likely that he continued to hear, read, and witness performances of Classical and Hellenistic Greek literature in his adult life, and if so, what works would have been most popular and accessible? In short, what Classical and Hellenistic Greek literary works resided in Luke's library, whether a "mental library," based on Luke's recollection of texts that he had read, studied, and even memorized, or a literal library of material texts that he could access or that he actually owned?

We have reconstructed the content of Luke's "library" from four separate sources: the literary works prescribed for students by ancient rhetoricians and grammarians; the remains of literary papyri from Hellenistic and Roman Egypt; the remains of school texts on papyrus, parchment, pottery, wood, and stone from Hellenistic and Roman Egypt; and the quotations and citations of ancient literary works by Luke's near contemporaries, especially those with educational backgrounds and cultural orbits similar to Luke's.

In the following chapters we shall examine the possible influence of a number of Classical and Hellenistic Greek literary works on the narrative of Luke-Acts: Homer's *Iliad* and *Odyssey*, Aesop's fables, Epimenides' *On Minos and Rhadamanthus*, Euripides' *Bacchae*, Plato's *Apology*, and Aratus's *Phaenomena*. Given our reconstruction of what Classical and Hellenistic works would have been accessible to someone like Luke in the first century CE, it should not be at all surprising to discover that he was influenced by Homer, Aesop, Euripides, and Plato, for they are some of the most commonly referenced authors from all the sources that we have examined. Aratus is a bit of a surprise, and Epimenides even more so; there must have been unique circumstances that caused Luke to invoke these authors in the speech that he attributes to Paul in Athens. We shall take these considerations into account as we continue to examine Luke's reliance on these specific authors one by one in the chapters that follow.

5

Luke and Homer

Much to the dismay of Plato, who in the early fourth century BCE attempted to design a salutary educational system for his ideal city-state that excluded Hesiod, Homer, and the poets (*Resp.* 376e–398b), the Homeric epics, with their scandalous stories about the gods and heroes, had been used for educational purposes in Greece already for at least a century. And much to the chagrin of St. Augustine, who in the late fourth century CE bitterly recalled being compelled to learn how to read Homer in Greek as a schoolboy (*Conf.* 1.14), these same epics would continue to serve these educational purposes in the Mediterranean world until the fall of the Roman Empire.

Anecdotes from two of Luke's contemporaries illustrate the pervasive influence of Homer both chronologically and geographically during the first century CE: from cradle to grave, on the one hand, and beyond the furthest reaches of the Roman Empire, on the other. The first-century CE Stoic philosopher and grammarian Heraclitus colorfully expresses how influential Homer has become throughout the entirety of one's life in the preface to his Homeric commentary, a defense of Homer by means of allegorical interpretation (*Homeric Questions* 1.5–7):

> For right away as infants in our first stage of life we are nursed by Homer in our rudimentary instruction, and while still in swaddling clothes we nourish our souls with his poetry as if with sweet milk. Homer stands by the side of each of us as we grow up and gradually become adults, and he is at the height of his power among us as we reach maturity. There is never too much Homer even in our old age, but rather when we stop reading Homer we begin to thirst for him all the more. There is only one end to Homer among humans, and that is the end of our life.
>
> (slightly paraphrased)

Dio Chrysostom, the first-century CE philosopher and rhetorician from Bithynia in Asia Minor, observes in his 53rd Oration, Περὶ Ὁμήρου, that Homer is well known throughout the entire world, even by people for whom Greek is not a native language (*Or.* 53.6):

> For it is simply impossible to create such sublime and magnificent and also sweet poetry without divine providence or without the inspiration of the Muses and Apollo. The result is that not only have those of the same tongue and language [as Homer] held it as a possession already for such a long time but so also have many

88 The Formal Education of the Author of Luke-Acts

non-Greeks. Those who speak two languages, and those of mixed race, and even some who have migrated very far away are acquainted with his verses, even though they are ignorant of many other Greek matters. They say that the poetry of Homer is sung even among the Indians, who have translated it into their own dialect and language.

As we have observed, Homer was the most ardently recommended author by the ancient rhetoricians and grammarians (e.g., Dionysius of Halicarnassus, Dio Chrysostom, Quintilian) who formulated essential reading lists for students, and commensurately, Homer was by far the most often-quoted poet both on the papyrological remains of ancient school texts and in the progymnastic exercises (e.g., Theon, "Hermogenes," Aphthonius) that composed the core of the ancient Greek educational curriculum. Homeric proper and place names were used at the most basic level of education in learning how to write and pronounce letters, syllables, and words. Individual lines from Homer's epics were used as simple writing and reading exercises. Longer Homeric passages were used to introduce grammar, syntax, and, eventually, rhetoric, to convey practical and technical information, and to teach good morals.[1]

Homer's *Iliad* and *Odyssey* were readily available throughout the Mediterranean world, as witnessed by the ubiquity of Homeric verses among the literary papyri, even in the most remote areas of Egypt in the far reaches of the Roman Empire, where actual texts of the Homeric epics far outnumber those of any other Greek author. As illustrated in the previous chapter, I count 1,624 Homeric papyri from Hellenistic and Roman Egypt dating to the period between 100 BCE and 200 CE (i.e., from around the time of the composition of Luke-Acts), of which 1,332 are identifiably from the *Iliad* and 223 from the *Odyssey*. Of these, 96 appear to be school texts, of which 73 are identifiably from the *Iliad* and 18 from the *Odyssey*. For the sake of comparison, the next most common authors on the Egyptian papyri from this period are Demosthenes (173 literary papyri, 5 school texts), Euripides (141 literary papyri, 17 school texts), Menander (125 papyri, 17 school texts), and Hesiod (130 papyri, 3 school texts).

Quotations and paraphrases of Homeric verses and various types of references and allusions to Homer appear regularly in Greek literature of the late Hellenistic and Roman Imperial periods (e.g., Plutarch, Lucian, and Athenaeus).[2] As we have seen, this holds true even among Hellenistic Jewish authors, such as the historian Josephus of Jerusalem and the philosopher Philo of Alexandria, who calls Homer the "greatest and most respected of the poets" (*Conf. Ling.* 2.4) and considers the *Iliad* and *Odyssey*

---

[1] On the Homeric epics as central texts in ancient Greek education, from the elementary to the most advanced levels, see H.-I. Marrou, *A History of Education*, 160–4; R. Cribiore, *Writing, Teachers, and Students*, 173–284; R. Cribiore, *Gymnastics of the Mind*, 137–43, 192–7, 204–5; T. Morgan, *Literate Education*, 105–15, 308–13 (tables 11–15), and 320 (tables 20–1); R. F. Hock, "Homer in Greco-Roman Education," 56–77. The centrality of Homer would, of course, have extended to the Greek education of Jews, both those in Palestine and those of the Diaspora—so M. Hengel, *Judaism and Hellenism*, 65–78.

[2] On the quotation of Homer among writers of the Second Sophistic, the literary elite of the first and second centuries CE, see J. F. Kindstrand, *Homer in der Zweiten Sophistik. Studien zu der Homerlektüre und dem Homerbild bei Dion von Prusa, Maximos von Tyros und Ailios Aristeides* (Uppsala: Almqvist & Wiksell, 1973).

Luke and Homer 89

centerpieces of a good education.[3] Among early Christian writers, such as Origen, Basil, and Gregory of Nazianzus, Homer continues to be a favorite object of commentary, whether for good or for ill.[4]

Of all the poets of antiquity, then, one would expect Homer to be the richest source for imitation and quotation for someone like the author of Luke-Acts, who almost certainly experienced the traditional Hellenistic Greek educational curriculum (ἐγκύκλιος παιδεία/*enkyklios paideia*) and consequently practiced a proper, sometimes even elevated, Greek writing style. The Homeric epics are eminently quotable, full of memorable aphorisms, from short phrases to multiple lines of verse, so we should not be surprised to find in the text of Luke-Acts actual quotations of the *Iliad* and *Odyssey*, or at least some references and allusions to Homer, as we do in the texts of many of Luke's contemporaries.

However, it is my assessment, after analyzing the entirety of the Greek text of Luke-Acts in the light of a familiarity with the Homeric epics that I have gained over some forty years of close study, that Homeric influence on the Gospel of Luke, at least, is very slight, and if there is in fact any influence, it is probably indirect. Like others, I perceive a possible Homeric echo in Luke's unique story about the appearance of the risen Jesus to two disciples on the road to Emmaus (Lk. 24:13-35), which is similar thematically and structurally to several Odyssean recognition scenes (e.g., Odysseus's appearances to Eumaeus, Philoetius, Eurycleia, Penelope, and Laertes): initial lack of recognition, testing of hospitality, recognition through a sign or token, humor achieved through dramatic irony.[5] However, we need to be very cautious about our assumptions here, keeping in mind that these are features that can be found also in stories from the Hebrew Scripture, which was well known to Luke in its Septuagintal form, such as in the memorable account of the angelic visitors to Abraham and Sarah in Genesis 18. Moreover, these same features are ubiquitous in ancient Greek literature generally, such as in the dramatic, fabulistic, and novelistic traditions, some of which were probably

---

[3] On the quotation of Homer by Josephus and Philo, see E. Koskenniemi, *Greek Writers and Philosophers*, 25–35, 158–63.

[4] G. Glockmann, *Homer in der frühchristlichen Literatur bis Justinus* (Berlin: Akademie Verlag, 1968), has traced the influence of Homer on early Christian literature up to the time of Justin Martyr (c. 150 CE). G. J. M. Bartelink, "Homer," *Reallexikon für Antike und Christentum* 121 (1991): 116–47, has documented the familiarity with Homer among early Christian writers from the philosopher Aristides of Athens in the early second century to the Empress Eudocia's Homeric centos in the mid-fifth century. K. O. Sandnes, *The Challenge of Homer*, has investigated how post-New Testament Christians, from the second century onward, regarded secular education generally: some rejected it entirely (e.g., Justin Martyr, Tertulian); others embraced it as a preparatory tool for larger Christian purposes (e.g., Clement of Alexandria, Origen, Basil, Gregory of Nyssa, and Gregory of Nazianzus, and, less so, Jerome and Augustine).

[5] On the formal components of Homeric recognition and hospitality scenes, see S. Reece, *The Stranger's Welcome: Oral Theory and the Aesthetics of the Homeric Hospitality Scene* (Ann Arbor: University of Michigan Press, 1993), 12–39. For some comparisons between various Homeric recognition scenes and Luke's account of the recognition of Jesus in Emmaus, see D. R. MacDonald, "The Ending of Luke and the Ending of the *Odyssey*," in *For a Later Generation: The Transformation of Tradition in Israel, Early Judaism and Early Christianity*, eds. R. A. Argall, B. A. Bow, and R. A. Werline (Harrisburg: Trinity Press International, 2000), 161–8; also C. T. McMahan, "More than Meets the 'I': Recognition Scenes in *The Odyssey* and Luke 24," *Perspectives in Religious Studies* 35 (2008): 87–107.

familiar to Luke. In the absence of any citation by Luke—contrast Luke's "as some of your poets have said" in Acts 17:28—and in the absence of any unique or even distinctive parallels between the recognition scenes in the *Odyssey* and in Luke, one cannot with any confidence trace the story in Luke 24 directly back to a Homeric archetype.

Caution also needs to be practiced in the identification of verbal parallels between the Homeric epics and Luke. As someone who has spent a great deal of time reading the Homeric epics in Greek and studying the formulaic language in which they are composed, I have from time to time supposed that I have perceived a Homeric verbal echo in the Gospel of Luke.[6] The formulaic phrases in Luke 4:36 καὶ ἐγένετο θάμβος ἐπὶ πάντας "and awe came upon everyone," and again in Luke 5:9 θάμβος γὰρ περιέσχεν αὐτὸν καὶ πάντας τοὺς σὺν αὐτῷ "for awe held him and everyone with him," for example, which occur in the New Testament only in Luke's gospel, appear to be echoes of the memorable formulas found so often in Homer's epics to describe the effect of heroic or miraculous events on those who witness them: "θάμβος 'awe' held/seized everyone" (e.g., *Il.* 23.815—θάμβος δ' ἔχε πάντας, *Od.* 3.372—θάμβος δ' ἕλε πάντας; cf. *Il.* 3.342, 4.79, 24.482; *Hymn* 28.6; Hesiod fr. 75.8). But caution needs to be practiced here, for the formula is not limited to early epic verse; it can be found in the imitative epic verse of the Hellenistic and Roman Imperial periods as well: Apollonius of Rhodes, *Argonautica* 2.681, 4.682; Quintus, *Posthomerica* 3.541 (cf. 4.218); Musaeus, *Hero and Leander* 95. The formula can be found even in prose literature: Chariton uses it in his novel *Callirhoe* (1.1.16) and Heliodorus in his novel *Aethiopica* (10.9.4.1). Even closer to Luke's milieu, similar formulas appear in the historical narrative of Josephus (*War* 5.324; 7.30) and in the biographical narrative of Plutarch (*Aemilius Paullus* 17.8). Closest of all to Luke's own time and milieu, the Acts of Andrew 6:5 describes the people of Patras in awe of Andrew as he heals the sick: θάμβος κατέλαβεν πάντας τοὺς κατοικοῦντας τὴν πόλιν "awe seized all the inhabitants of the city." In short, while the formulas in Luke 4:36 and 5:9 may initially strike a Homerist like me as epic in origin, it is impossible to reconstruct with certainty a direct line of influence from Homer to the Gospel of Luke. All we can say with any confidence is that Luke is using a literary formula that may have been Homeric in origin but that had by his time penetrated many other literary traditions as well.

It would be reasonable to assume that, of Luke's two works, we would be more likely to find Homeric influence in his Acts than in his gospel, for much of the narrative of Acts takes place in the Greco-Roman rather than Judaean world, and Luke was not so constrained in Acts, as he was in his gospel, to adhere to inherited material in an already established form. Yet, again, Homeric influence appears surprisingly slight even in Acts. It is absent in the early chapters (1–12), the narrative of which is situated in Judea, Samaria, and Syria in the East. Broader Greek literary and mythic influence appears to creep into the narrative beginning in chapter 13, when there is a shift geographically to Cyprus, Asia Minor, Greece, and Italy in the West, as well as a shift

---

[6] On formulaic language in Homer, see S. Reece, *Homer's Winged Words: The Evolution of Early Greek Epic Diction in the Light of Oral Theory* (Leiden: Brill, 2009); S. Reece, "Homer's *Iliad* and *Odyssey*: From Oral Performance to Written Text," in *New Directions in Oral Theory*, ed. M. Amodio (Tempe: Center for Medieval and Renaissance Studies, 2005), 43–89.

Luke and Homer 91

from travel primarily by land to travel primarily by sea. Once Paul and his companions leave the confines of the East, Luke's account begins to make many more connections to the Greco-Roman world: in Lystra Paul and Barnabas are mistaken for Hermes and Zeus, echoing a Greek tale that is attested also in the Roman poet Ovid's *Metamorphoses*; in Philippi Paul and Silas miraculously escape from a prison, much like Dionysus does in Euripides' *Bacchae*; on the Areopagus in Athens Paul defends himself against the charge of introducing new gods to the city, just as Socrates does in Plato's *Apology*, even quoting the Greek poets Epimenides and Aratus; in Ephesus Paul's companions encounter the enthusiasm of the devotees of the great goddess Artemis who fell from the sky; in Malta Paul boards a ship that has the Dioskouroi, the twin sons of Zeus, as a figurehead; and—with respect to the present topic treated at length below—in the vastness of the Adriatic Paul and his companions suffer a storm at sea that is worthy of Homer's *Odyssey*.

The reluctance, until fairly recently, among most New Testament scholars to acknowledge any Homeric influence on the New Testament, even in the second half of Acts, is somewhat surprising.[7] The few proposals offered have been very modest, and any perceived Homeric influence has generally been regarded as unconscious and/or indirect. Occasionally a word or phrase in Acts has been attributed to Homer: several commentators have observed, for example, that the phrase ἐπέκειλαν τὴν ναῦν "they ran the ship aground" in Acts 27:41 is a Homeric idiom;[8] a few commentators have traced the participle ἐρείσασα "having stuck fast" (of the prow of the ship) in the same verse back to Homer as well.[9] Occasionally a literary device or convention used in the latter part of Acts has been thought to be of Homeric origin. V. K. Robbins, for example, has observed that the shifts in narrative from third- to first-person in Acts—the notorious "we-passages"—occur only when Paul and his companions begin to travel by sea, just as sea voyages in ancient Greek literature (in epic, lyric, drama, history, novel, etc.), including most prominently in Homer's *Odyssey*, were often narrated in the first person. Robbins concludes that Luke is a versatile Hellenistic writer who has some familiarity with the conventions of Greek literature, including Homeric narrative.[10]

---

[7] Representative of this view is Glockmann, *Homer in der frühchristlichen Literatur*, 92, who does not detect any reference, quotation, or even allusion to Homer in the entire New Testament: "In den zahlreichen von mir untersuchten christlichen Schriften, die im 1. Jahrhundert und in der ersten Hälfte des 2. Jahrhunderts entstanden sind und unter dem Begriff 'urchristliche Literatur' zusammengefasst werden können, vermochte ich weder eine Äusserung über den Dichter der Ilias und Odyssee noch ein Zitat aus diesen beiden Epen oder irgendeine Anspielung auf eine Homerstelle zu finden." Glockmann proposes that the earliest reference to Homer among early Christian writers is to be found in Justin Martyr (e.g., 1 *Apol.* 18.5).

[8] E.g., F. Blass, *Acta apostolorum sive Lucae ad Theophilum liber alter: editio philologica* (Göttingen: Vandenhoeck & Ruprecht, 1895), 282; F. J. Foakes Jackson and K. Lake, eds., *The Beginnings of Christianity: The Acts of the Apostles* (London: MacMillan, 1933), 4:339; F. F. Bruce, *The Acts of the Apostles* (London: The Tyndale Press, 1951), 467.

[9] E.g., E. Haenchen, *The Acts of the Apostles* (Philadelphia: Westminster, 1971), 708; D. R. MacDonald, "The Shipwrecks of Odysseus and Paul," *New Testament Studies* 45 (1999): 94; K. L. Cukrowski, "Paul as Odysseus: An Exegetical Note on Luke's Depiction of Paul in Acts 27:1–28:10," *Restoration Quarterly* 55 (2013): 24.

[10] V. K. Robbins, "By Land and By Sea: The We-Passages and Ancient Sea Voyages," in *Perspectives on Luke-Acts*, ed. C. H. Talbert (Edinburgh: T&T Clark, 1978), 215–42.

92   *The Formal Education of the Author of Luke-Acts*

More recently, some have proposed that major themes in the narrative of the latter part of Acts are dependent, directly or indirectly, on Homer. S. M. Praeder has suggested that Homer's *Odyssey* is one of many ancient literary accounts of sea voyages, storms, and shipwrecks (in epics, histories, dramas, novels, elegies, satires, orations, and letters) that Luke used to varying degrees as models for his account of Paul's sea voyage in Acts 27:1–28:16. Given this extensive literary background, Praeder concludes, the account of the sea voyage in Acts should be read as a piece of literature, even allegorically and theologically, rather than as a record of a historical event.[11] K. L. Cukrowski has drawn parallels between the experiences and characters of Homer's Odysseus and Luke's Paul, in particular their endurance in the face of hardship and suffering. These parallels reach a climax toward the end of Acts, where Paul endures a storm and shipwreck. Cukroswki proposes that Luke is favorably comparing Paul's endurance with that of Odysseus.[12]

Finally, we cannot proceed much further without evaluating the considerable contributions of D. R. MacDonald, who has devoted much of his academic career to the contemplation of Homeric influence on the New Testament, especially on the entirety of the Gospel of Mark but also on substantial portions of Luke-Acts, and who has concluded that Homer's influence on the New Testament was direct and pervasive. MacDonald's corpus of work is much too vast to examine here *in toto*, but a summary and critique of his proposal that Luke modeled his account of Paul's sea voyage and shipwreck in Acts 27:1–28:16 on Homer's description of Odysseus's shipwrecks in *Odyssey* 5 and 12 will illustrate an early application of the methodology that MacDonald has continued to develop and use in his other publications on the topic.[13] This summary and critique will also help pave the way for my own treatment of this topic, and it will explain why MacDonald's work does not play a larger part in my own considerations of Homeric influence on Acts.

---

[11] S. M. Praeder, "Acts 27:1–28:16: Sea Voyages in Ancient Literature and the Theology of Luke-Acts," *Catholic Bible Quarterly* 46 (1984): 683–706.

[12] K. L. Cukrowski, "Paul as Odysseus," 24–34.

[13] MacDonald's publications on the influence of Homer in the New Testament include, in chronological order: "Luke's Eutychus and Homer's Elpenor: Acts 20:7-12 and *Odyssey* 10–12," *Journal of Higher Criticism* 1 (1994): 5–24; "Secrecy and Recognitions in the *Odyssey* and Mark: Where Wrede Went Wrong," in *Ancient Fiction and Early Christian Narrative*, eds. R. F. Hock, J. B. Chance, and J. Perkins (Atlanta: Scholars Press, 1998), 139–53; "The Shipwrecks," 88–107; "The Soporific Angel in Acts 12:1-17 and Hermes' Visit to Priam in *Iliad* 24: Luke's Emulation of the Epic," *Forum* 2, no. 2 (1999): 179–87; "The Ending of Luke and the Ending of the *Odyssey*," 161–8; *The Homeric Epics and the Gospel of Mark* (New Haven: Yale University Press, 2000); "Renowned Far and Wide: The Women Who Anointed Odysseus and Jesus," in *A Feminist Companion to Mark*, eds. A. J. Levine and M. Blickenstaff (Sheffield: Sheffield Academic Press, 2001), 128–35; *Does the New Testament Imitate Homer? Four Cases from the Acts of the Apostles* (New Haven: Yale University Press, 2003); "Paul's Farewell to the Ephesian Elders and Hector's Farewell to Andromache: A Strategic Imitation of Homer's *Iliad*," in *Contextualizing Acts: Lukan Narrative and Greco-Roman Discourse*, eds. T. Penner and C. V. Stichele (Atlanta: Society of Biblical Literature, 2003), 189–203; "The Breasts of Hecuba and those of the Daughters of Jerusalem: Luke's Transvaluation of a famous Iliadic Scene," in *Ancient Fiction: The Matrix of Early Christian and Jewish Narrative*, eds. J-A. A. Brant, C. W. Hedrick, and C. Shea (Atlanta: Society of Biblical Literature, 2005), 239–54; "Imitations of Greek Epic in the Gospels," in *The Historical Jesus in Context*, eds. A-J. Levine, D. C. Allison, and J. D. Crossan (Princeton: Princeton University Press, 2006), 372–84; *The Gospels and Homer; Luke and Vergil; Luke and the Politics of Homeric Imitation*.

Homeric Resonance in Luke's Account of Paul's Sea Voyage and Shipwreck (Acts 27:1–28:16)

The debate over the identification of the genre of the Acts of the Apostles has always been a dynamic one: is it a biography, history, travelogue, epic, novel, or acts (i.e., *res gestae*)? Or does it resist categorization into a single one of these specific genres? Recently, some New Testament scholars have ventured to categorize Acts as a Christianized prose epic. Most famously D. R. MacDonald has proposed in a series of publications that several episodes narrated in Acts are deliberate imitations of episodes from Homer's *Iliad* and *Odyssey* and that Luke expected his audience to recognize this. To use MacDonald's own terminology, Luke is waving "intertextual flags" that "advertise" the relationship between Acts, the "hypotext," and the Homeric epics, the "hypertexts," in an attempt to "emulate," "transvalue," and "christianize" them.[14] M. Bonz, on the other hand, has turned to Vergil as the primary inspiration for Luke, proposing that Acts is a prose epic modeled on Vergil's *Aeneid* (or perhaps, since Luke probably did not know Latin, on a Greek prose version of the *Aeneid*). Both Aeneas and Paul have a mission to go on a westward journey and found a new people in Italy. Both "epics" are characterized by ambiguous prophecies, dramatic reversals, insistence on moral rectitude, and heavenly beings serving as messengers at critical moments. Luke's agendum, Bonz concludes, is to replace the salvation claims of Imperial Rome with those of Christianity.[15]

But Acts is not an epic in any meaningful sense of the term: its form is plain prose rather than metrical verse, its diction is not archaic and grand, it lacks most of the recognizable poetic elements of epic (epithets, formulas, type-scenes, ring compositions, similes, priamels, ecphrases, narrative arrangement characterized by *in medias res* and *hysteron-proteron*, divine viewpoint), its characters are not heroic in any ancient sense of the term, it lacks mythical elements for the most part, and it does not have an epic scale or scope.[16] This is not to say, however, that Luke is not familiar with Greek epic, that he does not also assume a familiarity with Greek epic among his audience, and that he does not take advantage of that familiarity to embellish his narrative with epic resonance at certain critical points.

For over a century New Testament scholars have from time to time observed some similarities in Luke's description of Paul's sea voyage at the end of Acts and in Homer's accounts of sea voyages, storms, and shipwrecks in the *Odyssey*. These similarities have been marshaled most expansively in recent years by D. R. MacDonald. Among the many other comparisons that MacDonald makes between Homer's epics and the Gospel of Mark and Luke-Acts, he includes in his article "The Shipwrecks of Odysseus and Paul" a proposal that Luke deliberately used Homer's account of Odysseus's shipwrecks in *Odyssey* 5 and 12 as a model in his description of Paul's sea voyage and

---

[14] See the list of MacDonald's publications on this topic in the previous note.

[15] M. P. Bonz, *The Past as Legacy.*

[16] L. C. A. Alexander, *Acts in Its Ancient Literary Context: A Classicist Looks at the Acts of the Apostles* (London: T&T Clark, 2005), 165–82, has raised many important distinctions between ancient epic and the Acts of the Apostles and has severely criticized the notions of MacDonald and Bonz that the Acts of the Apostles, or for that matter any of the gospels, is an epic from the perspective of genre.

94   *The Formal Education of the Author of Luke-Acts*

shipwreck in Acts 27:1–28:16. By borrowing distinctive themes and diction from Homer, MacDonald concludes, Luke encouraged his readers to compare and contrast the two accounts so that they might realize that Paul and his God were greater than Odysseus and his gods.[17] In my view MacDonald vastly overstates his case, which is built on dubious assertions and fallacious assumptions. I begin by offering a synopsis of his proposals, then some criticisms of what I perceive to be his greatest fallacies and excesses; this will be followed by a presentation of some rather more modest proposals that I believe are built on a firmer foundation.

MacDonald makes much of the use of first-person discourse to narrate the sea voyages in both the *Odyssey* and Acts, proposing that the we-passages in Acts are imitations of Odysseus's first-person account of his voyages in books 9–12 (especially book 12). This echoes a proposal made earlier by V. K. Robbins, who claimed that the use of first-person discourse in ancient narratives about sea voyages generally, including in the *Odyssey*, inspired Luke's use of the first person in Acts.[18] There is, of course, a much simpler explanation: both the *Odyssey* and Acts include first-person discourse because those telling the stories in their own voices were present, or at least claimed to be present, at the events. Moreover, first-person discourse is not something unique to Odysseus's account of his voyages in *Odyssey* 9–12. Two-thirds of the *Odyssey*, and much of the *Iliad* too for that matter, is presented in the voices of its characters rather than in the third person of the external narrator. Already in our earliest surviving specimen of literary criticism, Aristotle expresses his great admiration for Homer's practice of allowing his characters to speak for themselves (*Poet.* 1460a). First-person discourse became a regular literary device in almost all genres of Greek literature, not just in epic, and certainly not just in narratives of sea voyages.

MacDonald places heavy emphasis on the detail that the narratives of the we-passages in Acts are all associated with Troas, which, MacDonald notes, is "a mere 10 miles south of ancient Troy."[19] MacDonald's purpose, of course, is to position the narrative of Acts in the locus of Homer's *Iliad*, and he makes every effort to fuse the two locations, incorrectly stating, for example, that "by placing the story of Eutychus in *Troy*, Luke seems to be hinting that one should read it in light of Troy's mythological traditions."[20] But Homer's Troy/Ilium, a Bronze Age inland city, and Luke's Troas, a major Hellenistic and Roman seaport widely known as Alexandria Troas, are not the same. It may seem a minor point, but Troas is more than "a mere 10 miles" from Troy; it is actually fifteen as a crow flies, and it would have been more than that by land travel in antiquity—in fact Troy and Troas were a full day's journey apart. Luke would not have been able to invoke the citadel of Homeric Troy/Ilium in the minds of his ancient audience simply by mentioning the Hellenistic/Roman seaport of Alexandria Troas. On the contrary, if Luke is invoking any event from ancient history or myth here in his description of the spread of the gospel from Troas to Macedonia, it seems much more

---

[17]   D. R. MacDonald, "The Shipwrecks," 95, 101, 106–7.
[18]   V. K. Robbins, "By Land and by Sea," 215–42.
[19]   D. R. MacDonald, "The Shipwrecks," 91.
[20]   D. R. MacDonald, "The Shipwrecks," 91–2.

Luke and Homer 95

likely that he is suggesting a reversal of the historical conquest of Asia by Alexander of Macedon than the mythical sack of Ilium by Agamemnon of Mycenae.[21]

Moreover, MacDonald's claim that "Luke narrates in the first person plural only those journeys related to the Troad" is incorrect.[22] Again, MacDonald has played fast and loose with the details here to serve his purposes. The first we-passage (16:10-17), from Troas to Philippi, indeed begins in Troas, but the town plays no further part in the passage, which is largely concerned with the events in Philippi. The second we-passage (20:5-15), from Philippi to Miletus, does pass through Troas and narrates the colorful story of Eutychus (whom MacDonald later claimed to be drawn from the Homeric character Elpenor—both being young men who fall from high places).[23] The third we-passage (21:1-18), from Miletus to Jerusalem, has nothing at all to do with Troas, but MacDonald tries to sidestep this aberration by considering the second and third we-passages as one and the same. The fourth we-passage (27:1-28:16), from Caesarea to Rome, has nothing to do with Troas, except that the ship that Paul and his party embark on for the first leg of their voyage, from Caesarea to Myra, on the southern coast of Lycia, is said to be a ship from Adramyttium.[24] MacDonald derives great significance from the identification of the port city of this ship: "Adramyttium was a port city in Mysia, viz. the Troad, at the base of Mt. Ida, famous in the *Iliad* as the gods' favourite lookout on Troy."[25] In reality, Adramyttium is not in the Troad. It is almost fifty miles southeast of Troas as a crow flies; it is more than seventy miles by the shortest ancient land route and even further by a combination of land and sea route—several days of travel in antiquity, in any event. Nor is Adramyttium at the base of Mt. Ida but rather fifteen miles south and across the Adramyttium Bay from the mountain; it would be more accurate to describe its location as at the base of Mt. Pindasos to the southeast. MacDonald has perhaps misidentified the ancient port of Adramyttium with the modern Turkish town of Edremit, an inland city to the northeast, which is named after ancient Adramyttium.[26] Here, as elsewhere, MacDonald has manipulated the details, in large and small ways, to buttress his proposal, as a result vastly overstating the evidence in support of his extravagant conclusions.

Regarding the themes that MacDonald points to as shared by the narratives of the sea voyages of Odysseus in the *Odyssey* and of Paul in Acts, most are very conventional and widespread throughout Greek literature: embarking, putting out to sea, furling and unfurling sails, confronting contrary winds and waves, experiencing darkness,

---

[21] On Luke's account of the spread of the gospel from Asia to Macedonia in Acts 16 as a reversal of Alexander's famous conquest of Asia from Macedonia, see C. S. Keener, *Acts: An Exegetical Commentary* (Grand Rapids: Baker Academic, 2014), 3:2334–47.

[22] D. R. MacDonald, "The Shipwrecks," 89.

[23] D. R. MacDonald, "Luke's Eutychus," 5–24.

[24] A fifth "we-passage," found in the reading of Acts 11:28 preserved in codex Bezae, has nothing to do with Troas but rather with Antioch.

[25] D. R. MacDonald, "The Shipwrecks," 93.

[26] The same misidentification of the location of Adramyttium can be found on the maps of several commentaries on Acts: e.g., F. J. Foakes Jackson and K. Lake, eds., *The Beginnings of Christianity: The Acts of the Apostles* (London: Macmillan, 1933), 5: back of volume ("Additional Notes to the Commentary"); H. Conzelmann, *Acts of the Apostles* (Philadelphia: Fortress, 1987), back of volume; C. K. Barrett, *A Critical and Exegetical Commentary on the Acts of the Apostles* (London: T&T Clark, 1994–1998), 2: front of volume.

96   *The Formal Education of the Author of Luke-Acts*

jettisoning cargo, abandoning hope of survival, shipwreck, and rescue.[27] These conventional themes are shared by many ancient accounts of sea voyages, not only in epics but, as S. M. Praeder has demonstrated (above), also in histories, dramas, novels, elegies, satires, orations, and letters. Two thematic parallels that MacDonald offers are somewhat more distinctive: the appearance of a supportive divinity (Ino in the *Odyssey*, the angel of the Lord in Acts) who comforts a sailor suffering through a storm (Odysseus, Paul); the shipwreck upon an unknown land where refuge and resources are offered to the sailor(s) by the inhabitants (the Phaeacians in the *Odyssey*, the Maltese in Acts).[28] Yet both parallels entail experiences that have been shared by multitudes of sailors throughout history, both in literature and in real life. A final parallel, that both Odysseus and Paul are supposed to be gods by the inhabitants of the unknown land, is certainly notable, but it is perhaps more remarkable to us as modern readers than it was to the ancient audience, for this is a theme that is not unique to the scenes of the Phaeacians in the *Odyssey* and the Maltese in Acts but is repeated several times throughout both works, as well as in many works, of various genres, of ancient literature. Finally, I note a particular deficiency in MacDonald's handling of themes with a view to drawing connections between Homer's *Odyssey* and Luke's Acts. In his eagerness to support his underlying premise, MacDonald selects certain details (and omits others) from several different Homeric episodes—here the episodes of the storms at sea in *Odyssey* 5, 12, and 14—and then he rearranges the sequence of details so that it matches up with the sequence of events in Acts 27, even displaying the sequences tidily side by side in two columns. This practice results in a shipshape presentation, but it also significantly distorts the evidence. Unfortunately, this has become MacDonald's *modus operandi* in all his subsequent work on Homer and the New Testament.

Regarding diction that is shared by the narratives of the sea voyages in the *Odyssey* and in Acts, MacDonald properly notes the possible Homeric origin of the expression in Acts 27:41 ἐπέκειλαν τὴν ναῦν "they ran the ship aground," as have many before him (F. Blass, F. J. Foakes Jackson and K. Lake, F. F. Bruce, E. Haenchen, S. M. Praeder, C. K. Barrett) and as I shall in my own treatment of this episode below. The rest of the vocabulary shared by Homer and Luke detected by MacDonald, however, is much less noteworthy. Of little significance are the two nautical words found in the *Odyssey* that MacDonald observes are found in the New Testament only in Acts 27:1–28:16—λιμήν, "harbour" and πρῷρα "prow"—for these words are extremely common in many ancient narratives that involve navigation: λιμήν occurs almost 1,200 times in extant literature between the time of Homer and Luke; πρῷρα occurs over 100 times. Even less significant are those nautical words found both in Acts 27:1–28:16 and the *Odyssey* but that MacDonald observes are seldom found elsewhere in the New Testament—κυβερνήτης "pilot," νότος "south wind," πέλαγος "open sea," πηδάλιον "rudder," and πρύμνη "stern"— all of which occur hundreds of times in ancient literature outside Homer and the New Testament. MacDonald marks as significant even such extremely common words as πλέω "to sail," ἀνάγομαι "to set sail," ἀναβαίνω/ἐπιβαίνω "to embark," and φέρομαι "to be

---

[27] D. R. MacDonald, "The Shipwrecks," 95–9. To be precise, the only occurrence of the word "waves" in Acts is as a manuscript variant of 27:41.

[28] D. R. MacDonald, "The Shipwrecks," 99–101, 101–3.

borne," but their ubiquity in ancient Greek literature generally—tens of thousands of attestations between the time of Homer and the time of Luke—renders them utterly inconsequential for the purpose of making a comparison between specific passages of the *Odyssey* and Acts. When two narratives, even narratives as far apart chronologically as Homer's *Odyssey* and Luke's Acts, describe a common event (a sea voyage, storm, and shipwreck) in a common language (Greek), it is inevitable that they will share common vocabulary. Such shared vocabulary, when it is the normal, colloquial vocabulary of the period, expressed in the dialect of its respective narrator, is no evidence of influence by one text on another. In Luke's narrative of Paul's sea voyage in Acts, he is for the most part (though not entirely) simply using the words and expressions commonly used in his own time to describe sea voyages. Of all the diction shared by the *Odyssey* and Acts that MacDonald marshals there is nothing, with the exception of the expression ἐπέκειλαν τὴν ναῦν "they ran the ship aground" in Acts 27:41, distinctive enough to support the assumption of a genetic connection between the two texts. MacDonald's practice of collecting a plethora of individual words that appear in common between two texts and then organizing these words neatly into two columns in order to highlight the commonalities of the two texts is another feature found in all his subsequent publications. It may appear impressive to someone simply glancing at the countless pages of columns, but the piling on of more and more commonly shared but insignificant vocabulary does nothing to improve his argument; it only results—to use a Vergilian metaphor—in burying any potential gold deeply in the dung.

In sum, while there may be some validity to MacDonald's essential proposal that Luke's account of the sea voyage in Acts 27:1–28:16 is dependent in some ways on Homer's *Odyssey*, he vastly overstates his case by inundating his readers with false connections and insignificant parallels, making it very difficult for them to isolate anything of value and leaving them perplexed rather than persuaded. I have included this critique of MacDonald's article "The Shipwrecks of Odysseus and Paul," at the risk of appearing mean and petty, chiefly because it relates directly to my own analysis below of possible Homeric influence on these episodes in Acts. I have offered the critique in such detail because its relevance is not limited to this article: the critique can be applied, by analogy, to MacDonald's next twenty years of publications on the topic of Homeric influence on the New Testament, all of which contain similarly extravagant claims built on a foundation undermined by flaws and distortions. Finally, I have offered the critique at this time because, oddly enough, few New Testament scholars have yet to offer substantial critical evaluations of MacDonald's practices, methodologies, and proposals.[29] The strategy apparently adopted by many New

---

[29] The most substantial critiques are those of M. M. Mitchell, "Homer in the New Testament," *Journal of Religion* 83 (2003): 244–60; K. O. Sandnes, "Imitatio Homeri? An Appraisal of Dennis R. MacDonald's 'Mimesis Criticism,'" *Journal of Biblical Literature* 124 (2005): 715–32; and K. Larsson, "Intertextual Density, Quantifying Imitation," *Journal of Biblical Literature* 133 (2014): 309–31. Meaningful critiques are offered also by J. B. Weaver, *Plots of Epiphany: Prison-Escape in Acts of the Apostles* (Berlin: Walter de Gruyter, 2004), 151–5; L. T. Johnson, "Review of *Does the New Testament Imitate Homer? Four Cases from the Acts of the Apostles*," *Christianity and Literature* 54, no 2 (2005): 285–7; P. R. Eddy and G. A. Boyd, *The Jesus Legend: A Case for the Historical Reliability of the Synoptic Jesus Tradition* (Grand Rapids: Baker Academic, 2007), 316–17, 340–3; and C. S. Keener, *Acts: An Exegetical Commentary* (Grand Rapids: Baker Academic, 2012), 1:83–7.

98   *The Formal Education of the Author of Luke-Acts*

Testament scholars of simply ignoring his work, as though it is some sort of idiosyncrasy that will go away on its own if ignored for long enough, does not seem to me a responsible one. MacDonald's work needs to be taken seriously, not just because his publications on the topic of Homeric influence on the New Testament are so substantial, and not just because his views are beginning to find their way into standard commentaries on Acts (e.g., the recent commentaries of R. I. Pervo and C. S. Keener),[30] but primarily because, if even a small fraction of his claims proves true, this should change the way the Gospel of Mark, the Gospel of Luke, and the Acts of the Apostles are read; that is to say, they should be read as pieces of deliberate literary fiction rather than as biographies or histories that claim to be accounts of actual events.

In what follows I aim for something more ambitious than the routine references of commentators who observe, without any further explication, a verbal or thematic similarity between Homer's *Odyssey* and the last two chapters of Acts, yet more modest than the extravagant claims of MacDonald that Homer's *Odyssey* wielded a direct and pervasive influence on Luke's account of Paul's sea voyage. I believe that there do exist in Luke's account of the sea voyage of Paul in Acts some purposeful environmental, thematic, verbal, and even metrical resonances of Homer's narrative of the sea voyages of Odysseus in the *Odyssey*. The milieu is similar: the sea voyages of both Odysseus and Paul pass from east to west (from Asia to Europe); they both experience storms as they pass by the island of Crete that throw them drastically off course; they both pass through the notorious straits between Italy and Sicily. More specifically, several themes are shared by the accounts of Odysseus's and Paul's experiences at sea: suffering a storm off the island of Crete; offering a speech on a storm-tossed ship; being visited by a divine messenger; awaiting eagerly the arrival of dawn; failing to recognize a strange land; and running a ship aground. Complementing these thematic resonances, as I shall illustrate thoroughly below, are some evocative snatches of epic diction and even of epic meter.

These Homeric resonances are complemented by the more elevated language that we witness in Acts 27:1–28:16 as a whole, where Classical and Hellenistic literary and even poetic Greek replaces some of the prosaic Septuagintal and Koine Greek that is the norm elsewhere in Acts.[31] The elevated language includes literary and poetic word forms: the literary and poetic comparative adverb ἆσσον "nearer" rather than the prosaic ἐγγυτέρον (27:13); the altogether poetic (epic) ἐπικέλλω "run aground" rather than the prosaic ἐποκέλλω (27:41). It includes complex syntax: numerous circumstantial participial clauses (81x), many of which are genitive absolute constructions (22x); two instances of the rare, and highly literary, oblique optative (27:12, 39); the only instance in the New Testament of the literary idiom πρός + genitive (27:34); the Classical Greek

---

[30] R. I. Pervo, *Acts: A Commentary* (Minneapolis: Fortress, 2009); C. S. Keener, *Acts: An Exegetical Commentary Volumes 1–4* (Grand Rapids: Baker Academic, 2012–2015).

[31] But one should keep in mind that the frequency of what appears to be elevated diction in Acts 27:1–28:16 may be attributable partly to the unusual context of a sea voyage, storm, shipwreck, etc., which requires a certain degree of technical language: e.g., κόλπος meaning a "bay" rather than a "bosom"; ἐκπίπτω meaning "run aground" rather than "fall off"; ἐρείδω meaning "stick fast" rather than "lean." Also, some of the diction remains overtly Septuagintal (Acts 27:35), and there even appear to be some echoes of the Septuagintal version of the sea voyage of Jonah (Jonah 1:5).

stylistic construction whereby a series of participial clauses are summed up with οὕτως + an indicative verb (27:17—elsewhere only in Acts 20:11 in the New Testament). It includes elegant idiomatic phrases: φιλανθρώπως ... χρησάμενος "having treated benevolently" (27:3); ἐπιμελείας τυχεῖν "to obtain care" (27:3); προθέσεως κεκρατηκέναι "to have achieved a purpose" (27:13); κατὰ τραχεῖς τόπους ἐκπέσωμεν "run aground upon rough places" (27:29); ηὔχοντο ἡμέραν γενέσθαι "pray for day to arrive" (27:29); μεταλαβεῖν τροφῆς "to take nourishment" (27:33, 34); ἄσιτοι διατελεῖτε "remain without food" (27:33); κορεσθέντες τροφῆς "satiated with food" (27:38); κατεῖχον εἰς τὸν αἰγιαλόν "head for the beach" (27:40); ἐπέκειλαν τὴν ναῦν "run the ship aground" (27:41); ἡ δίκη ζῆν οὐκ εἴασεν "justice did not allow him to live" (28:4);[32] ἔπαθεν οὐδὲν κακόν "suffer no evil" (28:5); φιλοφρόνως ἐξένισεν "entertain hospitably" (28:7). Finally, it includes a poeticism in the oxymoronic wordplay κερδῆσαι ὕβριν καὶ ζημίαν "to gain violence and loss" (27:21).[33] With this as a background, we shall now focus on Homeric resonance specifically, as we make our way through the account of Paul's sea voyage in Acts 27:1–28:16.

Acts 27:7-20: Cretan Storms

The account of Paul's voyage from Caesarea to Rome in Acts 27:1–28:16 begins with the narrative shifting, for the fourth and final time in Acts, to the first person plural (i.e., it is one of the "we-passages"). At first it reads very much like a historical account of experienced events, a first person travelogue essentially, with great attention to even the most mundane and seemingly insignificant details: that the centurion in command is Julius of the Augustan Cohort, that (the subsequently unmentioned) Aristarchus the Macedonian from Thessalonica accompanies them, that they are initially placed on an Adramyttian ship that is headed for the coast of Asia Minor, that they make a stop in Sidon, that they sail on the leeward side of Cyprus to avoid the headwinds, that they then make a switch in the port city of Myra, in Lycia, to a ship from Alexandria that is headed to Italy, and that contrary winds force them to sail south, on the leeward side of Crete, along Salmone, to a place called Fair Havens near the city of Lasaia. The account up to this point is written completely in standard prosaic Greek, with words, phrases, idioms, and grammatical and syntactical constructions commonly found in Classical, Hellenistic, and Roman Imperial-era prose authors such as Isocrates, Xenophon, Aristotle, Polybius, Diodorus Siculus, Dionysius of Halicarnassus, Strabo, Josephus, Plutarch, and Pausanias. It is not the Septuagintal and Koine Greek that we have witnessed in much of the earlier narrative of Luke-Acts. But neither is it the literary or poetic Greek that we shall witness in the narrative that follows. The island of Crete, however, serves as the locus for a transition to a different world, both geographically and literarily.

---

[32] Justice (Δίκη) should probably be capitalized here, as it appears to refer to the divinity—daughter of Zeus and Themis, as in Hesiod's *Theogony* 902, *Works and Days* 213-24, 256-62, and throughout subsequent Greek literature.

[33] C.f. μὴ κακὰ κερδαίνειν "don't gain evils" in Hesiod's *Works and Days* 352; δάκρυα κερδᾶναι "to gain tears" in Euripides' *Hecuba* 518; πᾶν κέρδος ἡγοῦ ζημιουμένη φυγῇ "consider it all a gain to be suffering exile" in Euripides' *Medea* 454.

100 *The Formal Education of the Author of Luke-Acts*

It is now autumn: the dangerous season for sailing has arrived (27:9), and a decision must be made whether to spend the winter in the harbor at Fair Havens, on the south coast of Crete, or to sail on in search of a safer harbor to the west. At this critical juncture the narrative undergoes a transformation from a mundane travelogue to an exciting tale of adventure. Luke offers the remarkable scenario of the prisoner Paul, in language evocative of his earlier public address to the Athenians on the Areopagus— Άνδρες ... θεωρῶ "Gentlemen ... I see" (Acts 17:22 = 27:10)—giving a formal exhortation (παραινέω "I exhort"—only here, in 27:9, and, again of Paul, in 27:22, in the New Testament) to the centurion, the pilot, the shipowner, and the entire crew, warning them that if they continue the voyage they will suffer damage and loss not only of the ship and its cargo but also their very lives. And though Paul's warning will prove to be largely correct, the centurion and the crew decide to ignore it in deference to the advice of the pilot and captain. A south wind lures them to set out from the harbor at Fair Havens, but soon, as Paul forewarned, a "typhonic" northeast wind called Euraquilo rushes down against them from inland Crete, and they are driven helplessly by the storm southwest in the direction of the Syrtis, the shallow bay full of sandbars off the coast of Libya. They take drastic measures against the storm, undergirding the ship with ropes, lowering the gear, and throwing the cargo and tackle overboard, but they continue to be driven by the storm, they see neither the sun nor the stars for many days, and they lose all hope of survival.

Anyone acquainted with Homer's *Odyssey* senses that they are in familiar territory here, beginning with the section of the narrative in which Paul's ship is driven by the wind southward toward the coast of Crete. For Crete plays a major role in the *Odyssey*, where the island is flaunted as a place of mythic proportions. Crete is that land "in the middle of the wine-dark sea, lovely, fertile, surrounded by water, where innumerable men live, who speak many tongues, and there are ninety cities" (*Od.* 19.172-7).[34] The island serves as a place of transition and transformation: sailors are driven off course by storms and forced to take refuge on Crete; they are also driven away from Crete by storms and carried by wind and waves southward to alien lands.

On Menelaus's sea voyage home from Troy, as Nestor relates in his tale to Telemachus in Pylos, Zeus sends a storm with monstrous waves that separates his ships and brings some to the southern coast of Crete, to the headlands of Gortys and Phaestos (very near where Paul's ship harbors at Fair Havens). The storm shatters most of Menelaus's fleet upon the reefs, but the wind and the waves carry five of the ships south to Egypt (3.276-302). There Menelaus experiences a transition to a world of "men with strange tongues" (3.302), where, as Menelaus himself tells Telemachus in Sparta, he is detained until he defeats the shape-shifting god Proteus in a wrestling match in order to find out how he can get successfully home (4.351-586).

In his first "Cretan lie," which he tells to Athena upon arriving in Ithaca, Odysseus claims that he is a Cretan, having fled because he had killed the son of Idomeneus, and now blown by the winds to this island unknown to him (13.256-86). In his second

---

[34] Crete naturally plays a smaller role in the *Iliad*, but it is still rich in myth: "Crete of the hundred cities" and of "eighty black ships" is listed in the Catalogue of Ships (2.645-57) as the home of the "god-like" (3.230) King Idomeneus, great-grandson of Zeus through Deucalion and Minos (13.450-3).

Luke and Homer

101

"Cretan lie," which he tells to the swineherd Eumaeus, Odysseus again claims to be a Cretan, who was captured by Egyptians and then led away by a Phoenician man who plots to send him under constraint by ship to Libya to be sold into slavery. But as the ship passes by Crete Zeus sends a storm that destroys the ship, and all the men drown except Odysseus, who holds onto the mast of the ship until he reaches Thesprotia, where King Pheidon treats him hospitably. Later King Pheidon sends him to Dulichion in a ship, but the sailors mistreat him and contrive to sell him as a slave. While the ship is docked in Ithaca he escapes and ends up at Eumaeus's hut (14.192–359).[35] Eumaeus responds to Odysseus's lie by telling a story about how an Aetolian man had once come to him with the news that Odysseus was in Crete with Idomeneus, repairing the ships that a storm had broken to pieces (14.379–85). In his third "Cretan lie," which he tells to his wife Penelope, Odysseus claims that he is Aethon, the brother of the Cretan king Idomeneus. He claims that he once saw Odysseus on his way to Troy, when the winds drove his ships off course to Crete. Odysseus managed to escape the storm and had anchored in the difficult harbor at Amnisos, where a north wind kept him stranded for twelve days (19.172–348).

For someone acquainted with these tales in the *Odyssey*, then, the narrative in Acts about Paul's ship being blown off course by contrary winds and forced to seek safe harbor in Crete would reverberate with epic resonance. Even more so would the subsequent narrative about a typhonic northeast wind arising against them and driving them southward from Crete, for they are in danger, like Menelaus and Odysseus in the *Odyssey*, of being driven to the alien lands of the south. In particular, the ship's crew dreads becoming marooned on the Syrtis, the bay full of sand bars off the coast of Libya, but, as events turn out, the storm drives them to the strange island of Malta, where they are granted hospitality by the "barbarian" inhabitants.

Acts 27:15 (Western Text) συστείλαντες τὰ ἱστία "having furled the sails"

Acts 27:13-15 describes how Paul's ship, as it coasts along the southern coast of Crete, is suddenly hit by a storm that throws it off course and forces it to drift southward with the wind. Some witnesses of the Western Text of Acts (82, 614, 1518, 2125, syr[h with *], Cassiodorus, Bede) include the following phrase at this point in the narrative: τῷ πνέοντι (πλέοντι 614, 1518) καὶ συστείλαντες τὰ ἱστία.[36] Verse fifteen in these manuscripts, then, reads: συναρπασθέντος δὲ τοῦ πλοίου καὶ μὴ δυναμένου ἀντοφθαλμεῖν τῷ ἀνέμῳ ἐπιδόντες τῷ πνέοντι (πλέοντι 614, 1518) καὶ συστείλαντες τὰ ἱστία ἐφερόμεθα. "Since the ship was thrown off course and could not face the wind, having given way to its blowing and having furled the sails we were borne along."

This formula στέλλω + ἱστίον "furl the sail," which occurs only here in the New Testament (and Septuagint), is largely poetic in Classical and Hellenistic Greek, both in its verb's simplex and compound forms. It appears to be drawn directly from Homer,

---

[35] A very similar "Cretan lie" is told by Demeter to the daughters of Celeus in the Homeric *Hymn to Demeter* 120–44.

[36] So B. M. Metzger, *A Textual Commentary on the Greek New Testament*, 2nd ed. (Stuttgart: Deutsche Bibelgesellschaft, 1994), 440.

102   *The Formal Education of the Author of Luke-Acts*

and, more specifically, from a formula that makes up part of the traditional Homeric type-scene for disembarking from a ship:[37] *Iliad* 1.433—ἱστία μὲν στείλαντο, θέσαν δ' ἐν νηῒ μελαίνῃ "they furled the sails and placed them in the black ship"; *Odyssey* 3.10–11—οἱ δ' ἰθὺς κατάγοντο ἰδ' ἱστία νηὸς ἐΐσης στεῖλαν ἀείραντες, τὴν δ' ὥρμισαν, ἐκ δ' ἔβαν αὐτοί "Straightway they made landfall, and they furled the sails of the well-balanced ship by lifting them up, and they moored the ship, and they themselves got out"; *Odyssey* 16.352—ἱστία τε στέλλοντας ἐρετμά τε χερσὶν ἔχοντας "furling the sails and holding the oars in their hands."

This formula made its way from Homer into the Greek epic tradition generally. We see imitations of it in Apollonius of Rhodes' *Argonautica* (2.1262–4), and again in the fifth-century CE epic poet Nonnus's *Dionysiaca* (3.43). The combination of στέλλω (or its compounds συστέλλω/ὑποστέλλω/ἀναστέλλω) + ἱστίον appears occasionally elsewhere in Greek literature, but where it does, it is almost always used metaphorically. Pindar praises Xenocrates' hospitality with this nautical metaphor (*Isthm.* 2.39–40): "a blowing wind never caused him to 'furl the sail' [i.e., penny-pinch] at his hospitable table"; Aristophanes uses the formula as a metaphor for checking one's anger (*Frogs* 999–1000): "furl the tips of your sails"; Dio Chrysostom uses it as a metaphor for the relationship between the ruler and the ruled (*Or.* 3.65): "furl the sail"; Plutarch uses it as a metaphor for how to take care of one's own body (*De tuenda sanitate praecepta* Stephanus page 128 F): "one must not furl the body like a sail."[38]

In sum, though I do not think that the reading συστείλαντες τὰ ἱστία 'having furled the sails', found in some manuscripts of Acts 27:15, is original to Luke's composition (the manuscript evidence argues against its inclusion), it is illuminating to witness how later revisers, editors, and/or scribes of the text of Acts freely embellished this scene of a storm at sea by drawing a formula from the traditional diction of Homeric epic. Homer must have resided in the recesses of their minds and on the tips of their tongues (and pens). I am supposing in what follows that this applies to Luke himself and that he embraced a similar practice on occasion in his account of Paul's sea voyage and shipwreck.

Acts 27:21-6: A Speech on a Storm-Tossed Ship

The *Odyssey* continues to exert its influence on the account of Paul's sea voyage in Acts, as the narrative takes on an adventurous, story-telling quality and is even embellished by a heroic speech, a prophecy, and a divine intervention.

Epic heroes are expected to deliver memorable speeches on the decks of ships in the midst of raging storms. Odysseus is the paradigm. He has been sailing on his raft from the island of Ogygia for eighteen days and is on the verge of reaching the land of the

---

[37] On the formal components of the Homeric type-scene of disembarkation, see W. Arend, *Die typischen Scenen bei Homer* (Berlin: Weidmann, 1933), 79–81 and plate 5.

[38] Elsewhere I find the phrase only in "Aristotle," *Mechanica* 851b and in Heliodorus, *Aethiopica* 5.17.4, where, in both cases, it is used literally, and, of course in later scholia, grammars, lexica, and commentaries that explain the phrase's literary usages: e.g., scholia to Homer and Pindar, Phrynichus's grammar, Julius Pollux's thesaurus, Eusthathius's commentaries on Homer.

Luke and Homer 103

Phaeacians, when Poseidon notices him and raises a great storm, turning day into night and blasting the raft with winds and waves. In his distress, Odysseus delivers a speech that captured the imagination of poets throughout antiquity:

> Alas, wretch that I am ... Zeus has churned up the sea, and the blasts of the wind are rushing upon me ... my destruction is certain ... thrice and four times blessed are those who died in Troy ... I wish that I had died there too ... for then I would have received a proper burial and widespread fame ... but now I am destined to suffer a miserable death.
>
> summary of *Od.* 5.299–312

Odysseus's speech became the literary model for Aeneas's speech in Vergil's *Aeneid*, when he is confronted with a similar storm raised against his ship by the wind god Aeolus (*Aen.* 1.81–101). The "speech on a storm-tossed ship" then became a literary motif among many first-century CE Latin poets: Lucan (*Phars.* 654–77); Seneca (*Ag.* 512–26); Silius Italicus (*Pun.* 17.260–7); Valerius Flaccus (*Arg.* 1.627–32).

In similarly dire circumstances Paul asserts himself heroically, and he delivers a speech offering a much more optimistic evaluation of the situation than had Odysseus. For the second time in this chapter (cf. 27:9-10) Luke presents the remarkable scenario of Paul, in language evocative of his address to the Athenians on the Areopagus— σταθεὶς δὲ ὁ Παῦλος ἐν μέσῳ ... ἔφη, Ἄνδρες Ἀθηναῖοι ... "Paul, standing in their midst, said 'Gentlemen of Athens ...'" (17:22) ≈ σταθεὶς (ὁ) Παῦλος ἐν μέσῳ αὐτῶν εἶπεν ... ὦ ἄνδρες ... "Paul, standing in their midst, said 'O gentlemen ...'" (27:21)— delivering a formal speech in the most unlikely of circumstances: on the deck of a ship in a raging storm. Paul's speech lacks verisimilitude as a historical account: it is not simply a record of an actual event; it is a literary topos.[39] Paul chastises the crew for not following his earlier advice and consequently suffering the violence and loss that he had predicted. This is a pleasing "I-told-you-so" moment for our hero. And Luke further embellishes his speech with the poetic, oxymoronic, wordplay: "to gain violence and loss" κερδῆσαι ὕβριν καὶ ζημίαν (27:21) (cf. the similar wordplays in Hesiod and Euripides cited above). He also embellishes Paul's speech with the literary motif of divine intervention in time of crisis: Paul exhorts the crew to take heart since he has just learned from a messenger of the God he worships that there will be no loss of human life, but just of the ship. Those familiar with the *Odyssey* will recall that after Odysseus's famous speech aboard his storm-tossed raft he too is visited by a divinity, the sea goddess Ino, who tells him not to fear, since it is not his fate to perish (5.333–50). The goddess's words prove true: while Odysseus's raft is destroyed by the storm,

---

[39] Commentators have observed the incongruity. E.g., E. Haenchen, *The Acts of the Apostles*, 704: "The author has no real idea of the situation: with the howl of the gale and the pitch of the ship Paul could not deliver an address as on the Areopagus." S. M. Praeder, "Acts 27:1–28:16: Sea Voyages," 696: "The speech in Acts 27:21-6 is not very credible as a historical record. It still needs to be recognized, however, that the speech corresponds to one of the conventions of storm scenes. Paul is not alone in his supposed ability to deliver a speech during a raging storm. This ability is something that he shares with Odysseus, Julius Caesar, the Greeks and the Trojans, Hannibal, the Argonauts, and Aeneas."

104   *The Formal Education of the Author of Luke-Acts*

he is eventually washed by the waves upon the shore of Scheria, the island of the Phaeacians.[40] Similarly, Paul reports that according to God's messenger he is fated to stand before Caesar, and so God has graciously decided to spare all of Paul's fellow travelers as well. They will wreck upon an island, Paul predicts.

As the narrative of Acts proceeds, there occur, in fact, many more notable similarities between the larger accounts of Odysseus's sea voyage and shipwreck on the island of Scheria (*Od.* 5.278–493) and Paul's sea voyage and shipwreck on the island of Malta (Acts 27:13–28:10). In summary: monstrous storms batter their ships; they give speeches while on the decks of their storm-tossed ships; divinities appear to assure them that it is their destiny to survive the storms; the waves shake their ships to pieces; at dawn they swim safely to shore; they seek shelter on land from the damp and cold; they are offered warm hospitality by the natives of the land, who suspect that they may be gods; they perform great deeds among the natives and are rewarded with many honors and provisions for their subsequent journeys.

This is not to say that Luke is slavishly modeling his narrative in Acts on this specific episode of the *Odyssey*, for there are also many differences between the two narratives. Moreover, in some respects Luke seems to be portraying Paul not as an epic hero, who rants and raves against the gods about his miserable fate, but rather as a Stoic philosopher, who remains unperturbed by evil fortune. The depiction of a wise man remaining calm in the face of a raging storm was a leitmotif in the philosophical writings of Luke's own time: e.g., Epictetus, *Dissertations* 2.19.15–19, where Epictetus gauges the true measure of a Stoic philosopher by how he responds to a storm at sea (cf. 2.5.12–14); Plutarch, *De tranquillitate animi* 475d–476a, where a wise man facing bad fortune is compared to a valiant pilot facing a raging storm; (later) Diogenes Laertius, *Lives of the Philosophers* 1.5.86 and 9.11.68, where anecdotes are recorded about the philosophers Bias and Pyrrho, who remained heroically unperturbed in the face of storms at sea.

So far as their speeches on their storm-tossed ships are concerned, Odysseus's speech is one of lament and despair, while Paul's is one of encouragement and hope: παραινῶ ὑμᾶς εὐθυμεῖν "I exhort you to take heart" (27:22); μὴ φοβοῦ "don't fear"(27:24—Paul's report of the angel's speech); εὐθυμεῖτε "take heart" (27:25). Paul's words here point us to what was surely the closest and most familiar model for his behavior in the face of the storm: namely, the gospel account of Jesus, who calmly sleeps through a storm on the Sea of Galilee, and, when awakened by his terrified disciples, commands the winds and the waves to cease, and, moreover, chides his disciples for their lack of faith (Mk 4:35-41; Mt. 8:23-7; Lk. 8:22-5). During another storm too Jesus offers encouragement to his disciples who are on a boat battered by the wind and waves of the Sea of Galilee, using words of encouragement similar to those of Paul to his shipmates: θαρσεῖτε ... μὴ φοβεῖσθε "be courageous ... don't fear" (Mk 6:50 = Mt. 14:27). Commentators have occasionally observed that Luke has embroidered a pattern that links Paul's "passion" in the latter chapters of Acts with Jesus's passion in

---

[40] Scheria is not specifically called an island in the *Odyssey*, but all indications are that it was to be understood as an island. The earliest post-Homeric traditions understand Scheria as a former name of the island of Corcyra (e.g., Hellanicus, Aristotle, and, later, Strabo).

Luke and Homer

the latter chapters of his own gospel (e.g., Acts 21:4, 10-14, and Lk. 18:31-4).[41] Their common experiences in the face of storms can be included as part of that larger pattern.

To someone wondering, then, what literary models—ancient epics, contemporary philosophical texts, or contemporary gospels—influenced Luke's depiction of Paul's actions and demeanor on board the storm-tossed ship in Acts, the best answer may very well be "all the above—and probably more."

Acts 27:29 ηὔχοντο ἡμέραν γενέσθαι "they prayed for day to arrive"

On the fourteenth night of being tossed about by a storm on the Adriatic Sea, around the middle of the night, the sailors begin to suspect that they are approaching land, a suspicion confirmed by two successive soundings. Dreading the prospect of being dashed against a rough shoreline in the dark of night, the sailors take the unusual step of casting four anchors from the stern of the ship and then "pray for day to arrive" (27:29 ηὔχοντο ἡμέραν γενέσθαι).[42] The language of this idiom is prosaic and is very much at home in the novelistic tradition. There are close parallels in two ancient Greek novels roughly contemporary with Luke's Acts, although the setting is not nautical in any case: Chariton's novel *Callirhoe* 6.1.6.3 ἡ μὲν βασιλὶς ηὔχετο ἡμέραν γενέσθαι τάχιον "the queen prayed for day to arrive quickly"; Longus's novel *Daphnis and Chloe* 2.8.2.5 θᾶττον εὐχόμεθα γενέσθαι τὴν ἡμέραν "we pray for day to arrive quickly," and 2.23.4.3 εὐχόμενος δὲ τὴν ἡμέραν γενέσθαι ταχέως "praying for day to arrive quickly."

Nonetheless, anyone acquainted with the Homeric epics will recall many memorable nocturnal scenes in which the arrival of dawn is eagerly or fearfully awaited. The Trojan warrior Hector, for example, "prays that divine dawn appear quickly" (*Il*. 9.240 ἀρᾶται δὲ τάχιστα φανήμεναι Ἠῶ δῖαν) so that he can destroy the Achaean ships that are beached on the shore (other examples in the *Iliad*: 8.565; 9.662; 11.723; 18.255). Several times in the *Odyssey* the nocturnal scene involves sailors on a ship or encamped next to a ship that is beached on a strange island, eagerly awaiting the arrival of dawn. Odysseus is rounding Cape Malea and on the verge of arriving home to Ithaca when a north wind blows him off course and drives his ships southward to the land of the Lotus Eaters and then to the land of the Cyclopes (*Od*. 9.76–192). In the dark of night his ships come upon an uninhabited island, with a sheltered harbor, and in spite of the waves crashing against the shore, they are able to beach the ship in the harbor. They fall

---

[41] The earliest systematic comparison that I have found of the parallels between the Gospel of Luke's account of the life of Jesus and Acts' account of the life of Paul is E. Zeller, *Die Apostelgeschichte nach ihrem Inhalt und Ursprung kritisch untersucht* (Stuttgart: Carl Mäcken, 1854), 425–32, whose main purpose is to prove the common authorship of the two works. For a survey of the history of criticism on the Jesus-Paul parallels generally, see A. J. Mattill, Jr., "The Jesus-Paul Parallels and the Purpose of Luke-Acts: H. H. Evans Reconsidered," *Novum Testamentum* 17 (1975): 15–46 (esp. 15–21). For a convenient list of parallels between Jesus and Paul's "passions" specifically, see R. I. Pervo, *Acts: A Commentary*, 533–4.

[42] The ancients realized that it was much safer and more effective to throw anchors off the prow than the stern. For a nautical circumstance similar to that of Paul's ship, cf. Pindar's *Pythian* 10.51-2: Κῶπαν σχάσον, ταχὺ δ' ἄγκυραν ἔρεισον χθονί πρῴραθε, χοιράδος ἄλκαρ πέτρας. "Let go your oar! Quickly drop the anchor down from the prow to the bottom, as a safeguard against the protruding rocks." The scholia on this passage note that "an anchor prevents ships from running aground on the rocks" and that it is "from the prow that anchors are cast into the sea."

106   *The Formal Education of the Author of Luke-Acts*

asleep there on the beach and "await the divine dawn" (*Od.* 9.151 ἐμείναμεν Ἠῶ δῖαν). The situation in the *Odyssey* and in Acts is remarkably similar: a ship finding shelter at night in the harbor/bay of an unknown island, with a beach upon which the sailors can drive the keel of their ship, and, most pertinent here, the sailors eagerly awaiting the arrival of daylight. The same formulaic phrase is used, in similar circumstances, to describe the arrival of Odysseus's ship on the beach of Aiaia, the island of Circe, and the sailors "awaiting the arrival of dawn" (12.7 ἐμείναμεν Ἠῶ δῖαν). In fact, the same, or very similar, formulas are used regularly in the *Odyssey* whenever someone is awaiting, with eagerness or trepidation, the arrival of daylight (9.306, 436; 16.368; 18.318; 19.50, 342). The effect of these Homeric echoes in Acts is to increase the level of anticipation and tension at this critical moment of the narrative.

Acts 27:34 οὐδενὸς γὰρ ὑμῶν θρὶξ ἀπὸ τῆς κεφαλῆς ἀπολεῖται "for the hair of not one of you will be lost from your head"

As dawn is about to break Paul delivers another speech to everyone on the ship, encouraging them to take some nourishment, since they have not eaten anything, he contends, for fourteen days. This, Paul asserts, is for the sake of their preservation, and he encourages them further by quoting a proverb "for the hair of not one of you will be lost from your head."

Paul's short speech here (27:33-4) is full of Classical and literary idioms: ἄσιτοι διατελεῖτε "you remain without food" (both words occur only here in the New Testament); μεταλαβεῖν τροφῆς "to take nourishment" (the expression occurs in the New Testament only in Acts); πρὸς τῆς ὑμετέρας σωτηρίας "for the sake of your preservation" (πρός + genitive is a high literary style, occurring only here in the New Testament). And the climax of this literary flourish is the proverb that Paul quotes, for, in the midst of their distress, Paul exhorts the crew by uttering what sounds like a snatch of heroic epic verse (27:34): οὐδενὸς γὰρ ὑμῶν θρὶξ ἀπὸ τῆς κεφαλῆς ἀπολεῖται "for the hair of not one of you will be lost from your head." The function of the conjunction γάρ "for" is simply to connect the proverb in the second half of Acts 27:34 to the narrative context of the first half. If we delete the conjunction we can see that Luke has presented us with a full dactylic hexameter verse:[43]

$$- \smile \smile / - - / - \| \smile \smile / - \smile \smile / - \smile \smile / - \circ$$

οὐδενὸς ὑμῶν θρὶξ ἀπὸ τῆς κεφαλῆς ἀπολεῖται

Not only does the verse scan perfectly from the perspective of external metrics (i.e., the combinations of long and short syllables), including the regularly dactylic fifth foot, but it observes several of the internal features of proper dactylic hexameter verse, most notably a third-foot masculine caesura, but also a diaeresis between the first and second foot and a masculine caesura in the fourth foot. It also properly avoids second- and

---

[43] I believe the first person to comment on the dactylic hexameter shape of this proverb is Th. Birt, "Ἄγνωστοι θεοί und die Areopagrede des Apostels Paulus," *Rheinisches Museum für Philologie* 69 (1914): 380, who simply notes it in passing.

Luke and Homer   107

fourth-foot feminine caesurae. Moreover, all of the diction of the verse, and even the positions of the words and phrases in the verse, are characteristic of dactylic hexameter poetry. That is to say, the four main words in the verse—οὐδενός, θρίξ, κεφαλῆς, and ἀπόλεῖται—all of which appear in extant dactylic hexameter verses, are here placed in metrical positions in which they also appear in those extant verses.[44]

I am not convinced that Luke is quoting an actual ancient epic verse here, for the use of the definite article τῆς is very prosaic, and the pronoun ὑμῶν does not have its usual epic form.[45] Rather, it appears that Luke is reformulating an inherited prosaic proverb into dactylic hexameter verse in order to embellish with another epic feature a scene that already has a certain level of epic resonance.

We do not have to search far to find possible prosaic sources for this proverb. A similar expression regarding the loss of the hair of the head, within a similar context of guaranteeing safety in a time of danger, occurs three times in the Septuagint: 1 Kingdoms 14:45 εἰ πεσεῖται τῆς τριχὸς τῆς κεφαλῆς αὐτοῦ ἐπὶ τὴν γῆν (with respect to the safety of Jonathan); 2 Kingdoms 14:11 εἰ πεσεῖται ἀπὸ τῆς τριχὸς τοῦ υἱοῦ σου ἐπὶ τὴν γῆν (with respect to the safety of the son of the woman of Tekoa); 3 Kingdoms 1:52 εἰ πεσεῖται τῶν τριχῶν αὐτοῦ ἐπὶ τὴν γῆν (with respect to the safety of Adonijah). Also, a similar expression, this one regarding the numbering of the hairs of the head, but again within a similar context of guaranteeing safety in a time of danger, occurs twice in the New Testament: Matthew 10:30 ὑμῶν δὲ καὶ αἱ τρίχες τῆς κεφαλῆς πᾶσαι ἠριθμημέναι εἰσίν (with respect to the safety of Jesus's disciples); Luke 12:7 ἀλλὰ καὶ αἱ τρίχες τῆς κεφαλῆς ὑμῶν πᾶσαι ἠρίθμηνται (with respect to the safety of Jesus's disciples).[46]

The closest parallel to Acts 27:34, however, is a similar version of the proverb in Luke's gospel, which also features a dactylic hexameter shape (Lk. 21:18): καὶ θρὶξ ἐκ τῆς κεφαλῆς ὑμῶν οὐ μὴ ἀπόληται (Jesus comforts his disciples). Unlike Lk. 12:7, which has a parallel in Matthew 10:30, this verse is unique to the Gospel of Luke. The passage as a whole, the eschatological discourse of Jesus to his disciples, in which he warns of future suffering, appears in all three synoptic gospels (Mk 13:3-13; Mt. 24:3-14; Lk. 21:7-19), but only in Luke are Jesus's warnings capped off by the aphorism "and the hair from your head will not perish." Either Luke has another source, or he is improvising here. The aphorism, in fact, seems a bit out of place, given the context. One might even say that it contradicts what immediately precedes. For Jesus has just cataloged all the terrible things that his disciples will suffer: wars and tumult, earthquakes, famine and pestilence, persecutions, the betrayal of friends and family,

---

[44] E.g., οὐδενός appears in this metrical position in Theognis 1.411, θρίξ appears in this metrical position in *Anthologia Graeca* 5.21.3, κεφαλῆς appears in this metrical position in Apollonius of Rhodes' *Argonautica* 2.1069, and ἀπόλεῖται appears in this metrical position in *Anthologia Graeca* Appendix 281.5.

[45] The closest actual Homeric verses are *Odyssey* 13.399 ξανθὰς δ᾽ ἐκ κεφαλῆς ὀλέσω τρίχας "I shall destroy the yellow hair from your head" and 431 ξανθὰς δ᾽ ἐκ κεφαλῆς ὄλεσε τρίχας "she destroyed the yellow hair from his head," but the context is very different (of Athena disguising Odysseus).

[46] The Syriac translation (Sinai ms.) of this aphorism in Matthew 10:30 includes a word play. Some have taken this to indicate that the proverb has an Aramaic origin: so M. Black, *An Aramaic Approach to the Gospels and Acts*, 3rd ed. (Oxford: Clarendon, 1967), 161. This would presumably apply to Luke 12:7 as well.

108   *The Formal Education of the Author of Luke-Acts*

and even the death of some of them. The aphorism "and the hair from your head will not perish" immediately follows. It appears, then, that Luke is quoting a proverb that is not entirely appropriate contextually.[47]

In sum, I do not think that Luke is quoting an actual epic verse in Acts 27:34. In spite of the meter and the other epic features, the diction is simply too prosaic. But he is perhaps striving for an epic flavor here by refashioning a popular aphorism into the shape of a dactylic hexameter verse.

Acts 27:39 τὴν γῆν οὐκ ἐπεγίνωσκον "they did not recognize the land"

When day finally arrives, Paul and his shipmates do not recognize the land (Acts 27:39): Ὅτε δὲ ἡμέρα ἐγένετο, τὴν γῆν οὐκ ἐπεγίνωσκον, κόλπον δέ τινα κατενόουν ἔχοντα αἰγιαλὸν εἰς ὃν ἐβουλεύοντο εἰ δύναιντο ἐξῶσαι τὸ πλοῖον. "When day arrived, they did not recognize the land, but they detected a bay that had a beach upon which they planned, if possible, to drive the ship."

Those familiar with the *Odyssey* will recall Odysseus's arrival at long last, after years of *Sturm und Drang*, to his homeland of Ithaca, having been deposited while still asleep on a beach within a calm harbor by the Phaeacian sailors who had escorted him there. When he awakes, though he has just slept through the night in his own fatherland, he does not recognize it, since he had been away a long time, and since the goddess Athena had spread a mist around it (*Od.* 13.187–90): ὁ δ' ἔγρετο δῖος Ὀδυσσεὺς εὕδων ἐν γαίῃ πατρωΐῃ, οὐδέ μιν ἔγνω, ἤδη δὴν ἀπεών· "God-like Odysseus awoke, having slept in his own fatherland, but he did not recognize it, since he had been away a long time."

The situation in the two scenes is quite similar: the first glimpse of a strange land in the morning by a sailor just arrived from the open sea. And the three words that compose the phrase are almost identical—γαίην + οὐδέ + ἔγνω ≈ γῆν + οὐκ + ἐπεγίνωσκον—though Luke has understandably used their more prosaic forms. Again, the effect of the Homeric echo in Acts is to increase the level of anticipation and tension at this critical moment of the narrative and, in this case, even to introduce a sense of adventure and mystique.

Acts 27:41 ἐπέκειλαν τὴν ναῦν "they ran the ship aground"

We conclude with Luke's use of a phrase that provides the strongest evidence in Acts that he knew Homer's *Odyssey* and was consciously drawing from the epic in his narrative of Paul's sea voyage in Acts 27:1–28:16. The unmistakable epic origin of this phrase renders all the more plausible the proposals of other Homeric resonances already offered above.

---

[47] Incidentally, the occurrence of this aphorism in Luke's gospel is pretty strong evidence—if any were needed—that in Acts 27:34 Luke is placing his own words into Paul's mouth rather than reporting a Pauline speech verbatim. But, of course, I am assuming that this is the case here, just as it is elsewhere in the many speeches of Acts. The view that the speeches in Acts are largely Lucan material has been the scholarly consensus for much of the past century: e.g., H. J. Cadbury, "Speeches in Acts," in *The Beginnings of Christianity*, eds. F. J. Foakes Jackson and K. Lake, 5:402–27; M. Dibelius, *Studies in the Acts of the Apostles*, 26–77, 138–91.

The actual shipwreck is described in Acts 27:40-1. This passage is full of technical nautical terms and phrases, some of which can be found in other ancient literary accounts of seafaring: casting the anchors into the sea, unleashing the crossbars of the rudders, hoisting the foresail to the breeze, holding course for the shore, encountering a crosscurrent, running the ship aground, getting the prow stuck firmly (in the sand), and experiencing the destruction of the stern by the force (of the waves). Among these nautical phrases, however, the antepenultimate one stands out as a distinctly Homeric idiom: ἐπέκειλαν τὴν ναῦν "they ran the ship aground."

The most startling feature of this phrase is the word that Luke uses for "ship"—ναῦς. This is the only occurrence of this word in the entire New Testament. Elsewhere, both in his gospel (8x) and in Acts (19x), Luke always uses the word πλοῖον. All three ships that transport Paul during his voyage from Caesarea to Rome in Luke's account in Acts 27:1–28:16 are called πλοῖα. This very Alexandrian ship that is called a ναῦς here in 27:41 has just been called a πλοῖον eleven times earlier in chapter 27, and it will shortly be called a πλοῖον again (27:44), even though it has been utterly destroyed by the storm. There is surely some purpose in Luke's decision to use ναῦς, the more poetic and literary word for "ship," in this particular idiom.

Almost as startling is Luke's use of the word for "to run aground"—ἐπικέλλω. Like ναῦς, this is the only occurrence of this word, and, in fact, even of any cognates of this word, in the entire New Testament. Other than this single instance in Acts 27:41 this form of the verb occurs in ancient Greek only in poetry and, specifically, in dactylic hexameter verse: Homer's *Odyssey*; Apollonius of Rhodes' *Argonautica*; Numenius's *Halieutikon*; Phanocles' *Erotes*; *Anthologia Graeca* 9.228. Its prose form is ἐποκέλλω (Herodotus, Thucydides, Polybius, etc.).[48] The simplex forms of the verb follow the same pattern as the compound forms, κέλλω being the usual form in poetry, ὀκέλλω in prose.[49] What we have here in Luke's phrase ἐπέκειλαν τὴν ναῦν (Acts 27:41) is a poetic idiom and, in particular, a Homeric idiom.

A Homeric origin for Luke's idiom has been conjectured for over a century. Back in the "good old days," when New Testament scholars were also Classicists and vice versa, those who encountered the phrase ἐπέκειλαν τὴν ναῦν in Acts 27:41 were reminded immediately of the Homeric formulas. The Classicist and New Testament scholar F. Blass, in his edition and commentary on Acts, recalls that the similar expression ἐπικέλλω + ναῦς occurs twice in book nine of Homer's *Odyssey*, notes that the poetic ἐπικέλλω always appears as ἐποκέλλω in prose, observes the sudden shift in Acts 27:41 from the common πλοῖον to the otherwise unattested (in the New Testament) ναῦς,

---

[48] The original reading of Acts 27:41 in Codex Vaticanus, ἐπέκειλαν, has been changed by a "corrector" of the manuscript to the regular prosaic form ἐπώκειλαν. John Chrysostom (Homily 53 on Acts) also quotes the prosaic form ἐπώκειλαν from his text of Acts, and many late manuscripts (*Byzantine Koine*) have made the same "correction." The early manuscripts, however, all read ἐπέκειλαν, and here, as usually elsewhere, *lectio difficilior est potior*.

[49] To speak more technically, Luke has created a unique hybrid form here that is somewhere between poetic and prosaic. He uses the poetic form of the verb, ἐπικέλλω, rather than the prosaic form, ἐποκέλλω, but instead of the sigmatic aorist tense form used in poetry, ἐπέκελσαν, he uses the liquid (i.e., asigmatic) aorist tense form used in prose, ἐπώκειλαν. The outcome is the utterly unique ἐπέκειλαν of Acts 27:41.

110 *The Formal Education of the Author of Luke-Acts*

and therefore suggests that this expression "may have been taken from Homer himself" (*potest hoc ex ipso Hom. desumptum esse*).[50] Commenting on the same verse (along with the reading of Lk. 23:53 preserved in codex Bezae) in a later work on the gospels, Blass declares more confidently: "Must we not accept it for a certainty that Luke, the physician of Antioch, had gone through his Homer?"[51]

Several later commentators on Acts have echoed Blass's evaluation but have not probed any further or ventured any proposals about the origin and nature of Luke's familiarity with Homer: F. J. Foakes Jackson and K. Lake: "Blass's suggestion that there is a conscious reminiscence of Homer in this collocation of two unusual words is very attractive. If Luke was acquainted with Aratus and Epimenides, his knowledge of Homer is easily credible."[52] And more laconically: F. F. Bruce, *The Acts of the Apostles*, 467: "plausibly ascribed to a Homeric reminiscence (cf. *Od.* 9.148, 546)"; E. Haenchen, *The Acts of the Apostles*, 708: "a literary expression (cf. *Od.* 9.546)"; C. K. Barrett, *A Critical and Exegetical Commentary on the Acts of the Apostles*, 2:1213: "Did Luke take it from Homer?"; R. I. Pervo, *Acts: A Commentary*, 666: "an undisputed dash of Homerica."

Recently, some New Testament scholars have relied on the apparent Homeric origin of this expression to draw a closer connection—to propose a greater level of influence—between Homer and Luke. As we have seen, S. M. Praeder acknowledges that there is a conscious linguistic echo of Homer's *Odyssey* in the distinctive phrase ἐπέκειλαν τὴν ναῦν in Acts 27:41, and she uses this as one piece of evidence for her proposal that Homer's *Odyssey* is one among many ancient literary accounts of sea voyages, storms, and shipwrecks that Luke used to varying degrees as models for his account of Paul's sea voyage.[53] D. R. MacDonald properly notes, among a host of less convincing parallels between the accounts of Odysseus's and Paul's sea voyages in the *Odyssey* and Acts, the Homeric origin of the expression ἐπέκειλαν τὴν ναῦν in Acts 27:41.[54] K. L. Cukrowski regards ἐπέκειλαν τὴν ναῦν in Acts 27:41 as a Lucan imitation of Homer, and he uses this as a foundation for drawing further parallels between the experiences and characters of Odysseus and Paul, in particular their endurance in the face of hardship and suffering.[55]

This remarkable phrase ἐπέκειλαν τὴν ναῦν in Acts 27:41 deserves some further consideration. I believe that it is almost certainly drawn from Homer's *Odyssey*, where the combination of the words (ἐπι)κέλλω and ναῦς occurs many times. The compound verb ἐπικέλλω occurs three times, all in passages describing the beaching of a ship (running a ship aground): 9.138 ἐπικέλσαντας μεῖναι χρόνον "having run (the ships—cf. 9.148-9) aground, to stay for awhile"; 9.148 νῆας ἐϋσσέλμους ἐπικέλσαι "to run the well-decked ships aground"; 13.113-14 ἣ μὲν ἔπειτα ἠπείρῳ ἐπέκελσεν "it (the ship) was then run aground on the dry land." The simplex κέλλω occurs five times in the *Odyssey*, again all in passages describing the beaching of a ship (running a ship aground): 9.149

---

[50] F. Blass, *Acta apostolorum*, 282.
[51] F. Blass, *Philology of the Gospels* (London: Macmillan and Company, 1898), 186.
[52] F. J. Foakes Jackson and K. Lake, eds., *The Beginnings of Christianity*, 4:339.
[53] S. M. Praeder, "Acts 27:1–28:16: Sea Voyages," 701.
[54] D. R. MacDonald, "The Shipwrecks," 94–5.
[55] K. L. Cukrowski, "Paul as Odysseus," 24–5.

κελσάσησι δὲ νηυσί "when the ships had been run aground"; 9.546 = 12.5 ≈ 11.20 νῆα μὲν ἔνθ' ἐλθόντες ἐκέλσαμεν ἐν ψαμάθοισιν "having arrived there we ran the ship aground upon the sand"; 10.511 νῆα μὲν αὐτοῦ κέλσαι "run the ship aground there."

Further, I suspect that Luke may have drawn the phrase specifically from one of the two scenes of sea voyages in the *Odyssey* that, as we have seen, have resonated elsewhere in Acts 27:1–28:16: Odysseus's arrival by ship at the land of the Cyclopes or his arrival by ship home in Ithaca. That is to say, it seems plausible to me that Luke is not simply incorporating broadly used epic diction here to create a general epic resonance but that he is actually invoking one of the more memorable scenes from the *Odyssey*. We noted above that the phrase "they prayed for day to arrive" (ηὔχοντο ἡμέραν γενέσθαι) in Acts 27:29 of the sailors waiting off the coast of the island of Malta sounds like a resonance of the phrase "we awaited the divine dawn" (ἐμείναμεν Ἠῶ δῖαν) in *Odyssey* 9.151 of Odysseus's crew when they arrive on the island off the coast of the land of the Cyclopes. This same Odyssean scene may also be the source of Luke's epic phrase ἐπέκειλαν τὴν ναῦν "they ran the ship aground" in Acts 27:41 (*Od.* 9.146–51):

> ἔνθ' οὔ τις τὴν νῆσον ἐσέδρακεν ὀφθαλμοῖσιν,
> οὔτ' οὖν κύματα μακρὰ κυλινδόμενα προτὶ χέρσον
> εἰσίδομεν, πρὶν νῆας ἐϋσσέλμους ἐπικέλσαι.
> κελσάσησι δὲ νηυσὶ καθείλομεν ἱστία πάντα,
> ἐκ δὲ καὶ αὐτοὶ βῆμεν ἐπὶ ῥηγμῖνι θαλάσσης·
> ἔνθα δ' ἀποβρίξαντες ἐμείναμεν Ἠῶ δῖαν.

> Then no one caught sight of the island with his eyes,
> nor did we see the long waves crashing against the dry land,
> before we ran the well-decked ships aground.
> And when the ships had been run aground, we took down all the sails,
> and we ourselves disembarked upon the breakers of the sea.
> And then, having fallen asleep, we awaited the divine dawn.

We also noted above that the phrase "they did not recognize the land" (τὴν γῆν οὐκ ἐπεγίνωσκον) in Acts 27:39 of the sailors when they finally see the coast of the island of Malta sounds like a resonance of the verse "having slept in his native land, not even so did he recognize it" (εὕδων ἐν γαίῃ πατρωΐῃ, οὐδέ μιν ἔγνω) in *Odyssey* 13.188 of Odysseus when he finally arrives home to the island of Ithaca. This scene too may be the source of Luke's epic phrase ἐπέκειλαν τὴν ναῦν "they ran the ship aground" in Acts 27:41 (*Od.* 13.113–16):

> ἔνθ' οἵ γ' εἰσέλασαν, πρὶν εἰδότες. ἡ μὲν ἔπειτα
> ἠπείρῳ ἐπέκελσεν ὅσον τ' ἐπὶ ἥμισυ πάσης,
> σπερχομένη· τοῖον γὰρ ἐπείγετο χέρσ' ἐρετάων.
> οἱ δ' ἐκ νηὸς βάντες ἐϋζύγου ἤπειρόνδε

> There they [Phaeacians] drove it [ship], before they knew it, and it [ship]
> was then run aground on the dry land, half of her whole length,
> as it ran in, so fast was it pushed by the hands of the rowers.
> And they disembarked the well-fitted ship onto dry land

112   *The Formal Education of the Author of Luke-Acts*

Yet it may be prudent to observe that a combination of three verses that describes the arrival of Odysseus's ship back from Hades to the island of Aiaia in *Odyssey* 12.5–7 also contains two of the motifs marshaled above: "running the ship aground" and "waiting for dawn to arrive":

νῆα μὲν ἔνθ' ἐλθόντες ἐκέλσαμεν ἐν ψαμάθοισιν,
ἐκ δὲ καὶ αὐτοὶ βῆμεν ἐπὶ ῥηγμῖνι θαλάσσης·
ἔνθα δ' ἀποβρίξαντες ἐμείναμεν Ἠῶ δῖαν.

Having arrived there we ran the ship aground upon the sand,
and we ourselves disembarked upon the breakers of the sea.
And then, having fallen asleep, we awaited the divine dawn.

This is not an important or memorable arrival scene in the *Odyssey*, the passage itself being very brief and perfunctory and the language completely formulaic: the first verse appears verbatim in *Odyssey* 9.546, the latter two verses appear verbatim in *Odyssey* 9.150–1, and the shorter phrases that compose the three-verse formula appear repeatedly throughout the *Iliad* and *Odyssey*. This is a precautionary reminder for us that it may have been Luke's familiarity with Homeric diction generally rather than his memory of a particular Homeric passage that resulted in his describing Paul's crew "waiting for day to arrive" or "running the ship aground" or "not recognizing the land" in the same scene, just as it may have been Luke's familiarity with Homeric themes generally rather than his memory of a particular Homeric episode that resulted in his describing Paul's crew "suffering a Cretan storm" or Paul "giving a speech on a storm-tossed ship."

Conclusion

In order to detect and appreciate the Homeric resonances in Luke's account of Paul's sea voyage and shipwreck one may conduct a thorough analysis, as we have done above, of the diction, idioms, and themes of the narrative. Or, for a more impressionistic approach, one may simply read Acts 27:1–28:16 side by side with one of the several Odyssean accounts of storms at sea (e.g., 9.62–84) and arrivals at a safe harbor (e.g., 9.136–51). This is, of course, best done in ancient Greek. I first detected and appreciated the Homeric resonances impressionistically: that is to say, I did not turn to commentaries, lexica, digital databases, and so forth to track down the Homeric resonances; I simply read the text of Acts with the text of Homer residing in my mind as a template. My experience reading Acts was probably not unlike the experience of many of Luke's ancient readers (and listeners). It is a little embarrassing to confess that even after forty years of devoting my life to the study of Greek literature I have obtained a proficiency in the language that is probably no greater, in some respects, than that of ancient students who completed the secondary level of the Hellenistic educational curriculum (ἐγκύκλιος παιδεία/*enkyklios paideia*). This would include the author of Acts and no doubt many of his contemporary readers (and listeners). In other words, given my academic background, I am probably as good an audience as any, so far as detecting and appreciating what Luke was trying to achieve by embellishing his narrative with Homeric resonance.

The Homeric resonances in Luke's account of Paul's sea voyage and shipwreck in Acts 27:1–28:16 had several effects on me, and I wonder if these effects were not the same for Luke's ancient audience. In general, as we have observed above, they embellish the entire narrative with a literary flourish. More specifically, again as we have observed above, they raise the level of tension and anticipation at critical moments of the narrative. But, even more specifically, they invite a comparison to be made between the central characters of Odysseus and Paul. As I was reading about Paul's experiences on his sea voyage, the specter of Odysseus was ever on my mind: the obstacles to Paul's successful sea voyage reminded me of the many obstacles to the return home of the "much-suffering" Odysseus; Paul's almost heroic intellectual prowess called to my mind the "much-devising" Odysseus; Paul's close connection to the divine caused me to equate him with the "god-like" Odysseus. In short, Paul, like, Odysseus, was πολύτλας "much-suffering," πολύμητις "much-devising," and δῖος "god-like."[56]

Odysseus is not a stereotypical epic hero. He is not distinctive for his physique, like Ajax, nor for his ruling power, like Agamemnon, nor for his martial prowess, like Achilles. Rather, he is a suffering hero who overcomes obstacles through his cunning, patience, and obstinacy. To probe the essence of Odysseus's heroic character, one can do no better than to catalogue the ornamental epithets that are so often attached to his name.

The most common epithets of Odysseus in Homer can be grouped into three categories.[57] The first category includes those epithets that honor his god-like qualities—that he is born from the gods, is favored by the gods, and is, in fact, very much like the gods: δῖος Ὀδυσσεύς (104x) "god-like," Ὀδυσσῆος θείοιο (31x) "godly," διογενὴς Ὀδυσσεύς (26x) "Zeus-born," ἀντιθέῳ Ὀδυσῆϊ (10x) "god-rivaling," Ὀδυσῆα Διΐ φίλον (3x) "dear to Zeus," θεοῖσ' ἐναλίγκιον "resembling the gods" (2x). Odysseus is distinguished for his closeness to the gods—especially to Athena—who frequently protect him from harm and advise him at critical moments, sometimes directly, other times through omens and dreams. Odysseus sometimes even plays the role of a god in

---

[56] I am focusing here on the characterization of Odysseus in Homer's *Odyssey*, not on his characterization during the many hundreds of years between Homer and Luke. Odysseus's reputation deteriorates in post-Homeric literature, both Greek (the Epic Cycle, Pindar, the tragedies of Sophocles and Euripides, etc.) and Latin (Vergil's *Aeneid*, Ovid's *Metamorphoses*, etc.), in which aspersions are cast on his character for feigning insanity in order to avoid participation in the expedition against Troy, lying to Clytemnestra that her daughter Iphigenia is to be married to Achilles, falsely accusing Palamedes of betrayal, deceiving Philoctetes to obtain his bow, usurping Ajax's rightful claim to Achilles' armor, stealing the Palladium from Troy, and abandoning his comrade Achemenides in the land of the Cyclopes on his return home. This deteriorating reputation might cause someone to wonder why Luke would have chosen Odysseus as a model for his hero, but Luke's decision is completely understandable if one focuses on his indebtedness specifically to the Odysseus of Homer.

[57] There are other epithets attached to Odysseus, of course, some particular to him, such as Λαερτιάδης Ὀδυσσεύς (34x) "son of Laertes" and Ὀδυσεὺς Ἰθακήσιος (2x) "Ithacan," but most of a more generic nature (i.e., ones that are readily attached to other characters as well): Ὀδυσῆα δαΐφρονα (9x) "war-minded," Ὀδυσῆος ἀμύμονος (9x) "blameless," Ὀδυσῆα μεγαλήτορα (8x) "great-hearted," πτολίπορθος Ὀδυσσεύς (7x) "city-sacker," φαίδιμ' Ὀδυσσεῦ (5x) "illustrious," πολύαιν' Ὀδυσεῦ (4x) "much-praised," ἐσθλὸς Ὀδυσσεύς (3x) "noble," Ὀδυσῆος κυδαλίμοιο (3x) "glorious," Ὀδυσεὺς δουρὶ κλυτός (3x) "famous for his spear," Ὀδυσεὺς δουρικλυτός (2x) "spear-famed."

114   *The Formal Education of the Author of Luke-Acts*

a "theoxeny" (the appearance of a god disguised as a stranger): the Phaeacians in Scheria honor him as a god (5.36; 19.280; 23.339), Telemachus initially thinks that he may be a god (16.178-9), and the suitors in Ithaca fear that he may be a god, come down from heaven, who has likened himself to a wandering stranger (17.484-7).

The second category includes those epithets that celebrate Odysseus's wisdom and cleverness: πολύμητις Ὀδυσσεύς (86) "of many devices," πολυμήχαν' Ὀδυσσεῦ (19x) "of many contrivances," Ὀδυσῆα ποικιλομήτην (6x) "of various plans," Ὀδυσῆα πολύφρονα (5x) "of many thoughts," Ὀδυσῆα Διὶ μῆτιν ἀτάλαντον (4x) "equal to Zeus in counsel," Ὀδυσσεὺς πολύτροπος (2x) "of many turns." The opening verse of the *Odyssey* refers to Odysseus as πολύτροπος, which refers literally to the "many turns" of his journey home but figuratively to the "many turns" of his mind. Odysseus is known for his μῆτις "wisdom," μήδεα "plans," and δόλοι "stratagems." Even before Odysseus is introduced in the *Odyssey*, Helen and Menelaus regale Telemachus with stories about his father's resourcefulness during two missions into Troy (4.240-59, 266-89). Odysseus introduces himself to the Phaeacians as one who is famous for his δόλοι "stratagems" (9.19-20). The many "stratagems" of Odysseus mentioned in the *Odyssey* include: his scheme to penetrate the walls of Troy with the wooden horse (8.492-520); his verbal trick on the Cyclops regarding his name (9.364-7); his ploy to make a comrade give up his cloak (14.495-502); his elaborate plot to overcome the suitors (16.267-307); his ruse to gain possession of his bow (19.582-7). Odysseus's intellectual prowess is complemented by a "hands-on" practical cleverness: e.g., he serves as a skilled carpenter in building his own raft to sail from Calypso's island (5.234-61).

The third category includes those epithets that pertain to Odysseus's suffering and to his endurance in the face of suffering: πολύτλας Ὀδυσσεύς (41x) "much-suffering," Ὀδυσσῆος ταλασίφρονος (12x) "of enduring mind," τλήμων Ὀδυσεὺς (2x) "enduring." The very name of Odysseus is folk-etymologized in the *Odyssey* as a "man of grief" (1.55 ὀδύρομαι), and, of course, the narrative illustrates time and again his role as a suffering hero: ten years of war and ten more years of wandering, having to overcome every conceivable obstacle to his return home: hostile gods, monsters, and humans; captivity; temptations; hunger, cold, and nakedness; and, especially, violent storms and shipwrecks.

If one allows these images of Odysseus to hover in the background while reading the narrative of Acts, one cannot help but be struck by how these three categories of Odyssean epithets—"god-like," "much-devising," and "much-suffering" can be attached equally well to the character of Paul.

Paul as "god-like"—Paul is described as having a distinctive relationship with God in Acts. The account of God appearing and speaking to him directly on the road to Damascus is so central to the narrative of Acts that it is related three times (9:1-9; 22:6-11; 26:12-18). Concurrent with this central event, God reveals to Ananias that Paul has been handpicked by God to know God's will and to hear God's voice (9:15; 22:14-15; cf. 26:16-18). As the narrative of Acts unfolds, then, we are not surprised to witness God appearing frequently to Paul in dreams and visions: in Troas (16:9), Corinth (18:9-10), and Jerusalem (22:17-21; 23:11). In the scene of sea voyage and shipwreck under consideration here, God's special favor toward Paul is expressed through a heavenly messenger, who appears in the midst of the storm and tells him not to fear, for he will

Luke and Homer   115

survive along with his companions (27:23-5). As we have observed, this scene appears to echo a similar divine intervention in a time of like crisis in the *Odyssey*: after Odysseus's speech aboard his storm-tossed raft, he too is visited by a divinity, the sea-goddess Ino, who tells him not to fear, since it is not his fate to perish (5.333–550).

Paul's "god-like" character is further manifested in the special powers that God grants to him throughout the narrative of Acts: miraculous healing, casting out of demons, escape from prison, and other signs and wonders. Paul is actually identified as a god twice in Acts: when he heals a crippled man in the town of Lystra, the townspeople suspect that he is the god Hermes, who has likened himself to a mortal and come down to earth, and they try to worship and sacrifice to him (Acts 14:11-13);[58] when he suffers no ill effects from a viper's bite on the island of Malta, the islanders begin to believe that he is a god (Acts 28:3-6). As we have observed above, these scenes echo the recurring theme of "theoxeny" found also in the *Odyssey*, where Odysseus is several times suspected by his hosts of being a god.

Paul as "much-devising"—Paul's cleverness of thought and speech is highlighted throughout the narrative of Acts: he confounds the Jews with his preaching ability in Damascus (9:22); he taunts the Roman officials who had illegally beaten and imprisoned him in Philippi (16:37-9); he outmaneuvers the Epicurean and Stoic philosophers in Athens by addressing them in their own terms (17:22-31); he cleverly splits the opposition against him by announcing that he is a Pharisee and is being judged for his belief in a resurrection (22:6-10); he matches wits with the professional orator Tertullus in his defense before Felix (24:1-24); he shrewdly appeals to Caesar in his defense before Festus (25:8-12); he presents an excellent and effective speech, tailored to his audience, in his defense before Herod Agrippa (26:1-32). In the scene of sea voyage and shipwreck under consideration here, he offers a practical and timely speech to the crew on the storm-tossed ship at a most critical moment (27:33-4). In short, Luke has gifted Paul with quick-wittedness and oratorical prowess in Acts that match those of Odysseus in Homer's epics.[59] The wise old man Phoenix once reminded Achilles what it means to be a true hero: "to be both a speaker of words and a doer of deeds" (*Il.* 9.443). Odysseus is, to be sure, a "doer of deeds," but in both the *Iliad* and *Odyssey* he holds a reputation as a "speaker of words" *par excellence* (e.g., *Il.* 3.221-4; *Od.* 13.291–302).

Paul's intellectual prowess in Acts is complemented by his practical knowledge: the τέχνη "craft" by which he supports himself while in Corinth is described as σκηνοποιός "tent-maker" or "leather-worker" (18:3); he reminds the Ephesians that there too he worked with his hands to support himself and his companions (20:34). In the scene of sea voyage and shipwreck Paul is depicted as a Renaissance man of sorts: he proves himself more knowledgeable about sailing than the ship's pilot and captain (27:10-11,

---

[58] It may not be insignificant that Odysseus was, according to the mythic tradition, the great-grandson of the god Hermes—through his maternal grandfather Autolycus (*Od.* 19.392–466; Hesiod fr. 64, and, later, in Apollodorus, Ovid, Hyginus, and Pausanias).

[59] This is all the more remarkable in view of Paul's own denial that he is a skillful public speaker in his letter to the Corinthians (2 Cor. 10:10-11; 11:6). Yet one may reasonably counter that by using the rhetorical device of denying his ability to speak in public, Paul is actually asserting that very ability! "Unaccustomed to public speaking as I am ... " is a rhetorical preamble as old as Socrates (Plato, *Apol.* 17a–18a).

116   *The Formal Education of the Author of Luke-Acts*

21), more alert to a treacherous plot of the sailors than the centurion or the soldiers (27:30-32), and more effective at calming the crew in the midst of the storm than their nominal leaders (27:21-6, 33-6), and when they do finally overcome the storm and land on the island of Malta Paul immediately makes himself useful by gathering firewood to fight off the rain and cold (28:1-3). These are all activities with which "much-devising" Odysseus would have been very much at home.

Paul as "much-suffering"—Shortly after Paul is introduced in Acts, God is described revealing to him how many things he will have "to suffer" ($\pi\alpha\theta\epsilon\tilde{\iota}\nu$ 9:16). And, indeed, Paul's suffering becomes a leitmotif in the subsequent narrative: he constantly encounters hostile audiences (13:45, 50; 14:2; 16:22; 17:5-9, 13, 18-19, 32; 18:5-6; 19:9, 30; 22:22-3; 23:1-2); he is subjected to physical abuse, suffering beatings (16:23; 21:32; 23:2), stoning (14:19), and imprisonment (16:23-34; 20:23; 21:33–23:30; 23:35–26:32; 28:16-31); there are even several attempts on his life—all of which he escapes (9:23-5, 29; 14:5, 19; 20:3, 19; 21:4, 10-14, 27-36; 23:12-30; 25:2-3; 27:42-4). Paul's suffering in the narrative of the sea voyage includes having to endure a violent storm (27:13-20), hunger (27:21, 33), a shipwreck (27:39-44), and yet another plot to kill him—along with the rest of the prisoners (27:42-4). Odysseus too, as we have seen, is the epitome of a suffering hero, and much of the suffering that he endures echoes that of Paul during his sea voyage: captivity, hunger, cold, nakedness, storms, shipwrecks, having to swim in the open sea, and the potential threat of hostile islanders.

I conclude with a reflective thought experiment: first, let us try to keep in mind Luke's depiction of the character of Paul in Acts while reading the proem of the *Odyssey*:

> Sing to me, Muse, about the man of many turns, who wandered much,
> when he had sacked the holy citadel of Troy.
> He saw the cities of many men, and he knew their minds,
> and he suffered many woes in his heart upon the sea,
> striving for his own life and the return of his companions.

Second, conversely, let us try to keep in mind Homer's depiction of the character of Odysseus in the *Odyssey* while reading about Paul's suffering in Acts, much of which is well summarized in Paul's own words in his letter to the Corinthians (2 Cor. 11:23-7) (*NIV*):

> I have worked much harder, been in prison more frequently, been flogged more severely, and been exposed to death again and again. Five times I received from the Jews the forty lashes minus one. Three times I was beaten with rods, once I was pelted with stones, three times I was shipwrecked, I spent a night and a day in the open sea, I have been constantly on the move. I have been in danger from rivers, in danger from bandits, in danger from my fellow Jews, in danger from gentiles; in danger in the city, in danger in the country, in danger at sea; and in danger from false believers. I have labored and toiled and have often gone without sleep; I have known hunger and thirst and have often gone without food; I have been cold and naked.

The overall effect of Homeric resonance in Acts, then, in addition to embellishing the narrative with a literary flourish, and beyond raising the level of tension at critical moments of the narrative, is to draw a comparison between the central characters of Odysseus and Paul. The presence of a Homeric hero hovering in the background serves to elevate Paul's stature as a hero. But Luke's use as a model here of a very different kind of epic hero, Odysseus, serves to highlight Paul's suffering as well as his heroism. Luke is depicting Paul, just as Homer had depicted Odysseus, as a suffering hero.

6

Luke and Aesop

Aesop is a very nebulous figure, and the hundreds of fables attributed to him that survive to this day have their origins in various places and periods. The earliest Aesopic fables are found embedded in the texts of some of the Greek poets, such as Hesiod, Archilochus, Semonides, Aeschylus, Sophocles, and Aristophanes, as well as in the narratives of Classical prose writers, such as Herodotus, Xenophon, Plato, and Aristotle. The fourth- to third-century BCE Athenian orator Demetrius of Phalerum was apparently the first to gather a collection of Aesopic fables in prose form, and though his work did not survive the medieval period his collection was probably the source for the first-century CE Latin poet Phaedrus, who produced five books of Aesopic fables in a Latin iambic meter called the senarius, and for the first- or second-century CE Greek poet Babrius, who produced two books of Aesopic fables in an offshoot of the Greek iambic meter called the choliambic. Aesopic fables continued to be referenced in Greek literature of the Hellenistic and Roman Imperial periods, both in poetry, such as in the poems from various periods that compose the Greek Anthology, and in prose, such as in the works of Diodorus Siculus, Plutarch, Lucian, Achilles Tatius, and Athenaeus. Throughout the medieval period Aesopic fables were copied and recopied, translated, reshaped into various metrical forms, adapted to new contexts, and weighed down with moralizing introductions (*promythia*) and summaries (*epimythia*), and these types of adaptations have continued even to this day. Great care needs to be taken, then, when attributing an Aesopic fable, or a specific verse or phrase of a fable, to a particular place of origin or period of time.[1]

---

[1] For an exhaustive collection of Aesopic fables embedded in Archaic, Classical, and Hellenistic Greek literature, see G.-J. van Dijk, *AINOI, ΛOΓOI, MYΘOI: Fables in Archaic, Classical, and Hellenistic Greek Literature* (Leiden: Brill, 1997), and F. R. Adrados, *History of the Graeco-Latin Fable: Volume One: Introduction and From the Origins to the Hellenistic Age* (Leiden: Brill, 1999). For a reconstruction of the prose collection of Demetrius of Phalerum, see B. E. Perry, "Demetrius of Phalerum and the Aesopic Fables," *Transactions and Proceedings of the American Philological Association* 93 (1962): 287–346. For a survey of the transmission of Aesopica, including in Babrius and Phaedrus, see B. E. Perry, *Babrius and Phaedrus* (Cambridge: Harvard University Press, 1965), xi–cii. For a critical edition of Phaedrus, see A. Guaglianone, *Phaedri Augusti Liberti Liber Fabularum* (Turin: Paravia, 1969). For a critical edition of Babrius, see M. J. Luzzatto and A. La Penna, *Babrii Mythiambi Aesopei* (Leipzig: Teubner, 1986). For the state of the collection during the Medieval and Byzantine periods, see F. R. Adrados, *History of the Graeco-Latin Fable: Volume Two: The Fable during the Roman Empire and in the Middle Ages* (Leiden: Brill, 2000). For a survey of the use of Aesop's fables in the Roman and Medieval educational systems, see B. F. Fisher, *A History of the Use of Aesop's Fables as a School Text from the Classical Era through the Nineteenth Century* (Bloomington: Indiana University Dissertation, 1987), 6–163. For some well-selected and annotated bibliography on all matters of Aesopica, see N. Holzberg, *The Ancient Fable* (Bloomington: Indiana University Press, 2002).

120 The Formal Education of the Author of Luke-Acts

The use of Aesop in the ancient educational curriculum, the ἐγκύκλιος παιδεία/*enkyklios paideia*, is of particular interest to us since, as we have observed, someone who was as proficient in the Greek language as the author of the Gospel of Luke and the Acts of the Apostles must have had the experience of a formal Greek education, at least through the primary and secondary levels. Aesopic fables were an important component of this curriculum at the primary level, and even the later *progymnasmata*, the graded series of exercises for teaching prose composition and elementary rhetoric at the secondary level, had as their simplest exercises the *mythoi*, of which the fables of Aesop were standard. The primary evidence for the centrality of Aesopic fables in the educational curriculum is substantial. The first-century CE rhetorician Quintilian, who prescribes the training of an aspiring orator from infancy onward in his long treatise titled *Institutio Oratoria*, suggests that a student of rhetoric should at an early stage study Aesop's fables, learning to paraphrase the verse forms in simple prose, analyzing each verse, giving its meaning in a different language, and then proceeding to a freer paraphrase in which the student abridges or embellishes the original (1.9.1–3). The second- to third-century CE sophist Philostratus records that the first-century CE philosopher Apollonius of Tyana recommended for the edification of children the tales of Aesop rather than those of the poets (*Vit. Apoll.* 5.14–15), since Aesop's falsehoods are explicit rather than deceptive and since they are concluded with a moral lesson. Aelius Theon, the first-century CE rhetorician from Alexandria in Egypt who offers the earliest surviving specimen of *progymnasmata*, quotes, refers to, or mentions Aesop six times. The progymnastic exercises of "Hermogenes" (second century CE?), Aphthonius (fourth century CE), and Nicolaus (fifth century CE) mention Aesop an additional seven times. From the Greek papyri of the period under consideration (100 BCE–200 CE), excavated from the sands of Egypt, there have survived nine manuscripts that include Aesop, two of them school texts, as well as three manuscripts that include Babrius, two of them school texts. Also, fourteen fables of Babrius have been found, most in meter but some in prose, badly written and with many errors, on some third-century CE wax tablets belonging to a young student's copy book.[2]

As a measure of the familiarity of the general reading public with Aesopic fables and proverbs during this period, we may simply observe that the philosopher and biographer Plutarch, a contemporary of Luke, quotes, refers to, or mentions Aesop fifty times in his various works. However, the popularity of Aesop in antiquity was not an exclusively pagan phenomenon; the Aesopic tradition had crept deeply into the Jewish and Christian milieu as well. As we shall see, the apocryphal work Sirach (also known as Ecclesiasticus), which was transmitted through the Greek Septuagint, uses a

---

[2] These are the so-called *Tabulae ceratae graecae Assendelftianae*, published by D. C. Hesseling, "On Waxen Tablets with Fables of Babrius," 293–314, which were acquired at Palmyra in Syria in 1881 and are now housed in the library at Leiden University. On the common use of Aesop's (and Babrius's) fables at the primary level of the ancient educational curriculum, see H.-I. Marrou, *A History of Education*, 160–4. R. Cribiore, *Gymnastics of the Mind*, 137–43, 192–201, observes that no prose was read in the primary and secondary schools except for fables, such as those of Aesop and Babrius, and gnomic works of Isocrates (e.g., *Demon., Nic.*). On the more general use in the literature of the period of maxims and morals, including Aesopic fables, see T. Morgan, *Literate Education*, 120–51.

metaphor of a clay pot and a metal cauldron (13.2) that appears to be drawn from Aesop's fable "Clay and Bronze Pots" (Chambry 355, Perry 378).[3] The Coptic Gospel of Thomas places a proverb in the mouth of Jesus (102) that appears to be drawn from Aesop's fable "Dog in the Manger" (Perry 74). The early Christian Church Father Clement of Alexandria mentions Aesop by name and paraphrases an Aesopic proverb in his explanation of why Jews refuse to eat swine (*Strom.* 7.6.33.3). According to the Babylonian Talmud (b. B. Qam. 60b) the Rabbi Itzhak Nafha once told a tale that is an almost verbatim translation of the widely known Aesopic fable "The Middle-Aged Man and his Two Mistresses" (Halm 56, Chambry 52, Hausrath 31, Perry 31; cf. Babrius 22, Phaedrus 2.2).

Some general similarities between the lives, teachings, and deaths of Aesop and Jesus have not escaped the notice of both Classicists and New Testament scholars. These tend to fall into two main categories: usually, and traditionally, a comparison of Aesop's fables with Jesus's parables as a genre, both being short, moralizing stories, rooted in oral tradition, that draw lessons from the natural world about human experience;[4] and, less frequently, and more recently, a comparison of the trajectory of Aesop's life in the novelistic *Life of Aesop* with that of Jesus's life as recorded in the gospels, both traditions portraying a righteous sage, acting as a representative of a god, who speaks truth to power in the form of stories and anecdotes, is unjustly brought to trial, is taken forcefully out of the city, and is executed, thus suffering the fate of a ritual scapegoat.[5]

---

[3] I refer in this chapter to the following editions of Aesopica: K. Halm, *Fabulae Aesopicae Collectae* (Leipzig: Teubner, 1852); E. Chambry, *Aesopi Fabulae* (Paris: Société d'Édition 'Les Belles Lettres,' 1925 (volume one), 1926 (volume two)); A. Hausrath, *Corpus Fabularum Aesopicarum* (Leipzig: Teubner, 1940); B. E. Perry, *Aesopica* (Urbana: University of Illinois Press, 1952). For a recent English translation of 600 Aesopic fables, collected from various Greek and Latin sources and arranged topically, see L. Gibbs, *Aesop's Fables* (Oxford: Oxford University Press, 2002).

[4] On the generic similarities between Aesop's fables and Jesus's parables, see, for example, A. Jülicher, *Die Gleichnisreden Jesu*, vol. 1, 2nd ed. (Tübingen: Mohr Siebeck, 1899), 94–115; R. Dithmar, ed., *Fabeln, Parabeln und Gleichnisse: Beispiele didaktischer Literatur* (Munich: Deutscher Taschenbuch-Verlag, 1970); M. A. Beavis, "Parable and Fable," *Catholic Biblical Quarterly* 52 (1990): 473–98; F. Vouga, "Die Parabeln Jesu und die Fabeln Äsops: Ein Beitrag zur Gleichnisforschung und zur Problematik der Literarisierung der Erzählungen der Jesus-Tradition," *Wort und Dienst* 26 (2001): 149–64.

[5] For some literary and thematic comparisons between the *Life of Aesop* and the gospels generally, see S. Salomone, "Esopo 'Capro espiatorio,'" in *Il Capro espiatorio: Mito, Religione, Storia*, ed. S. Isetta (Genova: Tilgher, 2007), 49–64; M. Andreassi, "The *Life of Aesop* and the Gospels: Literary Motifs and Narrative Mechanisms," in *Holy Men and Charlatans in the Ancient Novel*, eds. S. Panayotakis, G. L. Schmeling, and M. Paschalis (Eelde: Barkhuis Publishing, 2015), 151–66. For some literary, thematic, structural, and generic comparisons between the *Life of Aesop* and Mark's gospel specifically, see W. Shiner, "Creating Plot in Episodic Narratives: The Life of Aesop and the Gospel of Mark," in *Ancient Fiction and Early Christian Narrative*, eds. R. F. Hock, J. B. Chance, and J. Perkins (Atlanta: Scholars Press, 1998), 155–76; R. I. Pervo, "A Nihilist Fabula: Introducing the *Life of Aesop*," in *Ancient Fiction and Early Christian Narrative*, eds. R. F. Hock, J. B. Chance, and J. Perkins (Atlanta: Scholars Press, 1998), 77–120; S. S. Elliott, "Witless in your Own Cause: Divine Plots and Fractured Characters in the *Life of Aesop* and the Gospel of Mark," *Religion & Theology* 12 (2005): 397–418; D. F. Watson, "The *Life of Aesop* and the Gospel of Mark: Two Ancient Approaches to Elite Values," *Journal of Biblical Literature* 129 (2010): 699–716; L. M. Wills, *The Quest of the Historical Gospel: Mark, John, and the Origins of the Gospel Genre* (London: Routledge, 1997), 23–50, who includes John along with Mark in his comparison with the *Life of Aesop*; L. M. Wills, "The Aesop Tradition," in *The Historical Jesus in Context*, eds. A.-J. Levine, D. C. Allison, and J. D. Crossan (Princeton: Princeton University Press, 2006), 222–37, who, again, includes John along with Mark in his comparison.

122   *The Formal Education of the Author of Luke-Acts*

In the former category all four gospels have been invoked, while in the latter category most attention has been focused on the Gospel of Mark. I propose in what follows to take a close look at the Gospel of Luke, which, in its presentation of Jesus's life, teaching, and death, includes some very close similarities, not just in content but also in language, both to the trajectory of the life of Aesop and also to Aesop's teaching in his fables. There seems nothing more natural than that Luke, in crafting his own version of the gospel from his inherited sources, would have drawn from the fables and proverbs of Aesop, as well as from other *mythoi*, that were so central to his own educational training.

The Rejection of Jesus in Nazareth and Aesop in Delphi (Lk. 4:14-30)

The account of the rejection of Jesus in his hometown of Nazareth appears in all three synoptic gospels: Mark 6:1-6; Matthew 13:53-8; Luke 4:14-30. In all three accounts of the episode Jesus goes to Nazareth and teaches there in the synagogue on the Sabbath. Jesus's teaching astonishes his fellow townspeople, since they recognize him as the son of Joseph and Mary, and they take offense at him. Jesus then responds with an aphorism that a prophet is not honored in his own country and among his own people, and he does not perform great deeds there, as he has elsewhere.

Luke's account is almost three times longer than Mark's and Matthew's, however, and the material that appears uniquely in Luke includes some very puzzling features. First, the episode is placed very early in Luke's account, at the beginning of Jesus's ministry, while in Matthew and Mark the episode appears later in Jesus's ministry, after he has taught and performed great deeds around the Sea of Galilee, and especially in the city of Capernaum. In Luke's account, Jesus suspects that his audience is expecting him to perform in his hometown the kinds of deeds that he had performed in Capernaum. This produces a chronological inconcinnity, for according to Luke's account Jesus has not yet been to Capernaum.

Second, Luke alone offers an account of the content of Jesus's teaching. In an interpretation of Isaiah's prophecy about the arrival of a prophet who will come to the aid of those who suffer (Isa. 61:1-2), Jesus claims that he himself is that prophet and that his own work is the fulfillment of that prophecy. Jesus is portrayed as thinking quite highly of himself, and his audience is initially impressed by the words that flow from his mouth, but they also seem rather put off, given his humble origins: "Is this not Joseph's son?"

Third, Luke alone has Jesus, in response to the townspeople's disbelief, tell stories about how Elijah and Elisha chose to perform great deeds among gentiles in foreign lands rather than among Jews their own homeland of Israel. The townspeople of Nazareth perceive the intended offensiveness of the analogy, i.e., that likewise Jesus chooses not to perform great deeds in his hometown, and they are filled with anger at Jesus. In Matthew and Mark, the people are simply offended that a local boy of humble parentage is being so presumptuous. Their lack of faith results in Jesus's refusal/inability to do great deeds in Nazareth. Luke reverses the direction of causality: the people are gravely offended because Jesus refuses to do great deeds in Nazareth and because he equates his reluctance to that of the prophets Elijah and Elisha.

Finally, Luke alone has the townspeople become so angry at Jesus's words that they stand up, cast him out of the city, and lead him to the brow of the mountain upon which the city is built to throw him down headlong. As it turns out, Jesus simply passes through their midst and goes about his business. This addendum to the story is unexpected, remarkable, and indeed, most puzzling. Luke's description of the event produces a geographical inconcinnity: Nazareth is not built upon a mountain. Moreover, some of the language that Luke uses here is foreign to the language of the New Testament: ὀφρῦς "brow" occurs only here in the New Testament (it is a common word in Classical Greek, including in the metaphorical expression "brow of a mountain/cliff/bank, etc."); κατακρημνίζω "to throw down from a precipice" occurs only here in the New Testament (it too is a common word in Classical Greek).[6] Also, the extremely understated description of the escape of Jesus from their hands is a strange and unique feature.

Now, the first of these four puzzling Lucan features is simply a result of Luke deciding to move an episode in the life of Jesus inherited from his sources back much earlier in his gospel than it appears in Matthew and Mark, at the beginning of Jesus's ministry, perhaps for reasons of emphasis. For Luke the advantage of placing a story of such high programmatic value for the entire gospel, anticipating right at the beginning of his account of Jesus's ministry the rejection by his own people and the crucifixion that will serve as a culmination of that very ministry, must have outweighed the chronological problem that it presented. The three other puzzling features, however, can best be accounted for, I think, by appreciating that hovering in the background of Luke's account, and coloring his narrative, is the well-known story of the life, teaching, and death of antiquity's most famous fabulist Aesop.

Others have noticed that the story in the gospels of the life, trial, and execution of Jesus follows the pattern of the traditional ancient Greek tale of a scapegoat or *pharmakos*: a righteous poet/philosopher/wiseman, acting as a representative of a god, speaks truth to power in his own homeland, usually in the form of a story or fable, and is unjustly brought to trial for impiety/blasphemy, and is then cast out and killed by his own people; the people are consequently punished, as the poet/philosopher/wiseman

---

[6] The two words occur once each in the Septuagint but in very different contexts: ὀφρῦς occurs in a literal sense in Leviticus 14:9, of shaving off the eyebrows of a leprous person; κατακρημνίζω occurs in 2 Chronicles 25:12, of ten thousand captured enemies of Judah being pushed off a cliff to their deaths.

124　　　*The Formal Education of the Author of Luke-Acts*

has predicted.[7] Many ancient Greek poets/philosophers/wisemen, both mythical and historical (or some combination of the two), share in at least some of the elements of this traditional tale: Orpheus, Marsyas, Thamyris, Demodocus, Epimenides, Homer, Hesiod, Aesop, Archilochus, Hipponax, Theognis, Simonides, Sappho, Tyrtaeus, Aeschylus, Euripides, Socrates.[8] Aesop in particular serves as a paradigmatic scapegoat—and his story was known far and wide.[9]

The so-called *Life of Aesop* preserves several almost identical accounts, embedded with many fables, of Aesop's life and death. In its extant forms the *Life of Aesop* is a product of the first or second century CE, but it clearly draws on a wealth of earlier traditions: the murder of Aesop at the hands of the Delphians, as well as their

[7]　Early Christian writers made an association between Jesus's passion and the literal scapegoat ritual as described in Leviticus 16 (Barn. 7:7-8; Tertullian, *Marc.* 3.7.7, *Adv. Jud.* 14.9), but the depiction in the gospels of Jesus as a human scapegoat, similar in function to his pagan Greek predecessors, was first observed by Origen, who compares Jesus to "a just man dying willingly for the common good in order to remove plague, barrenness, tempests, and similar calamities" (paraphrase of *Cels.* 1.31). For influential treatments of Jesus as a scapegoat figure, or *pharmakos*, in the gospel tradition, see P. Wendland, "Jesus als Saturnalien Koenig," *Hermes* 33 (1898): 175–9; J. G. Frazer, *The Golden Bough: A Study in Magic and Religion*, vol. 3, 2nd ed. (London: Macmillan, 1900), 186–200; R. Girard, *The Scapegoat* (Baltimore: Johns Hopkins, 1986), 100–124; R. Girard, *Things Hidden Since the Foundation of the World* (London: Athlone Press, 1987), 167–70, 180–262. R. Schwager builds on Girard's scapegoat theory (especially in R. Girard, *Violence and the Sacred* (Baltimore: Johns Hopkins, 1977)) in his own analysis of Jesus as scapegoat in *Must there be Scapegoats? Violence and Redemption in the Bible* (San Francisco: Harper and Row, 1987), 136–227. Also building on Girard is R. G. Hamerton-Kelly, *The Gospel and the Sacred: Poetics of Violence in Mark* (Minneapolis: Fortress, 1994), in his application of Girard's scapegoat theory to the Gospel of Mark. Less explicitly beholden to Girard are L. M. Wills, *The Quest of the Historical Gospel*, 23–50; A. Y. Collins, "Finding Meaning in the Death of Jesus," *The Journal of Religion* 78 (1998): 175–96; D. J. Stökl, "The Christian Exegesis of the Scapegoat between Jews and Pagans," in *Sacrifice in Religious Experience*, ed. A. I. Baumgarten (Leiden: Brill, 2002), 207–32; R. E. DeMaris, *The New Testament in its Ritual World* (London: Routledge, 2008), 91–111.

[8]　Around the turn of the twentieth century the so-called "Cambridge Ritualists" paid special attention to the ritual of scapegoating in ancient Greek culture: J. G. Frazer, *The Golden Bough: A Study in Comparative Religion*, vol. 2 (London: Macmillan, 1890), 210–17; J. E. Harrison, *Prolegomena to the Study of Greek Religion* (Cambridge: Cambridge University Press, 1903), 95–119; L. R. Farnell, *The Cults of the Greek State*, vol. 4 (Oxford: Clarendon, 1907), 267–84; G. Murray, *The Rise of the Greek Epic* (Oxford: Clarendon, 1907), 12–16, 253–8. A renewal of interest in ancient Greek scapegoating rituals occurred in the 1970s and 1980s: J.-P. Vernant and P. Vidal-Naquet, *Tragedy and Myth in Ancient Greece* (Brighton: Harvester Press, 1981), 87–119; W. Burkert, *Structure and History in Greek Mythology and Ritual* (Berkeley: University of California Press, 1979), 59–77; R. Parker, *Miasma: Pollution and Purification in Early Greek Religion* (Oxford Clarendon, 1983), 24–6, 257–80; J. Bremmer, "Scapegoat Rituals in Ancient Greece," *Harvard Studies in Classical Philology* 87 (1983): 299–320. D. D. Hughes, *Human Sacrifice in Ancient Greece* (London: Routledge, 1991), 139–65, offers a thorough survey of the ancient Greek literary and archaeological evidence for scapegoating. On the poet's function as scapegoat in ancient Greek culture, see T. Compton, "The Trial of the Satirist: Poetic *Vitae* (Aesop, Archilochus, Homer) as Background for Plato's *Apology*," *American Journal of Philology* 111 (1990): 330–47; on the poet as scapegoat both in ancient Greek culture and in Indo-European comparands, see T. Compton, *Victim of the Muses: Poet as Scapegoat, Warrior and Hero in Greco-Roman and Indo-European Myth and History* (Washington, DC: Center for Hellenic Studies, 2006).

[9]　A. Wiechers, *Aesop in Delphi* (Meisenheim am Glan: Hain, 1961), 31–49, was the first to define Aesop as a *pharmakos*, followed by F. R. Adrados, "The 'Life of Aesop' and the Origins of the Novel in Antiquity," *Quaderni Urbinati di Cultura Classica*, n.s. 1, 30 (1979): 93–112. The subject is treated most thoroughly by T. Compton, "The Trial of the Satirist," 330–47, and T. Compton, *Victim of the Muses*, 19–40.

Luke and Aesop 125

compensation for his death, is known as early as Herodotus (2.134); the accusation that Aesop stole a bowl from the temple of Apollo at Delphi is known to Aristophanes (*Wasps* 1446-9). The account in the *Life of Aesop* of Aesop's later travels, his visit to the Greek sanctuary of Delphi, and his death at the hands of the Delphians includes many features that are similar to Luke's account of Jesus's visit and reception at his hometown of Nazareth, and an audience's awareness of the story of Aesop helps to color the episode in the gospel and resolve its several puzzling features. I take the following account from version W of the *Life of Aesop*; two other versions, G and Pl, give much the same account, and in similar language.[10]

According to the *Life of Aesop* Aesop visits a number of other cities throughout Greece, demonstrating his wisdom (τὴν ἑαυτοῦ ἐπιδεικνύμενος σοφίαν), before eventually ending up in Delphi. He demonstrates his wisdom there too, and the people gladly listen to him at first, but they neglect to grant him due honor (οἱ δὲ ὄχλοι ἡδέως μὲν αὐτοῦ ἠκροῶντο, οὐδὲν δὲ αὐτὸν ἐτίμησαν). Aesop responds in kind by telling the Delphians some fables and stories that illustrate their low status and humble origins: Delphi is the least of cities, and the Delphians are the offspring of slaves. The Delphians are so offended that they conspire against Aesop, arrest him, convict him of blasphemy and desecration of Apollo's temple, and arrange for him to be thrown down from a cliff (ἀπὸ κρημνοῦ βληθῆναι). The Delphians themselves drag him by force in order to throw him down from the precipice (εἷλκον μετὰ βίας ἐπὶ τὸ κρημνίσαι αὐτόν). They lead him to the cliff and place him at its summit (ἀπήγαγον αὐτὸν ἐπὶ τὸν κρημνὸν καὶ ἔστησαν αὐτὸν ἐπὶ τοῦ ἄκρου). Aesop utters a curse against the Delphians, predicting that those who learn of his unjust death will avenge him. Then the Delphians push him and throw him down from the cliff (οἱ δὲ ὠθήσαντες ἔρριψαν αὐτὸν κατὰ τοῦ κρημνοῦ). Thus Aesop dies. He does get the last laugh, however, as Delphi suffers from a plague, and the Delphians must propitiate for his unjust death.

Some of Luke's audience, upon hearing about the people of Nazareth leading Jesus forcibly out of the city to the brow of a mountain in order to push him off, may very well have been reminded of the well-known story of Aesop. Both the vocabulary and the context are remarkably similar. The resonance of the colorful compound κατακρημνίζω is particularly notable: it occurs only here in the New Testament, but this verb, and various related forms in -κρημν-, serves as a virtual leitmotif in the account of Aesop's death in the *Life of Aesop*. From version W of the *Life of Aesop* we have the following: the Delphians arrange for Aesop to be thrown down "from a cliff" (ἀπὸ κρημνοῦ); they drag him by force in order "to throw" him down from the precipice (κρημνίσαι); they lead him to the "cliff" and place him at its summit (κρημνόν); they push him and throw him "down from the cliff" (κατὰ τοῦ κρημνοῦ). Also, in version Pl of the *Life of Aesop* the compound verb κατακρημνίζω is used in a fable that anticipates

---

[10] A critical edition of version *W*, represented by several medieval manuscripts, can be found in B. E. Perry, *Aesopica*, 81–107, and, more recently, in M. Papathomopoulos, ed., Ὁ βίος τοῦ Αἰσώπου: ἡ παραλλαγή *W*: *Editio Princeps* (Athens: Papadimas, 1999), and K. Grammatiki, *Vita Aesopi: Überlieferung, Sprache und Edition einer frühbyzantinischen Fassung des Äsopromans* (Wiesbaden: Reichert, 2001).

126   *The Formal Education of the Author of Luke-Acts*

Aesop's impending fate: shortly before Aesop is cast off the cliff by the Delphians he warns them by relating a fable of an old farmer who "is cast off" (κατακρημνίζεσθαι) a "cliff" (κρημνός) by some worthless little donkeys. This compound verb—κατακρημνίζω—is a favorite in Aesop's fables as well, where we find a dog "casting" itself into a well (κατακρημνίσαντος Chambry 155), hares intending to commit suicide by "casting" themselves off a "bank" into a pond (κατακρημνίσαι; κρημνόν, κατακρημνίσωμεν Chambry 191), and an ass "falling down" and dying under the weight of his load (κατακρημνισθεὶς Hausrath 192; cf. 197).[11] The resonance of the verb in describing Jesus's impending death at the hands of his own townspeople may have triggered in Luke's audience a memory of the most famous scapegoat figure of antiquity, the sage Aesop, who is unjustly executed by being cast off a cliff by the people of Delphi.

If we recognize that Luke is modeling Jesus's reception in Nazareth on Aesop's reception in Delphi, the uniquely puzzling features in Luke's version of the story become understandable. Like Aesop in the *Life of Aesop*, Jesus in Luke's gospel gains a great reputation for his words and deeds as he travels throughout the surrounding lands (Lk. 4:14-15). When he arrives in his hometown of Nazareth Jesus, like Aesop, initially finds a receptive audience, but soon his prophecies, aphorisms, and stories, all of which carry with them underlying criticisms of his audience, cause grave offense to his fellow townspeople (Lk. 4:16-28). Like Aesop, who was of very low social status, in fact a notoriously ugly slave, Jesus is considered by his audience to be of too humble an origin to merit much honor (Lk. 4:22).

Luke's reliance on the story of Aesop appears to have inspired him to reverse the chain of events as they are arranged in Matthew and Mark. In Matthew and Mark the lack of faith of the people of Nazareth results in Jesus's refusal/inability to do great deeds in Nazareth. In the Gospel of Luke, as in the *Life of Aesop*, the causality is reversed: Jesus's refusal to do great deeds in Nazareth, as he has done elsewhere, results in the people being gravely offended (Lk. 4:23-8).

Finally, the end of the *Life of Aesop* is particularly useful in illuminating the end of Luke's account of Jesus's rejection in Nazareth. Luke alone of the synoptic gospels has the townspeople of Nazareth become so angry at Jesus's words that they stand up, cast him out of the city, and lead him to the brow of the mountain upon which the city is built to throw him down headlong (καὶ ἀναστάντες ἐξέβαλον αὐτὸν ἔξω τῆς πόλεως, καὶ ἤγαγον αὐτὸν ἕως ὀφρύος τοῦ ὄρους ἐφ’ οὗ ἡ πόλις ᾠκοδόμητο αὐτῶν, ὥστε κατακρημνίσαι αὐτόν Lk. 4:29). In its New Testament context (i.e., compared to the parallel accounts in Mark and Matthew), the end of Luke's story is unexpected and puzzling. Why are the people of Nazareth so angry that they attempt to murder Jesus? Why is Nazareth described as built upon a mountain? Why is the language in which the story is told foreign to New Testament vocabulary and diction? As we have seen, these questions are resolvable if we recognize that the *Life of Aesop* inspired Luke's

---

[11] The verb κατακρημνίζω is used broadly elsewhere to describe the fate of those who commit sacrilege against the cult of Apollo at Delphi (Demosthenes, *Fals. leg.* 327; Diodorus Siculus, *Bibliotheca historica* 16.28, 31; Philo, *Prov.* fr. 2.33; Aelian, *Var. hist.* 11.5). The *Suda sub* Αἴσωπος and Φαιδριάς uses the verb to describe the murder of Aesop by the Delphians.

Luke and Aesop

account of Jesus's rejection in Nazareth, for both Luke's story and the language in which he tells it have uncanny parallels in the story of the fate of Aesop.[12]

The big difference between the two accounts, of course, is that Aesop is thrown from the cliff and dies, while, in perhaps the most understated but impressive sentences in Luke's gospel, Jesus simply passes through the middle of the crowd and goes away (αὐτὸς δὲ διελθὼν διὰ μέσου αὐτῶν ἐπορεύετο Lk. 4:30). Jesus is eminently greater than Aesop. Yes, he will eventually suffer the fate of Aesop—accused of being a blasphemer and a desecrater of the temple, put on trial, convicted, and executed—but not yet. Jesus's death as a scapegoat, already anticipated programmatically by Luke here at the beginning of Jesus's ministry, will have to wait until the end of the gospel story.

Two Possible Quotations from Aesop's Fables in the Double Tradition

According to Luke's gospel, only after his escape from the hands of his own people in his hometown of Nazareth does Jesus begin his major ministry throughout the Galilee, teaching, performing miracles of healing, and attracting disciples. Before long Jesus's activities attract the attention of John the Baptist, who sends two messengers to ask him if he is the expected Messiah. Jesus points to his miracles of healing as an answer, and after John's two messengers leave he speaks about John to the crowd in a series of aphorisms, drawing his words in at least two instances from aphorisms that are embedded in the fables of Aesop.

Now, before we look at these two instances in Luke, we should note that New Testament scholars have from time to time perceived themes that are shared by Aesop's fables and Jesus's parables and have even proposed that Jesus's parables have drawn from the Aesopic tradition. However, the points of contact are usually very few and the comparisons very loose: e.g., that the Aesopic fable of the miser who buries a lump of gold in the ground (Chambry 345) is paralleled in Jesus's parable of the talents, in which one of the three servants buries his master's money in the ground rather than

---

[12] M. Froelich and T. E. Phillips, "Throw the Blasphemer off a Cliff: Luke 4:16-30 in Light of the *Life of Aesop*," *New Testament Studies* 65 (2019): 21–32, have recently examined side by side these two accounts of the death sentences of Jesus and of Aesop, emphasizing that both are being condemned to the same fate (to be cast from a precipice) for the same crime (blasphemy). Jesus has blasphemously insulted the Jews of Nazareth by extending God's mercy to the gentiles, while Aesop has maligned the special status of the Delphians before Apollo. I believe that their conclusion—that Luke is drawing on the account of the death of Aesop here—is correct, but they significantly overstate the uniqueness in antiquity of accounts of execution by lethal fall. This mode of execution is attested in many literary sources other than the *Life of Aesop*: one need only recall the Athenian Barathron (Herodotus 7.133, etc.), the Spartan Kaiadas (Thucydides 1.134.4, etc.), Cape Leukatas on the island of Leukas (Strabo 10.2.9), the Typaion mountain in Elis (Pausanias 5.6.7), the Tarpeian rock in Rome (Dionysius of Halicarnassus, *Ant. rom.* 7.35.4; 8.78.5, etc.), and the emperor Tiberius's favorite execution spot high on a cliff on Capri (Suetonius, *Tib.* 62), along with the many executions, besides Aesop's, that took place off the cliffs at Delphi (Euripides, *Ion* 1222, 1266; Demosthenes, *Fals. leg.* 327; Aeschines, *Fals. leg.* 143; Diodorus Siculus, *Bibliotheca historica* 16.28, 31; Pausanias 10.2.4; Philo, *Prov.* fr. 2.33; Plutarch, *Praec. ger. rei publ.* 825b (Stephanus); Aelian, *Var. hist.* 11.5).

128   *The Formal Education of the Author of Luke-Acts*

risk investing it (Mt. 25:14-30).[13] The similarities between the vocabulary and details of these two stories, not to speak of their underlying messages, are very slight indeed.

Other even looser parallels have been proposed: e.g., that Aesop's fable of the fisherman whose net is able to capture the large but not the small fish (Chambry 25) shares a common setting with Jesus's parable of the fishermen who pick through the results of their catch (Mt. 13:47-8); that Aesop's fable of the bird catcher who resorts to serving his tame partridge as a meal to an unexpected guest (Chambry 286) shares a common situation with Jesus's parable of the man who asks his friend for three loaves of bread to feed an unexpected guest (Lk. 11:5-8); that Aesop's fable of the farmer who takes his axe to a barren fruit tree until he discovers honey inside (Chambry 85) shares some common features with Jesus's parable of the man who intends to cut down a barren fig tree (Lk. 13:6-9).[14] In all these perceived parallels, however, the similarities in vocabulary and detail are very slight, and in most cases the underlying thrusts of their messages are completely different.[15]

In short, most parallels that have been perceived between Aesopica and the gospels simply share common themes, situations, customs, etc. that are universal in nature and do not require an assumption of a genetic connection between the texts. What we need to establish a genetic connection are not simply commonly used expressions but actual verbal parallels, ideally sequences of identical words that are atypical rather than trite in nature: I believe that such is the case in two examples that I shall propose from the seventh chapter of Luke. Further, if these sequences of identical words are ensconced in identical meters, a genetic connection seems all the more probable: I believe that such is the case in the third example that I shall propose from the twenty-fourth chapter of Luke.

"A reed shaken by the wind" (Lk. 7:24 and Mt. 11:7)

Having entertained an inquiry from two messengers of John the Baptist as to whether he (Jesus) is the expected Messiah, Jesus addresses his own followers with some

---

[13] Cf. D. Flusser, "Aesop's Miser and the Parable of the Talents," in *Parable and Story in Judaism and Christianity*, eds. C. Thoma and M. Wychogrod (Mahwah: Paulist Press, 1989), 9–25.

[14] These three parallels, among others, are marshaled by M. Wojciechowski, "Aesopic Tradition in the New Testament," *Journal of Greco-Roman Christianity and Judaism* 5 (2008): 99–109. On the basis of such parallels Wojciechowski has proposed a genetic connection between the Aesopica and the gospels, i.e., that the gospel writers, or even that Jesus himself, actually knew the Aesopic tales and were drawing from them.

[15] Some perceived parallels have bordered on the absurd: e.g., Aesop's fable of the beaver who bites off its own testicles and casts them aside in order to avoid capture is compared to Jesus's advice on several occasions to cut off a limb if it is causing someone to stumble (Mt. 5:29-30, 18:8-9; Mk 9:43-7) and to Jesus's praise of eunuchs who have castrated themselves for the kingdom of heaven (Mt. 19:12) (so Wojciechowski, "Aesopic Tradition," 105). The *Neuer Wettstein* draws a few parallels between Aesopic fables and stories recorded in the gospels, but these parallels arise simply as a result of sharing a common situation or context: e.g., the story in the three synoptic gospels about Jesus calming the storm (Mk 4:35-41; Mt. 8:23-7; Lk. 8:22-5) and two Aesopic fables about shipwrecked sailors praying to the gods for help (Chambry 53, 309) are cited as parallels in U. Schnelle, M. Lang, and M. Labahn, eds., *Neuer Wettstein* I/1.1, 196–7, on Mk 4:35-41. But a shipwrecked sailor praying for help must have been one of the most commonplace occurrences in antiquity! Such "parallelomania" is so prevalent in the *Neuer Wettstein* that it is difficult, as Vergil is said to have once remarked of Ennius's poetry, "to find the gold amidst the dung" (Cassiodorus, *Institutiones* 1.1.8: *aurum in stercore quaero*).

Luke and Aesop   129

rhetorical questions in very aphoristic language about their reception of John as a prophet (Lk. 7:24-5):

Τί ἐξήλθατε εἰς τὴν ἔρημον θεάσασθαι; κάλαμον ὑπὸ ἀνέμου σαλευόμενον; ἀλλὰ τί ἐξήλθατε ἰδεῖν; ἄνθρωπον ἐν μαλακοῖς ἱματίοις ἠμφιεσμένον; ἰδοὺ οἱ ἐν ἱματισμῷ ἐνδόξῳ καὶ τρυφῇ ὑπάρχοντες ἐν τοῖς βασιλείοις εἰσίν.

"What did you go out into the desert to look at? A reed shaken by the wind? But what did you go out to see? A man wrapped in soft clothes? Behold, those who dress in costly clothing and luxury live in royal (houses)."

An almost verbatim parallel in Matthew (11:7-8) indicates that the gospel writers are probably drawing from a common source (i.e., "Q").[16] The passage's credentials as a saying very early ascribed to Jesus are further burnished by a close parallel in the Gospel of Thomas 78: "Jesus said, 'Why have you come out to the countryside? To see a reed shaken by the wind? Or to see a m[an] who is wearing a soft garment li[ke your] kings and your nobles? They have soft garments on, but they are unable to know the truth.'"[17]

There is little doubt, then, that the gospels of Matthew, Luke, and Thomas have preserved a very early tradition about Jesus. But what is the origin of the colorful language of Jesus's rhetorical questions? No close Septuagintal parallels for any of the expressions present themselves, and in fact, the expressions all seem more comfortable in a pagan than in a Jewish or Christian context.[18] Most conspicuously, there is an entire family of fables attributed to Aesop that are centered precisely on the image of a reed being shaken by the wind (Halm 179, Chambry 101, Hausrath 71, 239, Perry 70; cf. Babrius 36, Aphthonius 36, Avianus 16). Many versions of these fables entail a contest of sorts between a slender reed and a large tree: an oak, an olive, or a cypress. The reed, though criticized for its weakness, manages to withstand the wind much more successfully than the larger trees.

The version of the fable closest verbally to the expression in Matthew and Luke is a prose version of the Fable of the Oak and the Reed in the sixteenth-century manuscript Parisinus 105:

---

[16] The Synoptic Problem pertains at some level to the following consideration of double tradition material (Lk. 7:24, 32 and Mt. 11:7, 17). I use the shorthand "Q" in a very inclusive sense, to signify not a single recoverable Greek manuscript but rather a complex array of oral traditions and written documents, mostly in Greek, to be sure, but some, perhaps, in Aramaic. "Q-skepticism," along the lines of the Farrer hypothesis, has perhaps drawn in the reins on some of the extravagances of those wishing to reconstruct the text of a specific, tangible artifact, lay it out on a page with chapter and verse numbers, and study it in isolation from the extant gospels (viz. some of the fellows of The Jesus Seminar and their *epigoni*), but it has not, in my view, undermined the fundamental building blocks of the almost two centuries old two-source theory.

[17] Translation of the Coptic text by S. J. Gathercole, *The Gospel of Thomas: Introduction and Commentary* (Leiden: Brill, 2014), 496.

[18] Passages in the Septuagint that contain one or two of the lexical items of the expression "a reed shaken by the wind" are sometimes offered as parallels (e.g., Isa. 7:2, 17:13, 42:3; Ps. 83:13 (= LXX 82:14); Wis. 4:4), but the contexts are usually quite different, and the noun κάλαμος "reed" is never paired with the verb σαλεύω "shake" in the Septuagint.

130   *The Formal Education of the Author of Luke-Acts*

Δρῦς καὶ κάλαμος περὶ ἰσχύος ἤριζον. ἀνέμου δὲ σφοδροτάτου ἐπιπνεύσαντος ὁ μὲν κάλαμος σαλευόμενος καὶ συγκλινόμενος ταῖς πνοαῖς τῶν ἀνέμων τὴν ἐκρίζωσιν ἔφυγεν, ἡ δὲ δρῦς δι᾽ ὅλου ἀντιστᾶσα ἑαυτὴν ἐκ ῥιζῶν κατηνέχθη.

ὁ λόγος δηλοῖ ὅτι οὐ δεῖ τοῖς κρείττουσιν ἀντιπίπτειν.

An oak and a reed were quarreling about their strength. But when a very strong wind began to blow, the reed, though shaken and bent by the gusts of the winds, escaped being uprooted, while the oak, though having stood up entirely against the wind, was completely uprooted.

The story shows that one must not resist those who are stronger.

That there is a genetic relationship between Aesop and the gospels in the particular expression "a reed shaken by the wind" is supported by the fact that in all of surviving Greek literature only in the Aesopic fable (ἀνέμου . . . ὁ μὲν κάλαμος σαλευόμενος) and in the gospel passages (κάλαμον ὑπὸ ἀνέμου σαλευόμενον) does the combination of these three specific Greek words occur: κάλαμος, ἄνεμος, σαλεύω (reed, wind, shake).

The reverberation of the Aesopic fable serves to complicate the audience's understanding of Jesus's rhetorical questions about John. Jesus is implying much more than that John is not weak and wavering or soft and decadent. He is reminding his audience that John, like Aesop, is a lowly, unsightly outsider and a sage who speaks truth to power, even at great risk. This unwavering prophet, who lifts his voice in the wilderness against the establishment, is not like a reed that bends with the wind, for he offers his opponents no quarter. John is more like the mighty oak that utterly resists the wind and refuses to bend to its will, even though this will lead eventually to its destruction. Like the oak, John will be uprooted by strong external forces: decapitated by the hands of Herod Antipas.

"We played the aulos ('reed-pipe') for you, and you did not dance" (Lk. 7:32 and Mt. 11:17)

Jesus continues to address his audience, censuring the "men of this generation" by likening them to children sitting in the marketplace who call to one another (Lk. 7:32):

Ηὐλήσαμεν ὑμῖν καὶ οὐκ ὠρχήσασθε· ἐθρηνήσαμεν (ὑμῖν some mss.) καὶ οὐκ ἐκλαύσατε.

"We played the aulos ('reed-pipe') for you, and you did not dance; we lamented (for you), and you did not weep."

Again, an almost verbatim parallel in Matthew (11:17), which occurs in the same thematic context, indicates that the gospel writers are probably drawing from a common source (i.e., "Q"). Jesus's expression, with its metaphoric quality, vivid vocabulary and imagery, and parallelism between the two clauses of the couplet, appears to be a quotation of a proverb in some poetic form, but it does not draw obviously from the Septuagint or any other Semitic source. The first clause is foreign to the Septuagint, with the two verbs never occurring in combination there—though they occur in combination very commonly in Classical and Hellenistic Greek literature, including in Aesop's fables. The two verbs of the second clause are occasionally paired in the Septuagint and elsewhere in the New Testament (e.g., Mic. 1:8; Jer. 10:1; Lk. 23:27; Jn 16:20), but they are not uncommonly paired in Classical and Hellenistic Greek literature as well, including, again, in Aesop's fables.[19]

The meaning of the introduction to the proverb (Lk. 7:31-2; Mt. 11:16) and indeed, of the two-part proverb itself (Lk. 7:32; Mt. 11:17) is not transparent. What is the significance of the children calling to one another as they sit in the marketplace? Who are the "we" and the "you" of the proverb, both literally and metaphorically? What is the symbolism behind playing the aulos, dancing, lamenting, and weeping?[20] The gospel writers attribute a rather perplexing interpretation to Jesus in the two verses that follow (Lk. 7:33-4; cf. Mt. 11:18-19): "For John the Baptist has come neither eating bread nor drinking wine, and you say 'He has a demon!' The Son of Man has come eating and drinking, and you say 'Look at this glutton and wine-bibber, a friend of tax collectors and sinners!'" Those who play the aulos and those who lament, then, are apparently to be understood as the prophets, and more specifically Jesus and John, and those who fail to respond by dancing and by weeping are the people of this generation, who do not heed the prophets. It is critical to observe that Jesus's addendum forms a chiastic response to the two-part proverb: the abstemious John is the one who lamented; the hedonistic Jesus is the one who played the aulos. In neither case did the people of this generation respond correctly or in a timely fashion to the prodding of the prophet.

In the absence of any obvious Semitic source, it is worth considering if a very early Christian tradition is placing a Classical or Hellenistic proverb in the mouth of Jesus

---

[19] This has not kept some from creating their own hypothetical Semitic sources for the proverb. J. Wellhausen, one of the earliest and strongest advocates for an Aramaic model underlying the Greek gospels, proposed that this verse reproduced an Aramaic proverb, offering in support the wordplay *raqedton* "dance" and *arqedton* "lament" in the various later Syriac translations (both the Old Syriac and Peshitta): *Der syrische Evangelienpalimpsest vom Sinai* (Göttingen: Dieterichschen Verlagsbuchhandlung, 1895), 11. Wellhausen later backtracked a bit, in "Review of A. Meyer's *Jesu Muttersprache*," *Göttingische gelehrte Anzeigen* 158 (1896): 265-8, conceding that the term *arqedton* is Syriac (i.e., Mesopotamian), not Palestinian Aramaic. In fact both words are Syriac, and their reconstruction as first-century Palestinian Aramaic is mere conjecture. Nonetheless, several scholars have followed Wellhausen's initial lead, reproducing in their hypothetical Aramaic models not only wordplay but even rhyme and rhythm: M. Black, *An Aramaic Approach*, 161; J. Jeremias, *New Testament Theology* (New York: Charles Scribner's Sons, 1971), 26. M. Casey, *An Aramaic Approach to Q* (Cambridge: Cambridge University Press, 2002), 105, 129-32, offers a slightly different Aramaic reconstruction that lacks the wordplay. It seems highly speculative and, in my view, unnecessary to reconstruct the wording of a hypothetical, pre-Greek, Palestinian Aramaic model for the Greek proverb in "Q" (i.e., in Matthew and Luke) based on later Syriac translations of the very Greek text under consideration! Motivated by a passion to resurrect the *ipsissima verba* of the historical Jesus, some have invented a *hypothetical* Aramaic model for the proverb when an *actual* Greek model—in Herodotus and in Aesop, as we shall see—is staring them right in the face.

[20] A concise summary of the various solutions that have been offered for this notorious *crux* can be found in U. Luz, *Matthew 8-20: A Commentary* (Minneapolis: Augsburg Fortress, 2001), 145-50; these solutions are somewhat more fleshed out in D. Zeller, "Die Bildlogik des Gleichnisses Mt 11:16/ Lk 7:31," *Zeitschrift für die neutestamentliche Wissenschaft* 68 (1977): 252-7. M. Casey, *An Aramaic Approach to Q*, 129-42, has recently added a new and intriguing interpretation of the two-part proverb, understanding it as an address directed *at* John and Jesus respectively rather than spoken (metaphorically) *by* them.

132   *The Formal Education of the Author of Luke-Acts*

here. And one readily finds a possible model—at least for the first clause of Jesus's expression—in a very popular and well-attested Aesopic fable: There once was a man who saw some fish swimming in the sea and played a tune on his aulos in an effort to entice them to come ashore. When his hopes were unrealized he resorted to his net. As the captured fish were flopping about on the shore, the man chastised them, saying, Ὑμεῖς, ὅτε μὲν ηὔλουν, οὐκ ὠρχεῖσθε, νῦν δέ, ὅτε πέπαυμαι, τοῦτο πράττετε. "When I was playing the aulos you did not dance, but now, when I cease playing, you do" (Halm 27, Chambry 24, Hausrath 11, Perry 11; cf. Babrius 9; Aphthonius 33).

If there is a genetic connection here, the direction of influence is clear, for the fable is attested already as early as the fifth century BCE. Herodotus (1.141) places the fable (he calls it a λόγος/logos) in the mouth of King Cyrus in his report of the fate of the Ionian and Aeolian Greeks of Asia Minor, who had previously refused Cyrus's request to switch their allegiances from the Lydian king Croesus (cf. 1.76) but are now, in the face of Cyrus's conquest of Lydia, very eager to obtain his favor. Cyrus dismisses them by relating the tale: An aulos player once saw some fish in the sea and began playing his aulos to them in the hope that they would be drawn willingly to shore. When this ruse failed the aulos player instead cast a net and forcefully hauled a great number of the fish to shore. When he saw the fish flopping about on the shore, he censured them, saying, Παύεσθέ μοι ὀρχεόμενοι, ἐπεὶ οὐδ᾽ ἐμέο αὐλέοντος ἠθέλετε ἐκβαίνειν ὀρχεόμενοι. "Stop dancing for me, since when I was playing my aulos you were unwilling to come out and dance." Both the context (i.e., "you should have heeded my words sooner," "you would have been better off had you complied willingly") and the vocabulary ("playing an aulos' to those who "refuse to dance") are similar to the proverb in the gospels. Also, Herodotus, like Luke and Matthew, proceeds to explain the meaning of the proverb—although Matthew and Luke put the explanation in Jesus's mouth, while Herodotus uses his own authorial voice.

The gospel writers need not have been familiar with the text of the Histories of Herodotus himself. The first-century CE rhetorician Aelius Theon includes this Herodotean tale of the aulos-player in his *progymnasmata* as one of four examples of fables from Classical historians that he considers worthy of imitation by students in their rhetorical exercises (vol. 2, p. 66 in L. Spengel's edition). This is an indication that the fable was a commonplace in the educational curriculum of the time and that the author(s) of the source(s) of this "double tradition material" could have been recalling it from school exercises that they had once performed as students. Moreover, while Herodotus's version is the earliest extant attestation of the fable, it survives, as noted above, in several later Aesopic collections as well: e.g., Babrius 9; Aphthonius 33. The wording that is most similar to that of the gospels is a prose version found in many manuscripts that appear to owe their origin to a very early collection of Aesopic tales (Halm 27, Chambry 24, Hausrath 11, Perry 11). In this prose version the fisherman chastises the netted fish: Ὦ κάκιστα ζῷα, ὑμεῖς, ὅτε μὲν ηὔλουν, οὐκ ὠρχεῖσθε, νῦν δέ, ὅτε πέπαυμαι, τοῦτο πράττετε. "Oh most evil creatures, when I was playing the aulos you did not dance, but now, when I cease playing, you do." It is possible, therefore, that the author(s) of the source(s) of this "double tradition material" drew from a popular Aesopic fable or proverb rather than from the specific passage of Herodotus's Histories.

Luke and Aesop 133

This parallel is seldom observed in New Testament commentaries;[21] likewise in commentaries on Herodotus.[22] But greater attention has been paid to the parallel over the past century in specialized studies of Jesus's parables: A. Jülicher observes the parallel but without any comment.[23] A. A. T. Ehrhardt acknowledges that Jesus's expression may have been influenced either by Herodotus or Aesop.[24] M. Wojciechowski considers this among the stronger parallels between Aesop's fables and Jesus's parables and sayings, claiming that here Jesus is alluding to this very fable of the fisherman, and noting that the fable furnishes a background and an explanation for Jesus's saying: i.e., ignoring the aulos player will result in a fate similar to that of the fish in the fable.[25]

D. Flusser has been one of the strongest advocates for a genetic relationship between Aesop's fables and the two passages that we have been considering from the double-tradition material.[26] He proposes that Jesus himself knew the Aesopic fables and, in particular, used Aesopic associations on three occasions in the gospels in connection with his interactions with Herod Antipas, Tetrarch of the Galilee. In the first instance, Jesus calls Herod Antipas a "fox" (Lk. 13:32), which is the most ubiquitous animal in Aesop's fables, and which is associated with craftiness and lack of true nobility, in contrast, for example, to a lion. Secondly, about John the Baptist, whom Herod Antipas eventually executed, Jesus asks the crowd: "What did you go into the desert to see? A reed shaken by the wind?" (Mt. 11:7; Lk. 7:24). Flusser proposes that the imagery is taken from Aesop's fable of the Oak and the Reed (Chambry 101 = Hausrath 71), and he speculates that the Oak represents John the Baptist, the Reed the members of the court of Herod. Thirdly, referring to the rejection of John the Baptist, Jesus puts a proverb in the mouths of some children at play in the marketplace: "We played the aulos for you but you did not dance" (Mt. 11:17; Lk. 7:32). Flusser notes the parallel in Aesop's fable of the Fisherman who Plays the Aulos for the Fish (Chambry 24 = Hausrath 11), and also its occurrence in Herodotus's story of Cyrus and the Ionians, noting that the combination of both aulos-playing and dancing occurs only in Aesop-Herodotus and in the gospels. He suggests that the scene of the children at play caused Jesus to think of the Aesopic proverb.

Several of Flusser's contentions appear untenable (or are patently incorrect): that Jesus himself, rather than the gospel writers, knew and quoted Aesop; that a simple

---

[21] Th. Zahn, *Das Evangelium des Matthäus* (Leipzig: G. Böhme, 1903), 430–1, note 27, mentions it in passing but then dismisses it: "There is nothing to learn from the parallel in Herodotus 1.141, cf. Aesop, Fab. 27b (Halm), except that playing a flute meant an invitation to dance." A few more recent commentaries note the parallel but do not broach the question of influence: W. D. Davies and D. C. Allison, *A Critical and Exegetical Commentary on the Gospel According to Saint Matthew*, vol. 2 (Edinburgh: T&T Clark, 1991), 263, for example, succinctly note that the expression "seems to have been proverbial" and cite Herodotus 1.141 and Aesop 27 (Halm) along with some other loose parallels (e.g., Eccl. 3:4); J. A. Fitzmyer, *The Gospel According to Luke I–IX* (New York: Doubleday, 1981), 680, simply advises "See Herod. 1.141, Aesop 27b."

[22] W. W. How and J. Wells, *A Commentary on Herodotus* (Oxford: Clarendon, 1912), 118, laconically remark "The fable [i.e., in Herodotus] is part of a collection bearing Aesop's name. For it cf. St. Matt. xi. 17."

[23] A. Jülicher, *Die Gleichnisreden Jesu*, 26–7.

[24] A. A. T. Ehrhardt, "Greek Proverbs in the Gospel," *Harvard Theological Review* 46 (1953): 66–8.

[25] M. Wojciechowski, "Aesopic Tradition," 104–5.

[26] D. Flusser, *Die rabbinischen Gleichnisse und der Gleichniserzähler Jesus* (Bern: Peter Lang, 1981), 52, 151–4.

134   *The Formal Education of the Author of Luke-Acts*

reference to a fox in the Gospel of Luke would of itself suffice to evoke Aesop's fables in the minds of the audience; that the quotation of a mere four Greek words in the gospels of Matthew and Luke—reed shaken by wind"—would not only evoke a particular Aesopic fable but would also cause the audience of the gospels to extrapolate that the oak in Aesop's fable represents John the Baptist and the reed the court of Herod (even though in the fable the oak is weak and the reed strong!); that aulos-playing and dancing occur only in Aesop-Herodotus and in the gospels (they also occur in combination in Anacreon, Xenophon, Plato, Theocritus, etc.). But one need not accept all of Flusser's contentions in order to subscribe to his basic proposition that the gospel writers drew from the rich well of Aesopic tradition.

It would certainly be appropriate thematically here, in this self-contained discourse (Lk. 7:24-35; Mt. 11:7-19), for the gospel writers to evoke the figure of Aesop as a counterpart to the figures of Jesus and John the Baptist: all three are sages/prophets, who function as social outsiders from the periphery of civilized life, and who eventually suffer as scapegoats, executed by unjust societies for their righteous words and actions.

An Aesopic Quote Unique to the Gospel of Luke

"Oh foolish ones, and slow in heart" (Lk. 24:25)[27]

In an account unique to the Gospel of Luke the crucified and risen Christ is described joining two disciples on their way from Jerusalem to the village of Emmaus, appearing bewildered by their failure to recognize the significance of the events of the past few days, and chastising them for not comprehending the full meaning of the ancient prophecies (Lk. 24:25-7):

> (25) καὶ αὐτὸς εἶπεν πρὸς αὐτούς, Ὦ ἀνόητοι καὶ βραδεῖς τῇ καρδίᾳ τοῦ πιστεύειν ἐπὶ πᾶσιν οἷς ἐλάλησαν οἱ προφῆται· (26) οὐχὶ ταῦτα ἔδει παθεῖν τὸν Χριστὸν καὶ εἰσελθεῖν εἰς τὴν δόξαν αὐτοῦ; (27) καὶ ἀρξάμενος ἀπὸ Μωϋσέως καὶ ἀπὸ πάντων τῶν προφητῶν διερμήνευσεν αὐτοῖς ἐν πάσαις ταῖς γραφαῖς τὰ περὶ ἑαυτοῦ.

> (25) And he said to them, "Oh foolish ones, and slow in heart to believe in all the things that the prophets spoke. (26) Was it not necessary that the Christ suffer these things and come into his glory?" (27) And beginning from Moses and all the prophets he explained to them the matters concerning himself in all the scriptures.

So far as I am aware, no commentator has ever observed that Jesus's expression Ὦ ἀνόητοι καὶ βραδεῖς τῇ καρδίᾳ "Oh foolish ones, and slow in heart" occurs verbatim in two versions of animal fables attributed to Aesop.[28] In "The Fox and the Goat in the

---

[27] An earlier version of my proposal that Luke 24:25 is an Aesopic quote appeared in S. Reece, "Aesop, Q, and Luke," *New Testament Studies* 62 (2016): 357–77.

[28] Shortly after I brought attention to the Aesopic parallels of Luke 24:25 in "Aesop, Q, and Luke," 357–77, W. Ross published an article on the same topic: "'Ὦ ἀνόητοι καὶ βραδεῖς τῇ καρδίᾳ': Luke, Aesop, and Reading Scripture," *Novum Testamentum* 58 (2016): 369–79. He came—very tentatively— to conclusions regarding the direction of influence that are precisely the opposite of mine.

Well" a fox uses precisely these words to chastise a goat for jumping into a well for a drink without making any provision for how he will get back out. In "The Frogs at the Wedding of the Sun" a wiser-than-average frog uses precisely these words to chastise his companions for celebrating the wedding of the sun since, he predicts, if the sun were to produce any offspring, it would become too hot and dry for the frogs to survive. That commentators have neglected to note these parallels is understandable: the versions of the fables that include the verbatim expression have survived in only two manuscripts, the fourteenth- to fifteenth-century Codex Vaticanus graecus 777 and the early fifteenth-century Codex Parisinus graecus 2991 A, and they have been published only in an appendix to O. Crusius's 1897 Teubner edition of Babrius and as variants in E. Chambry's 1925 Budé edition of Aesop.

The popular Aesopic fable of how a fox trapped in a well tricks a goat into jumping in to facilitate her escape occurs in several slightly different prose versions attested in a few dozen manuscripts (Halm 45, Chambry 40, Hausrath 9, Perry 9). If further proof of the fable's antiquity were needed, the fact that it occurs in Latin translation already in the early first century CE (Phaedrus 4.9) serves to remove all doubt.[29] The fable probably originated in the Classical period, perhaps even as early as the Archaic period.[30] In the most common version of the fable the fox uses the goat as a stepladder and, having escaped from the well, taunts the trapped goat by saying something like: "Hey you (Ὢ οὗτος), if only you had as many wits as you have hairs in your beard, you would have thought about how you were going to get out of the well before jumping in." In a shorter prose version of the fable that survives in two manuscripts, the fox introduces her taunt of the trapped goat by calling him a fool (using the same two introductory words that Luke places in the mouth of Jesus in his excoriation of his disciples on their way to Emmaus): "Oh foolish one (Ὢ ἀνόητε)."[31] A metrical version of the fable poses a slightly different situation: a fox, while passing by a well, catches sight of a goat trapped within and taunts him from above. This version elaborates the fox's initial taunt a bit further to include the entire verse Ὢ ἀνόητε καὶ βραδὺς τῇ καρδίᾳ "Oh foolish one, and slow in heart," which, other than being in the singular rather than plural, is identical to Jesus's expression in the Gospel of Luke. This metrical version, published in E. Chambry's 1925 edition (as fable 40 *aliter*), is preserved in Codex Vaticanus graecus 777 (labeled Mb in Chambry), a fourteenth- or fifteenth-century manuscript containing 244 fables in alphabetical order, many metrical, thirty or so in the choliambics of Babrius, and about fifty others, including this one, in a Byzantine dodecasyllabic verse form in which the old iambic meter has devolved into

---

[29] O. Crusius, *Babrii Fabulae Aesopeae* (Leipzig: Teubner, 1897), 165, includes a version of the fable in his collection of Babrius's choliambics (as number 182), but only two, possibly three, lines in its surviving form can be manipulated to scan as choliambics.

[30] F. R. Adrados, *History of the Graeco-Latin Fable: Volume One*, 437, places the origin of the fable back at least into the Classical period, based on its typically Classical, three-part structure. He proposes that the fable may even be pre-Classical, based on its similarities to the archaic poet Archilochus (*Volume One* 495).

[31] Cf. fable number 134 in the fifteenth-century codex Bodleianus Auct. F. 4.7 (Ba) and fable number 81 in the thirteenth-century codex Palatinus 367; printed in Halm 45b, Chambry 40 *aliter*, and O. Crusius, *Babrii Fabulae Aesopeae*, 182 (as noted above Crusius includes this version in his collection of Babrius's choliambics).

136   *The Formal Education of the Author of Luke-Acts*

mere "syllable counting." This dodecasyllabic rendition of the fable is numbered 205 in this manuscript:

Τράγος δὲ πάλιν διψήσας ἐν τῷ θέρει [πάλιν in ms.; Chambry prints πάλαι]
κάτω κατῆλθε πιεῖν εἰς φρέαρ ὕδωρ.
Ὁ δὲ κορεσθεὶς ἀνελθεῖν οὐκ εὐπόρει,
ὃς μετενόει καὶ βοηθὸν ἐζήτει,
ὅπως ἀνέλθῃ ἐκ τοῦ βάθους ὁ τράγος. (5)
Ἡ δὲ ἀλώπηξ τοῦτον ἐκβλεψαμένη
ἐμειδίασε καὶ πρὸς αὐτὸν ἐλάλει·
Ὦ ἀνόητε καὶ βραδὺς τῇ καρδίᾳ, [βραδὺς in ms.; Chambry prints βραδὺ]
εἰ εἶχες φρένας ὡς ἐν πώγωνι τρίχας,
οὐκ ἂν κατῇεις, εἰ μὴ ἄνοδον οἶδας.' (10)

Οὕτω τῶν ἀνθρώπων τοὺς φρονίμους δεῖ πρῶτον τὰ τέλη τῶν πραγμάτων σκοπεῖν, εἶθ' οὕτως αὐτοῖς ἐπιχειρεῖν.

A goat, having again grown thirsty in the summer heat,
Climbed down into a well to drink some water.
Having quenched his thirst he could not find a way to climb out,
So the goat had a change of mind and began to seek some help,
So that he might climb out from the depths of the well.
But a fox, having caught sight of him,
Smiled and began to speak to him:
"Oh foolish one, and slow in heart,
If you had as many wits as hairs in your beard,
You would not have climbed down before figuring out a way back up."

Prudent people should consider the outcome of their actions before attempting them.[32]

An altogether different Aesopic fable, about frogs celebrating the wedding of the sun, also contains a verbatim expression of the phrase under consideration. This fable occurs in both prose and poetic versions. The fact that the fable occurs both in the

---

[32] As mentioned above, a version of the fable with but a few verbal differences, and slightly shorter because it appears to be missing two verses, is recorded in Codex Parisinus graecus 2991 A, an early fifteenth-century codex that includes an appendix of several four-, five-, and eight-line Aesopic fables in the tradition of Ignatius the Deacon's *tetrasticha iambica*—but rather more dodecasyllabic than truly iambic. These fables are edited by C. F. Müller and included at the end of a collection of iambic fables published by him in O. Crusius, *Babrii Fabulae Aesopeae*, 249–96. Müller does not attribute the fable to anyone in particular, but he includes it in his collection of *tetrasticha iambica* that he considers later imitations of those of the ninth-century cleric and fabulist Ignatius the Deacon, who composed four-line (*tetrasticha*) Aesopic fables in iambic trimeter (*iambica*)—though ones influenced by the metrical conventions of the *politici dodecasyllables* (i.e., no resolution, accent on penultimate syllable). Müller prints two other *tetrasticha iambica* versions of the fable of the Fox and Goat (II 15 and II 31b) that do not include the line in question (ὦ ἀνόητε καὶ βραδὺς τῇ καρδίᾳ), and—what is pertinent for our purposes—he also prints a version (II 31a) that does include the line. This version is neither built upon a four-line structure (*tetrasticha*) nor composed in a proper iambic meter (*iambica*) but is rather, like the version of the fable in Codex Vaticanus graecus 777, in a stichic dodecasyllabic verse form.

Luke and Aesop

Greek choliambics of the first- to second-century CE poet Babrius (24) and in the Latin iambic senarii of the early first-century CE poet Phaedrus (1.6) attests to its antiquity. In the prose version of the fable, which survives in two manuscripts (Halm 77, Chambry 128), an exceptionally prudent frog points out to his companions that this wedding is not an occasion to rejoice since, if the sun marries and has a son like himself, the increased heat will dry up their ponds all the more quickly. The frog chastises his companions with the words "Oh fools, for what reason do you rejoice?" (Ὦ μῶροι, εἰς τί ἀγάλλεσθε;) A dodecasyllabic version of the fable takes the frog's warning a bit further. This version is preserved only in Codex Vaticanus graecus 777 and is published only in E. Chambry's 1925 edition (as fable 128 *aliter*). This dodecasyllabic rendition of the fable is numbered 63 in this manuscript:

Ἡλίῳ ποτὲ γάμος θέρους ὑπῆρχε.
Οἱ δὲ βάτραχοι ἠγάλλοντο μεγάλως
ἐπὶ τῇ λαμπρᾷ τραπέζῃ τοῦ Ἡλίου.
Εἷς δὲ ἐξ αὐτῶν μέγα ἀναστενάξας
ἀνακέκραγε καὶ πρὸς αὐτοὺς ἐβόα· (5)
Ὦ ἀνόητοι καὶ βραδεῖς τῇ καρδίᾳ,
εἰς τί βοᾶτε μεγάλα κεκραγότες
ὡς ἐπ᾽ ἀγάθῳ τινὶ προσδοκωμένῳ;
Εἰ οὖν Ἥλιος μονώτατος ὑπάρχων
ὕλην ἅπασαν καὶ τὴν γῆν καταφλέγῃ, (10)
εἰ γήμας παῖδα ἀνθόμοιον ποιήσει,
τί μὴ πάθωμεν ἡμεῖς κακόν, εἰπέ μοι.

Ὅτι πολλοὶ τῶν τὸ φρόνημα κουφότερον ἐχόντων χαίρουσιν ἐπ᾽ ἀδήλοις.

Once, during the summer, the sun held a wedding.
The frogs were greatly delighted
At the brilliant feast of the sun.
But one of them, letting out a great groan,
Lifted up his voice and shouted to them.
"Oh foolish ones, and slow in heart,
For what reason do you shout out with your loud croaking,
As though you were expecting something good?
If the sun, while all by himself,
Burns up all the woodland and the earth,
If he marries and has a son like himself,
Tell me what evil we shall not suffer."

Many people who have vain thoughts rejoice in unknown things.

Given the very close similarities between the expressions Ὦ ἀνόητε/ἀνόητοι καὶ βραδὺς/βραδὺ/βραδεῖς τῇ καρδίᾳ in the Aesopic fables and in the Gospel of Luke, all with exactly the same vocabulary, arranged precisely in the same order, and poured into the same meter, we can conclude with some certainty that they did not arise in complete isolation from one another. Rather, we appear to be dealing here with a

138   *The Formal Education of the Author of Luke-Acts*

genetic relationship between these texts. This must be a case of "Luke" quoting "Aesop," "Aesop" quoting "Luke," or both quoting a common source.[33]

"Christianization" of the Aesopic Corpus

It is likely, and entirely reasonable, that the first inclination of most readers, when faced with these circumstances, is to assume that a Byzantine poet (or poets) contrived to add a Christian flavor to these two ancient Aesopic tales by interpolating an expression from a well-known story in the Gospel of Luke.[34] The fact that the expression occurs only in the dodecasyllabic versions of the two fables, not in the choliambics of Babrius or (translated) in the iambic senarii of Phaedrus, or in the various Greek prose versions, points to this direction of influence. Aesopic fables reformulated as dodecasyllabic verses, such as the two fables under consideration here, are clearly a Byzantine innovation. This syllable-counting verse form, sometimes called the *politici* (i.e., "popular") *dodecasyllables*,[35] was an offspring of the ancient iambic trimeter via the choliambics of a Babrian type. But while the ancient iambics and choliambics were based on variations of syllabic quantity and pitch accent, the dodecasyllables were based on the dynamic rhythm of stress accent, and while the syllables of the ancient iambics and choliambics could be resolved (i.e., two short syllables could be substituted for a long syllable in some metrical positions), thereby allowing some variation in the number of syllables in each verse, the dodecasyllables entailed mere syllable-counting, with a caesura separating the initial five syllables from the subsequent seven (or, sometimes, the reverse). Also, the dodecasyllables shared a feature of Babrian choliambics in accenting the penult of the final word of every verse. The dodecasyllabic

---

[33] More complicated, yet still genetic, relationships can be imagined, unlikely though they may seem: e.g., "Luke" quoted from an earlier Aesopic, or possibly non-Aesopic, iambic verse, and the dodecasyllabic "Aesop" quoted from "Luke" without any awareness of the earlier iambic verse.

[34] This is W. Ross's tentative conclusion in his recent article "'Ὦ ἀνόητοι καὶ βραδεῖς τῇ καρδίᾳ': Luke, Aesop, and Reading Scripture." He argues for this direction of influence based on the lateness of the Aesopic manuscripts that contain the expression (he seems to think that there is but one manuscript instead of two; in any case, the accident of attestation is not a strong argument for the date of composition of any work, as all who work with ancient manuscripts know well), on the fact that the entire phrase occurs nowhere else in extant Greek literature (but this is not surprising, given that only a fraction of Greek literature has survived to our time), and on the fact that an adjective plus the phrase "in heart" appears to be a Semitic construction (this is Ross's strongest argument, for indeed similar constructions occur regularly in the Septuagint—e.g., ὅσιοι καὶ ταπεινοὶ τῇ καρδίᾳ, σοφὸς τῇ καρδίᾳ, δειλὸς τῇ καρδίᾳ—but they are not utterly foreign to ancient Greek—e.g., δειλοὶ τῇ καρδίᾳ in a fragment attributed to the philosopher Pythagoras).

[35] One finds some discrepancies in the use of this term. The dodecasyllable was included among the στίχοι πολιτικοί "political verses" by the Byzantines themselves, but today the term "political verse" is used primarily of the fifteen-syllable verse form that became the most common meter of Byzantine and Modern Greek poetry: e.g., M. D. Lauxtermann, *The Spring of Rhythm. An Essay on the Political Verse and Other Byzantine Metres* (Österreichische Akademie der Wissenschaften: Vienna, 1999), 21–40.

verse form began to appear in the sixth or seventh century.[36] Thus the Byzantine poet(s) who refashioned the prose versions, or iambic trimeter or choliambic versions (cf. Babrius), of the two Aesopic fables certainly had the opportunity, and perhaps the motivation, to have interpolated a memorable expression from the Gospel of Luke.

In fact, it is clearly demonstrable that words, phrases, and, in at least one case, even entire stories from the Septuagint and New Testament have from time to time crept into the massive and ever-evolving corpus of Aesopic fables. Most notorious, albeit idiosyncratic, is an entire fable about the trees in search of a king, which appears as the 133rd fable in Codex Vaticanus graecus 777 (Chambry 253, Hausrath 293, Perry 262), the fourteenth- or fifteenth-century manuscript containing 244 Aesopic fables in alphabetical order that we have referenced above, for this fable is drawn wholesale, almost verbatim, from the Greek Septuagint (Judg. 9:8-15).[37] A century or two earlier Odo of Cheriton, an early thirteenth-century English cleric and fabulist, had translated this story from the Septuagint into Latin and placed it as the headpiece in his heavily Christianized collection of Aesopic fables in Latin prose.[38]

While the texts of the bodies of Aesopic fables in the Greek tradition tend to remain thoroughly pagan, the moral addenda (*epimythia*) attached at various periods are naturally susceptible to interpolations from the Septuagint and New Testament. Passing through the Greek tradition since antiquity, for example, was an Aesopic fable about two roosters who fought for dominance over the hens: the victorious rooster flew to the rooftop to exult and was seized by an eagle; the defeated rooster retreated to an inconspicuous place and survived to mount the hens (Babrius 5, Aphthonius 12, "Syntipas" 7). The fifteenth-century manuscript Trivultianus 775 (T), which contains only six Aesopic fables, attaches as an *epimythion* to this fable (Halm 21, Chambry 20, Hausrath 266) a quotation of the Septuagint Greek version of Proverbs 3:34 (quoted in

---

[36] A more precise date for the origin of the dodecasyllable appears elusive, since it probably arose in an oral rather than written medium: E. Chambry, *Aesopi Fabulae*, 28, suggests the fourth or fifth century; U. Ursing, *Studien zur griechischen Fabel* (Lund: H. Ohlsson, 1930), 13, concurs; F. R. Adrados, *History of the Graeco-Latin Fable: Volume Two*, 513, favors the sixth or seventh. Some fairly normal-looking dodecasyllables can be seen already in the poetry of Georgios of Pisidia (seventh century), who wrote poetry in a form evolutionarily between the ancient quantitative iambic trimeter and the Byzantine dodecasyllable. P. Maas, "Der byzantinische Zwölfsilber," *Byzantinische Zeitschrift* 12 (1903): 278–323, is still the most thorough analysis of the development of the meter, as well as the foundation of modern study of Byzantine metrics generally; he projects the origin of the Byzantine dodecasyllable back to a century before Georgios of Pisidia, i.e., the sixth century.

[37] On this direction of influence, see E. Kellenberger, "Once Again: the Fable of Jotham (Judg. 9), and Aesop," *Semitica* 60 (2018): 131–7; Z. Margulies, "Aesop and Jotham's Parable of the Trees (Judges 9:8-15)," *Vetus Testamentum* 69 (2019): 81–94. A rendition of the fable also occurs in Josephus's *Antiquities* 5.236-8.

[38] Christian influence was much more pervasive in the Medieval Latin tradition of Western Europe than in the Byzantine Greek traditions of Eastern Europe. Odo of Cheriton composed/adapted many Aesopic fables in Latin prose, setting them in a Christian context and adding Christian *epimythia* and even short sermons: e.g., "The Heretic and the Fly" (Odo 12), "The Cat who Made himself a Monk" (Odo 15), and "The Fox who Confessed his Sins to the Rooster" (Odo 25). The numeration of Odo's fables here is based on the edition of L. Hervieux, *Les fabulistes latins depuis le siècle d'Auguste jusqu'à la fin du moyen âge*, vol. 4 (Paris: Firmin-Didot, 1896). English translations of Odo's fables are available in J. C. Jacobs, *The Fables of Odo of Cheriton* (Syracuse: Syracuse University Press, 1985).

140   *The Formal Education of the Author of Luke-Acts*

Jas 4:6 and 1 Pet. 5:5): ὁ μῦθος δηλοῖ ὅτι Κύριος ὑπερηφάνοις ἀντιτάσσεται, ταπεινοῖς δὲ δίδωσιν χάριν. "The fable shows that the Lord opposes the haughty but gives grace to the humble."

Another Aesopic fable with a Christian *epimythion* is "The Bull, the Lioness, and the Wild Boar" (Halm 395, Hausrath *sub* "Syntipas" 11, Perry 414). This fable has survived not through the usual transmission of the Greek Aesopic corpus but rather through a collection of Aesopic fables in Syriac, which were, in turn, translated back into Greek by Michael Andreopoulos, a Byzantine scholar of the eleventh century. The fable is about a bull that gores a lion to death while he is sleeping. As the lion's mother is lamenting her son's death a wild boar commiserates facetiously from afar: "How many men are lamenting the deaths of their children whom you and your son killed!" The *epimythion* includes an almost verbatim version of the "golden rule" from Mark 4:24 (cf. Mt. 7:2 and Lk. 6:38): ὁ μῦθος δηλοῖ ὅτι ἐν ᾧ μέτρῳ μετρεῖ τις μετρηθήσεται αὐτῷ. "The fable shows that by whatever measure someone measures it will be measured out to him."

In sum, the footprint of Christianity on the Byzantine Greek tradition is relatively light: the form, the content, and the language of the Greek fables, both in prose and poetic form, are thoroughly pagan, and it is remarkable how tenaciously they remained so even through centuries of Byzantine transmission. When Christianization does occur, it always happens very late in the process, and it tends to be focused not on the bodies of the fables but on the *epimythia*, where Christian elements could be interpolated most easily without disrupting the integrity of the fables.

What does this mean for our consideration of the relationship between the expression Ὦ ἀνόητε/ἀνόητοι καὶ βραδὺς/βραδὺ/βραδεῖς τῇ καρδίᾳ "Oh foolish one(s), and slow in heart" in the dodecasyllabic versions of the two Aesopic fables, "The Fox and the Goat in the Well" and "The Frogs at the Wedding of the Sun," and in the story of Jesus meeting two of his disciples on their way to Emmaus as recorded in the Gospel of Luke? It means that what may have been quite reasonably our first inclination, i.e., to assume that the author(s) of the dodecasyllabic fables was (were) interpolating a New Testament passage, has little to recommend it. Such an interpolation into the text of the body of a fable would be not just remarkable, not just unusual, but utterly unique in the entire Greek Aesopic tradition, even in the late adaptations by Byzantine Christians like Ignatius the Deacon and "Syntipas." That a verbatim interpolation of a New Testament passage would have occurred twice, independently, in two different Aesopic tales is hardly imaginable.

"Aesopification" of the Christian Corpus

Therefore, we should not dismiss out of hand the possibility that the expression in question did once exist, quite apart from the Gospel of Luke, embedded in a prose or poetic version of an ancient Aesopic fable, or perhaps in a popular Classical or Hellenistic proverb or aphorism, and that it happened to survive only in these two late dodecasyllabic versions of the Aesopic tales. The extant Aesopic corpus is massive, but what has been lost would surely dwarf what has survived. Expressions in later versions

Luke and Aesop 141

of the fables, like the one under consideration here, that do not happen to have parallels in the ancient Aesopic corpus, need not be regarded as innovations—or as interpolations from extra-Aesopic sources. These late versions may simply have been drawing from versions of fables that survived to their time but have not survived to ours.

Consequently, we should give serious consideration to the possibility that the direction of influence that we have assumed up to this point should be reversed. The author(s) of the dodecasyllabic fables did not draw the expression Ὦ ἀνόητε/ἀνόητοι καὶ βραδὺς/βραδὺ/βραδεῖς τῇ καρδίᾳ "Oh foolish one(s), and slow in heart" from the Gospel of Luke. Rather, the Gospel of Luke drew this expression from an ancient, i.e., pre-Christian, version of these Aesopic fables.

There are several features of the expression that recommend this direction of influence. The expression as a whole occurs nowhere else in Jewish or Christian literature, so it is not particularly at home there. The use of Ὦ "Oh" with the vocative is rare in the New Testament, as in Koine Greek generally, in contrast to its regular usage in Classical Greek. It occurs in only three different passages in the gospels: Jesus addresses the Canaanite woman Ὦ γύναι "Oh woman" (Mt. 15:28); Jesus addresses the crowd Ὦ γενεὰ ἄπιστος "Oh faithless generation" (Mk 9:19—from which the expression is drawn verbatim in Lk. 9:41 and Mt. 17:17); and Jesus addresses his two disciples in the passage under consideration here. The first half of the expression, Ὦ ἀνόητε / Ὦ ἀνόητοι, with "Oh" + "fool(s)" in the vocative, is very rare in Jewish or Christian literature: never in the Septuagint, only once in Philo (*Somn.* 2.181), and only once elsewhere in the New Testament, when Paul addresses the Galatians thus Ὦ ἀνόητοι Γαλάται "Oh foolish Galatians" (Gal. 3:1). On the other hand, this word combination is fairly common in Classical and Hellenistic Greek literature: Sophocles, Aristophanes (three times—contracted ὤνόητε / ὤνόητοι), Plutarch (twice), Maximus the Sophist (twice), Chariton, Philostratus, Alciphron, etc. The second half of the expression, βραδεῖς τῇ καρδίᾳ "slow in heart," occurs nowhere else in Jewish or Christian literature. In fact, in the entire Septuagint and New Testament the adjective βραδύς occurs only here and in James 1:19, in an equally aphoristic expression, again with Classical rather than Septuagintal or New Testament resonance: ἔστω δὲ πᾶς ἄνθρωπος ταχὺς εἰς τὸ ἀκοῦσαι, βραδὺς εἰς τὸ λαλῆσαι, βραδὺς εἰς ὀργήν· "Let every man be swift to listen, slow to speak, slow to anger."[39] From Classical and Hellenistic literature, on the other hand, one can compare such similar expressions as προνοῆσαι βραδεῖς "slow to understand" (Thucydides 3.38.6) and βραδὺς πρὸς ὀργὴν "slow to anger" (Menander's *Sententiae* 60). In short, the expression Ὦ ἀνόητε/ἀνόητοι καὶ βραδὺς/βραδὺ/βραδεῖς τῇ καρδίᾳ "Oh foolish one(s), and slow in heart" is lexically and syntactically more Classical than Koine, and it resides more comfortably in a pagan context, such as in Aesop's fables, than in a Jewish or Christian context, such as in the Gospel of Luke.

More noteworthy than the language and syntax of the expression, however, is the meter in which it is ensconced: within the prose of the Gospel of Luke the expression sticks out as an almost perfectly crafted, full iambic trimeter verse: - ◦ ⌣ - / - ‖ - ⌣ - / - - ⌣ - (Ὦ ἀνόητοι καὶ βραδεῖς τῇ καρδίᾳ). Moreover, the main caesura falls in its

---

[39] Other forms of the root (e.g., the verbal form βραδύνω, the adverbial form βραδέως, the nominal form βραδυτής) do occur in the Septuagint and the New Testament, though very infrequently.

142   *The Formal Education of the Author of Luke-Acts*

regular place after the anceps of the second metron, and Porson's law regarding the anceps of the third metron is observed (i.e., that if long, and if followed by a word break, it must be a monosyllable).[40] The only possible blemish is that the alpha privative of ἀνόητοι, which is a naturally short vowel, should scan as a long syllable here. But this is permissible: the lengthening of the alpha privative for metrical purposes is a liberty taken regularly in ancient Greek poetry (epic, lyric, tragedy, and comedy)—e.g., in the adjective ἀθάνατος "deathless."

The iambic trimeter is, of course, the meter most like natural human speech, as Aristotle reminds us in his *Poetics* (1449a), and so it is possible that Luke at some point in his life blurted out a full iambic trimeter verse entirely by accident. It seems most unlikely, however, that this event, remarkable as it was on its own, would have coincided, again entirely by accident, with the utterance of a rhetorical and poetic expression like this one—and, moreover, that this expression would then appear in two Aesopic fables in a metrical form that evolved from the iambic trimeter. It seems more likely that Luke is quoting a Classical or Hellenistic Greek poetic expression here, and, given that the expression occurs verbatim in the two later versions of Aesop's fables, it seems plausible that Luke is drawing from an ancient version of an Aesopic fable or proverb.

Let us assume for a moment that Luke is, in fact, quoting here from an Aesopic fable—or at least from a free-floating Aesopic proverb. It may seem strange to some that the gospel writer would put the words of Aesop into the mouth of Jesus. But should it? Luke was not an eyewitness to the events that he is narrating, and he makes no claim to be recording the *ipsissima verba* of his subjects. On the contrary, as he confesses in the prologue to his gospel (1:1-4), he is writing at some distance from the events and is therefore relying on a potpourri of oral and written traditions. Moreover, in his gospel, and even more so in Acts, Luke, like many Classical and Hellenistic historians, ornaments the speeches of his internal narrators by putting into their mouths what he deems most appropriate to the occasion. Sometimes what Luke deems most appropriate is a quotation from a Classical or Hellenistic poet: he places part of a very suitable dactylic hexameter verse from the Hellenistic poet Aratus's eulogy to Zeus (*Phaenomena* 5) in the mouth of Paul on the occasion of his speech to the Athenians (Acts 17:28: τοῦ γὰρ καὶ γένος ἐσμέν "for we too are his offspring"); he appears to place part of an iambic trimeter verse from the Classical tragedian Euripides (*Ion* 8) in the mouth of Paul on the occasion of his address to the Roman tribune in the Antonia fortress in Jerusalem (Acts 21:39: οὐκ ἀσήμου πόλεως πολίτης "I am a citizen of no mean city"); and he appears to place part of an iambic trimeter proverb from the Classical poetic tradition (probably Euripides' *Bacchae* 795, possibly Aeschylus's *Agamemnon* 1624 or Pindar's *Pythian* 2.172-3) in the mouth of the resurrected Jesus in Paul's account before King Agrippa of his experience on his journey to Damascus (Acts 26:14: σκληρόν σοι πρὸς κέντρα λακτίζειν "it is difficult for you to kick against the goad"). And, as we have seen, he appears to place two aphorisms from Aesop's fables in the mouth of Jesus in his evaluation of John the Baptist (Lk. 7:24: κάλαμον ὑπὸ ἀνέμου σαλευόμενον "a reed

---

[40] Or, put another way, when an iambic trimeter verse ends in a word forming a cretic ($-\,\smile\,-$), it is regularly preceded either by a short syllable or, if long, by a monosyllable.

shaken by the wind"; Lk. 7:32: ηὐλήσαμεν ὑμῖν καὶ οὐκ ὠρχήσασθε "we played the aulos for you, and you did not dance"). Likewise, here at the end of his gospel, in crafting the details of his version of the story about the events on the way to Emmaus, Luke appears to place in the mouth of the resurrected Jesus a well-known Aesopic proverb in metrical form.

If indeed Luke was drawing from a well-known Aesopic proverb here, how would this have affected the reception of this passage by Luke's audience? In their use of the proverb Ὦ ἀνόητε/ἀνόητοι καὶ βραδὺς/βραδὺ/βραδεῖς τῇ καρδίᾳ "Oh foolish one(s), and slow in heart" both Aesopic fables depict a bewildered speaker chastising his listener(s) for his (their) naiveté, general lack of insight, and obtuseness regarding the wider ramifications of the situation. Hence, when Luke, who was familiar with the resonance of this proverb, was faced with circumstances in his own narrative in which he wanted to emphasize the bewilderment of Jesus in the face of the naiveté, lack of insight, and obtuseness of his disciples, it was natural that he drew from the well of literary and oratorical conventions in which he had been thoroughly immersed. The proverb would, of course, have had a similar resonance for Luke's literate audience.

Aesopic Influence within the Context of Luke's Cultural Milieu

We have proposed that the general popularity of Aesop's fables in the first century CE, and especially the considerable role they played in the educational curriculum of the time, lends plausibility to the assumption that the gospel writers were familiar with them and would have shown no hesitancy to incorporate Aesopic vocabulary, verbal combinations, and proverbial expressions in their own narratives. It may lend some further credibility to the idea that the gospel writers were drawing from Aesopica if we were able to isolate similar Aesopic parallels in the writings of other Jewish and Christian writers within their cultural milieu. And, indeed, we do not have to search very far afield to find them. I offer, as a conclusion, four examples arranged chronologically.

The apocryphal work Sirach (i.e., Ecclesiasticus), which was transmitted through the Greek Septuagint, advises its readers not to associate with people who are stronger and richer than they are, offering the following metaphor (13:2): "What will a clay pot have in common with a metal cauldron? It will strike against it and be shattered." This appears to be an allusion to Aesop's fable of the Clay and Bronze Pots (Chambry 355, Perry 378), which offers the same advice illustrated by the same metaphor: "Two pots, one clay and one bronze, were floating down a river. The clay pot said to the bronze: 'Swim far away from me, and not nearby, for if you touch me I shall break, and I would not willingly touch you.' This fable teaches that life is precarious for a poor man who lives near a rapacious master." The imagery of the metaphor is so distinctive that it seems very unlikely that these two expressions arose independently. Elsewhere the author of Sirach advises that a wise man should seek out the wisdom of all the ancients and that he should travel in foreign lands and learn what is good and evil in the human lot (39:1-4): perhaps this allusion to an Aesopic fable is an illustration of the author following his own advice.

144   *The Formal Education of the Author of Luke-Acts*

The Coptic Gospel of Thomas appears to draw from Aesopica—in addition to the "reed shaken by the wind" proverb in 78 discussed above—a proverb placed in the mouth of Jesus (102): "Jesus said, '[W]oe to those Pharisees, for they are like a dog sleeping in the manger of so[me] cattle, for it neither eats nor al[low]s the cattle to feed.'"[41] That this was a saying very early ascribed to Jesus receives support from two passages in the gospels of Matthew and Luke that provide a context for the proverb: "Woe to you, scribes and Pharisees, hypocrites, since you close the kingdom of heaven to humankind, for you do not enter yourselves nor do you allow entrance to others wishing to enter (Mt. 23:13)." "Woe to you, lawyers, since you have taken the key of knowledge; you yourselves have not entered, and you have prevented others wishing to enter (Lk. 11:52)." Among a large body of proverbs attributed to Aesop we find one almost identical: Κύων ἀναπεσὼν εἰς φάτνην αὐτός τε οὐκ ἐσθίει τῷ τε ὄνῳ ἐμποδίζει. "A dog lying next to a manger does not eat himself and also prevents the donkey (from eating)."[42] This Greek proverb was well known in late antiquity and widely quoted, although the second animal appears sometimes as a horse, cow, or ox rather than a donkey.[43] Whatever the immediate source of the proverb was for the Gospel of Thomas, this little nugget offers an intriguing link between the Jesus and Aesopic traditions.[44]

The early Christian Church Father Clement of Alexandria mentions Aesop by name and paraphrases an Aesopic proverb in his explanation of why Jews refuse to eat swine (*Strom.* 7.6.33.3): "Whence Aesop too did not badly say that swine cry out very loudly when they are seized, for they know that they are good for nothing except for sacrifice." Clement appears to be referring here to an account in the *Life of Aesop* (48) in which Aesop is explaining that sheep remain silent when they are seized because they have become accustomed to the harmless process of being sheared or milked, whereas swine cry out loudly because their only useful function is to be sacrificed for their meat.

According to the Babylonian Talmud (b. B. Qam. 60b) a tale was once related by the second-generation Amoraic Rabbi Itzhak Nafha to illustrate a point to two of his disciples, each of whom had been insisting on a lesson in his particular field of interest: "This is like a man who had two wives, a young one and an old one. The young one would pluck out her husband's white hair, whereas the old one would pluck out his

---

[41]   Translation of the Coptic text by S. J. Gathercole, *The Gospel of Thomas*, 569.

[42]   The Greek proverb appears in the fourteenth-century manuscript Mosquensis 239; it is catalogued as proverb number 74 in B. E. Perry, *Aesopica*, 276. J. F. Priest, "The Dog in the Manger: In Quest of a Fable," *Classical Journal* 81 (1985): 49–58, catalogues all the attestations of the proverb but comes to no definite conclusions about the directions of influence.

[43]   *Greek Anthology* 12.236 (probably Strato of Sardis); Lucian, *Adversus Indoctum* 30, *Timon* 14; Diogenianus the Grammarian, *Paroemiae* 2.83; many of the medieval Greek lexica, beginning with Hesychius. A version in the form of a proper fable (rather than a simple proverb) appears only in a very late Latin prose version among the so-called "Fabulae Extravagantes" (listed as fable 702 in B. E. Perry, *Aesopica*, 696). The directions of influence among the various quotations of the proverb are impossible to determine since no single attestation is clearly earlier than another: perhaps something can be elicited from the coincidence that the four earliest attestations of the proverb—*Greek Anthology* (Strato), Lucian (twice), and the *Gospel of Thomas*—all appear to date to the second century CE and have connections with the East (Asia Minor, Syria, Egypt) rather than the West (Greece and Italy).

[44]   S. J. Gathercole, *The Gospel of Thomas*, 233–8, 505–8, detects the possible exertion of the Aesopic fable tradition elsewhere in the *Gospel of Thomas*: (8) the fable of the small fish that slip through the net; (82) Jesus's expression "He who is near me is near the fire."

black hair. Thus he finally became bald on both sides." The Rabbi's tale is an almost verbatim translation of a widely known Aesopic fable "The Middle-Aged Man and his Two Mistresses" (Halm 56, Chambry 52, Hausrath 31, Perry 31; cf. Babrius 22, Phaedrus 2.2). In the Aesopic tradition the fable is intended to illustrate the perils of falling prey to two overly eager women; Rabbi Nafha uses the tale to illustrate the inappropriate behavior of his overly zealous disciples. Similar expropriation of the Aesopic tradition appears fairly frequently in Jewish Rabbinic literature.[45]

Conclusion

It seems prudent to remain open to the possibility, then—indeed, I would say, the plausibility—firstly, that Luke's account of the rejection of Jesus by his own townspeople in Nazareth (Lk. 4:14-30), and, in particular, the specific details about Jesus being cast out of the city and led to the brow of a mountain to be pushed off, is partly modeled on the account of Aesop's rejection and execution by the townspeople of Delphi in the *Life of Aesop*, and, secondly, that the two aphoristic expressions about John the Baptist attributed by Luke to Jesus, κάλαμον ὑπὸ ἀνέμου σαλευόμενον "a reed shaken by the wind" (Lk. 7:24) and ηὐλήσαμεν ὑμῖν καὶ οὐκ ὠρχήσασθε 'we played the aulos for you, and you did not dance" (Lk. 7:32), are drawn ultimately from aphorisms in Aesop's fables, and, thirdly, that the expression attributed to Jesus on his way to Emmaus, Ὦ ἀνόητοι καὶ βραδεῖς τῇ καρδίᾳ "Oh foolish ones, and slow in heart" (Lk. 24:25), is an actual quotation of a verse from a poetic version of an early Aesopic fable.

As we have noted, Aesopic fables were immensely popular at this time throughout the Mediterranean world. They are regularly referenced in Greek literature of this period, both in poetic and prosaic form, such as in the verses of the Greek Anthology and in the narratives of Diodorus Siculus, Lucian, and Achilles Tatius. We have already observed that Luke's exact contemporary Plutarch quotes, refers to, or mentions Aesop fifty times in his various works. Aesopic fables were also being refashioned *in toto* in various metrical forms during this period, in both Greek and Latin, by poets such as Babrius and Phaedrus. Aesopic fables and proverbs had also become a regular feature of primary and secondary school exercises during this period, as attested both by the instruction of teachers like Quintilian (*Inst.* 1.9.1–3), as well as by the records of actual school exercises that have survived on papyrus sheets and on wax tablets.

The popularity of Aesop was not an exclusively pagan phenomenon. The Aesopic tradition had crept deeply into the Jewish and Christian milieu as well, as attested by Aesopic allusions in the Jewish apocryphal work Sirach and the Christian Gospel of Thomas, and, later, in the writings of the early Christian Fathers and Jewish Rabbis.

In short, we should not be surprised to discover that Luke was familiar with the Aesopic tradition and referenced it in his gospel. On the contrary, we should be surprised if we were to discover that he did not.

---

[45] So H. Schwarzbaum, "Talmudic-Midrashic Affinities of Some Aesopic Fables," *Laographia* 22 (1965): 466–83, who offers a dozen or so parallels.

7

Luke and Epimenides and Aratus
(Acts 17:23, 28a, and 28b)

The narrative of the Acts of the Apostles, like that of many ancient prose works of a historical nature, is punctuated by numerous speeches delivered by internal narrators. Major speeches in *oratio recta* by Paul, Peter, and Stephen constitute about 25 percent of the text of Acts; shorter speeches—e.g., by James, Gamaliel, Demetrius, Tertullus, and Festus—add slightly to this percentage. Nonetheless, almost all the speeches in Acts appear in the form of précis and are, from the perspective of actual rhetorical practice, unrealistically short. Paul's actual speeches would certainly have been much longer—even soporifically so: one thinks of poor Eutychus falling asleep on the windowsill as Paul extends his speech in Troas far into the night (Acts 20:7-9) or of Paul's students in Ephesus enduring his five-hour lectures in the school of Tyrannus (Western text of Acts 19:9). The speeches in Acts do not pretend to be verbatim transcriptions of actual speeches; rather, they appear to be fashioned by Luke to fit the purposes of the speakers on the particular occasions of the speeches and thereby to serve the central function of advancing the action at critical points in the narrative. Moreover, the speeches in Acts are generally presented in the diction, syntax, and style of Luke; there is little to differentiate them linguistically or stylistically from one another or from the larger narrative in which they are embedded. In other words, Luke does not make any discernible effort to preserve the language and style of the speakers. Therefore, when we consider the incidences of Classical and Hellenistic quotations embedded in the speeches in Acts, as in Paul's speech to the Athenians in Acts 17, we can reasonably attribute their inclusion to the author of Acts (Luke—the external narrator) rather than to a speaker embedded in the narrative of Acts (Paul—an internal narrator). M. Dibelius's conclusions on this topic have been influential for almost a century—namely, that the literary aims of the author sometimes overrode historical veracity so that the words of the historical Paul, for example, are not always recorded literally in the speeches attributed to him in Acts.[1]

---

[1] M. Dibelius, "Paul on the Areopagus," in *Studies in the Acts of the Apostles*, 26–77, and M. Dibelius, "The Speeches in Acts and Ancient Historiography," in *Studies in the Acts of the Apostles*, 138–91. Even before Dibelius, the influential German Classical scholars U. von Wilamowitz-Moellendorff and E. Norden, who kept the texts of the ancient historians at their fingertips, had already explicitly expressed their conviction that the speeches in Acts were the invention of a "compiler" or "editor": U. von Wilamowitz-Moellendorff, *Die Griechische Literatur des Altertums* (Leipzig: Teubner, 1907),

148 *The Formal Education of the Author of Luke-Acts*

Paul's speech to the Athenians in Acts 17—whether it is understood to have occurred more publicly, on the Hill of Ares, to the Epicureans and Stoics, among other Athenians and visitors who regularly frequented the Agora, or more privately, within the confines of the Stoa Basileios, exclusively to the Areopagite Council—is situated by Luke in a manner that offers the most suitable occasion in the entire narrative of Acts to portray Paul drawing from the rich tradition of Classical and Hellenistic Greek poetry. And he does so explicitly. For almost two millennia—since at least the time of Clement of Alexandria in the second century CE—Acts 17:28b τοῦ γὰρ καὶ γένος ἐσμέν "for we too are his offspring," a phrase that Paul himself attributes to τινὲς τῶν καθ᾽ ὑμᾶς ποιητῶν "some of your (the Athenians') poets," has been recognized as the beginning of a dactylic hexameter verse (- - / - ◡ ◡ / - ◡) from the astronomical poem *Phaenomena* by the third-century BCE Cilician poet Aratus.[2] But there are probably at least two other quotations earlier in Paul's speech. The first is Paul's reference to an inscription that he had observed on an altar in Athens reading Ἀγνώστῳ Θεῷ "to the unknown god" (Acts 17:23). The second is Paul's poignant description, immediately preceding his

---

190–1; E. Norden, *Agnostos Theos*, 1. The American New Testament scholar H. J. Cadbury too had already proposed that all the speeches in Acts, like those in ancient histories generally, were largely inventions of the author: H. J. Cadbury, "Speeches in Acts," 402–27. This viewpoint is most commonly associated with Dibelius, though, and his conclusions have strongly influenced many New Testament scholars: e.g., U. Wilckens, *Die Missionsreden der Apostelgeschichte* (Neukirchen-Vluyn: Neukirchener Verlag, 1961); E. Plümacher, *Lukas als hellenistischer Schriftsteller*, 32–79, and, later, E. Plümacher, "Die Missionsreden der Apostelgeschichte und Dionys von Halikarnass," *New Testament Studies* 39 (1993): 161–77; the commentaries on Acts of E. Haenchen and H. Conzelmann. For a more recent treatment of the matter that shifts slightly back toward a more traditional and "conservative" view, see the lively presentation by C. Gempf, "Public Speaking and Published Accounts," in *The Book of Acts in its Ancient Literary Setting*, eds. B. W. Winter and A. D. Clarke (Grand Rapids: Eerdmans, 1993), 259–303, who concludes that the speeches in Acts, like those embedded in Greco-Roman historical writing, are not, on the one hand, faithful transcripts of the speeches given on the occasion of their delivery, but neither are they simply fabrications of the author; they are rather documentations of speeches that faithfully record the contexts of the original speeches, including their strategies, tactics, and results (though not, of course, the exact wording). This is, more or less, the view of many "conservative" New Testament scholars with respect to the speeches in Acts: F. F. Bruce, *The Speeches in the Acts of the Apostles* (London: The Tyndale Press, 1944); F. F. Bruce, "The Speeches in Acts—Thirty Years After," in *Reconciliation and Hope*, ed. R. Banks (Grand Rapids: Eerdmans, 1974), 53–68; C. Hemer, *The Book of Acts in the Setting of Hellenistic History* (Tübingen: Mohr Siebeck, 1989), 415–27; C. Hemer, "The Speeches of Acts: I. The Ephesian Elders at Miletus," *Tyndale Bulletin* 40 (1989): 77–85; C. Hemer, "The Speeches in Acts: II. The Areopagus Address," *Tyndale Bulletin* 40 (1989): 239–59; C. S. Keener, *Acts: An Exegetical Commentary*, 1:258–319. This is also the view of the Classicist and scholar of ancient rhetoric G. A. Kennedy, *New Testament Interpretation through Rhetorical Criticism* (Chapel Hill: University of North Carolina Press, 1984), 114–40.

[2] The early Christian tradition is unanimous in its attribution of Acts 17:28b to Aratus: Clement of Alexandria (second century CE), *Stromata* 1.19.91; Origen (second to third century CE), *Commentarii in evangelium Joannis* 10.7; Didymus Caecus (fourth century CE), *In Genesim* (p. 227 in the edition of L. Doutreleau and P. Nautin); Socrates Scholasticus (fourth to fifth century CE), *Historia ecclesiastica* 3.16.25; John Chrysostom (fourth to fifth century CE), *Homiliae in Acta apostolorum* 38 and *Homiliae in epistulam ad Titum* 3; Jerome (fourth to fifth century CE), *Epistulae* 70; the so-called "Euthalian Apparatus" (fourth to seventh century CE) (Migne 85.640); Isho'dad of Merv (ninth century CE Nestorian Commentator), probably quoting Theodore of Mopsuestia (fourth to fifth century CE) (which passage can be found in M. D. Gibson, *The Commentaries of Isho'dad of Merv: Volume IV: Acts of the Apostles and Three Catholic Epistles* (Cambridge: Cambridge University Press, 1913), 29).

quotation of Aratus, of the relationship between the human and the divine: Ἐν αὐτῷ γὰρ ζῶμεν καὶ κινούμεθα καὶ ἐσμέν "For in him (God) we live and move and are" (Acts 17:28a). The two earlier quotations appear to be related, inasmuch as they both pertain in some way to the ancient Cretan prophet Epimenides, and the two later quotations are related, inasmuch as they both describe the relationship between the human and the divine and, of course, inasmuch as they reside in the syntax of a single verse (Acts 17:28):

> Ἐν αὐτῷ γὰρ ζῶμεν καὶ κινούμεθα καὶ ἐσμέν, ὡς καί τινες τῶν καθ' ὑμᾶς ποιητῶν εἰρήκασιν, τοῦ γὰρ καὶ γένος ἐσμέν.

> "For in him (God) we live and move and are [Epimenides]," as some of your poets have said, "for we too are his offspring [Aratus]."

We shall begin our examination of Paul's speech with his explicit quotation of Aratus's *Phaenomena*, and we shall then examine the two earlier quotations that can, with somewhat less certainty, be associated with Epimenides.

Aratus Τοῦ γὰρ καὶ γένος ἐσμέν (Acts 17:28b) "For we too are his offspring"

Born in the province of Cilicia in Asia Minor in the late fourth century BCE, Aratus studied in Ephesus and Cos before making his way to Athens, where he was introduced to Stoicism by the school's founder Zeno, who regularly taught at the Stoa Poikile in the Athenian Agora. Aratus is reported to have dabbled in many genres of literature: astronomical and medical works, funeral elegies, epigrams, letters, hymns, even an edition of Homer's *Odyssey*. But his most famous composition, and the only one that has survived through a manuscript tradition, is a didactic poem on the constellations called the *Phaenomena* ("Appearances"), which was combined with a complementary didactic poem on the weather called the *Diosemeia* ("Signs"), together comprising 1,154 dactylic hexameter verses.

Aratus's *Phaenomena* was highly regarded in its own time, and it became even more popular in subsequent generations. It was even included in a second wave of entries into the literary canon for students advocated by ancient rhetoricians and grammarians. That is to say, in the genre of epic poetry, the Hellenistic poets Aratus, Apollonius of Rhodes, and Theocritus were added to an earlier list of recommended epic poets that included Homer, Hesiod, Panyassis, and Antimachus (e.g., Quintilian, *Inst.* 10.1.55). The use of Aratus's *Phaenomena* in schools led to the publication throughout the eastern Mediterranean of many grammatical and exegetical commentaries on the work (e.g., the second-century BCE commentaries of Attalus of Rhodes, Boethus of Sidon, and Hipparchus of Nicaea). The *Phaenomena* became well known in the western Mediterranean as well, where it was admired and used by Cicero, Vergil, and Ovid, among many other Roman literary figures.

150 *The Formal Education of the Author of Luke-Acts*

There is ample evidence for the popularity of Aratus's *Phaenomena* during Luke's own lifetime. His contemporary Plutarch references Aratus seventeen times in his works, always with respect to the *Phaenomena*. Quotations from Aratus (almost all from the *Phaenomena*) appear on eleven Egyptian papyri from around the time of Luke (100 BCE–200 CE), signaling the work's continued popularity even in the furthest reaches of the Mediterranean world. Like other works in the literary canon, the *Phaenomena* continued to be used also in school texts during the Hellenistic and Roman Imperial periods: *P.Hamb.* 2.121, a papyrus roll written in Herakleopolites, Egypt during the first half of the second century BCE, contains an anthology of verses for use in schools that includes verses 480–94 of Aratus's *Phaenomena*; *P.Berol.* inv. 5865, a papyrus codex from the third to fourth century CE, contains a handbook geared toward making the *Phaenomena* intelligible, presumably to students in a classroom.[3] The second- to third-century CE Christian scholar Origen even suggests that in his speech to the Athenians Paul is remembering a Greek lesson from his preparatory schooling when it occurs to him to spring the quotation of Aratus in Acts 17:28 on his Athenian audience.[4]

So far as Paul's—or rather Luke's—familiarity with, and use of, Aratus's *Phaenomena* is concerned, a helpful analogue can be found in the second-century BCE Jewish apologist Aristobulus of Alexandria, whose aim it was to reconcile Greek philosophical concepts with the Hebrew Scripture and who even ventured that Pythagoras and Plato were familiar with the writings of Moses. In an exposition about Judaism addressed to King Ptolemy, Aristobulus quotes several verses of the invocation to Zeus in Aratus's *Phaenomena* but renders the invocation more acceptable to Jewish sensibilities by substituting "God" for "Zeus" (Θεοῦ for Διός) in the first, second, and fourth verses. For example, he replaces Aratus's first line Ἐκ Διὸς ἀρχώμεσθα ... "From Zeus let us begin ..." with Ἐκ Θεοῦ ἀρχώμεσθα ... "From God let us begin ..."[5] Building a bridge between Greek and Judeo-Christian religious concepts is, of course, Paul's ostensible aim as well in his speech to the Athenians in Acts 17. Similar aims can be observed among other early Christian theologians: the second-century CE Christian patriarch Theophilus of

---

[3] On *P.Hamb.* 2.121, see B. Snell, ed., *Griechische Papyri der Hamburger Staats- und Universitäts-Bibliothek* (Hamburg: J. J. Augustin, 1954), number 121 and plate 3; on *P.Berol.* inv. 5865, see M. Maehler, "Der 'wertlose' Aratkodex P. Berol. Inv. 5865," *Archiv für Papyrusforschung und verwandte Gebiete* 27 (1980): 19–32. H.-I. Marrou, *A History of Education*, 184–5, proposes that Aratus's *Phaenomena* was used to teach astronomy at the secondary level of the *enkyklios paideia*; R. Cribiore, *Gymnastics of the Mind*, 142–3, suggests that the work was linguistically approachable for students because it drew mainly from Homer, with whom they were intimately familiar.

[4] Origen, *Fragmenta ex commentariis in epistulam 1 ad Corinthios* (on 1 Cor. 9:19-23 = section XLIII in C. Jenkins, "Documents: Origen on I Corinthians. III.," *Journal of Theological Studies* 9 (1908): 513): ἀλλ' εἴ που ἦν ἐκ προπαιδεύσεως μάθημα Ἑλληνικὸν τοῦτο ὑπομνησθεὶς ἔλεγεν πρὸς Ἀθηναίους "but if perchance there was a Greek lesson from his preparatory schooling, having remembered this he quoted it to the Athenians."

[5] Aristobulus's comments are preserved in Eusebius's *Praeparatio evangelica* 13.12.6. On quotations of Greek literature by Hellenistic Jewish literary figures, including Aristobulus, see E. S. Gruen, "Jewish Perspectives on Greek Culture," in *Hellenism in the Land of Israel*, eds. J. J. Collins and G. E. Sterling (Notre Dame: University of Notre Dame Press, 2001), 72–6. Some have suggested, without evidence, that in Acts 17:28b Luke is quoting Aristobulus rather than Aratus: M. J. Edwards, "Quoting Aratus: Acts 17:28," *Zeitschrift für die neutestamentliche Wissenschaft* 83 (1992): 266–9; R. I. Pervo, *Acts: A Commentary*, 439; V. Wittkowsky, "'Pagane' Zitate im Neuen Testament," *Novum Testamentum* 51 (2009): 109–10.

Antioch (*Autol.* 2.8) and the second- to third-century CE Christian theologian Clement of Alexandria (*Protr.* 7.73; *Strom.* 5.14.101) both quote several verses of the invocation to Zeus in Aratus's *Phaenomena*. Theophilus contrasts the worldview of the Greek poets to that of the Hebrew Scripture, pointing out the inherent contradictions among the pagans—although he treats Aratus much more charitably than other pagan poets. Clement's approach is much closer to that of Aristobulus, since he offers Aratus as an example of the adage that even pagan philosophers and poets have at times chanced upon divine truth (cf. *Strom.* 1.19.91). It is remarkable that both an earlier Jewish apologist and a later Christian theologian found in Aratus's invocation to Zeus an instrument for rapprochement between Judeo-Christian and Greek religious views. By positioning Aristobulus and Clement's use of Aratus as bookends in our consideration of Acts 17, we are provided with a context for better understanding Paul's motives for quoting Aratus in his speech to the Athenians.

Aratus's *Phaenomena* is introduced with an eighteen-verse proem that is essentially an invocation to Zeus:

> Ἐκ Διὸς ἀρχώμεσθα, τὸν οὐδέποτ' ἄνδρες ἐῶμεν
> ἄρρητον· μεσταὶ δὲ Διὸς πᾶσαι μὲν ἀγυιαί,
> πᾶσαι δ' ἀνθρώπων ἀγοραί, μεστὴ δὲ θάλασσα
> καὶ λιμένες· πάντη δὲ Διὸς κεχρήμεθα πάντες.
> Τοῦ γὰρ καὶ γένος εἰμέν. Ὁ δ' ἤπιος ἀνθρώποισι (5)
> δεξιὰ σημαίνει, λαοὺς δ' ἐπὶ ἔργον ἐγείρει
> μιμνήσκων βιότοιο· λέγει δ' ὅτε βῶλος ἀρίστη
> βουσί τε καὶ μακέλῃσι, λέγει δ' ὅτε δεξιαὶ ὧραι
> καὶ φυτὰ γυρῶσαι καὶ σπέρματα πάντα βαλέσθαι.
> Αὐτὸς γὰρ τά γε σήματ' ἐν οὐρανῷ ἐστήριξεν (10)
> ἄστρα διακρίνας, ἐσκέψατο δ' εἰς ἐνιαυτὸν
> ἀστέρας οἵ κε μάλιστα τετυγμένα σημαίνοιεν
> ἀνδράσιν ὡράων, ὄφρ' ἔμπεδα πάντα φύωνται.
> Τῷ μιν ἀεὶ πρῶτόν τε καὶ ὕστατον ἱλάσκονται.
> Χαῖρε, πάτερ, μέγα θαῦμα, μέγ' ἀνθρώποισιν ὄνειαρ, (15)
> αὐτὸς καὶ προτέρη γενεή. Χαίροιτε δὲ Μοῦσαι
> μειλίχιαι μάλα πᾶσαι. Ἐμοί γε μὲν ἀστέρας εἰπεῖν
> ᾗ θέμις εὐχομένῳ τεκμήρατε πᾶσαν ἀοιδήν.

> From Zeus let us begin; never should we mortals let him remain
> unmentioned. All the streets are full of Zeus,
> and all the marketplaces of men; the sea is full,
> and the harbors; all of us, in every way, have need of Zeus.
> For we too are his offspring. He, in his kindness to mortals,
> grants favorable signs, and he awakens the people for work,
> reminding them of their livelihood. He tells us when the soil is best
> for the oxen and the mattocks, and he tells us when the seasons are favorable
> for trenching round the trees and sowing all sorts of seeds.
> For he himself established the signs in heaven,
> having set apart the constellations, and he considered for each year
> the stars that would especially signal the establishment

152   *The Formal Education of the Author of Luke-Acts*

of the seasons for mortals, so that everything might grow steadfastly.
Therefore mortals always propitiate him first and last.
Hail, father, great wonder, great boon to men,
you yourself and the earlier generation. May you Muses rejoice,
all of you most gracious. And for me, as I pray that I speak of the stars
in a manner that is right, guide my entire song.

It is notable that Paul, Aristobulus before him, and Theophilus and Clement after him, all quote exclusively from this proem of Aratus's *Phaenomena*, the invocation to Zeus: Paul, of course, quotes only verse 5; Aristobolus had quoted verses 1–9; Theophilus would quote verses 1–9; Clement would quote verses 13–15 in his *Protrepticus* and verses 1–6 and 10–15 in his *Stromata*. It is possible that the invocation to Zeus was the only part of Aratus's *Phaenomena* that these writers knew or at least knew well enough to quote. The rest of the *Phaenomena* is a very detailed, and rather tedious, description of the northern and southern constellations, the planets, the celestial circles, the rising of the zodiac, and the phases of the moon and movement of the sun; the *Diosemeia* is then introduced with a second (shorter) invocation to Zeus, followed by a treatment of weather signs. Stoic cosmology permeates the entire work: the cosmos is viewed as ordered and knowable, as it is a manifestation of the divine; Zeus is viewed as a personification of the heavens, and so the movements of the heavenly bodies serve as Zeus's signs of guidance to humanity.

It is altogether suitable that Luke would have Paul quote Aratus in his speech to the Athenians since Paul and Aratus are both from Cilicia (Aratus's hometown of Soli was just twenty miles from Paul's hometown of Tarsus), since their philosophical and theological views overlap in significant ways, and since the audience of Paul's speech, delivered just a stone's throw from where Aratus studied with the Stoic philosopher Zeno, includes some who are themselves Stoics. Paul's quotation of verse five of the *Phaenomena* in Acts 17:28 is not, as some have supposed, simply an offhand quotation lifted from an anthology or a collection of aphorisms that had entered the popular culture.[6] Rather, Paul appears to have in mind here as a context for the quotation the entire invocation of Aratus's *Phaenomena* and, by extension, the poem as a whole. He incorporates the essence of Aratus's *Phaenomena* seamlessly in his speech by picking up on the very language of the quotation in what follows: he rephrases Aratus's poetic τοῦ γὰρ καὶ γένος ἐσμέν "for we too are his offspring" in verse 28 with a more prosaic γένος οὖν ὑπάρχοντες τοῦ θεοῦ ... "therefore being the offspring of God ..." in verse 29, which in turn leads directly to the central theme of his speech: his condemnation of idolatry.

Much of Paul's speech to the Athenians could, in fact, have been comfortably spoken by a Stoic like Aratus: the underlying assumption of monotheism; the argument for the

---

[6]   That Paul is quoting an aphorism divorced from its original literary context is a view already expressed long ago by F. W. Farrar, *The Life and Work of St. Paul*, vol. 1 (New York: E. P. Dutton & Company, 1879), 630–2, and more recently by A. J. Malherbe, *Social Aspects of Early Christianity*, 2nd ed. (Philadelphia: Fortress, 1983), 41–5; K. Berger, "Hellenistische Gattungen im Neuen Testament," *Aufstieg und Niedergang der römischen Welt* II 25, no. 2 (1984): 1055; J. E. Stambaugh and D. L. Balch, *The New Testament in Its Social Environment* (Philadelphia: Westminster, 1986), 121–2; H. Chadwick, "Some Ancient Anthologies and Florilegia, Pagan and Christian," in *Studies on Ancient Christianity*, ed. H. Chadwick (Aldershot: Ashgate Publishing, 2006), 7; C. S. Keener, *Acts: An Exegetical Commentary*, 3:2659–61.

Luke and Epimenides and Aratus   153

existence of god from design in nature; the belief that god transcends but at the same time permeates his entire creation; the idea of a creation of everything from one; the trust in god's establishment of seasons and boundaries; the perception that god is not far from each of us and that we should strive to seek and find him; the assurance that in god we live and move and are; the conviction that we are god's offspring; the notion that god does not need anything from humankind; the attendant criticism of popular religion, with its man-made idols, altars, etc.; and, finally, the anticipation of a righteous judgment at the end of time.[7]

The only stumbling block for Paul's Athenian audience, really, is his assertion of a resurrection of a man (Jesus) from the dead, an idea introduced by Paul at the very end of his speech (17:31). This idea is met immediately by ridicule from his Athenian audience (17:32). Though the ancient Greeks speculated philosophically about the reincarnation of the soul, they did not embrace a physical resurrection. Paul's concept of ἀνάστασις ("resurrection") would have struck them as something foreign, even inimical, to their fundamental beliefs.

Addendum on Cleanthes' *Hymn to Zeus*

Some commentators on Acts have attributed Paul's quotation in Acts 17:28b τοῦ γὰρ καὶ γένος ἐσμέν "for we too are his offspring" to Cleanthes of Assos, the fourth- to third-century BCE Stoic philosopher and successor to Zeno of Citium as the head of the Stoic school in Athens, who composed a *Hymn to Zeus* whose fourth line begins ἐκ σοῦ γὰρ γένος ἐσμέν "for from you are we the offspring."[8] Cleanthes' *Hymn to Zeus* has

---

[7]   Stoic themes in Paul's speech have been identified and traced by several scholars over the past century: e.g., E. Norden, *Agnostos Theos*, 3–140; M. Pohlenz, "Paulus und die Stoa," *Zeitschrift für die neutestamentliche Wissenschaft* 42 (1949): 69–104; M. Dibelius, "Paul on the Areopagus," 26–77; H. Hommel, "Neue Forschungen zur Areopagrede Acta 17," *Zeitschrift für die neutestamentliche Wissenschaft* 46 (1955): 145–78; D. L. Balch, "The Areopagus Speech: An Appeal to the Stoic Historian Posidonius against Later Stoics and the Epicureans," in *Greeks, Romans, and Christians*, eds. D. L. Balch et al. (Minneapolis: Fortress, 1990), 52–79; E. J. Schnabel, "Contextualising Paul in Athens: The Proclamation of the Gospel Before Pagan Audiences in the Graeco-Roman World," *Religion and Theology* 2 (2005): 172–90.

[8]   The following commentators on Acts 17:28b have at least entertained the possibility of Cleanthes as a source of the quotation (in chronological order): J. B. Lightfoot, *Biblical Essays* (London: Macmillan, 1893), 206; Th. Zahn, *Introduction to the New Testament*, vol. 1 (New York: Charles Scribner's Sons, 1909), 52, 71; P. H. Ling, "A Quotation from Euripides," *The Classical Quarterly* 19 (1925): 26; F. J. Foakes Jackson and K. Lake, eds., *The Beginnings of Christianity*, 4:218; R. Renehan, "The Collectanea Alexandrina Selected Passages," *Harvard Studies in Classical Philology* 68 (1964): 385—though Renehan appears to have changed his mind a decade later in R. Renehan, "Classical Greek Quotations in the New Testament," in *The Heritage of the Early Church: Essays in Honor of Georges Vasilievich Florovsky on the Occasion of his Eightieth Birthday*, eds. D. Neiman and M. Schatkin (Rome: Pontificium Institutum Studiorum Orientalium, 1973), 40, when he declares that the words in Acts 17:28b "belong to Aratus and to no one else"; H. R. Minn, "Classical Reminiscence in St. Paul," *Prudentia* 6 (1974): 95–6; R. Pesch, *Die Apostelgeschichte II* (Zurich: Benziger, 1986), 139; D. Kidd, *Aratus: Phaenomena* (Cambridge: Cambridge University Press, 1997), 166; C. K. Barrett, *A Critical and Exegetical Commentary on the Acts of the Apostles*, 2:848; J. C. Thom, *Cleanthes' Hymn to Zeus* (Tübingen: Mohr Siebeck, 2005), 65. The apparatus to Acts 17:28b in the United Bible Societies' *Greek New Testament* practices a diplomatic ambivalence with the laconic notation: "Cleanthes? Aratus, *Phaenomena* 5" (likewise in its index of allusions and verbal parallels).

154   *The Formal Education of the Author of Luke-Acts*

not survived through a manuscript tradition, but its thirty-nine verses are quoted in full in the fifth-century CE *Anthology* of Stobaeus (1.1.12). What follows is the invocation of Cleanthes' hymn as recorded in the single manuscript of Stobaeus's *Anthology* that includes the hymn, the fourteenth-century Codex Farnesinus III D 15 currently housed in the Biblioteca Nazionale di Napoli:

Κύδιστε[9] ἀθανάτων, πολυώνυμε, παγκρατὲς αἰεί,
Ζεὺς[10], φύσεως ἀρχηγέ, νόμου μετὰ πάντα κυβερνῶν,
χαῖρε· σὲ γὰρ πᾶσι[11] θέμις θνητοῖσι προσαυδᾶν.
ἐκ σοῦ γὰρ γένος ἐσμὲν ἤχου μίμημα λαχόντες[12]
μοῦνοι, ὅσα ζώει τε καὶ ἕρπει θνήτ' ἐπὶ γαῖαν·
τῷ σε καθυμνήσω καὶ σὸν κράτος αἰὲν ἀίδω[13].

Most honored of immortals, you of many names, always all-powerful,
Zeus, first cause of nature, who guides everything lawfully,
Hail! For it is right for all mortals to call upon you.
For from you are we the offspring, having chanced upon an imitation of your voice,
we alone of all the mortal creatures that live and creep upon the earth.
Therefore, I shall hymn you and always sing of your might.

There are indeed some broad themes shared by Cleanthes' *Hymn to Zeus* and Paul's speech to the Athenians in Acts 17, most notably that a single god created the cosmos and now sustains everything in it. But there are no exact quotations of Cleanthes' hymn in Paul's speech. The original reading of verse four of the hymn is unclear—ἐκ σοῦ γὰρ γένος ἐσμέν? ἐκ σοῦ γὰρ γένος εἶσ'? ἐκ σοῦ γὰρ γενόμεσθα/γενόμεσθ'?—but, whatever it was, it was not identical to Acts 17:28b. Paul's quotation in Acts 17:28b is clearly from verse five of Aratus's *Phaenomena*, with which it is identical (save for the substitution of ἐσμέν for Aratus's εἰμέν). Moreover, as observed above, ancient commentators on Acts from as early as Clement and Origen are unanimous in attributing the quotation to Aratus, while no one in antiquity ever suggested any connection with Cleanthes.

---

[9] Κύδιστε should be elided as Κύδιστ' in order for the verse to scan properly.
[10] The vocative Ζεῦ would fit the syntax better than the nominative Ζεύς.
[11] The third verse does not scan properly in the manuscript, but this is easily resolved by substituting the alternative epic form πάντεσσι for πᾶσι.
[12] The fourth verse does not scan properly in the manuscript, and the meaning is unclear. O. Hense and C. Wachsmuth's edition of Stobaeus (*Ioannis Stobaei anthologium*, vol. 1 (1884; repr., Berlin: Weidmann, 1958), 25), which aims to record the actual readings of Stobaeus rather than "corrected" readings, records the verse thus, in its unmetrical form. J. von Arnim's edition of the fragments of Cleanthes (*Stoicorum veterum fragmenta*, vol. 1 (Leipzig: Teubner, 1905), 103–137) reconstructs the verse as ἐκ σοῦ γὰρ γένος εἶσ' ἤχου μίμημα λαχόντες. J. U. Powell's edition of the fragments of Cleanthes (*Collectanea Alexandrina* (Oxford: Clarendon, [1925] 1970), 227–231) reconstructs the verse as ἐκ σοῦ γὰρ γενόμεσθα, θεοῦ μίμημα λαχόντες. Many other emendations have been proposed: a dozen or so are evaluated in R. Renehan, "The Collectanea Alexandrina," 382–6. The newest edition, translation, and commentary of Cleanthes' hymn by J. C. Thom, *Cleanthes' Hymn to Zeus*, 54–66, offers a full repertory of conjectures for the fourth verse: twenty-seven different conjectures proposed between the time of Joseph Scaliger in 1573 and Hans Schwabl in 2001.
[13] This should be corrected to ἀείδω or ἀείσω.

Scholars who attribute Paul's quotation to Cleanthes (often along with Aratus) seem to be motivated by two considerations: 1) Paul introduces the quotation in Acts 17:28b by saying "As some of your *poets* have said," with *poets* in the plural, so Paul must be quoting more than one poet here (Aratus *and* Cleanthes); 2) Paul's expression "*your* poets," addressed to an Athenian audience, implies that he is quoting Athenian poets, and Cleanthes, as the head of the Stoic school in Athens for the last third of his life, was more closely associated than Aratus with Athens.[14] However, the plural *poets* is not a determining factor here, as the plural form of ποιητής is commonly used in antiquity to introduce a quotation of just one poet.[15] Moreover, if a second poet were needed to justify the phrase, Paul's expression could be understood to refer backward to the quotation of Epimenides, as we shall see below, as well as forward to the quotation of Aratus. The issue of "*your* poets" is not a determining factor either, for Aratus too spent time in Athens, where he studied with Peripatetic and Stoic philosophers, including Zeno, the founder of Stoicism.

Epimenides Ἀγνώστῳ Θεῷ (Acts 17:23) "To the unknown god"

Before the explicit quotation of Aratus's *Phaenomena* (Acts 17:28b), which occurs halfway through Paul's speech to the Athenians, there occur at least one and possibly two other quotations. The first is Paul's reference at the beginning of his speech to an inscription reading Ἀγνώστῳ Θεῷ "to the unknown god" that he claims to have observed earlier on an altar in Athens (Acts 17:23). The second resides in the first half of the verse that, as we have seen, also contains a quotation of Aratus (Acts 17:28a): Ἐν αὐτῷ γὰρ ζῶμεν καὶ κινούμεθα καὶ ἐσμέν "for in him (God) we live and move and are." Both can be associated in some respect with the ancient Cretan prophet Epimenides; the first reference, which is a more oblique allusion to an Epimenidean altar to an unknown god, prepares Paul's audience for the quotation, or at least paraphrase, of an actual epic verse of Epimenides that follows.

A rich tradition arose in antiquity about the life and deeds of Epimenides, some of it perhaps historical but much of it mythical: that he was a prophet from Knossos on Crete who as a boy, while tending his father's sheep, fell asleep in a cave for many years,

---

[14] The variant "*our* poets" (ἡμᾶς) found in a few manuscripts is surely a result of itacism, which was the source of many similar textual variants in the New Testament: ὑμᾶς "your" and ἡμᾶς "our" were pronounced alike by the early centuries of the Christian era. In such cases of phonetic ambiguity a *lectio difficilior* is sometimes to be preferred but not a *lectio impossibilis*: it is hardly possible that Paul would have included himself among the Athenians whom he was addressing.

[15] E.g., Lycurgus, *Contra Leocratem* 92 and 132 (citing single tragedies), Aristotle, *Politica* 1252b (citing Euripides), and 1335b (citing Solon), Aristotle, *Magna Moralia* 2.15.1 (citing Euripides), Plutarch, *Adversus Colotem* 1113a (citing Homer). Some additional plural constructions are noted by M. Dibelius, *Studies in the Acts of the Apostles*, 51 (Philo and Ps.-Aristotle) and some from even later antiquity by R. Renehan "Classical Greek Quotations in the New Testament," 41 (Simplicius) and R. Renehan, "Acts 17:28," *Greek, Roman, and Byzantine Studies* 20 (1979): 347–53 (Zenobius).

156   *The Formal Education of the Author of Luke-Acts*

awoke with the gift of prophecy, and lived to an astonishingly old age.[16] His primary encounter with Athens entailed his purification of the city after the sacrilege of the Alcmaeonidae (late seventh century BCE), who had murdered the followers of Cylon while they sat as suppliants at the altars on the Acropolis.[17] At that time Epimenides was said to have placed altars to various local divinities all around the Areopagus. Diogenes Laertius (*Lives* 1.110) adds an interesting detail that is pertinent to our understanding of Paul's speech in Acts 17: "even to this day there are to be found throughout the demes of the Athenians 'anonymous altars' (βωμοὶ ἀνώνυμοι) that are memorials of this purification."

There are at least three other ancient references, independent of Luke's account of Paul's speech in Acts 17, to altars in Athens set up to honor unknown divinities. The second-century CE geographer Pausanias, who spent a considerable amount of time in Athens, mentions, among the temples, sanctuaries, and statues of many other divinities, some "altars of gods called Unknown" (βωμοὶ θεῶν ὀνομαζομένων Ἀγνώστων) near Athens' harbor at Phalerum (1.1.4). The Athenian sophist Philostratus (second to third century CE) records a conversation of the neo-Pythagorean philosopher Apollonius of Tyana, a contemporary of Luke, in which Apollonius, recalling the mythic Hippolytus's disdain for the goddess Aphrodite, advises that "it is prudent to speak well of all the gods, and especially in Athens, where altars even of unknown divinities (ἀγνώστων δαιμόνων) have been set up" (*Vit. Apoll.* 6.3.5). The Christian apologist Tertullian (second to third century CE) on two occasions mentions that there is in Athens an altar with the inscription "to the unknown gods" (*ignotis deis*) (*Nat.* 2.9; *Marc.* 1.9). In neither passage is Tertullian alluding to Paul's speech in Acts 17; rather, he is remarking generally on the idolatry of the Athenians.[18]

---

[16] The details of Epimenides' life and works are most fully narrated in Diogenes Laertius's *Lives of the Philosophers* 1.109-15. Additional accounts of his life and deeds, sometimes with conflicting details, are included in Plato, *Laws* 642d-e and 677d-e; Aristotle, *Constitution of the Athenians* 1 and *Rhetorica* 1418a; Apollonius (the second-century BCE? paradoxographer), *Historiae mirabiles* 1.1-4; Plutarch, *Life of Solon* 12.7-12 (and in several of Plutarch's minor works). Also, several anecdotal comments about Epimenides appear in Cicero, *De legibus* 2.28 and *De divinatione* 1.34; Strabo, *Geographica* 10.4.14; Valerius Maximus, *Facta et dicta memorabilia* 8.13(ext).5; Lucian, *Timon* 6 and *Philopseudes* 26; Pausanias 1.14.4, 2.21.3-4, 3.11.11, 3.12.11, 8.18.2; Maximus of Tyre, *Dissertationes* 10.1, 38.3-4; and in medieval grammars, lexica, and scholia, as well as in some of the early Church Fathers, to whom we shall turn shortly.

[17] Cf. Herodotus 5.71; Thucydides 1.126; Aristotle, *Constitution of the Athenians* 1; Plutarch, *Life of Solon* 12.

[18] Altars to unknown gods are known from elsewhere in the ancient Mediterranean as well: Pausanias (5.14.8) observes an altar of unknown gods (ἀγνώστων θεῶν βωμός) in Olympia; Strabo (3.4.16) reports that the Celts living in Iberia sacrifice to an anonymous god (ἀνωνύμῳ τινὶ θεῷ); a dedicatory inscription erected in the precinct of the temple of Demeter in Pergamum in the second century CE (?) and excavated in 1909 has plausibly been reconstructed as:

ΘΕΟΙΣΑΓ[ΝΩΣΤΟΙΣ
ΚΑΠΙΤ[ΩΝ
ΔΑΔΟΥΧΟ[Σ
Kapiton the Torch-Bearer (dedicated this altar) to the unknown gods.

This inscription was first published in H. Hepding, "Die Arbeiten zu Pergamon 1908–1909, II: Die Inschriften," *Mitteilungen des kaiserlich deutschen archäologischen Instituts, Athenische Abteilung* 35 (1910): 454-7, who provides a photograph, reconstructed text, and some commentary. Hepding

Luke and Epimenides and Aratus 157

There is, of course, no explicit reference to the Cretan prophet Epimenides in Paul's quotation of the inscription Ἀγνώστῳ Θεῷ in Acts 17:23. However, the story of Epimenides' deeds in Athens was probably so well known among Paul's (and Luke's) audience that an association could have been taken for granted. Some of the Church Fathers appear to have made the association. Didymus Caecus (fourth century CE), *In Genesim* (p. 227 in the edition of L. Doutreleau and P. Nautin), mentions together Paul's quotations Ἀγνώστῳ Θεῷ in Acts 17:23 and Κρῆτες ἀεὶ ψεῦσται "Cretans are always liars" in Titus 1:12 (along with the quotation of Aratus τοῦ γὰρ καὶ γένος ἐσμέν in Acts 17:28b). The quotation about the Cretans is attributed by the author of Titus himself to a Cretan prophet, and it is attributed specifically to Epimenides by several Church Fathers: Clement of Alexandria, Epiphanius, John Chrysostom, Socrates Scholasticus, Augustine, and Oecumenius. Epiphanius (fourth century CE), *Panarion* (p. 169 in K. Holl's 1922 edition), and John Chrysostom (fourth to fifth century CE), *Homiliae in epistulam ad Titum* 3, are even more explicit than Didymus about the association: they present the quotations in Acts 17:23 and Titus 1:12 together and attribute the latter specifically to Epimenides.

We shall consider below the question of what poetic work of Epimenides is being quoted in Titus 1:12 and, by extension, in Acts 17:28a. For now it is sufficient to mention that Epimenides was thought in antiquity to have written many poetic works, including, according to Diogenes Laertius, a *Theogony*, an *Argonautica*, a poem *On the Birth of the Curetes and Corybantes*, and a poem *On Minos and Rhadamanthus*, as well as some prose works *On Sacrifices* and *The Cretan Constitution*.[19] Other titles mentioned in antiquity are a *Cretica* and a *Chresmoi* ("Oracles").[20] And the tenth-century CE lexicon, the *Suda* (*sub* Ἐπιμενίδης), mentions in addition some prose works by Epimenides on religious mysteries, on purificatory rites, and on riddles.

It is possible, of course, that these are all later works attributed to the semi-mythical Epimenides in order to elevate their status.[21] Works of the Classical, Hellenistic, and

---

concedes, however, that the first line of the inscription could also be reconstructed as ΘΕΟΙΣΑΓ[ΙΩΤΑΤΑΙΣ, i.e., θεοῖς ἁγιωτάταις "to the two most holy goddesses," referring to Demeter and Persephone. The superlative form of this adjective is fairly common in descriptions of divinities on dedicatory inscriptions, including ones to Demeter and Persephone (*IG* V,1 594), and the location of the altar in the precinct of the temple of Demeter favors this latter reconstruction. For a more accessible presentation of the inscription, including a photograph, transcription, and discussion, see A. Deissmann, *St. Paul: A Study in Social and Religious History* (London: Hodder and Stoughton, 1912), 261–6. For a catalog of ancient evidence for an altar to an unknown god, or rather gods, in Athens, see F. J. Foakes Jackson and K. Lake, eds., *The Beginnings of Christianity*, 5:240–6. For a more recent survey of comparative inscriptional material, see P. van der Horst, "The Altar of the 'Unknown God' in Athens (Acts 17:23), and the Cults of 'Unknown Gods' in the Hellenistic and Roman Periods," *Aufstieg und Niedergang der römischen Welt* II 18, no. 2 (1989): 1426–56.

[19] Diogenes Laertius's account (*Lives* 1.111–12) is contradictory, however, as he lists *On Minos and Rhadamanthus* among the prose works (καταλογάδην) *On Sacrifices* and *The Cretan Constitution* but then states that *On Minos and Rhadamanthus* comprised 4000 (epic) verses (ἔπη).

[20] Eratosthenes (*Catasterismi* 1.27) mentions a *Cretica* (τὰ Κρητικά), and Diodorus Siculus (*Bibliotheca historica* 5.80.4) appears to reference an Epimenidean *Cretica* as well. This is perhaps the same as the work titled *On Minos and Rhadamanthus* by Diogenes Laertius. In his commentary on Titus Jerome attributes Titus 1:12 to Epimenides' work *Oraculorum* or perhaps *De oraculis*, which would be a Latin translation of a Greek Χρησμῶν or perhaps Περὶ Χρησμῶν.

[21] M. L. West, *The Orphic Poems* (Oxford: Clarendon, 1983), 45–53, locates these works in the fifth century—and later.

158   *The Formal Education of the Author of Luke-Acts*

even Roman Imperial periods tended to become attached to such figures as Epimenides: one may compare the many works attributed throughout antiquity to Orpheus, Homer, Hesiod, Pythagoras, and Aesop. For our purposes, none of this really matters: only the fact that in the first century CE certain works were thought by many to have been composed long ago by the Cretan prophet Epimenides.

Epimenides Ἐν αὐτῷ γὰρ ζῶμεν καὶ κινούμεθα καὶ ἐσμέν (Acts 17:28a) "For in him we live and move and are"

There is no record of any commentator on Acts between the beginnings of the tenth and the twentieth centuries identifying Paul's words in Acts 17:28a Ἐν αὐτῷ γὰρ ζῶμεν καὶ κινούμεθα καὶ ἐσμέν "For in him we live and move and are" as a quotation of Greek poetry. And for good reason. First of all, the phrase does not scan in any poetic meter in its inherited form; it is straight prose. Secondly, most of the Patristic commentators who identify 17:28b τοῦ γὰρ καὶ γένος ἐσμέν as a quotation of Greek poetry, some even offering its source as Aratus, do not make similar claims about 17:28a: so Clement of Alexandria, Origen, Jerome, Didymus Caecus, Socrates Scholasticus, John Chrysostom.[22]

However, it should be kept in mind that many ancient Greek verses that are embedded in prose texts have lost their metrical shapes, either in the initial act of the poetic verse being quoted or paraphrased or in the process of scribal transmission. At any point the original poetic form could have been altered for a variety of reasons. The person could be changed, from second to third person, for example, as perhaps here in Acts 17:28a, where, as we shall see, Ἐν γὰρ σοὶ ζῶμεν of Epimenides' verse has been changed to Ἐν αὐτῷ γὰρ ζῶμεν of Paul's speech. The dialect could be changed from Ionic to Attic or Koine, for example, as in Acts 17:28b, where the epic form εἰμέν of Aratus's poem has been changed to the prosaic form ἐσμέν of Paul's speech (though in this case the meter is not affected by the change). It was also common in prose to write out in full (*scriptio plena*) those words whose vowels had been elided in their original poetic form: Paul, or his amanuensis, or a later scribe, quotes χρῆσθ' ὁμιλίαι of Euripides' and/or Menander's iambic trimeter verse as χρηστὰ ὁμιλίαι in 1 Corinthians 15:33, thereby undermining the poetic meter. Likewise, when Justin Martyr embeds within his prose Euripides' famous iambic trimeter verse ἡ γλῶσσ' ὀμώμοχ', ἡ δὲ φρὴν ἀνώμοτος "My tongue swore, but my mind was unsworn" (*Hipp.* 612), he undermines

---

[22] Clement of Alexandria, while identifying Acts 17:28b "for we too are his offspring" as drawn by Paul from Aratus's *Phaenomena* (*Strom.* 1.19.91), draws no connection to Epimenides in Acts 17:28a "for in him we live and move and are." The fact that Clement explicitly demonstrates his familiarity with Epimenides by identifying Titus 1:12 "Cretans are always liars, evil beasts, lazy bellies" as drawn by Paul from Epimenides (*Strom.* 1.14.59) makes the absence of any reference by him to Epimenides in relation to Acts 17:28a all the more significant. But it is possible that Clement regards Acts 17:28a as a second quotation from Aratus, for he claims that Paul is "making use of poetic models (plural) from Aratus's *Phaenomena*" (ποιητικοῖς χρώμενος παραδείγμασιν ἐκ τῶν Ἀράτου Φαινομένων) (*Strom.* 1.19.91).

Luke and Epimenides and Aratus 159

the meter by failing to observe two elisions: ἡ γλῶσσα ὀμώμοκεν ἡ δὲ φρὴν ἀνώμοτος (*1 Apol.* 39.4). Also, prosaic quotations regularly write out in full words that have suffered crasis (τὰ ἄλλα for τἄλλα) or apocope (κατά for κάτ) in their poetic forms, and they regularly contract combinations of vowels that had appeared uncontracted in the poetic form, as here, for example, in Acts 17:28a, where the uncontracted poetic form κινεόμεσθα of Epimenides' verse has been changed to a contracted prosaic form κινούμεθα of Paul's speech. As we shall see below, a metrical form of Acts 17:28a can quite easily be reconstructed.

Also, the frequently repeated claim that the Patristic commentators regarded Acts 17:28b but not 17:28a as a quotation does not appear to be entirely correct. Augustine (fourth to fifth century CE) appears to think that 17:28a is a quotation of Greek literature, while, surprisingly, he does not seem to realize that 17:28b is a quotation of the Greek poet Aratus.[23] Augustine cites 17:28a many times, along with the claim in Acts "as some of the poets among you have said," but without even mentioning 17:28b. In his *Confessions* 7.9.15, for example, Augustine, speaking about the knowledge he has acquired through pagan literature, quotes only the first half of Acts 17:28 and attributes it to the Greeks:

> et dixisti Atheniensibus per Apostolum tuum, quod in te vivimus et movemur et sumus; sicut et quidam secundum eos dixerunt.

> And you spoke to the Athenians through your apostle that "in you we live and move and are," as also some among them have said.[24]

It is perhaps significant for our purposes that in two passages Augustine defends Paul's quotation of a Greek source in Acts 17:28a immediately after he has defended his quotation of the "prophet of Crete" in Titus 1:12.[25]

Athanasius (fourth century CE) too appears to be aware of a Greek saying that he understands as the source behind what he regards as a quotation in Acts 17:28a. Athanasius has been speaking about what the Greek philosophers believe, or should believe, concerning the relationship between the divine Logos, the universe, and humanity (*Inc.* 41–2). Then, as evidence of his contention that the Logos resides in humanity, Athanasius, referring to these Greek sources, declares: καθὼς καὶ οἱ παρ' αὐτοῖς συγγραφεῖς φασιν ὅτι ἐν αὐτῷ ζῶμεν, καὶ κινούμεθα, καὶ ἐσμέν "just as the writers among them say that 'in him we live and move and are'" (*Inc.* 42.4). Athanasius elsewhere uses this precise phrase οἱ παρ' αὐτοῖς συγγραφεῖς "the writers among them" to refer to the Greek poets, including Homer (*C. Gent.* 16.33). He also uses the similar phrase οἱ παρ' αὐτοῖς θαυμαστοὶ ποιηταί "the marvelous poets among them" to refer to pagan Greek sources (*C. Gent.* 17.11).

---

[23] Augustine knows Aratus—he mentions him in passing in *De civitate Dei* 16.23, apparently referring to his *Phaenomena*—but Augustine makes no reference in any of his works to Aratus as author of Acts 17:28b.

[24] Similarly in *De civitate Dei* 8.10; *Expositio quarumdam propositionum ex epistula ad Romanos* 3; *Contra Gaudentium* 2.10.11; *Sermones de novo testamento* 68.6; *De unico baptismo contra Petilianum* 4.6; *Contra litteras Petiliani* 2.30.69; *Contra adversarium legis et prophetarum* 2.4.13.

[25] *Contra litteras Petiliani* 2.30.69; *Contra adversarium legis et prophetarum* 2.4.13.

160   *The Formal Education of the Author of Luke-Acts*

Augustine's "some among them" (*quidam secundum eos*) and Athanasius's "writers among them" (οἱ παρ' αὐτοῖς συγγραφεῖς) are apparently identified as the Cretan prophet Epimenides himself by the ecclesiastical writer Theodore (*c.* 350–428 CE), Bishop of Mopsuestia in Cilicia, who attributes 17:28a to Minos, presumably a speaker in a work by Epimenides. The path to this conclusion is a circuitous one, but it is extremely important to my contention that Acts 17:28a is a quotation of Epimenides, so I shall grant it an extended explanation in what follows.

In 1906, the New Testament scholar J. R. Harris chanced upon a copy of an anonymous Syriac commentary on the Nestorian lectionary called the *Gannat Bussame* "Garden of Delights" that includes in one family of manuscripts some commentary on Paul's speech to the Athenians in the Acts of the Apostles. The commentary as a whole incorporates many passages from Theodore of Mopsuestia—referred to anonymously as "the Interpreter" in order to avoid too close an association with someone who was thought to hold unorthodox theological views—among which is the following passage on Acts 17:28:

> "In Him we live and move and have our being." The Cretans used to say of Zeus, that he was a prince and was ripped up by a wild boar, and he was buried: and lo! his grave is with us. Accordingly Minos, the son of Zeus, made over him a panegyric and in it he said: "A grave have fashioned for thee, O holy and high One, the lying Kretans, who are all the time liars, evil beasts, idle bellies; but thou diest not, for to eternity thou livest, and standest; for in thee we live and move and have our being."
>
> translation of the Syriac text by J. R. Harris[26]

Harris recognized immediately, of course, that the purported panegyric of Zeus by his son, the Cretan king Minos, included versions of two passages that also occurred in the New Testament: "Paul's" quotation of a dactylic hexameter verse by a Cretan prophet in his letter to Titus (1:12) Κρῆτες ἀεὶ ψεῦσται, κακὰ θηρία, γαστέρες ἀργαί "Cretans are always liars, evil beasts, lazy bellies," and "Paul's" declaration to the Athenians in Acts 17:28a Ἐν αὐτῷ γὰρ ζῶμεν καὶ κινούμεθα καὶ ἐσμέν "For in him we live and move and are." What is this panegyric of Zeus by the Cretan king Minos that appears to have been the source of these two New Testament passages? Likely none other than a work of the Cretan prophet and poet Epimenides. The dactylic hexameter verse in Titus 1:12 is attributed by the author of that letter to a Cretan prophet, and the verse has been broadly attributed to Epimenides by the Church Fathers since at least the time of Clement of Alexandria. Theodore of Mopsuestia's commentary on Acts 17:28 preserved in the *Gannat Bussame* suggests that Acts 17:28a is from the same source. As we have already observed, Diogenes Laertius (*Lives* 1.112) reports that,

---

[26] See J. R. Harris, "The Cretans Always Liars," *The Expositor* 7, no. 2 (1906): 305–17; "A Further Note on the Cretans," *The Expositor* 7, no. 3 (1907): 332–7; "St. Paul and Epimenides," *The Expositor* 8, no. 4 (1912): 348–53; "Once More the Cretans," *The Expositor* 8, no. 9 (1915): 29–35; *St. Paul and Greek Literature* (Cambridge: W. Heffer & Sons, 1927) 1–25. The quoted passage is not explicitly attributed to "the Interpreter," but it follows immediately upon an extract from Theodore, and it is clearly a translation of a Greek source.

Luke and Epimenides and Aratus

among several other works, Epimenides composed a 4000-verse work called *On Minos and Rhadamanthus*. Perhaps it was in this work that Epimenides included a poetic denunciation of the Cretans as liars and placed it in the mouth of his internal narrator Minos.[27]

Further light was shed on this matter a few years later when the Semitic scholar M. D. Gibson published a text and translation of a Syriac commentary on Acts by the ninth-century CE Nestorian Church Father Isho'dad of Merv. In the section on Acts 17 Isho'dad, like the author of the *Gannat Bussame*, quotes "the Interpreter," presumably Theodore of Mopsuestia, as follows:

> About this altar on which was written "To the hidden God" Mar Ephraim and others say that want of rain and earthquakes sometimes happened at Athens. And when they took counsel to make prayers collectively every day, they changed the altars of all their gods. And when altars were at an end, and there were no helps, they overturned them and threw them down. And again they congregated and took counsel saying, "If there are no others, who is this one who does not cease to trouble us?" And they carved and set up altars to the hidden God, whoever He was. And when the mercies of Grace revealed about the anguish of their minds, He sent them help. But the Interpreter says that the Athenians were once upon a time at war with their enemies, and the Athenians retreated from them in defeat. Then a certain Demon appeared and said unto them, "I have never been honoured by you as I ought; and because I am angry with you, therefore you have a defeat from your enemies." Then the Athenians were afraid and raised up to him the well-known altar. And because they dreaded lest this very thing should happen to them, having secretly neglected [one] who was unknown to them, they erected for themselves one altar more and wrote upon it "Of the Unknown and Hidden God." And when they wished to say this, that though there is a God in whom we do not believe, we raise this altar to His honour that He may be reconciled to us, although He is not honoured as known, therefore Paul did well to take a reason from this and said before them, "This hidden God, to whom ye have raised an altar without knowing Him, I have come to declare unto you. There is no God whom ye know not, except the true God, who hath appointed the times by His command, and hath put bounds, etc." This "He hath determined the times," that is to say, the variations of summer and winter, spring and autumn.
>
> This "In Him we live and move and have our being," and this, "As certain of your own sages have said, We are His offspring." Paul takes both of these from certain heathen poets. Now about this, "In Him we live, etc.," because the Cretans said as truth about Zeus that he was a lord, he was lacerated by a wild boar and buried, and, behold, his grave is known amongst us, so therefore Minos, son of Zeus, made a laudatory speech on behalf of his father, and he said in it: "The Cretans carve a

---

[27] H. Diels, *Die Fragmente der Vorsokratiker*, vol. 2, 2nd ed. (Berlin: Weidmann, 1907), 493–4, conjectures that the verse quoted in Titus 1:12 came from a *Theogony* attributed in antiquity to Epimenides that because of its oracular content was sometimes called *Chresmoi*.

162   *The Formal Education of the Author of Luke-Acts*

tomb for thee, O holy and high, liars, evil beasts, and slow bellies; for thou art not dead forever; thou art alive and risen; for in thee we live and are moved and have our being." So therefore the blessed Paul took this sentence from Minos. For he took again "We are the offspring of God" from Aratus, a poet, who wrote about God, and about the seven [planets] and the twelve [signs], saying, "From God we begin, from the Lord of heaven, that is Zeus. For all markets and seas and havens are filled with His name. And also in every place all men are in want of Him, because we are His offspring. And He out of His goodness giveth good signs to us and to all men. He moves us to come forward to work, and He ordains all that is visible and invisible. And because of this we all worship Him, and say, 'Hail to thee, our Father, wonderful and great!'" Plato also and others say that souls are of the nature of God.

translation of the Syriac text by M. D. Gibson[28]

To this evidence from Isho'dad's commentary on Acts should be added a comment from his very short commentary on Titus in which he claims that the verse about Cretan liars in Titus 1:12 is to be attributed to a poet of Crete, who was considered a prophet, whom some call Maxanidus (a Syriac corruption of Epimenides),[29] others call Minos, son of Zeus.[30] Given Isho'dad's attribution of the verse "Cretans are all liars . . ." in Titus 1:12 to the Cretan king Minos, whom he equates with Epimenides, the panegyric of Zeus that Isho'dad places in the mouth of the Cretan king Minos in his commentary on Acts can reasonably be attributed to the same "heathen poet": namely, the Cretan prophet and poet Epimenides. In his commentary on Acts 17:28 Isho'dad is completely accurate in his extended analysis of Aratus as the source of Acts 17:28b; there is little reason to suspect that he was not equally accurate in his analysis of Epimenides as the source of Acts 17:28a.

Even before he had seen Gibson's text and translation of Isho'dad's commentary, Harris had attempted to reconstruct the Greek original of the Syriac translation in the *Gannat Bussame* as follows, basing his second line on the quotation of "a prophet of their own" in Titus 1:12, which had long been identified as a verse of Epimenides, the fourth line on the unattributed expression in Acts 17:28a, and the rest on snatches of verse at the beginning of the Hellenistic poet Callimachus's *Hymn to Zeus* (i.e., lines eight and nine), which was modeled on an earlier poem by the Cretan Epimenides:[31]

Τύμβον ἐτεκτήναντο σέθεν, κύδιστε μέγιστε,
Κρῆτες, ἀεὶ ψευδεῖς, κακὰ θηρία, γαστέρες ἀργαί.
Ἀλλὰ σὺ γ᾽ οὐ θνῄσκεις, ἕστηκας γὰρ ζοὸς αἰεί,

---

[28] M. D. Gibson, *The Commentaries of Isho'dad of Merv: Volume IV*, 39–40 (Syriac) and 28–29 (English).
[29] So J. R. Harris, "Once More the Cretans," 34.
[30] Isho'dad's commentary on Titus can be found in M. D. Gibson, *The Commentaries of Isho'dad of Merv: Volume V: The Epistles of Paul* (Cambridge: Cambridge University Press, 1916), 146–7 (Syriac) and 99 (English).
[31] Harris's Greek reconstruction can be found in J. R. Harris, "A Further Note," 336; his English translation of this section of the Syriac commentary *Gannat Bussame* can be found in J. R. Harris, "The Cretans Always Liars," 310.

Ἐν γὰρ σοὶ ζῶμεν καὶ κινύμεθ᾽ ἠδὲ καὶ ἐσμέν.

A grave have fashioned for thee, O holy and high One,
the lying Kretans, who are all the time liars, evil beasts, idle bellies;
but thou diest not, for to eternity thou livest, and standest;
for in thee we live and move and have our being.

One can take issue with several features of Harris's Greek reconstruction: εἰμέν rather than ἐσμέν (line four) is the proper form for epic verse; ἠδὲ καί (line four) joins pairs of nouns or adjectives in epic verse but never, as here, a series of verbs. Also, since there is no Greek model on which to base two verses of the reconstruction other than Callimachus's hymn, which was based on Epimenides, it would seem advisable to follow Callimachus's diction more closely. Callimachus uses τάφον rather than τύμβον (line one), the aorist θάνες rather than the present θνῇσκεις (line three), and he calls the Cretans ψεῦσται rather than ψευδεῖς (line two), as, more importantly, does the author of Titus (Callimachus, *Hymn to Zeus* 8–9):

‘Κρῆτες ἀεὶ ψεῦσται᾽· καὶ γὰρ τάφον, ὦ ἄνα, σεῖο
Κρῆτες ἐτεκτήναντο· σὺ δ᾽ οὐ θάνες, ἐσσὶ γὰρ αἰεί.

"Cretans are always liars." For your tomb, Oh Lord,
Did the Cretans build. But you did not die, for you always are.

A few years after Harris's attempt at a reconstruction, the Classical scholar A. B. Cook, who agreed heartily with Harris's theory about an Epimenidean source for the panegyric to Zeus recorded in Isho'dad's commentary on Acts, offered a better Greek reconstruction:

Σοὶ μὲν ἐτεκτήναντο τάφον, πανυπέρτατε δαῖμον,
Κρῆτες ἀεὶ ψεῦσται, κακὰ θηρία, γαστέρες ἀργαί.
Ἀλλὰ γὰρ οὐ σὺ θάνες, ζώεις δὲ καὶ ἵστασαι αἰεί.
Ἐν σοὶ γὰρ ζῶμεν καὶ κινεόμεσθα καὶ εἰμέν.[32]

Two years later, the Reverend T. Nicklin, who also thoroughly embraced Harris's theory, offered some minor refinements in his reconstruction of the fourth verse:

Ἐν γὰρ (or γ᾽ ἄρα) σοὶ ζῶμεν καὶ (or τ᾽ ἰδὲ) κινεόμεσθα καὶ ἐσμέν.[33]

But there is nothing to recommend the word order of Nicklin's Ἐν γὰρ σοὶ ζῶμεν over Cook's Ἐν σοὶ γὰρ ζῶμεν. Also, the ἄρα in the expression γ᾽ ἄρα is never unelided in epic verse, while the τε in the expression τ᾽ ἰδέ is never elided.

It is impossible, of course, to be absolutely confident in any poetic Greek reconstruction based on a prosaic Syriac paraphrase. Whatever the precise wording of

[32] A. B. Cook, *Zeus: A Study in Ancient Religion*, vol. 1 (Cambridge: Cambridge University Press, 1914), 664, note 1.

[33] T. Nicklin, "Epimenides' *Minos*," *Classical Review* 30 (1916): 36.

164 *The Formal Education of the Author of Luke-Acts*

the original poem, I am convinced that in his account of Paul's speech to the Athenians in Acts 17 Luke has consciously and deliberately placed in Paul's mouth a saying— Ἐν αὐτῷ γὰρ ζῶμεν καὶ κινούμεθα καὶ ἐσμέν "For in him we live and move and are"— that was already in antiquity, certainly by the first century CE, associated with Epimenides. Whether it was really composed by a historical seventh- or sixth-century BCE Cretan prophet named Epimenides is irrelevant. I am also convinced that Luke expected at least some of his audience to recognize the Epimenidean source of Paul's saying. Indeed some readers and commentators of Acts over the next millennium continued to recognize the source: Augustine, Athanasius, Theodore of Mopsuestia, Isho'dad of Merv. Most, apparently, then forgot about it for another millennium until being reminded by the discovery and dissemination of two Syriac commentaries on Acts in the early twentieth century by J. R. Harris and M. D. Gibson.[34]

If Paul's declaration at Acts 17:28a Ἐν αὐτῷ γὰρ ζῶμεν καὶ κινούμεθα καὶ ἐσμέν "For in him we live and move and are" was perceived by Paul's (or Luke's) first-century CE audience to be echoing Epimenides, how would this have informed their understanding of Paul's speech? In other words, what would be the point of all this? Obviously, if in the

---

[34] There is, of course, no unanimity among commentators that Acts 17:28a had as its source a verse of the Cretan poet Epimenides. While a fairly steady stream of commentators over the last century have embraced Harris's proposal—H. J. Lawlor, "St. Paul's Quotations from Epimenides," *Irish Church Quarterly* 9, no. 35 (1916): 180–93; W. M. Ramsay, "A Cretan Prophet," *Quarterly Review* 231, no. 459 (1919): 378–95; Th. Zahn, *Die Apostelgeschichte des Lucas*, vol. 2 (Leipzig: A. Deichert, 1921), 621–5; F. J. Foakes Jackson and K. Lake, eds., *The Beginnings of Christianity*, 5:246–51; M. Dibelius, *Studies in the Acts of the Apostles*, 47–51 (but note his change of mind on 187–8); F. F. Bruce, *The Acts of the Apostles*, 338; P. Courcelle, "Un vers d'Épiménide dans le 'discours sur l'Aréopage,'" *Revue des Études Grecques* 76 (1963): 404–13; E. B. Howell, "St. Paul and the Greek World," *Greece & Rome* 11 (1964): 18–19; L. T. Johnson, *The Acts of the Apostles* (Collegeville, Minnesota: Liturgical Press, 1992), 316; J. L. Moles, "Jesus the Healer in the Gospels, the *Acts of the Apostles*, and Early Christianity," *Histos* 5 (2011): 155; C. K. Rothschild, *Paul in Athens: The Popular Religious Context of Acts 17* (Tübingen: Mohr Siebeck, 2014), 24—many have remained ambivalent, considering Epimenidean influence possible but unprovable, and some have objected strongly to the notion of any Epimenidean influence whatsoever on the grounds that the sentiment of 17:28a is more philosophic and Stoic than poetic. Among those who have objected over the past century, some have held Harris's proposal up to ridicule: three quite influential scholars, H. Gressmann, "Review of M. D. Gibson, The Commentaries of Isho'dad of Merv," *Berliner Philologische Wochenschrift* 30 (1913): 935–9, M. Pohlenz, "Paulus und die Stoa," 101–4, and R. Renehan, "Classical Greek Quotations in the New Testament," 17–45, 34–42, are representative of this group. Following the lead of E. Norden's *Agnostos Theos*, they have become heavily invested in the belief that Paul's entire speech to the Athenians is indebted to Stoic philosophy and so have concluded that Acts 17:28b is not a direct quotation of the *Phaenomena* of Aratus but rather a formula from the Stoic philosopher Posidonius (so Pohlenz). Similarly, they conclude that Acts 17:28a is a pantheistic Stoic formula, perhaps from the Stoic philosopher Chrysippus (so Renehan). They explain the testimony of the Syriac commentaries, which they perceive as a threat to their theory of Stoic influence, with a fanciful and unbelievable solution: namely that some anonymous medieval Christian, who was ignorant of Greek meter and had scant Classical learning, for some inexplicable reason took the verse from Titus 1:12, incorporated it into a watered-down version of some verses from the Hellenistic poet Callimachus, then appended the prose expression in Acts 17:28b, which he mistook for a metrical verse, and, finally, attributed this composite monstrosity to the mythic Cretan king Minos. This fabrication, they claim, fooled the authors of the Syriac commentaries, including Isho'dad of Merv, who mistakenly took it as an Epimenidean passage that was the source of Paul's quotations in Acts 17:28a and in Titus 1:12.

middle of Paul's speech to the Athenians (Acts 17:28a) he reminds his audience of a verse from a poem by Epimenides, this serves to strengthen the association with Epimenides that he has already made at the beginning of his speech with his reference to an altar to an unknown god (Acts 17:23). Paul cleverly uses this association as a tool, of course, by claiming that the new divinity that he is introducing to the Athenians is both that very unknown god and the one "in whom we live and move and are." There are, however, several subtler associations in this scene with Epimenides, as Paul is, in some respects, envisioned as walking in the footsteps of the Cretan prophet. Both Epimenides and Paul are strangers from abroad who are introducing a cult of an unknown god to the Athenians (Diogenes Laertius, *Lives* 1.110; Acts 17:23). And both Epimenides and Paul go about their business, their "missionary work," by beginning at the Areopagus in the middle of Athens (Diogenes Laertius, *Lives* 1.110; Acts 17:19, 22).

Another association requires a somewhat longer explanation. Luke reveals a penchant for etymological wordplay, both in his gospel and in Acts, and he has a special fondness for the folk-etymologizing of proper names: e.g., the personal names Barnabas "son of exhortation" and Jesus "healer"; the name of the city Gaza "treasure"; the name of the festival Pascha "suffering."[35] In this light, I wonder if Luke may have been attracted to Epimenides' verse Ἐν σοὶ γὰρ ζῶμεν καὶ κινεόμεσθα καὶ εἰμέν partly because it contains a popular, folk-etymological connection between the name "Zeus" (Ζεὺς) and the verb "to live" (ζάω) (cf. Acts 17:25, where the etymological association is again picked up: "he gives to all life and breath and all things"). This popular folk etymology had its most prominent expression in Plato's *Cratylus* 395e–396b, where, in his analysis of the name of Zeus, Socrates declares: οὐ γὰρ ἔστιν ἡμῖν καὶ τοῖς ἄλλοις πᾶσιν ὅστις ἐστὶν αἴτιος μᾶλλον τοῦ ζῆν ἢ ὁ ἄρχων τε καὶ βασιλεὺς τῶν πάντων. "For certainly no one is more the cause of 'life' (ζῆν—the infinitive of ζάω) for us and for all others than the ruler and king of all."[36] In his account of Paul's speech to the Athenians, then, Luke appears to be replacing Epimenides' folk etymology on the name of Zeus as the source of "life" with one of his own on the name of Jesus as the source of "healing." For Paul had presumably been speaking to the Athenians about the bodily resurrection (ἀνάστασις) of Jesus (Ἰησοῦς), but then in an authorial aside at the end of Acts 17:18 Luke portrays the Athenian philosophers naively misunderstanding Paul's teaching as an attempt to introduce two foreign divinities into the city: Ἰησοῦς "Healing" (cf. the Greek healing divinity Ἰασώ/Ἰησώ) and Ἀνάστασις "Resurrection." Thus, the Athenians' perception that Paul is introducing two new divinities into the city (Ξένων δαιμονίων δοκεῖ καταγγελεὺς εἶναι Acts 17:18) and that the divinities' names are Ἰησοῦς "Healing" and Ἀνάστασις "Resurrection" seem to echo the device of folk-etymologizing also used by Epimenides, for these two etymologized divinities of Luke, "Healing" and "Resurrection," overlap in important thematic ways also with the story of Epimenides: Epimenides' primary interaction with Athens was to *heal* the people and the land of a

---

[35] See S. Reece, "Jesus as Healer: Etymologizing of Proper Names in Luke-Acts," *Zeitschrift für die neutestamentliche Wissenschaft* 110 (2019): 186–201, and S. Reece, "Passover as 'Passion': A Folk Etymology in Luke 22:15," *Biblica* 100 (2019): 601–10.

[36] This etymology is invoked explicitly also in Pseudo-Aristotle, *De mundo* 401a; Diogenes Laertius, *Lives of the Philosophers* 7.147; the *Letter of Aristeas* 16.

166 *The Formal Education of the Author of Luke-Acts*

plague; Epimenides' primary theological claim was that Zeus was not dead, as the Cretans claimed, but had *risen* from his tomb.[37]

Having drawn these connections with Epimenides, Luke then has Paul go one step further and strive to emulate the Cretan prophet. Paul audaciously claims to be making known to the Athenians Epimenides' unknown god (Acts 17:23). Moreover, Paul claims that this unknown god is emphatically not honored/elevated by objects made by human hands (like Epimenides' altar) (Acts 17:24-5). Finally, Paul replaces Epimenides' main divinity, Zeus, who is echoed also in his quotation of Aratus's invocation to Zeus in the *Phaenomena*, with his own divinity: a god who created the cosmos and everything in it (Acts 17:25-6).[38]

I am obligated here, as elsewhere, to offer a possible scenario whereby Luke came to know the story and possibly these very words, of Epimenides. Unlike the works of other ancient authors that I have proposed/shall propose Luke is quoting—Homer, Aesop, Euripides, Plato, and even Aratus to some degree—there is no evidence of any specific works of Epimenides being studied in the school curriculum during Luke's lifetime. Nor is there any evidence of any specific works of Epimenides serving as popular reading material among the reading public during Luke's lifetime. Luke's contemporary Plutarch, for example, references Epimenides only eight times in the massive corpus of his works. All that actually survives from antiquity of Epimenides' works are some lists of titles. If Epimenides' works were not well known to Luke or to his audience, what were Luke's special motivations for including a paraphrase of a verse from one of them? Part of the answer, as we have seen, is that Luke had a very strong motivation for including Epimenides in his description of Paul's experiences in Athens

---

[37] The ancient Greek theogonic tradition had accepted from the earliest times a Minoan version of the myth of Zeus's birth in a Cretan cave (Hesiod, *Theog.* 453–506), but only among the Cretans was Zeus, like the Semitic Adonis or the Egyptian Osiris, worshipped as a dying and rising god associated with the cycle of the seasons, a practice that elicited scorn among other Greeks and tarnished the Cretans' reputation (Callimachus, *Hymn to Zeus* 1–9 and *Iambi*, fr. 202.15–16; *Certamen Homeri et Hesiodi* 94–101; Lucian, *Philopseudes* 3, *De sacrificiis* 10, *Timon* 6; *Anthologia Graeca* 275; as well as, of course, many early Christian apologists: Tatian, Athenagoras, Theophilus of Antioch, Clement of Alexandria, Origen). A. B. Cook, *Zeus: A Study*, 1:644–65, collects some of the ancient literary and material evidence for the Cretan myth of a dying and rising Zeus. This is expanded and updated in E. F. Bloedow, "Evidence for an Early Date for the Cult of Cretan Zeus," *Kernos: Revue Internationale et Pluridisciplinaire de Religion Grecque Antique* 4 (1991): 139–77; M. Kokolakis, "Zeus' Tomb. An Object of Pride and Reproach," *Kernos: Revue Internationale et Pluridisciplinaire de Religion Grecque Antique* 8 (1995): 123–38; N. Postlethwaite, "The Death of Zeus Kretagenes," *Kernos: Revue Internationale et Pluridisciplinaire de Religion Grecque Antique* 12 (1999): 85–98. An ancient hymn to the Cretan Zeus that was found on a second- to third-century CE inscription at the site of the temple of Dictaean Zeus at Palaikastro (housed now in the Heraklion Archaeological Museum), invokes the "Great Youngster," "the Son of Kronos," and invites him to come back from the earth at year's end to invigorate the crops and flocks. While the inscription itself is relatively late, the text goes back to the Hellenistic, perhaps even the Classical, period. M. L. West, "The Dictaean Hymn to the Kouros," *Journal of Hellenic Studies* 85 (1965): 149–59, offers a text, translation, and commentary.

[38] C. K. Rothschild, *Paul in Athens*, has detected some of these traces of Epimenides in Luke's account of Paul in Athens, and she proposes that the author of Acts, whom she suggests may have been a pseudo-Titus writing in the early second century CE, actually presents Paul as a second Epimenides (p. 24): "For Luke, both Paul and Epimenides are strangers from afar summoned to Athens to fix a mistake; both announce that the tomb of their god is a lie; and, both transfer eastern cult traditions to Greece through Asia."

Luke and Epimenides and Aratus   167

because of his legendary association with the Athenians, because of his theology of Zeus, which Luke wished to present as an earlier manifestation of Paul's theology of God, and because of the clever use which Luke wished to make of an Epimenidean altar as a jumping-off point for the introduction of a new unknown god to the Athenians.

To the more specific question of how Luke was familiar with some verses of Epimenides, however, I wonder if Luke could have known the story of Epimenides' visit to Athens and the verses about the Cretans' belief in a tomb of Zeus, which was the basis for Acts 17:28a, from the progymnastic exercises that were at the core of his curricular education in school. Among the progymnastic exercises used at an early stage of instruction were the ἀνασκευή "refutation" and κατασκευή "affirmation" of the credibility of stories drawn from ancient myths, legends, fables, maxims, and anecdotes. The first-century CE rhetorician Aelius Theon mentions several such exercises in his *Progymnasmata* (94–5): How plausible is it that Locrian Ajax, after committing such a sacrilege against the goddess Athena, would arrive safely home and live to a happy old age? How plausible is it that Medea would kill her own children? How plausible is it that hybrid creatures like Pegasus ever really existed? Theon praises the refutation of such myths in the past by Herodotus, Plato, and Ephorus, including the refutation of such stories as are found "regarding Lycurgus and Minos and Rhadamanthys and Zeus and the Curetes and the other mythic stories in Crete" (*Progymnasmata* 96). Thus, one can easily imagine a progymnastic exercise that posed questions about Cretan myth: How plausible is the Cretan claim that Zeus was born on Mt. Ida in Crete rather than on Mt. Lycaeon in Arcadia? How plausible is the Cretan claim that there exists a tomb of Zeus in Crete? As we may witness in the proem of his hymn to Zeus the Hellenistic poet Callimachus was torn between different versions of these myths, and he evokes disputes that occurred well before his time and continued to occur long after his time, including, no doubt, in progymnastic exercises (*Hymn to Zeus* 4–9):

πῶς καί νιν, Δικταῖον ἀείσομεν ἠὲ Λυκαῖον;
ἐν δοιῇ μάλα θυμός, ἐπεὶ γένος ἀμφήριστον.
Ζεῦ, σὲ μὲν Ἰδαίοισιν ἐν οὔρεσί φασι γενέσθαι,
Ζεῦ, σὲ δ' ἐν Ἀρκαδίῃ· πότεροι, πάτερ, ἐψεύσαντο;
"Κρῆτες ἀεὶ ψεῦσται"· καὶ γὰρ τάφον, ὦ ἄνα, σεῖο
Κρῆτες ἐτεκτήναντο· σὺ δ' οὐ θάνες, ἐσσὶ γὰρ αἰεί.

How shall we sing of him [Zeus]? As lord of Dicte or of Lycaeum?
My soul is split in two, since his birth is a matter of debate.
Some, O Zeus, say that you were born in the mountains of Ida;
Others, O Zeus, in Arcadia. Which of the two, O Lord, lied?
"Cretans are always liars." For your tomb, O Lord,
Did the Cretans build. But you did not die, for you always are.

There is some additional evidence that progymnastic exercises about the tomb of Zeus in Crete constituted part of the educational curriculum. The second- to third-century CE Greek sophist Philostratus writes about the particular skill in declamation of Antiochus, a second-century CE sophist from Aegae in Cilicia (Philostratus, *Vit.*

168   *The Formal Education of the Author of Luke-Acts*

soph. 569). Among some other themes of declamation in which Antiochus particularly excelled—Should a child born of rape be brought up by the family of the father or the mother? Should someone forced to become a eunuch by a tyrant who has abdicated on condition of immunity be punished for murdering that tyrant?—Philostratus praises Antiochus's skill in defending the Cretans for claiming that there existed a tomb of Zeus in Crete:

> ἄριστα δὲ καὶ ὑπὲρ τῶν Κρητῶν ἀπολελόγηται τῶν κρινομένων ἐπὶ τῷ τοῦ Διὸς σήματι φυσιολογίᾳ τε καὶ θεολογίᾳ πάσῃ ἐναγωνισάμενος λαμπρῶς.

> He made a most skillful defense too on behalf of the Cretans, who were being judged in the matter of the tomb of Zeus, when he argued brilliantly on the basis of natural philosophy and the entirety of theology.

Since the question of whether or not the Cretans were blameworthy for their claim about the existence of a tomb of Zeus in Crete was a theme of declamation among the sophistic orators, it could very well have been a topic also in the *progymnasmata* used in the *enkyklios paideia* of the schools at which these aspiring orators were trained. This is perhaps where Luke became familiar with the verses of Epimenides that raise this very question of the culpability of the Cretans.

Another, less explicit, indication that the matter of a tomb of Zeus in Crete may have been a topic in the *progymnasmata* can be found in a passage from the second-century CE satirist and rhetorician Lucian (*Philops.* 3). Here Lucian lists some examples from myth that can be used to debate whether certain lies are shameful or not:

> The Cretans exhibit a tomb of Zeus.
> The Athenians assert that Erichthonius sprang from the earth.
> The Thebans claim that the Spartoi were born from serpents' teeth.

These topics of debate too could very well have had their origin in progymnastic exercises, the first example perhaps having been proposed by a teacher to a student in the form: "Should the Cretans be ashamed or not to exhibit the tomb of Zeus?" Ancient teachers, and perhaps their students too, appear to have had all sorts of fun with this rhetorical question. A scholium to Callimachus's *Hymn to Zeus* 8 rationalizes that the story of a Cretan tomb to Zeus arose because an inscription on Minos's tomb in Crete that read Μίνωος τοῦ Διὸς τάφος "tomb of Minos, the son of Zeus" became effaced over time and lost its first two words, resulting in the inscription Διὸς τάφος "tomb of Zeus." Another possibility, the scholium continues, is that the priests of Cybele made a fictitious tomb for Zeus in an attempt to protect him from his father Kronos.

In sum, the setting and content of Paul's speech in Acts 17 generated a strong motivation for echoing the story of Epimenides and for including a quotation of a verse attributed to him. Where did Luke encounter this verse of Epimenides? Likely he encountered it as a student, finding it useful material for fulfilling a progymnastic exercise. To the rhetorical question "How plausible is the Cretan claim that there exists a tomb of Zeus in Crete?" Luke, as a student, could marshal as evidence in his refutation the respected verses of the Cretan prophet Epimenides himself that lay behind his later paraphrase, in a different sort of refutation, in Acts 17:28a and, even later, behind the passage preserved in translation in the Syriac commentaries on Acts 17:

Σοὶ μὲν ἐτεκτήναντο τάφον, πανυπέρτατε δαῖμον,
Κρῆτες ἀεὶ ψεῦσται, κακὰ θηρία, γαστέρες ἀργαί.
Ἀλλὰ γὰρ οὐ σὺ θάνες, ζώεις δὲ καὶ ἵστασαι αἰεί.
Ἐν σοὶ γὰρ ζῶμεν καὶ κινεόμεσθα καὶ εἰμέν.

They built a tomb for you, most high god,
The Cretans, always liars, evil beasts, lazy bellies.
However, you did not die, but you live and stand always.
For in you we live and move and are.

8

Luke and Euripides—Part One: How Did Luke Know the Dramas of Euripides?

I recently heard an American politician utter the hackneyed lines: "Be not afraid of greatness. Some are born great, some achieve greatness, and some have greatness thrust upon them." The politician may have been recalling a theatrical performance that he had witnessed of Shakespeare's comedy *Twelfth Night*, and he may have been fully aware that he was quoting Malvolio reading from Maria's false letter in Act 2, Scene 5. On the other hand, he may have never in his entire life set foot in a live theater setting. Instead, he may have seen a production or adaptation of the drama in a movie theater or on television, or heard it broadcast on the radio. Or he may have experienced the comedy only as a text rather than as a performance, having studied the drama formally in an academic setting, or having read it for pleasure privately and at his leisure. He may have found these lines of Shakespearean drama quoted in a collection of aphorisms or witticisms, or encountered them embedded in a written or oral version of any number of artistic genres and media that express our commonly shared cultural heritage quite divorced from their original Shakespearean context; if so, he was possibly unaware of the source of the lines that he was quoting.

A modern American politician is about as distant from Shakespeare as Luke was from the Athenian tragedian Euripides both chronologically—about half a millennium—and linguistically—vernacular American English in contrast to literary Elizabethan English; vernacular Koine Greek in contrast to literary Attic Greek. So, when we observe, as we shall shortly, that Luke appears to have quoted part of a verse of Euripides' *Bacchae* in his Acts of the Apostles, we should not assume without further reflection that he was recalling his experience of a live theatrical performance of the tragedy or that he had even read the text of the tragedy in its entirety. Indeed, as we shall see, while it is possible that Luke did in fact attend a live performance of the drama or that he did in fact read the drama in its entirety, the connection between Euripides' *Bacchae* and Luke's Acts, as in the connection between Shakespeare's *Twelfth Night* and the American politician's speech, is probably more complicated than that.

How Might Luke Have Been Exposed to Euripides?

Euripides was not the most highly revered dramatist of his own time. That honor goes to Sophocles, who won first prize with almost 80 percent of his productions, and then

172   *The Formal Education of the Author of Luke-Acts*

to Aeschylus, with almost 60 percent. Euripides comes in a distant third, with a little over 20 percent. His relatively poor reputation in his own time is also well illustrated by the fact that he and his dramas served as the butt of many jokes in contemporary comedies, most notoriously in Aristophanes' *Frogs*. His flight to Macedonia late in life may also have been related to his poor standing in Athens.

Euripides' popularity boomed in later centuries, however, while Aeschylus's and Sophocles' dramas became regarded as remote and antiquated. The social and political problems that Euripides posed remained relevant in later generations, his plots were more universal in scope, and his somewhat prosaic style and diction were more accessible to non-native Greek speakers throughout the Mediterranean world. Euripides' popularity in later centuries is partly responsible for the higher survival rate of his dramas: seventy-eight of his ninety-two dramas survived intact into the Hellenistic period and were available in the library of Alexandria in Egypt; seventeen or eighteen tragedies and one satyr play have survived to our own time, compared to only six or seven of Aeschylus's and only seven of Sophocles'.

Euripides' dramas were well known throughout the Mediterranean world during the Hellenistic and Roman Imperial periods, and they were accessible to any educated, Greek-speaking resident of the eastern Mediterranean, like the author of Luke-Acts, through a variety of media. Firstly, they were commonly used as textual material for study in the primary and secondary levels of schooling. As we have seen, the papyrological remains of school texts from Egypt indicate that Homer, Euripides, and Menander were the most commonly used poetic texts in primary and secondary schools. While Euripides is a distant second to the ubiquitous Homer, there survive 141 Euripidean papyri from Hellenistic and Roman Egypt dating to the period between 100 BCE and 200 CE (i.e., from around the time of the composition of Luke-Acts), of which seventeen appear to be school texts. The following Euripidean dramas are specifically quoted in surviving school texts: *Phoenissae* (the most common), *Hecuba*, *Hippolytus*, *Autolycus*, *Bacchae*, *Electra*, *Temenidae*, and *Troades*. Dramatic passages of Euripides were used in school texts for pedantic and practical matters such as teaching the syllabification of words and the metrical scansion of verses. Euripides' dramas were also mined for moralizing speeches, maxims, and gnomic phrases that were suitable for school-age children. In the progymnastic exercises that constituted the core of the educational curriculum in later antiquity, Euripides continued to play an influential role, as illustrated in the *progymnasmata* of Theon, Aphthonius, and "Libanius." As students advanced in learning, the Euripidean dramas must have been read and studied for grander poetic and literary purposes; they are prominent in all the reading lists (canons) of Greek literature recommended for students by the ancient grammarians and rhetoricians: e.g., Dionysius of Halicarnassus, Dio Chrysostom, and Quintilian. There is even good reason to believe that most of the Greek tragedies that survive to our time—all seven attributed to Aeschylus, all seven attributed to Sophocles, and ten of the eighteen attributed to Euripides—owe their survival precisely to the fact that they were selected to be included in anthologies of dramas used in the schools.[1]

---

[1] On the transmission of the texts of Euripides' tragedies, see G. Zuntz, *An Inquiry into the Transmission of the Plays of Euripides* (Cambridge: Cambridge University Press, 1965).

Luke and Euripides—Part One   173

The popularity of Euripidean drama in school texts is mirrored in the general reading habits of the adult populace, for the educational experiences of students must have played a part in shaping their literary tastes as adults. The literary papyri of the period—i.e., the physical remains of books that were being read in Egypt—include Homer, Hesiod, Euripides, and Menander most frequently of the poets. As just noted, there survive 124 Euripidean papyri from Hellenistic and Roman Egypt dating to the period between 100 BCE and 200 CE that do not have the typical features of school texts; they appear instead to be fragments of popularly read literary texts. Of Euripides' dramas the following are the most often referenced or quoted in the literary papyri: *Phoenissae* (the most common), *Orestes, Hecuba, Medea, Andromache,* and *Bacchae.* Further indication of the popularity of Euripides among the reading public of the ancient Mediterranean world during the time of Luke is offered by the high frequency of quotations from his dramas by authors roughly contemporary with Luke: Dionysius of Halicarnassus, Dio Chrysostom, Plutarch, Longinus, Aelius Aristides, Lucian of Samosata, and Hermogenes of Tarsus. Notably, Luke's contemporary Plutarch quotes, paraphrases, or refers to Euripides 367 times, 20 of which are from the *Bacchae,* a drama that, as we shall see, Luke too seems to know. Even Jewish writers, like Philo, and Christian exegetes, like Clement of Alexandria, quote from the dramas of Euripides, and, most notably, Luke's putative mentor and traveling companion Paul appears to quote a Euripidean iambic trimeter verse in his first letter to the Corinthians (15:33): Φθείρουσιν ἤθη χρηστὰ ὁμιλίαι κακαί ($- - \smile - / - - \smile - / \smile - \smile -$) "Evil communications corrupt good manners." As we noted earlier, while most commentators have with little evidence attributed Paul's quotation to Menander' comedy *Thais,* the beginning of this quotation has been discovered among some actual extracts of Euripidean verses on the very fragmentary late 3rd-century BCE papyrus *P.Hib.* 1.7. Of course, this does not exclude the possibility that Menander later adopted the Euripidean verse in one of his own comedies. In any case, Paul seems to be quoting the verse as an aphorism, without any reference to its earlier literary context, as though he knows it from popular culture, while Luke, as we shall see, appears to know both the actual text and the larger literary context of Euripides' *Bacchae.*

Finally, Euripides' dramas would have been known in Luke's time from their frequent reproduction as live performances in the ubiquitous theaters around the Mediterranean world. To some it may seem an unlikely scenario: a first-century Christian, steeped in Judaism, from the eastern Mediterranean attending pagan Greek performances of the sort that had been, were, and would be despised for their immorality and idolatry by Jews and Christians alike. And, indeed, later Jewish and Christian religious authorities vehemently condemned all forms of pagan entertainment—those that occurred in the theaters, amphitheaters, and hippodromes— as forms of idolatry.[2] But we should be wary about projecting these ideological condemnations back to Luke's particular situation in the first century; attitudes toward the theater were complex and must have been determined to a great extent by time

---

[2]   E.g., t. 'Abod. Zar. 2:5, 7; b. 'Abod. Zar. 18b; y. 'Abod. Zar. 1:7, 40a; Tertullian, *De spectaculis* 3.2, 8.10, *Apologeticum* 38.4; Clement of Alexandria, *Paedagogus* 3.11.76.3, *Stromata* 2.15.67.4.

174   *The Formal Education of the Author of Luke-Acts*

period and locale. Jewish engagement during this period with theaters in several cities throughout the eastern Mediterranean is attested, for example, in the less ideological archaeological evidence.[3] Also, according to later Talmudic sources—b. Shab. 66b; y. Shab. 6:8, 8c; y. Ta'an. 1:4, 64b—Jews were sometimes employed as mimes and pantomimes even in the theater at Caesarea. Moreover, and ironically, the very condemnations and warnings of Jewish and Christian religious authorities against the theater serve as testimony that members of their "flocks" found the theater attractive; the Jewish Rabbis and Christian Patristics were surely, in some cases, waging a battle, an uphill battle, against their followers' attraction to these forbidden places. Even some Jewish religious authorities confess to feeling an attraction to the theater: it is instructive to consider the behavior of Luke's contemporary, the Jewish philosopher Philo, who writes about his enjoyment of theatrical productions of Greek drama (*Ebr.* 177, etc.) and even quotes verses from a production of Euripides' *Auge* that he had witnessed at the theater in Alexandria (*Prob.* 141). Luke too would have encountered theaters in almost every town and city that he visited in the eastern Mediterranean, and it seems unlikely that a well-educated, Greek-speaking man traveling through the major cities of the Mediterranean, who for rhetorical purposes was trying to find points of contact and understanding between the pagan world and his own religious beliefs, would have abstained from attending the events that took place in what was a focal point of communal activity.

Luke demonstrates his familiarity with the theater as a public building when he describes in great detail the riot that took place in the famous theater at Ephesus (Acts 19:28-40), a Hellenistic and then Roman theater that could accommodate well over 20,000 spectators in Luke's day. Given his extensive travels through the towns and cities of the Mediterranean world, Luke must have visited many other theaters as well. According to the narrative of Acts, Luke spent significant time in Philippi (and, likely, throughout larger Macedonia), in Jerusalem and Caesarea (and, likely, throughout Judaea), and in Rome. According to early Christian traditions about Luke, he also spent significant time earlier in his life in Syrian Antioch and later in his life in Greece (in Boeotia, and, particularly, Thebes). All of these places had prominent, centrally located theaters. The physical remains of many of these theaters have been discovered and excavated, although the remains of others have left little or no trace, their marble and limestone having been reused throughout history as building material for other purposes, sometimes even for newer theaters on the same sites. It is perhaps worthwhile to lay out what we know about the theaters that Luke may have seen and perhaps entered, and then to consider what sorts of performances he would have been able to witness there.

---

[3] A second-century BCE inscription from the town of Iasos in Ionia (*CIJ* II 749) mentions a Jew named Nicetas, son of Jason the Jerusalemite, who supported the feast of Dionysus with a contribution of 100 drachmas; a first-century BCE inscription from Berenice in Cyrenaica (*SEG* 16.931 = *CJZC* 70) mentions a financial contribution by a Jew named D. Valerius Dionysius for plastering the floor and painting the walls of the amphitheater; a Roman Imperial-era inscription from the theater of Miletus (*CIJ* II 748) designates a specific seating area in the theater for "Jews and God-fearers" (or perhaps "Jews who are also God-fearers").

Theaters that Luke Likely Encountered

Syrian Antioch, which was Luke's native home according to early Christian tradition, was in Luke's day a populous cosmopolitan and multicultural center of the eastern Mediterranean, a pivotal educational, cultural, and commercial hub, a major Roman military and administrative base, and a focal point of Hellenistic Judaism and early Christianity. Since its founding by the Macedonian general Seleucus at the end of the fourth century BCE, it had prided itself particularly in its Hellenic background, and this played out in the prominence of its Hellenic cultural events, including Greek theatrical performances. Antioch had at least one theater during Luke's lifetime. The evidence is literary; the theater itself has not survived.[4] There was also a smaller theater associated with the temple of Zeus in the suburb of Daphne, built in the last quarter of the first century CE. The people of Antioch were famous in antiquity for their fondness of theatrical performances (Lucian, *Salt.* 76), some of which, surely, were in the form of mime and pantomime, others, apparently, in a more traditional dramatic format. This fondness is colorfully illustrated by the many Roman Imperial-era mosaics excavated in Antioch, in its port Seleucia, and in nearby Daphne, several of which depict actual scenes from ancient Greek theater, with the dramas of Euripides and Menander especially notable.[5]

Philippi, a prosperous and historical Greek city located strategically on the east-west artery *Via Egnatia*, where, according to the narrative of Acts, Luke apparently stayed for an extended period during Paul's second and third missionary journeys, had a large, centrally located Greek theater since the city's founding in the fourth century BCE that was further enlarged and refashioned during the Roman period, beginning in the first century BCE. Some of the ancient structure survives; the rest has been reconstructed in modern times, and ancient Greek drama continues to be performed there to this day.

Jerusalem, where, if we take the narrative of Acts at face value, Luke would have spent up to two years awaiting the outcome of Paul's trial, had over time become a thoroughly Hellenized and then Romanized city. Herod the Great had built a Roman theater in the city and an amphitheater (actually probably a hippodrome[6]) "on the

---

[4] The sixth-century CE chronicler Malalas of Antioch records that Julius Caesar built a theater in Antioch when he visited the city in 47 BCE and that Tiberius later continued work on the theater (*Chronographia* 9.5; 10.10). Josephus mentions a gathering at the theater during the time that Vespasian was in Syria, shortly before the destruction of Jerusalem (*War* 7.43), and again during the time that Titus was in Antioch, shortly after the destruction of Jerusalem (*War* 7.100).

[5] Cf. K. Weitzmann, "Illustrations of Euripides and Homer in the Mosaics of Antioch," in *Antioch-on-the-Orontes III The Excavations of 1937–1939*, ed. R. Stillwell (Princeton: Princeton University Press, 1941), 233–47; D. Levi, *Antioch Mosaic Pavements Volumes 1 and 2* (Princeton: Princeton University Press, 1947), 68–87; J. Huskinson, "Theatre, Performance and Theatricality in Some Mosaic Pavements from Antioch," *Bulletin of the Institute of Classical Studies* 46 (2002): 131–65; K. Gutzwiller and Ö. Çelik, "New Menander Mosaics from Antioch," *American Journal of Archaeology* 116 (2012): 573–623.

[6] The Herodian-era "amphitheaters" in Caesarea, Jerusalem, and Jericho were oval in shape, more in line with Roman hippodromes: so J. H. Humphrey, "'Amphitheatrical' Hippo-Stadia," in *Caesarea Maritima—Retrospective after Two Millennia*, eds. A. Raban and K. G. Holum (Leiden: Brill, 1996), 121–9; Y. Porath, "Why Did Josephus Name the Chariot-Racing Facility at Caesarea 'Amphitheatre'?" *Scripta Classica Israelica* 24 (2004): 63–7.

176 *The Formal Education of the Author of Luke-Acts*

plain" to celebrate the battle of Actium in 31 BCE. The evidence is literary (Josephus, *Ant.* 15.268); no certain archaeological remains have been found.[7] This—and general incredulity that the Jews would allow a theater to be constructed in the shadow of the Jerusalem temple—has led some to suppose that the theater was a temporary wooden rather than a permanent stone structure.[8] But this was not Herod's practice anywhere else, and Josephus's description of the costly, elaborate theater and its accoutrements points to a more permanent structure (*Ant.* 15.268, 272).[9]

Caesarea Maritima, through which, according to the narrative of Acts, Luke passed on his way to and from Jerusalem, and where he may have spent some time awaiting the outcome of Paul's trial, was essentially a Roman city superimposed on a Judaean landscape. It was Herod the Great's showcase to the world of Judaea's status as part of the Hellenistic and Roman world and of Caesarea's status as one of the great coastal cities of the eastern Mediterranean. Herod built a Roman-style theater there between 19 BCE and 9 BCE—the first theater in Palestine—that could accommodate up to four thousand spectators in more than thirty rows of seats.[10] The theater was just one facet of Herod's ambitious building program in Caesarea, which included an artificial harbor, a system of aqueducts, his own palace, an amphitheater or hippodrome, a temple for Roma and Augustus, an agora, and many other public buildings. The evidence for the theater is both literary (Josephus, *War* 1.415; *Ant.* 15.341) and archaeological: material from Herod's theater was reused in the theater's later reconstructions, including in its complete reconstruction in the twentieth century, where musical concerts continue to be performed to this day.

Rome, where, according to the account at the end of Acts, Luke spent at least two years with Paul, who appears to have had a relatively high degree of freedom while awaiting his trial there (Acts 28:30-1), had three permanent, i.e., stone, theaters at this time, all centrally located in the Campus Martius: the very large Theater of Pompey (built in 55 BCE); the Theater of Balbus (built in 13 BCE); and the Theater of Marcellus (built in 11 BCE). The literary, inscriptional, and archaeological evidence for all three theaters is considerable, and a substantial edifice of the Theater of Marcellus can still be seen.

---

[7] But see now R. Reich and Y. Billig, "A Group of Theater Seats Discovered Near the South-Western Corner of the Temple Mount," *Israel Exploration Journal* 50 (2000): 175–84 (though these seats cannot be dated precisely and may be from a later building). Also, a small 200-seat theater-like structure has even more recently (October or 2017) been discovered in the excavations beneath Wilson's Arch, although the structure is thought to be from the second century CE, after the destruction of Jerusalem by the Romans, and was apparently left unfinished. See J. Uziel, T. Lieberman, and A. Solomon, "The Excavations beneath Wilson's Arch: New Light on Roman Period Jerusalem," *Tel Aviv: Journal of the Institute of Archaeology of Tel Aviv University* 46 (2019): 237–66.

[8] So, for example, A. Lichtenberger, "Jesus and the Theater in Jerusalem," in *Jesus and Archaeology*, ed. J. H. Charlesworth (Grand Rapids: Eerdmans, 2006), 283–99, who believes that the wooden structure was taken down soon after its construction; so too J. Patrich, "Herod's Theatre in Jerusalem: A New Proposal," *Israel Exploration Journal* 53 (2002): 231–9.

[9] Z. Weiss, "Buildings for Mass Entertainment: Tradition and Innovation in Herodian Construction," *Near Eastern Archaeology* 77 (2014): 100–102, marshals some literary and archaeological evidence for a stone rather than wood construction.

[10] On the dimensions of the theater, see A. Segal, *Theatres in Roman Palestine and Provincia Arabia* (Leiden: Brill, 1995), 64–9.

Thebes, in the region of Boeotia in Greece, where according to early Christian tradition Luke spent the last years of his life, must have had, like any self-respecting Greek city, a substantial theater in a central location, but Thebes was sacked and razed repeatedly throughout its history and has been built over continuously from antiquity to modern times, so any physical remains of a theater are inconsiderable. Pausanias (9.16.6) locates a theater near the so-called gates of Proetides and a temple of Dionysus; however, the only remains of a theater ever found in Thebes are located 600 meters north of these gates.[11]

According to the narrative of the "we-passages" in Acts Luke may also have visited, or at least seen, the theaters in Assos, Mytilene, Miletus, Patara, and Myra in Asia Minor, and Syracuse, Rhegium, and Puteoli in Italy. All the theaters in these locations existed during Luke's lifetime.

In sum, Luke was probably born near a theater, spent his entire life near a theater, and died near a theater. He would have encountered theaters wherever he traveled, whether in Judaea, Syria, Asia Minor, Greece, or Italy. It does not seem likely that a well-educated and curious person like Luke, who had surely read and studied some drama in school as a youth and who no doubt continued to have some interest in it in his adult life, would have declined an opportunity to attend a theatrical performance from time to time. If so, what sort of theatrical performance would he have witnessed? What was performed in these many theaters throughout the Mediterranean world in the time of Luke?

What Was Performed in First-Century CE Theaters?

Tastes in theater had changed over the centuries, with traditional comedy and tragedy giving way to mime and pantomime. Mimes were lighthearted sketches of ordinary life played by large troops of actors without masks; pantomimes were dramatic performances on mythological themes with dancing and formalized gestures by a single mute actor who played several parts by changing his (sometimes her) mask and voice, all to the accompaniment of musical instruments and a chorus. In another derivative and somewhat mixed genre, solo performers (*tragoedi*) recited and sang extracts from traditional tragedies with musical accompaniment. First-century CE theaters also housed musical performances, athletic competitions, and other "spectacles," and they served as meeting places for religious, political, legal, and commercial activities.

Some scholars of ancient theater have asserted categorically that full-length reproductions of ancient tragedies and comedies were not a feature of Roman-era theaters. B. Gentili states that from at least the third century BCE, while actors would use texts of dramatic performances from the Classical period, they would combine scenes drawn from more than one drama and would set to music parts that in Classical theater were intended for dialogue (iambic trimeters) and recitative (anapaests).[12]

---

[11] So S. Symeonoglou, *The Topography of Thebes from the Bronze Age to Modern Times* (Princeton: Princeton University Press, 1985), xviii and 190.

[12] B. Gentili, *Theatrical Performances in the Ancient World: Hellenistic and Early Roman Theatre* (Amsterdam: Gieben, 1979), 30–3.

178   *The Formal Education of the Author of Luke-Acts*

These practices during the Hellenistic period served as a background for the tendency during the Roman period to mix dramas by turning originally recited verses into songs. A. Dihle states that while there was some restaging of entire tragedies in fourth- and third-century Athens and in the festivals of other wealthy cities, this was already in the early Hellenistic period the exception rather than the rule.[13] Certainly by the Roman Imperial period the technical requirements and the appropriate public for the production of entire Greek dramas were no longer present, and what one would find performed on stages were prologues, short scenes, messenger reports, stichomythic sections, and choral odes. A. Segal states categorically that in Syria-Palestine, at least, tragedy and comedy were never performed, especially Classical Greek tragedy and comedy, whose context and language would have been foreign to most of the population.[14] Theaters continued to be used for simple drama like the mime, but they were primarily used for meetings, worship, and necrology. Indeed, it is worth noting that all thirty theaters located in the Levant by A. Segal are "Roman" theaters: the orchestra area does not form a complete circle; the *scaena* (stage) encroaches on the orchestra's circumference; the *cavea* (seating complex) does not extend beyond the semicircle of the orchestra. Obviously these theaters were not built to accommodate Classical Greek drama, with its emphasis on the dancing and singing of the chorus in a circular orchestral area.[15]

However, I am skeptical of broad generalizations about what was or was not staged in Roman-era theaters, and I am especially skeptical of categorical assertions that full-length reproductions of traditional Greek tragedies and comedies were excluded altogether. S. Nervegna has recently marshaled and reevaluated the literary and inscriptional evidence and concluded that full-length reproductions of traditional tragedies and comedies continued to be performed in theaters through the Hellenistic and Roman Imperial periods.[16] Artistic evidence from many parts of the Mediterranean world, especially of tragic and comic scenes depicted in paintings on vases and walls as

---

[13] A. Dihle, *Der Prolog der "Bacchen" und die antike Überlieferungsphase des Euripides-Textes* (Heidelberg: Carl Winter, 1981), 29–30, 37.

[14] A. Segal, *Theatres in Roman Palestine*, 12–15; A. Segal, "Theatre," in *Oxford Encyclopedia of Archaeology of the Near East*, vol. 5, ed. E. M. Meyers (Oxford: Oxford University Press, 1997), 199–202.

[15] The view that full-length reproductions of ancient Greek tragedies and comedies were no longer a feature of theater by the Roman Imperial era goes back at least to L. Friedländer, *Darstellungen aus der Sittengeschichte Roms*, 6th ed. (Leipzig: S. Hirzel, 1888–1890), 1:118–19; 2:443–4. Recent advocates of this view include W. Beare, *The Roman Stage: A Short History of Latin Drama in the Time of the Republic*, 3rd ed. (London: Methuen, 1964), 233–40; B. Leyerle, *Theatrical Shows and Ascetic Lives: John Chrysostom's Attack on Spiritual Marriage* (Berkeley: University of California Press, 2001), 21.

[16] S. Nervegna, *Menander in Antiquity*, 63–119, examines revivals of Menander's comedies in the Hellenistic and Roman Imperial periods and concludes that entire comedies of Menander, "full-length and fully staged," not just extracts, continued to be performed in the theaters until the second century CE. Nervegna comes to the same conclusion with respect to ancient tragedies in S. Nervegna, "Staging Scenes or Plays? Theatrical Revivals of 'Old' Greek Drama in Antiquity," *Zeitschrift für Papyrologie und Epigraphik* 162 (2007): 14–42.

Luke and Euripides—Part One 179

well as in mosaics, seems to support this conclusion.[17] A short summary of the inscriptional, artistic, and literary evidence will be sufficient to show that ancient drama, both tragedy and comedy, was not only well known throughout the Mediterranean in the first century CE, including in many of the cities visited by Luke, but that full-length productions of such tragedies as Euripides' *Bacchae* continued to be a component of the many activities conducted in theaters, including those situated in the eastern Mediterranean.

Inscriptional Evidence

The strongest inscriptional evidence is the lists of winners of "archaic" or "old" comedy (ἀρχαία/παλαία κωμῳδία) and "archaic" or "old" tragedy (ἀρχαία/παλαία τραγῳδία) at theatrical performances during the Hellenistic and Roman Imperial periods. Such inscriptions have been found in many different locations, and they date from many different periods: e.g., *SEG* 19.335 and 25.501—*c.* 85 BCE from Tanagra in Boeotia; *IG* XII,4 2:845—first century CE from the island of Kos in the Dodecanese; *CIG* 2759— late second century CE from Aphrodisias in Asia Minor.[18]

S. Nervegna, as mentioned above, has examined the literary and inscriptional evidence for revivals of ancient drama during the Roman period, from Rome in the West to Asia Minor in the East, and visualizes a lively theatrical tradition within which revivals of old plays went hand in hand with performances of new ones.[19] Old tragedies and comedies were included in the programs of a number of festivals in the Hellenistic and Roman Imperial periods as well as in the repertoire of traveling actors. Euripides' tragedies and Menander's comedies in particular continued to be staged as full-length productions at least until the time of Plutarch.

---

[17] So T. B. L. Webster, *Monuments Illustrating Tragedy and Satyr Play* (London: University of London Institute of Classical Studies, 1967), 10, 16–20, 22, and varia; T. B. L. Webster, J. R. Green, and A. Seeberg, *Monuments Illustrating New Comedy*, vol. 1, 3rd ed. (London: University of London Institute of Classical Studies, 1995), 85–98; C. P. Jones, "Greek Drama in the Roman Empire," in *Theater and Society in the Classical World*, ed. R. Scodel (Ann Arbor: University of Michigan Press, 1993), 39–52; J. R. Green, *Theatre in Ancient Greek Society* (London and New York: Routledge, 1994), 142–71; P. E. Easterling, "Menander: Loss and Survival," in *Stage Directions. Essays in Ancient Drama in Honour of E. W. Handley*, ed. A. Griffiths (London: University of London Institute of Classical Studies, 1995), 153–60: K. Gutzwiller and Ö. Çelik, "New Menander Mosaics," 614; K. M. D. Dunbabin, *Theater and Spectacle in the Art of the Roman Empire* (Ithaca: Cornell University Press, 2016), 51–84.

[18] There are many others. Thespiae in Boeotia is especially rich in inscriptions, dating from the second century BCE to the second century CE, that record performances of "old tragedies" and "old comedies": *IThesp* 168 (146–95 BCE); *IG* VII 1760 (early first century BCE); *SEG* 3.334 (*c.* 160 CE); *IG* VII 1773 (*c.* 160 CE); *IThesp* 177, 178, and 179 (all second half of the second century CE). A recently published early second-century CE inscription (*SEG* 38.1462B) from Oenoanda, a small city in Lycia in Asia Minor, includes a record of prizes for various musical, literary, and theatrical competitions, including, among the richest, those for comic and tragic poets (translation and commentary in S. Mitchell, "Festivals, Games, and Civic Life in Roman Asia Minor," *Journal of Roman Studies* 80 (1990): 183–93). For commentary on several pertinent inscriptions, see E. Csapo and W. J. Slater, *The Context of Ancient Drama* (Ann Arbor: University of Michigan Press, 1994), 39–52, 186–206.

[19] S. Nervegna, *Menander in Antiquity*, 63–119; S. Nervegna, "Staging Scenes or Plays?" 14–42.

180　　　*The Formal Education of the Author of Luke-Acts*

Some inscriptions are particularly evocative for our purposes of connecting Luke with the performance of Classical tragedies. According to a very fragmentary inscription (*IGUR* I 223), heavily reconstructed by G. Kaibel in the late nineteenth century, a dramatic contest in Rhodes in the first century BCE included an entire trilogy and satyr play by Sophocles: the tragedies *Peleus*, *Odysseus Gone Mad*, and *Iberai*, followed by the satyr play *Telephus*.[20] This is a unique testimony, for there is no other evidence of revivals of the tragedies of Sophocles after the fourth century BCE, and there is no evidence at all of revivals of the tragedies of Aeschylus. Reproductions of "archaic" or "old" tragedy (ἀρχαία/παλαία τραγῳδία) in the later Hellenistic and Roman Imperial periods came to mean the tragedies of Euripides alone. An especially informative late third- or early second-century BCE inscription from Tegea in Arcadia (*SIG³* 1080), for example, records revivals of Euripidean tragedies in Athens (*Orestes*), Delphi (*Heracles*), Argos (*Heracles and Archelaos*), and Dodona (*Archelaos*).

Along with the evidence of inscriptions, we should consider the evidence of the texts on the Egyptian papyri that contain passages from ancient dramas. Almost all of these point, of course, to a literary reception of the dramas rather than to a theatrical performance. But there are some exceptions. *P.Oxy.* 3533, from the second century CE, for example, includes marks above the lines of a text of Menander's *Epitrepontes* that the editor, E. G. Turner, considers to be marks to help actors in their delivery.[21] *P.Oxy.* 2458, from the third century CE, also has actors' marks above the lines of a text of Euripides' *Cresphontes*, as well as some marks in the margins of the text that appear to denote the distribution of parts in a stichomythic section.[22] Also, the recently published *P.Oxy.* 4546, from the first century BCE or CE, looks like the actual script of an actor playing Admetus in a performance of Euripides' *Alcestis*, for it contains the thirty lines spoken by Admetus within the block of verses numbered *Alcestis* 344–82 in our surviving manuscripts, but it omits two lines of choral ode and seven lines spoken by Alcestis in a stichomythic section of this same block of verses. C. W. Marshall has argued that this text was used by an actor playing the role of Admetus in a revival of Euripides' *Alcestis* in Roman Egypt.[23] Though such documents are rare, it should not surprise us to find actors' librettos of Menandrian comedy and Euripidean tragedy among the Egyptian papyri, for, as we have observed, Philo, who lived in Alexandria at the time of the composition of *P.Oxy.* 4546, quotes two verses from a production of Euripides' *Auge* that he had actually witnessed at the theater (*Prob.* 141).

Artistic Evidence

There are many depictions of what look like performances of ancient tragedy and comedy in the various art forms of the Mediterranean world throughout antiquity,

---

[20]　G. Kaibel, "Aufführungen in Rhodos," *Hermes* 23 (1888): 268–78 (esp. 273–5).

[21]　E. G. Turner, "P.Oxy. L 3533: Menander's *Epitrepontes*," *The Oxyrhynchus Papyri* 50 (1983): 36–48.

[22]　E. G. Turner, "Dramatic Representations in Graeco-Roman Egypt: How Long Do They Continue? *L'Antiquité Classique* 32 (1963): 120–8, was the first to identify this papyrus as an excerpt of Euripides' tragedy made for acting purposes.

[23]　C. W. Marshall, "*Alcestis* and the Ancient Rehearsal Process (*P.Oxy.* 4546)," *Arion* 11, no. 3 (2004): 27–45.

Luke and Euripides—Part One   181

from Italy to the Levant, especially on vase paintings, fresco wall paintings, and mosaics. It is a challenge, of course, to distinguish scenes that are depicting dramatic performances from scenes that are simply depicting myths that also happened to be used as material in drama. The former is indicated by the inclusion of characters and objects unique to dramatic performance: a satyr, an aulos player, an actor's mask, etc. But even in those scenes that can clearly be determined to depict dramatic performances there remains the question as to whether the artists are attempting to depict performances from their own time or ones from earlier antiquity (e.g., Classical Athens). There is also the possibility that the artists are simply following an iconographic tradition and are therefore being inspired by earlier artistic depictions of dramatic performances rather than by actual dramatic performances of any period. Finally, there is the possibility that the artists are imagining a performance based on their familiarity with a dramatic text rather than on their experience of a live performance. Hence, artistic evidence for the performance of ancient dramas during the time of Luke is more evocative than determinative.

The comedies of Menander are the most commonly depicted dramas in ancient art, followed at some distance by the tragedies of Euripides and then Sophocles. There survive on various artifacts from the period between around 300 BCE and 300 CE, from all over the Mediterranean world, several dozen illustrations of scenes from Greek comedy, probably all from Menander.[24] The first-century CE fresco wall paintings from Pompeii in Italy and the third-century CE mosaics from Mytilene on the island of Lesbos and from Daphne, a suburb of Syrian Antioch, are the most conspicuous, but there have survived illustrations of comic scenes also on terracotta and stone reliefs, clay molds, drawings on papyrus, and paintings on glass.[25] Of special interest for our purposes, because of the tradition of Luke's connection to Syrian Antioch, is the large mosaic pavement at ancient Daphne discovered in 1999 and excavated in 2007 under the direction of Ö. Çelik of the Hatay Archaeological Museum, which includes four figured panels representing scenes from four different comedies of Menander. Each panel is inscribed with the name of the play and the number of the act: Act 1 of *Perikeiromene* "Girl whose Hair is Shorn"; Act 1 of *Philadelphoi* "Sisters who Love Brothers"; Act 1 of *Synaristosai* "Women at Lunch"; Act 3 of *Theophoroumene* "Possessed Girl." This artistic evidence suggests that comedies of Menander continued

---

[24] T. B. L. Webster, J. R. Green, and A. Seeberg, *Monuments Illustrating New Comedy*, 1:85–98, catalogs fifty-two of these scenes, to which can now be added four recently discovered mosaics from Daphne in Syria and two from Kissamos in Crete.

[25] On the fresco wall paintings from Pompeii depicting comedies of Menander, or at least Latin revisions of them, see M. Bieber, *The History of the Greek and Roman Theater*, 2nd ed. (Princeton: Princeton University Press, 1961), 227–34. On the mosaics from Mytilene of labeled scenes from eleven comedies of Menander, see S. Charitonidis, L. Kahil, and R. Ginouvès, *Les mosaïques de la maison du Ménandre à Mytilène* (Bern: Francke, 1970), 98–9, plate 27, 1. On the mosaics from Daphne of labeled scenes from four comedies of Menander, see K. Gutzwiller and Ö. Çelik, "New Menander Mosaics," 573–623. For a comprehensive list of wall paintings and mosaics of New Comedy generally, see S. Nervegna, "Menander's *Theophoroumene* between Greece and Rome," *American Journal of Philology* 131 (2010): 23–68.

182   *The Formal Education of the Author of Luke-Acts*

to be performed in theaters as far east as Antioch during the time of Luke and beyond, just as they were in Athens and elsewhere.[26]

Artistic depictions of scenes from tragic drama, though much fewer in number than those of comedies, are still found all over the Mediterranean world until at least the third century CE. The following list of examples from the entire periphery of the Mediterranean, beginning in the west and proceeding east, is illustrative: some first-century CE wall paintings from Pompeii that depict tragedies of Euripides, or perhaps Latin revisions of them, including *Hercules Furens, Heraclidae, Medea, Alcestis, Peliades, Hypsipyle, Iphigenia in Aulide*, and *Iphigenia in Tauris*;[27] a second-century CE wall painting from a grave in the necropolis of Cyrene that shows three tragic actors, one apparently representing Herakles, another Hermes, a chorus, and cithara and aulos players;[28] some later third-century CE wall paintings from Ephesus that depict scenes from tragedies of Euripides, including *Orestes* and an *Iphigenia*.[29] Finally, of special interest for our purposes, again because of the tradition of Luke's connection to Syrian Antioch, are some mosaics from Antioch, its suburb Daphne, and its port Seleucia, discovered during the Princeton University excavations in the 1930s and dated to the second and third centuries CE, depicting various generic theatrical scenes: a stage, actors' masks and costumes, satyrs in theatrical costume, maenads, etc. A performance of Euripides' *Hippolytus* is likely depicted on a mosaic from the "House of the Red Pavement" in Daphne; less clear are adjacent mosaics that appear to depict performances of Euripides' *Troades* and *Medea*, and his lost tragedies *Meleager* and *Stheneboea*. A performance of Euripides' *Iphigenia in Aulide* is likely depicted on a mosaic from the "House of Iphigenia" in Antioch; a performance of Euripides' *Helen* is possibly depicted on another.[30]

In sum, artistic depictions of drama in performance suggest an active tradition of reperformance of Classical Greek tragedies and comedies during the time of Luke and

[26] This is the conclusion of K. Gutzwiller and Ö. Çelik, "New Menander Mosaics," 614. For the view that the artistic depictions of Menandrian comedies generally, throughout the Mediterranean world, serve as evidence of an active tradition of reperformance of these dramas during the later Roman period, see T. B. L. Webster, J. R. Green, and A. Seeberg, *Monuments Illustrating New Comedy*, 1:85–98; C. P. Jones, "Greek Drama in the Roman Empire," 39–52; K. M. D. Dunbabin, *Theater and Spectacle*, 57–77. For the view that these artistic depictions could instead be depicting performances as they would have appeared in the Classical and Hellenistic Greek world rather than in the artists' own time, and that they are dependent upon an iconographic tradition entirely independent of performance in a contemporary theater, see E. Csapo, "Performance and Iconographic Tradition in the Illustrations of Menander," *Syllecta Classica* 10 (1999): 154–88, esp. 155–7.

[27] On these, see M. Bieber, *The History of the Greek and Roman Theater*, 227–34.

[28] On this, see M. Bieber, *The History of the Greek and Roman Theater*, 238–9.

[29] On these, see V. M. Strocka, *Die Wandmalerei der Hanghäuser in Ephesos* (Vienna: Österreichische Akademie der Wissenschaften, 1977), 45–56.

[30] On these mosaics as illustrations of Euripidean theatrical scenes, see K. Weitzmann, "Illustrations of Euripides and Homer," 233–47. D. Levi, *Antioch Mosaic Pavements*, 68–87, pl. XI–XIII, offers different explanations of the scenes on the "Red Pavement" and attributes them to general myth rather than to performances of tragedies. J. Huskinson, "Theatre, Performance and Theatricality," 131–65, takes a middle road, proposing that since theater had taken many forms by the third century CE—performed at banquets, readings, discussions, as well as for dramatic competitions of pantomime and recitations of solo tragic actors—these mosaics should be evaluated with various performative backgrounds in mind, not just traditional tragic drama.

Luke and Euripides—Part One   183

beyond. As noted above, however, the evidence is more evocative than determinative, since it remains possible that the artists have been inspired by a dramatic text or an iconographic tradition rather than by an actual experience of a live performance, or that the artists, rather than depicting a performance from their own time, are imagining how a performance would have appeared in its original setting during the Classical Greek period.

Literary Evidence

Contemporaries of Luke from throughout the Mediterranean world offer descriptions in both Greek and Latin of dramatic performances of various kinds that they witnessed at the many theaters they attended.[31] They mention the genres of contemporary theater, of course, such as mimes, pantomimes, and recitations, but they also mention features that are fundamental components of Classical tragedy and "old comedy" (what we now call "new comedy"): costumed actors, singers, dancers, players of the cithara and the aulos, choruses of young men and women, and even tragic actors singing with these choruses. The descriptions of these performances tend to be tangential to the main topics being addressed by these writers, however, and as a result are usually cursory and nebulous; it sometimes remains unclear, for example, whether the performances they describe were in Greek or Latin, whether they were reproductions of old dramas or productions of new ones, and whether they were full-length dramas or simply recitations of scenes. Most illuminating for our purposes are some passages from Dio Chrysostom, Plutarch, and Philo that point to the likelihood that full-length performances of Classical dramas, both tragedies and comedies, continued to be performed in the time of Luke even in the furthest reaches of the eastern Mediterranean.

Dio Chrysostom, the first-century CE philosopher and rhetorician from Bithynia in Asia Minor, who by his own account had traveled all over the Mediterranean world and had witnessed many theatrical performances (e.g., *Or.* 7.24, 119; 10.27; 11.9; 32.4, 35, 40, 55, 94; 77/78.18), is particularly informative about the nature of theatrical performances of his own time. In *Orationes* 19.5 he states that in the ancient dramas that have been passed down from the poets of the past all the components of comedy, but only the iambic portions of tragedy, have been preserved, the lyric songs of the tragic choruses having disappeared.[32] If this was the case, it would have been a natural and expectable evolution, for in the most primitive forms of ancient tragedy, the songs of the chorus had been essential, and the chorus even played the part of an actor. When Aeschylus introduced a second actor and Sophocles a third, the role of the chorus was diminished. Euripides' choruses became even more divorced from the action of the

---

[31] E.g., in chronological order, Cicero (*Fam.* 7.1.3); Philo (numerous passages—see below); Quintilian (*Inst.* 11.3.91; 11.3.178–80); Plutarch (numerous passages—see below); Dio Chrysostom (numerous passages—see below); Suetonius (*Jul.* 39.1; *Aug.* 43.1, 89.1); Epictetus (*Diss.* 1.24.15; 3.14.1); Apuleius (*Metam.* 10.29–34); Lucian (*Salt.* 27; *Nigr.* 11; *Pisc.* 31; *Nec.* 16; *Gall.* 26; *Anach.* 23; [*Encom. Demosth.*] 27); Philostratus (*Vit. Apoll.* 7.5; *Vit. soph.* 2.16, 23, 27).

[32] Elsewhere, however, Dio speaks vaguely of tragic performances accompanied by the aulos and song (*Or.* 11.7–9).

184   *The Formal Education of the Author of Luke-Acts*

drama. Finally, by the time of Agathon, the choruses had evolved into musical interludes that had no direct relevance to the action of the drama (so Aristotle, *Poet.* 1456a). It is easy to imagine, then, that some reproductions of ancient tragedy during the Roman Imperial era would have dispensed with the chorus altogether, as Dio asserts. Dio specifically reports that he has witnessed at least two reproductions of the ancient tragedies of Euripides in contemporary theaters: *Orestes* or *Iphigenia in Tauris* (*Or.* 10.27) and *Hercules Furens* (*Or.* 32.94—where he quotes three iambic verses of the tragedy).

Plutarch, the first-century CE philosopher and biographer from Chaeronea in Boeotia, also writes as though he has actually witnessed performances of Euripidean tragedies in the theater (*Crass.* 33; *Mor.* 63a, 473b, 556a, 854a–c, 998e). He recalls having heard the character of Ino, the heroine of Euripides' lost tragedy *Ino*, speaking in the theater, and he quotes two and a half iambic trimeter verses of the tragedy (*Mor.* 556a). He also recalls witnessing Euripides' lost tragedy *Cresphontes* and reports that a particularly dramatic speech of Merope, one iambic verse of which he quotes, brought the audience to its feet in terror (*Mor.* 998e).[33]

Finally, Philo (20 BCE–50 CE), the Jewish philosopher from Alexandria, offers clear descriptions of ancient Greek tragedies being performed in Roman-era theaters during his own lifetime. Several times Philo describes the activities of the contemporary theater as though he and his audience are very familiar with it from firsthand experience. He writes often about the structure of theaters, the dramatic activities that occurred there, and the effects these activities had on their audiences.[34] The most telling description of Philo for our purposes is his report that on one occasion (he does not say when or where) he witnessed an audience in a theater burst into a spontaneous standing ovation at the performance of Euripides' lost tragedy *Auge*, and he quotes two iambic verses from the tragedy (*Omn. Prob. Lib.* 141).[35]

In sum, the literary evidence correlates with the inscriptional and artistic evidence to indicate that Classical drama, both tragedy and comedy, was not only well known throughout the Mediterranean in the first century CE, including in many of the cities visited by Luke, but that full-length productions of such tragedies as Euripides' *Bacchae* would have been readily available for Luke to experience, if he had chosen to do so. Luke had almost certainly encountered Euripides' tragedies in the course of his traditional Greek education (ἐγκύκλιος παιδεία/*enkyklios paideia*), had perhaps continued to read them in his adult life, and may have even witnessed performances of

---

[33] P. de Lacy, "Biography and Tragedy in Plutarch," *American Journal of Philology* 73 (1952): 159–71, notes that Plutarch writes about tragedies—even the ancient tragedies of Aeschylus, Sophocles, and Euripides—in terms of staging and performance, indicating that he had witnessed first hand many dramatic performances, including performances of the ancient dramas.

[34] E.g., *De ebrietate* 177; *De opificio mundi* 78; *De posteritate Caini* 104; *De agricultura* 35; *Legatio ad Gaium* 78–9.

[35] On Philo's attitude toward the theater, see E. Koskenniemi, "Philo and Classical Drama," 137–52; J. Jay, "The Problem of the Theater in Early Judaism," *Journal for the Study of Judaism in the Persian, Hellenistic, and Roman Periods* 44 (2013): 218–53, who suggests that Jews in general, both those in Palestine and those of the Diaspora, had a complex relationship with the theater: some resisted Hellenization, while others participated fully in theatrical activities.

them in the theater. Euripides' dramas were eminently quotable, full of memorable aphorisms and speeches, from short phrases to several lines of verse. We should not be surprised, then, that the tragedies of Euripides would serve as a source of inspiration for a writer like Luke, and we should not be surprised to find in Luke-Acts allusions to, and even actual quotations of, Euripidean verse, just as we do in the writings of many of Luke's contemporaries. This holds true particularly for one of Euripides' most popular dramas: the *Bacchae*.

9

Luke and Euripides—Part Two: Thematic and Verbal Echoes of Euripides' *Bacchae* in the Acts of the Apostles

Was Luke Familiar with the Cult of Dionysus?

Euripides' *Bacchae* is the richest literary expression of the cult of Dionysus in antiquity. Before examining whether or not Luke knew this tragedy specifically, however, it is worthwhile to consider how familiar he may have been with the cult of Dionysus generally. The answer, as we shall see, is that the cult of Dionysus would have been very familiar to someone like Luke, just as it was familiar to most of his contemporaries in the eastern Mediterranean, including many Jews and Christians.

The worship of Dionysus was a central feature of Hellenization, and since the third century B CE Judaism had become thoroughly Hellenized, both among Jews in Palestine and among those of the Diaspora.[1] King Ptolemy IV Philopator ordered that Jews in Alexandria who registered to pay a poll tax be branded on their bodies with an ivy leaf symbol of Dionysus and that those who agreed to be initiated into the Dionysiac mysteries gain equal status with Alexandrian citizens (*3 Macc.* 2:28-30). King Antiochus IV Epiphanes compelled the Jews in Palestine to wear wreaths of ivy and join in processions in honor of Dionysus (2 Macc. 6:7). The Seleucid general Nicanor threatened to destroy the Jerusalem temple and replace it with one to Dionysus (2 Macc. 14:33). Some Greeks and Romans even considered the Jewish religion to be a form of Dionysiac worship.[2] Plutarch, who had himself been initiated into the mysteries of Dionysus (*Mor.* 611d), catalogs his impressions of the similarities between Jewish worship and Dionysiac rites—imbibing wine, carrying the thyrsus, playing the trumpet, cithara, and tympany, wearing the fawnskin—and he concludes that the Jews were actually worshipping Dionysus (*Quaest. Conv.* 4.6). Tacitus reports that some thought that the Jews worshiped Liber (Dionysus) because of some similarities in worship: Jewish priests chant to the music of pipes and cymbals, they wear garlands of ivy, and

---

[1] For a short survey of some of the points of contact between Judaism and the cult of Dionysus, with bibliography, see P. Wick, "Jesus gegen Dionysos? Ein Beitrag zur Kontextualisierung des Johannesevangeliums," *Biblica* 85 (2004): 183–8.

[2] On the identification of the Jewish god with the Greek conceptions of gods, including Dionysus, see M. Hengel, *Judaism and Hellenism*, 261–7.

188 *The Formal Education of the Author of Luke-Acts*

there is a golden vine in their temple. But Tacitus disagrees because he regards the worship of Liber festive and cheerful, while the Jewish religion is uncouth and shabby (*Hist.* 5.5).

By the early Christians, the cult of Dionysus would likely have been regarded with some fascination, as the figures of Jesus and Dionysus and the cults that they spawned shared many similarities.[3] Both gods were believed to have been born of a divine father and a human mother, with suspicion expressed by those who opposed the cults, especially in their own homelands, that this story was somehow a cover-up for the child's illegitimacy. They were both "dying gods": they succumbed to a violent death but were then resurrected, having suffered a *katabasis* into Hades, managing to overcome Hades' grasp, and then enjoying an *anabasis* back to earth. Both gods seemed to enjoy practicing divine epiphanies, appearing to and disappearing from their human adherents. The worship of both gods began as private cults with close-knit followers, sometimes meeting in secret or at night, and practicing exclusive initiations (devotees were a mixture of age, gender, and social class—in particular there were many women devotees). Both cults offered salvation to their adherents, including hope for a blessed afterlife, and warned of punishment to those who refused to convert. Wine was a sacred element in religious observances, especially in adherents' symbolic identification in their gods' suffering, death, and rebirth; devotees symbolically ate the body and drank the blood of their gods; and they experienced a ritual madness or ecstasy that caused witnesses to think that they were drunk.

These similarities were not lost on the Romans as well, who, when they first came into contact with Christians in substantial numbers in the latter half of the first century, were inclined to lump them together with the adherents of other mystery religions of the East and primarily with the worshipers of Dionysus. Tacitus appears to associate the followers of Christ with the followers of Dionysus in his colorful description, in Dionysiac terms, of the punishment Nero meted out on the Christians, ostensibly for setting Rome ablaze in 64 CE: an immense multitude of them (*multitudo ingens*) is dressed in wild animal skins and torn apart by dogs (*Ann.* 15.44; cf. Livy, *Ab urbe condita* 39.13).

Already in the second century, the early Christian apologist Justin Martyr was noting some of the similarities between Jesus and Dionysus (among other sons of Zeus): divine birth, death and resurrection, associations with wine, the vine, and the foal of an ass (*1 Apol.* 21, 25, 54). Also in the second century the Christian theologian Clement of Alexandria, who frequently references Euripidean maxims, and actually quotes *Bacchae* 470–2, 474, and 476 (*Strom.* 4.25.162.3–4), *Bacchae* 918–19 (*Protr.* 12.118.5), and *Bacchae* 1388 (*Strom.* 6.2.14.1), was asserting the superiority of the "mysteries of the Word" over the "mysteries of Dionysus" by appropriating the language of the Dionysiac cult in the service of the mysteries of Christianity (e.g., *Protr.* 12.118–23; *Strom.* 4.25.162). The third-century Church Father Origen, in his response to the

---

[3] For two short surveys of some of the similarities between Christianity and Dionysiac myth and ritual, with bibliography, see P. Wick, "Jesus gegen Dionysos?" 189–97, and C. J. P. Friesen, *Reading Dionysus: Euripides'* Bacchae *and the Cultural Contestations of Greeks, Jews, Romans, and Christians* (Tübingen: Mohr Siebeck, 2015), 19–23.

scathing attacks of the Greek philosopher Celsus that Jesus did not have the power of Greek divinities such as Dionysus, reminds Celsus that Jesus too caused earthquakes, liberated his followers from prison, and punished those who failed to believe in him be rending them into pieces (figuratively of the Jews) (*Cels.* 2.33–5; 8.42).

These perceived similarities between Dionysus and Jesus inspired someone in the Byzantine period to compose the cento *Christus patiens*, a Passion of Christ in 2,602 iambic trimeter verses, for which the author claims to have used Euripides as a model (κατ' Εὐριπίδην in verse three of the hypothesis). The *Christus patiens* in fact draws some 300 verses almost verbatim from the *Bacchae*, and it uses the characters of both Pentheus and Dionysus in the *Bacchae* as paradigms of Christ. One of the true oddities of Classical scholarship is that some verses at the end of Euripides' *Bacchae* that were corrupted or lost in the manuscript tradition have been reconstructed on the basis of verses that appear in this Byzantine-era Passion of Christ.[4]

Certainly, then, someone like Luke, a Christian steeped in Judaism and living in the eastern Mediterranean during the first century CE, could readily have become familiar with the cult of Dionysus by witnessing the actual practices of the cult. But the cult of Dionysus could have been experienced indirectly as well: in the theater, in literature, and in art.

Did Luke Know the *Bacchae* of Euripides Specifically?

One of the most popular expressions of the cult of Dionysus was Euripides' tragedy *Bacchae*, which could have been encountered in large public theatrical performances, in smaller private performances at dinner parties, in public or private readings, in a variety of textual forms, and in artistic depictions on vase and wall paintings, mosaics, and sculptures. Could Euripides' *Bacchae* have been known in one or more of these forms to the author of Luke-Acts? The answer, surely, is a resounding "yes."

Euripides composed the *Bacchae* late in life while living in Macedonia, having been exiled by his fellow Athenians, but the drama was staged in Athens after his death at the festival of the Greater Dionysia in 405 BCE. It won first prize—along with the three other unrelated Euripidean dramas that accompanied it. At the beginning of the drama Dionysus, son of the mortal Semele and the god Zeus, has returned from Asia and arrived in his homeland of Thebes in Greece. The ancient hypothesis of the drama runs as follows (my translation and paraphrase):

---

[4] Much more recently, the many perceived similarities between the cult of Dionysus and Christianity have led early twentieth-century scholars of the *religionsgeschichtliche Schule* to trace the origins of Christianity, including Pauline theology, historically back to the Hellenistic mystery cults: so F. Cumont, *Les religions orientales dans le paganisme romain* (Paris: E. Leroux, 1906), R. Reitzenstein, *Die hellenistischen Mysterienreligionen: Ihre Grundgedanken und Wirkungen* (Leipzig: Teubner, 1910), H. Böhlig, *Die Geisteskultur von Tarsos*, and, even more recently, R. Bultmann, *Das Urchristentum im Rahmen der antiken Religionen* (Zurich: Artemis, 1949), and H. Maccoby, *Paul and Hellenism* (London: SCM Press, 1991).

190 *The Formal Education of the Author of Luke-Acts*

Dionysus's kin denied that he was a god, so he inflicted a fitting punishment upon them. He made the women of Thebes mad, and the daughters of Cadmus [Autonoe, Ino, and Agave], the former king of Thebes, led the women as a troop of Bacchants to Mt. Cythaeron. But Pentheus, son of Agave, who had succeeded as king of Thebes, was vexed at what was happening, and he arrested and bound some of the Bacchants, and he sent messengers to the god himself. The messengers arrested the god, who remained passive, and led him to Pentheus, who ordered them to bind him and guard him within the palace, not only asserting that Dionysus was not a god, but even daring to treat him in every way as though he were a man. But Dionysus caused an earthquake and destroyed the palace. Then he led Pentheus to Mt. Cythaeron and persuaded him to put on women's clothes and spy on the women. But the women tore him limb to limb, with his mother Agave leading the way. Cadmus learned what had happened and gathered together Pentheus's scattered limbs, discovering Pentheus's head last of all in the hands of his own mother. Dionysus then revealed himself and gave instructions to everyone, making clear what was in store for each of them, so that he might never be despised as a human again by anyone either in word or in deed.

Many ancient Greek tragedies were performed but once, on the occasion of a major dramatic festival, and then never again. Others, the *Bacchae* among them, were produced over and over throughout the Classical, Hellenistic, and Roman periods. Soon after its initial production at the festival of the Greater Dionysia in Athens in 405 BCE Euripides' *Bacchae* was probably reproduced in the dramatic festivals of the Rural Dionysia in the various demes of Attica, and surely it was part of the revival of old tragedies that were incorporated into the Greater Dionysia in Athens beginning in the archonship of Theodotus in 387/386 BCE (on which see *IG* II² 2318, col. viii). We know that Euripides' tragedies were reproduced for three consecutive years in 342/341 (an *Iphigenia*), 341/340 (*Orestes*), and 340/339 (the name of the tragedy is missing) (on which see *IG* II² 2320).[5] Around 330 BCE the Athenian statesman Lycurgus had official texts of the three great fifth-century tragedians placed in the public archives of Athens; public officials were required to read from these copies as the tragedies were performed in order to preserve them from the contamination of actors' interpolations (Pseudo-Plutarch, *Mor.* 841f). According to an ancient tradition these official copies were the very ones that ended up in the library at Alexandria, thanks to a trick pulled by Ptolemy on the Athenians (Galen, *Commentary on the Epidemics of Hippocrates* 2.4). During the Hellenistic period, Greek tragedies, especially those of Euripides, began to be performed increasingly in cities outside Attica: we have already mentioned the late third- or early second-century BCE inscription from Tegea in Arcadia (*SIG*³ 1080), which records revivals of Euripidean tragedies in Athens, Delphi, Argos, and Dodona.

---

[5] For a recent edition of this inscription, with commentary, see B. W. Millis and S. D. Olson, *Inscriptional Records for the Dramatic Festivals in Athens* (Leiden: Brill, 2012), 61–9.

Along with the conquests of Alexander in the East came Greek theaters and dramas. Plutarch praises Alexander for having the children of his new subjects sing the tragedies of Sophocles and Euripides (*Fort.* 328d), and he reports that Alexander himself once quoted part of Euripides' *Bacchae* at a banquet (*Alex.* 53.4). Plutarch himself makes references to Euripidean dramas hundreds of times in his works, twenty of which are to the *Bacchae*. He had more than a textbook knowledge of Euripidean drama, for he reports that he had witnessed performances of Euripides' *Ino* and *Cresphontes* in the theater (*Mor.* 556a, 998e). Likely he had witnessed the *Bacchae* as well, for he models his account of the life of the Roman general Crassus on the fate of King Pentheus in the *Bacchae*, even relating a fanciful story about the severed head of the recently defeated Crassus being tossed into the middle of some banqueteers in the house of the Armenian King Artabazes just at the moment when a tragic actor was singing the part of Euripides' *Bacchae* where Agave appeared carrying the severed head of Pentheus. The tragic actor, who had been playing the role of Pentheus, opportunistically took on the role of Agave, picked up the head of Crassus, and used it as a prop for the remainder of the performance (*Crass.* 33)!

Thus it is clear that in Luke's lifetime Euripides' *Bacchae* would have been known even in the most eastern frontiers of the Roman Empire. The status of the *Bacchae* in Egypt, for example, as indicated by several references to the drama during the period between 250 BCE and 250 CE, is representative of the drama's status during that time all over the Mediterranean. In Epigram 48 (R. Pfeiffer's edition) of the third-century BCE scholar-poet Callimachus, a librarian at the famed library of Alexandria in Egypt, a mask of Dionysus is visualized gaping at a group of children who are reciting verse 494 of the *Bacchae*: "sacred is my hair." And, indeed, as we have previously noted, the papyrological evidence from Egypt reveals that during this period Euripides' *Bacchae* was studied in the schools at the primary and secondary levels and that it was also one of the more popularly read literary texts. Some generations later we witness the Christian scholars Clement and Origen, both of Alexandria, still quoting and referencing the *Bacchae* regularly (Clement, *Strom.* 4.25.162.3–4, 6.2.14.1; *Protr.* 12.118–23; Origen, *Cels.* 2.33–5, 8.42).

In sum, Luke had likely read and studied extracts of Euripides' *Bacchae* as a primary- and secondary-level school student. He may have read the entire tragedy at some point as an adult. He had access to performances of the entire tragedy—or at least excerpts of the tragedy—in the theater and elsewhere. Further, he would have encountered artistic depictions of Dionysus, and perhaps even scenes from the *Bacchae*, everywhere he traveled throughout the Mediterranean, on coins, vase and wall paintings, mosaics, and statuary.[6]

---

[6] For numerous ancient artistic depictions of the scene of Pentheus being torn limb from limb while dressed as a maenad, for example, see J. Bazant and G. Berger-Doer, "Pentheus," in *Lexicon Iconographicum Mythologiae Classicae*, vol. 7.1, eds. Christoph Ackerman and Jean-Robert Gisler (Zurich: Artemis, 1994), 306–17.

192   *The Formal Education of the Author of Luke-Acts*

Some Thematic and Verbal Echoes of the *Bacchae* in the Acts of the Apostles

The Greek Response to a New and Strange Cult from Asia

The prologue of Euripides' *Bacchae* begins with a stranger—the god Dionysus in disguise—presenting himself as someone who is introducing a new religion, the Dionysiac mysteries, from Asia to Greece. This, in essence, is the situation that the author of the Acts of the Apostles presents in his account of Paul's second missionary journey, when Paul, who is instructed in a vision by a Macedonian man to cross over from Asia, introduces the new religion of Christianity to Greece.

Both "divinities" δαίμονες/δαιμόνια are characterized from a Greek perspective as "new" νέος and/or "foreign" ξένος and their teaching as "strange" καινός. Pentheus, as king of Thebes, represents the Greek perspective on Dionysus in the *Bacchae*, and he refers to the "divinity" δαίμων throughout the drama in what must be regarded as negative terms—"new" νέος, "newly arrived" νεωστί, and "foreigner/stranger" ξένος— while he refers to Dionysus's mysteries as "strange" καινός.[7] Dionysus's adherents never refer to him in these negative terms. In the Acts of the Apostles the most striking clash between the Greek and Christian perspective occurs when Paul introduces this new religion from Asia into the heart of Greek culture: the Agora of Athens (Acts 17:16-34). There Paul confronts the Greek intellectual and civic establishment. The Epicurean and Stoic philosophers accuse Paul of being a "messenger of foreign divinities" ξένων δαιμονίων δοκεῖ καταγγελεὺς εἶναι because he preaches Jesus and Resurrection (17:18), and they accuse him of introducing "foreign matters" ξενίζοντά τινα into their hearing (17:20). They apprehend Paul and lead him to the Areopagus to learn what "strange teaching" ἡ καινὴ διδαχή he is promoting (17:19), for the Athenians are fond of learning about that which is "strange" καινότερον (17:21).

Paul tries to make some points of contact between the Greek and Christian divinities by quoting the Greek poets to his audience (17:28):

Ἐν αὐτῷ γὰρ ζῶμεν καὶ κινούμεθα καὶ ἐσμέν,
ὡς καί τινες τῶν καθ' ὑμᾶς ποιητῶν εἰρήκασιν,
Τοῦ γὰρ καὶ γένος ἐσμέν.

"For in him we live and move and are,"
As even some of your own poets have said,
"For we too are his offspring."

The second quotation, as we have seen, is clearly from Aratus's *Phaenomena* and refers to Zeus, and the first quotation, if it is a quotation, is possibly from a poem by

---

[7] Dionysus is referred to as a δαίμων "divinity" at *Bacchae* 22, 42, 219, 256, 272, 298, 378, 413, 417, 481, 498, 769. Dionysus is called ξένος "foreigner/stranger" at *Bacchae* 233, 247, 353, 441, 453, 642, 800, 1047, 1059, 1063, 1068, 1077—seven times by Penthus, four times by Pentheus's messenger, and once by Pentheus's attendant. Dionysus is called "newly arrived" νεωστί at *Bacchae* 219 by Pentheus. Dionysus is called "new" νέος at *Bacchae* 256, 272, and 467—twice by Pentheus, once by Teiresias. Dionysus's mysteries are called καινός "strange" at *Bacchae* 354 and 650, both times by Pentheus.

Luke and Euripides—Part Two

Epimenides, and it also refers to Zeus. But it is possible that Luke is also evoking Euripides' *Bacchae* here, for one of the more memorable passages of the drama is the stichomythic verbal duel between Dionysus and Pentheus in which Dionysus asserts (506):

οὐκ οἶσθ' ὅ τι ζῇς οὐδ' ὃ δρᾷς οὐδ' ὅστις εἶ

You do not know what life you live, nor what you are doing, nor who you are.[8]

If Luke is evoking the *Bacchae* here in Paul's speech to the Athenians—and the references in both texts to a "new/foreign" god being introduced to Greece offer some support for this view—his response to the drama is clear, triad for triad: it is in the one God, who made the cosmos and everything in it, who is lord of heaven and earth (17:24), who does not dwell in temples made by hand (17:24), and who is not someone served by human hands, as though he needs someone (17:25), that we as humans "live and move and are."

It is remarkable that just as there are three different responses in the *Bacchae* to the introduction of Dionysus to Greece, so here in Paul's speech to the Athenians there are three different responses:

1. The Critics—Acts 17:32: some scoff at him (as Pentheus does in the *Bacchae*).
2. The Cautious—Acts 17:32: some are noncommittal but agree to hear Paul again later (like Cadmus and Teiresias, who wish to keep their options open, in the *Bacchae*).
3. The Adherents—Acts 17:34: some believe and join the new cult (like the chorus of Bacchants and the women of Thebes in the *Bacchae*).

Aptly, of the two new adherents to Christianity named in Acts 17, one is an Areopagite named Διονύσιος/Dionysius "follower of Dionysus," and the other is a woman named Δάμαρις/Damaris "the subdued." It is clear enough that the name Dionysius evokes the god of the *Bacchae*; it is less clear but still notable that the name Damaris, "subdued" woman, evokes the female adherents of the god of the *Bacchae*.[9] If so, the underlying message appears to be that a new cult has already begun to encroach upon the territory of the cult of Dionysus.

---

[8] P. Colaclides, "Acts 17,28A and Bacchae 506," *Vigiliae Christianae* 27 (1973): 161–164, observes the verbal parallel (observed earlier also in the old *Wettstein*) between Acts 17:28 and *Bacchae* 506. Colaclides attributes the similarity to a common source, not to direct dependence of Luke on Euripides. J. L. Moles, "Jesus and Dionysus in *The Acts of the Apostles* and Early Christianity," *Hermathena* 180 (2006): 73–4, picks up on this verbal parallel, among several other verbal and thematic parallels between the *Bacchae* and Acts, and offers the dubious suggestion that a reference to the *Bacchae* here in Acts is supported by Paul's attribution of the phrase to "your (i.e., the Athenians') poets."

[9] E. Renan, *Saint Paul* (Paris: Michel Lévy Frères, 1869), 209, note 3, was the first to offer a possible association with the feminine name Δάμαλις, which means heifer or girl, both in the sense of being "tamed" or "subdued" (Horace mentions a drunken Greek woman named Damalis in *Carm.* 1.36). J. L. Moles, "Jesus and Dionysus," 74, also relates the name Δάμαρις to δάμαλις "heifer" and sees a parallel in Dionysus's association with a bull in the *Bacchae* (100, etc.); this seems to me an exegetical leap too far.

194   *The Formal Education of the Author of Luke-Acts*

Opposition to the New God as a Form of *Theomachia*

Euripides' *Bacchae* begins with a soliloquy by Dionysus, who complains that the Thebans do not revere him as a god (23–42), and that their king Pentheus, in particular, is participating in a θεομαχία, "the waging of a war against a god" (ὃς θεομαχεῖ τὰ κατ' ἐμέ 45), by driving him away from the sacrifices and failing to mention him in his prayers (43–6). This concept of θεομαχία, a futile resistance against an overwhelming power, becomes a leitmotif in the drama. The more prudent prophet Teiresias asserts that he will not, like Pentheus, "wage a war against the god" (κοὐ θεομαχήσω 325). Dionysus describes Pentheus's vain attempt to fight the god in similar terms, censuring him for "going to war against the god," even though he is just a man (πρὸς θεὸν γὰρ ὢν ἀνὴρ ἐς μάχην ἐλθεῖν ἐτόλμησε 635–6). The punishment for θεομαχία is anticipated throughout the *Bacchae*, and at the end of the drama Pentheus's mother Agave blames her son for "waging a war against the god" (ἀλλὰ θεομαχεῖν μόνον οἵός τ' ἐκεῖνος 1255–66), even as she unknowingly holds his severed head in her arms.

The compound verb θεομαχέω, as well as its nominal form θεομαχία and adjectival form θεομάχος, is surprisingly rare in ancient Greek generally.[10] Its first occurrence in surviving Greek literature is in Euripides' *Bacchae*, where it plays such a central role that some have even thought that Euripides himself coined the term.[11] Hence, it is remarkable to encounter the term, unique in the New Testament, at Acts 5:39.[12] In Acts 5:17-42, Peter and others of the apostles have been arrested and imprisoned by the Jewish authorities but then, like Dionysus's followers in the *Bacchae* (226–7, 443–50), miraculously escape from prison by means of divine aid. Also, as in the *Bacchae*, their escape from prison is reported to the authorities by some subordinates. The Jewish authorities are outraged and wish to kill them, but a Pharisee named Gamaliel advises caution, suggesting that if this new religious movement is of human origin, it will, like others, perish, but if it is of divine origin, they will not be able to destroy it, and they will risk becoming "wagers of war against god" (θεομάχοι 5:39). Given the rarity of this word, and given its prominent association with Euripides' *Bacchae*, it is plausible that Luke is consciously recalling the drama here and is offering an echo of it for the consideration of his audience, expecting that they will make a connection between the two episodes.

Both Classicists and New Testament scholars have observed the parallel, and some have regarded it as a deliberate echo of the *Bacchae* by Luke. The first to propose that Luke had actually read Euripides' *Bacchae* and was referencing it here in Acts 5:39 was the eminent Classical philologist W. Nestle, younger half-brother of the New Testament

---

[10]   J. C. Kamerbeek, "On the Conception of ΘΕΟΜΑΧΟΣ in Relation with Greek Tragedy," *Mnemosyne* 1 (1948): 271–83, traces the usage of the term in Greek literature, noting that it is first attested in the *Bacchae* and is key to the drama but that the concept is central to the subject matter of tragedy more broadly.

[11]   First proposed by W. Nestle, "Anklänge an Euripides in der Apostelgeschichte," *Philologus* 59 (1900): 49.

[12]   The verb form (μὴ θεομαχῶμεν) occurs in the Byzantine text at the close of Acts 23:9, but this simply looks like an effort to construct an apodosis, perhaps under the influence of Acts 5:39, for what was construed by someone as an incomplete conditional construction.

Luke and Euripides—Part Two　　　　195

textual critic E. Nestle of Nestle-Aland fame. W. Nestle proposed that Euripides coined the terms θεομάχος and θεομαχέω, since his entire tragedy *Bacchae* epitomizes this concept, and he categorized Luke's use of the term as one of the several deliberate *Reminiszenzen* of the *Bacchae* in Acts.[13] Other Classicists have embraced this view, though perhaps with somewhat less confidence. In his study of the concept of θεομαχία in Greek tragedy J. C. Kamerbeek remarks that "it looks far from impossible that the author of the Acts when using the term θεομάχοι . . . has Euripides' *Bacchae* in mind."[14] In his standard text and commentary of Euripides' *Bacchae* E. R. Dodds draws attention to three verbal echoes of the tragedy in Acts, θεομάχος among them: "The author of Acts may have had echoes of the *Bacchae* in his head when he wrote Acts 5:39; he had probably read the play."[15]

Several New Testament scholars have concurred, though generally with even less confidence than the Classicists. In an appendix to his justly famous article on the literary qualities of the speeches in Acts, M. Dibelius considers Gamaliel's use of θεομάχοι as possible evidence that Luke had read the *Bacchae*: "Here, it is not only the word, but also the *ethos* which is to some extent connected. This suggests that Luke himself may possibly have used the *Bacchae*."[16] In his definition of the term θεομαχέω in the *Theological Dictionary of the New Testament*, O. Bauernfeind asserts that Luke's use of the term at Acts 5:39 "is not due to LXX influence but to the direct or indirect influence of Euripides."[17] In his recent commentary on Acts R. I. Pervo offers some muted support: "It is possible that Luke took his inspiration from Euripides, indirectly if not directly."[18] So does C. S. Keener in his recent voluminous commentary: "Luke might expect much of his audience to catch it [viz. the allusion to Euripides' *Bacchae*]."[19] Nor has Luke's use of θεομάχος in Acts 5:39 escaped the eyes of D. R. MacDonald— "likely points to the *Bacchae*"—who includes this among a plethora of imitations and emulations of Greek literature that he claims to have identified in the New Testament.[20]

Other New Testament scholars have asserted that there is no direct literary dependence here on Euripides' *Bacchae*: instead Luke is simply using a proverbial Greek expression that encapsulates the mythic theme of human resistance to the divine, a theme that arose spontaneously and independently in a number of literary works including the *Bacchae* and Acts. Often marshaled in support for this view is the account in Second Maccabees of King Antiochus IV Epiphanes' persecution of a Jewish family who refused to eat swine: the king is warned that his attempt "to wage a war against god" (θεομαχεῖν) will not go unpunished (2 Macc. 7:19).

---

[13] W. Nestle, "Anklänge an Euripides," 48–50.
[14] J. C. Kamerbeek, "On the Conception of ΘΕΟΜΑΧΟΣ," 279.
[15] E. R. Dodds, *Euripides: Bacchae* (Oxford: Clarendon, 1944), 66. The two other echoes of the *Bacchae* in Acts identified by Dodds are the miraculous freeing of Peter in Acts 12:7 and the use of the aphorism "to kick against the goad" in Acts 26:14 (both of which will be treated at length below).
[16] M. Dibelius, "Literary Allusions in the Speeches in the Acts," in *Studies in the Acts of the Apostles*, 190.
[17] O. Bauernfeind, "θεομαχέω," in *Theological Dictionary of the New Testament*, eds. G. Kittel and G. Friedrich (Grand Rapids: Eerdmans, 1967), 4:528.
[18] R. I. Pervo, *Acts: A Commentary*, 148.
[19] C. S. Keener, *Acts: An Exegetical Commentary* (Grand Rapids: Baker Academic, 2013), 2:1239.
[20] D. R. MacDonald, *Luke and Vergil*, 37–8.

196 *The Formal Education of the Author of Luke-Acts*

A seminal article by A. Vögeli is often cited as a counterpoint to the proposal of W. Nestle.[21] Vögeli catalogs the attestations of the specific terms θεομάχος and θεομαχέω, as well as the larger mythic theme of human resistance to the divine, in Hellenistic and Roman-era Greek literature: Xenophon, Menander, Plutarch, Epictetus, Plutarch, Lucian, etc., including, in a Jewish context, Second Maccabees and Josephus. Given the pervasiveness of the term and the mythic theme, Vögeli is skeptical of drawing any direct connections between specific works. He does not categorically exclude the possibility of Euripidean influence on Luke, however; he is rather objecting to the idea that Luke is slavishly modeling his narrative of Christ after Euripides' narrative of Dionysus, with the character of Paul representing Pentheus, Gamaliel representing Teiresias, and so forth.

Vögeli's critical response to Nestle is seminal, not because it is devastating, or even very convincing, but because it is cited by so many commentators on Acts as though it closes the book on the matter. E. Haenchen: "As A. Vögeli appears to have established once and for all, this only signifies a 'convergence of theme' and the adoption by Luke of expressions that had become proverbial." H. Conzelmann: "There is, however, no literary dependence." C. K. Barrett: "The thought is … too popular to prove literary dependence." D. Marguerat: "Luc ne l'a pas emprunté directement à Euripide, mais qu'il l'a reçu par l'intermédiaire du judaïsme hellénistique."[22] In a recent monograph that examines the three prison escapes in Acts with a view to their religious context, J. B. Weaver proposes that Luke is evoking here the larger mythic concept of the fate of "god-fighters" in ancient Greek myth and literature generally. Thus, he too is not committed to a direct echo of Euripides' *Bacchae* (though he does not exclude the possibility).[23]

My own judgment is that if the term θεομάχος in Acts 5:39 had appeared in isolation we could only venture that Gamaliel's use of the term is suggestive of the *Bacchae*, just as it might be suggestive of other passages of ancient literature that also contain the term: e.g., a Menandrian comic verse or a passage from Plato or Xenophon. But since the verbal parallel in Acts 5:39 resides in a context very similar to that of the *Bacchae*— the introduction of a new God, the persecution and imprisonment of the new God's followers by the city authorities, a miraculous escape from prison by means of divine aid—I think that we can state with some confidence that it is a deliberate echo of the *Bacchae*. In fact Gamaliel's advice not to risk becoming θεομάχοι epitomizes the same range of responses to the new religion that we have observed above, both in the *Bacchae* and in Acts:

1. The Critics—the Jewish establishment: the Chief Priest, the Sanhedrin, the Sadducees, the captain of the temple guard (like King Pentheus, who represents the Theban establishment, along with the Theban military, in the *Bacchae*).

---

[21] A. Vögeli, "Lukas und Euripides," *Theologische Zeitschrift* 9 (1953): 415–38.

[22] E. Haenchen, *The Acts of the Apostles*, 254, cf. 685; H. Conzelmann, *Acts of the Apostles*, 43; C. K. Barrett, *A Critical and Exegetical Commentary on the Acts of the Apostles*, 1:298; D. Marguerat, *Les Actes des Apôtres (1–12)* (Genève: Labor et Fides, 2007), 190.

[23] J. B. Weaver, *Plots of Epiphany*, 132–48.

Luke and Euripides—Part Two   197

2. The Cautious—the Pharisaic teacher Gamaliel (like the old king Cadmus and the old prophet Teiresias in the *Bacchae*). Gamaliel's advice to "wait and see" (Acts 5:34-9) is, in fact, quite reminiscent of the reactions of Cadmus and Teiresias. While the two old men acknowledge the power of Dionysus, Cadmus advises his grandson Pentheus to accept Dionysus as a god even if he proves not to be one, since, as the son of Semele, his divinity will bring glory to their family (330-6), while Teiresias reduces Dionysus to an abstraction—wine (278-85)—and rationalizes his miraculous birth from Zeus's thigh as a lexical error (286-97).

3. The Adherents—Peter and the other apostles, the crowds of people in the temple (like the chorus of Bacchants and many of the women of Thebes in the *Bacchae*). The crowds of people in the temple, in fact, serve as a sort of dramatic chorus in the narrative of Acts 5.

Miraculous Prison Escapes

Some of the most remarkable similarities between Euripides' *Bacchae* and the Acts of the Apostles occur in their descriptions of the adherents of these new religions being persecuted by figures of authority and even arrested, bound (forms of the root δεσμ-), and imprisoned (forms of the root φυλακ-). But the divinities whom they worship watch over them and render their restraints ineffective: they are miraculously freed from their bonds and released from prison, with the barriers to their freedom giving way αὐτόματος "of their own accord." This is a concatenation of themes that runs throughout the entirety of the *Bacchae*, with two specific prison escapes described in detail: first the women followers of Dionysus escape from the public prison of Thebes (226-7, 443-50), and then the god Dionysus escapes from the confines of Pentheus's palace (352-7, 497-514, 576-659). A similar concatenation occurs in the Acts of the Apostles, with three different prison escapes spaced throughout the narrative: first, as we have already noted, Peter and some other apostles escape from the prison of the Chief Priest and Sanhedrin at the temple in Jerusalem (5:17-42); next Peter escapes from the prison of King Herod in Jerusalem (12:1-19); finally Paul and Silas escape from the public prison in Philippi (16:16-40).

In what follows I describe the most significant components of this concatenation of themes that is shared by the narratives of Euripides' *Bacchae* and Acts in their descriptions of the many prison escapes: I am comparing details from the two examples in the *Bacchae* as a whole with those from the three examples in Acts as a whole. As remarkable as the similar themes are, however, most telling are the shared diction and expressions used to compose these themes, so I accentuate these lexical similarities where they exist.

1. Dionysus claims that his mysteries are most appropriately observed at night (485-6: νύκτωρ), and, indeed, it is by night that the god's power is most efficacious (187: νύκτα, 425: νύκτας, 862: παννυχίοις, 1008: ἐς νύκτα).[24] The three prison escapes narrated in Acts, divinely inspired and miraculously effected, all occur during the night (5:19: διὰ νυκτός, 12:6: τῇ νυκτὶ ἐκείνῃ, 16:25: κατὰ τὸ μεσονύκτιον).

---

[24] Hence the appropriateness of Dionysus's epithet Νυκτέλιος ("the night-time one") in Plutarch, Pausanias, Nonnus, etc.

198   *The Formal Education of the Author of Luke-Acts*

2. Forms of φυλάσσω "to imprison," φύλαξ "prison guard," and φυλακή "prison" are used to describe the imprisonment of the adherents of the new religions, or of the god himself: φυλάσσω (*Bacch.* 497; Acts 12:4); φύλαξ (*Bacch.* 959; Acts 5:23, 12:6, 12:19, 16:23, 16:27, 16:36); φυλακή (*Bacch.* 869; Acts 5:19, 5:22, 5:25, 12:4, 12:5, 12:6, 12:10, 12:17, 16:23, 16:24, 16:27, 16:37, 16:40). Thus the root φυλακ- encapsulates a leitmotif shared by the two works.

3. The adherents of the two new religions are described as "bound" (δέω), their movements restricted by "bonds" or "chains" (δέσμος): δέω (*Bacch.* 444; Acts 12:6, cf. 9:2, 9:14, 9:21, 21:11, 21:13, 22:5, 24:27), δέσμος (*Bacch.* 444, 447, 518, 634, 643, 648, 1035; Acts 16:26, cf. 20:23, 23:29, 26:29, 26:31). Thus the root δεσμ- too encapsulates a leitmotif shared by the two works.

4. The chains that bind the women followers of Dionysus in the public prison in Thebes are said to have been loosened αὐτόματα "automatically" (i.e., of their own accord) from their feet, and the door bolts are said to have sprung open without human assistance (*Bacch.* 448–9):

αὐτόματα δ' αὐταῖς δεσμὰ διελύθη ποδῶν
κλῇδές τ' ἀνῆκαν θύρετρ' ἄνευ θνητῆς χερός.

Their chains, of their own accord, were loosened from their feet,
and without a human hand the door bolts sprang open.

Thematically, this scene has a parallel in the description of Paul and Silas's escape from the public prison in Philippi (Acts 16:26):

ἄφνω δὲ σεισμὸς ἐγένετο μέγας ὥστε σαλευθῆναι τὰ θεμέλια τοῦ δεσμωτηρίου, ἠνεῴχθησαν δὲ παραχρῆμα αἱ θύραι πᾶσαι, καὶ πάντων τὰ δεσμὰ ἀνέθη.

And suddenly there was an earthquake so great that the foundations of the prison were shaken, and immediately all the doors were opened, and everyone's chains were unfastened.

But even more similar lexically is the description of Peter's escape from King Herod's prison in Jerusalem with the help of an angel who miraculously causes his chains to fall from his hands and then leads him through the guard posts to the gate which opens for them αὐτομάτη "automatically" (i.e., of its own accord) (Acts 12:7, 10):

καὶ ἐξέπεσαν αὐτοῦ αἱ ἁλύσεις ἐκ τῶν χειρῶν . . . διελθόντες δὲ πρώτην φυλακὴν καὶ δευτέραν ἦλθαν ἐπὶ τὴν πύλην τὴν σιδηρᾶν τὴν φέρουσαν εἰς τὴν πόλιν, ἥτις αὐτομάτη ἠνοίγη αὐτοῖς.

And his chains fell from his hands . . . and passing through the first guard post and the second they came to the iron gate leading into the city, which of its own accord opened for them.

The adjective αὐτόματος is remarkable, as it occurs only here in the *Bacchae* and only here in Acts, both times with respect to the removal of barriers in an escape from prison, and so it offers a lexical parallel within a thematic parallel between the two works that appears to be deliberate rather than coincidental.

Luke and Euripides—Part Two 199

5. A miraculous earthquake shakes and destroys Pentheus's palace, enabling Dionysus, who is imprisoned within, to escape captivity (*Bacch.* 576–603). A miraculous earthquake shakes the foundation of the public prison in Philippi, causing the doors to open and freeing Paul and Silas from their chains (Acts 16:26).

6. The authorities in both the *Bacchae* and in Acts are notified of their prisoners' miraculous escapes by servants who have been sent to fetch the prisoners (*Bacch.* 443–8; Acts 5:21-3, cf. 12:18-19, 16:35-6).

7. Finally, the authorities who are responsible for the imprisonments are subverted, punished, or even destroyed in some appropriate way, or, alternatively, they are actually converted to the new religion. In the *Bacchae*, Pentheus is enticed to participate voyeuristically in the new cult, appearing silly and powerless in women's dress, before he is torn apart by his own mother; his entire extended family is banished and dishonored for their initial rejection of the god. In Acts 5, the temple authorities are portrayed as perplexed and ineffective, while Gamaliel is described as at least open to the possibility of being converted to the new religion. In Acts 12, the prison guards are said to have been executed, and King Herod suffers an unseemly death, its description aptly placed immediately following the prison escape, as though the two are to be understood as related. In Acts 16, the jailer, along with his family, is converted to the new religion; the Philippian magistrates are humbled and forced to apologize.

The essence of both Dionysus and Jesus as divinities who liberate people from what constrains them and, who, more specifically, have an uncanny ability to free themselves and/or their followers from prison, has been a topic of discussion since antiquity. As already noted, the third-century Church Father Origen, in his response to Celsus's question as to why Jesus did not simply free himself from his bonds, as Dionysus had done in the *Bacchae*, counters that Jesus too liberated his followers, namely Peter, Paul, and Silas, from prison (*Cels.* 2.34). Modern scholars too have observed the parallel theme of miraculous prison escapes in the two works and particularly the remarkable shared use of the term αὐτόματος "automatically" to describe the release from what constrains the prisoners. Some have regarded the broader theme's occurrence, and especially the specific term's occurrence, in Acts as a deliberate echo of the occurrences in the *Bacchae*.

O. Weinreich was the first modern scholar to give serious consideration to the parallel in a form-critical approach to the miraculous escapes (*Befrieungswunderen*) that can be found in many ancient authors, most frequently in a Dionysiac context (Pindar, Aeschylus, Euripides, Pacuvius, Ovid, Nonnus) but also in the following accounts: the escape of Moses by the Jewish historian Artapanus (preserved in Eusebius, *Praep. ev.* 9.27.23-4); the two escapes of Apollonius in Philostratus's *Life of Apollonius of Tyana*; the three escapes of Peter and the other apostles and of Paul and Silas in the Acts of the Apostles.[25] Weinreich proposes that Luke made direct use of Euripides'

---

[25] O. Weinreich, "Gebet und Wunder," in *Genethliakon Wilhelm Schmid*, eds. F. Focke et al. (Stuttgart: W. Kohlhammer, 1929), 280-341. The similarities between Artapanus's account of Moses's escape from prison and Luke's account of the three prison escapes in Acts have led some to imagine that the latter was dependent on the former, but while the similarities may be due to a genetic relationship between the two works, that relationship is probably best defined as a shared dependence on Euripides' *Bacchae*. so O. Weinreich, "Gebet und Wunder," 298 309, 313 41; J. B. Weaver, *Plots of Epiphany*, 64–78; C. J. P. Friesen, *Reading Dionysus*, 136–48.

200 *The Formal Education of the Author of Luke-Acts*

Bacchae—der Verfasser der Apg. hat die Bakchen unmittelbar benutzt (341)—the strongest evidence for a genetic relationship being the shared theme of the introduction of a new god, the common use of the rare term θεομάχος, and the use in similar contexts of the specific expression "to kick against the goads," in addition to the several similarities in the descriptions of the prison escapes. Many commentators, both Classicists and New Testament scholars, have embraced Weinreich's conclusion that Luke made direct use of the *Bacchae* in his three accounts of miraculous prison escapes.[26]

More recently, R. Kratz has expanded on Weinreich's form-critical approach by examining miraculous escapes (*Rettungswunderen*) in ancient Mediterranean literature and highlighting a concluding motif that entails the punishment and/or repentance of the opponents of the imprisoned subjects following their miraculous escapes.[27] This concluding motif plays itself out in the subversion or conversion of the new God's opponents in Acts: the subversion of the Jewish authorities, and the "conversion" of Gamaliel in chapter 5, the subversion of Herod in chapter 12, and the subversion of the Philippian authorities and the conversion of the jailer in chapter 16.[28] Because Kratz strictly embraces a form-critical approach, however, the question of Luke's relative dependence on Euripides is not of primary concern in his study.

Most recently J. B. Weaver has followed a similar approach but one that is more myth-critical than form-critical.[29] He proposes that both in the *Bacchae* and in Acts a prison escape is "a sacred event in which a deity's power to save is reenacted in propagation of the cult."[30] Weaver's mythic framework for cult foundation involves a progressive narrative that follows the following pattern: Arrival of New God/Cult > Conflict with Impious Ruler(s) > Imprisonment > Epiphanic Deliverance from Prison > Death or Repentance of Oppressor > Establishment of Cult. Weaver concludes that while narrative correspondences between the *Bacchae* and Acts are striking in the scenes of prison escape, most of the correspondences are also attested in other ancient Greco-Roman drama and mythography as well; hence Luke cannot be said to be dependent on any one text.[31] Many commentators, both Classicists and New Testament

---

[26] E. R. Dodds, *Euripides: Bacchae*, 125: "Memories of the present passage [*Bacchae* 443–8] may have helped to shape the story of the miraculous freeing of Peter in Acts 12:7 and 12:10." R. Renehan, "Classical Greek Quotations in the New Testament," 22: "Some of the details of Peter's deliverance from prison in Acts seem modelled on the liberation of the women in *Bacchae* 443–8." O. Bauernfeind, *Kommentar und Studien zur Apostelgeschichte* (Tübingen: Mohr Siebeck, 1980), 163: "Ein direkter Einfluss des Euripides mag bei Lk selbst anzunehmen sein." J. L. Moles, "Jesus and Dionysus," 74: "Thus in my view the verbal parallels prove use of *Bacchae* and of more general Dionysiac material." C. S. Keener, *Acts: An Exegetical Commentary*, 3:2495: "A general evocation of Dionysus's escape is clear in Luke's prison escapes in general and is likely here as well [i.e., in the earthquake scene in Acts 16:26]."

[27] R. Kratz, *Rettungswunder: Motiv-, traditions- und formkritische Aufarbeitung einer biblischen Gattung* (Frankfurt: Lang, 1979), 446–99.

[28] R. Kratz, *Rettungswunder*, 457, 473, 498–9. This concluding motif was a component that O. Weinreich, "Gebet und Wunder," 313–41, had missed in his analysis but one that J. B. Weaver, *Plots of Epiphany*, esp. 49–53, 57–9, picks up on as an important component of his framework for the establishment of a new cult.

[29] J. B. Weaver, *Plots of Epiphany*, 29–64.

[30] J. B. Weaver, *Plots of Epiphany*, 197.

[31] J. B. Weaver, *Plots of Epiphany*, 271.

Luke and Euripides—Part Two

scholars, have subscribed to this view that the similarities in the accounts of the prison escapes in Euripides' *Bacchae* and in Luke's Acts of the Apostles are simply formal in nature and do not require an awareness of the drama itself on the part of Luke.[32]

As already noted, because of the many close parallels, both thematic and lexical, I favor the view that Luke's Acts is to a certain degree directly dependent on Euripides' *Bacchae*. The effect of the parallels with Euripides' *Bacchae* is to give an apologetic angle to the narrative of Acts. This is Luke's subtle and artistic way of declaring to his audience that the Christian God is as powerful as—in fact even more powerful than—Dionysus. The Christian God too is a "liberator"; the Christian God too can control the natural forces of earthquakes; and the Christian God too loyally watches over his followers. This apologetic message is most explicit in Acts 16, the account of Paul and Silas's experiences in Philippi. Here at their first stop in Greece their God is placed in direct competition with two Greek divinities: first with Apollo and then with Dionysus. Acts 16:16-24 relates the story of a young girl with a "Pythian spirit" πνεῦμα πύθωνα who brings in much business by "manticizing" μαντευομένη for her masters. Both of these are pagan expressions, occurring only here in the New Testament, and they are closely associated with the cult of Apollo at Delphi. Paul casts out this Pythian spirit in the name of Jesus (16:18), an action that leads to Paul and Silas's arrest and imprisonment, which, as we have seen, leads to a second competition with a Greek divinity, namely Dionysus. Like Dionysus in the *Bacchae*, the Christian God responds to his followers' imprisonment by causing an earthquake that shakes the prison to its foundations, opens its doors, and loosens the prisoners' bindings (Acts 16:23-34).

As a final echo of Euripides' *Bacchae* in the account of the miraculous prison escapes in Acts—and as a segue to our next and final section on divine madness—it is worthwhile to consider what happens after Peter's escape in Acts 12. Once Peter has been miraculously freed from the prison of Herod by an angel of the Lord, he makes his way to the house of Mary, the mother of John Mark, where some of the believers are gathered in prayer. A young girl named Rhoda responds to Peter's knocking at the door, but when she recognizes Peter's voice she is so overcome by joy that she neglects to open the door and instead runs back inside to report the news. The others are incredulous, however, and accuse her of "being mad" (μαίνη). She keeps insisting that what she reports is true, but the others object that it must be an ἄγγελος, a "ghost" or

---

[32] A. Vögeli, "Lukas und Euripides," 436: "Zur Erklärung der Epiphanien, der Befreiungs- und Strafwunder der Apostelgeschichte ist der Regress auf Euripides in literarischer Hinsicht überflüssig." E. Haenchen, *The Acts of the Apostles*, 383: "this surely represents no more than literary convention in the rendering of detail." H. Conzelmann, *Acts of the Apostles*, 94: "there is no literary dependence of Luke upon Euripides here, but rather the appropriation of a widespread motif." R. I. Pervo, *Profit with Delight*, 18–24, and R. I. Pervo, *Acts: A Commentary*, 410: "Because of the proliferation of this originally mythic theme, it is not necessary to hypothesize that Luke made direct use of the *Bacchae*, but use is not unlikely." R. Seaford, "Thunder, Lightning, and Earthquakes in the *Bacchae* and the Acts of the Apostles," in *What is a God? Studies in the Nature of Greek Divinity*, ed. A. B. Lloyd (London: Duckworth, 1997), 142: "I suggest that the power and persistence of the pattern may derive, at least in part, from its relation with the powerful and persistent ritual of mystic initiation." J. Hackett, "Echoes of the *Bacchae* in the Acts of the Apostles?" *Irish Theological Quarterly* 23 (1956): 366: "The parallels of Acts with the *Bacchae* are individually so faint that it seems quite reasonable to maintain that these New Testament phrases could have been written so had the play never existed."

202 *The Formal Education of the Author of Luke-Acts*

"vision," of Peter. Finally they respond to Peter's continued knocking and when they open the door and see him are "ecstatic" (ἐξέστησαν). The verb μαίνομαι "to be mad," which is very rare in Acts (three times) and in the New Testament (two additional times), is itself evocative of the women followers of Dionysus, as well as of others affected by the power of the god. Words for "madness"—μαίνομαι, ἐμμαίνομαι, μανία—occur frequently in the *Bacchae*, describing Dionysus's followers generally (130, 301, 305) and the Bacchants specifically (34, 1094, 1295). In fact "Maenads" (μαινάδες "mad ones") is a name commonly attached to the followers of Dionysus in the *Bacchae* (18 times), and these "Maenads" are said "to be mad" (μαίνομαι) when under the influence of Dionysus. And "ecstasy"—the response of the believers to Peter's appearance—is, of course, often paired with "madness" as among the effects of Dionysus, including in Euripides' *Bacchae* (358–9, 850).

Words for "madness"—μαίνομαι, ἐμμαίνομαι, μανία—occur in Acts only here, of Rhoda, and in Acts 26, of Paul, in his defense before King Agrippa, to which we turn next. The rarity of the word in Acts, combined with its ubiquity in the *Bacchae*, suggests that here, the young girl Rhoda, who is the only one of the group to maintain her faith in the mysteries of this new religion, believing that Peter has miraculously been freed from the bonds of prison, is being implicitly associated with the Maenads of the *Bacchae*, for she, like the Maenads, is a joyful and naïve believer who has truly "gone mad."[33]

Acts 26:14: σκληρόν σοι πρὸς κέντρα λακτίζειν "it is difficult for you to kick against the goads"

Paul is the only person in Acts, other than Rhoda, who is accused of "being mad" (26:24), and he too in a Dionysiac context, shortly after he quotes what appears to be an actual verse from Euripides' *Bacchae* in his formal defense before King Agrippa (26:14). This is the most explicit and remarkable verbal echo of Euripides' *Bacchae* in Acts, and the several thematic and verbal echoes of the *Bacchae* in the three preceding accounts of prison escapes in Acts serve as its background. Both gods of these new religions, Dionysus and Jesus, directly confront their primary opponents, who are violently persecuting their followers, and warn them not to resist by "kicking against the goads" πρὸς κέντρα λακτίζειν.

In response to the raging Pentheus's threats to pursue the followers of Dionysus into the mountains and to arrest, even to massacre, them, Dionysus himself confronts him directly and warns him not to resist his power by "kicking against the goads" (794–5):

θύοιμ' ἂν αὐτῷ μᾶλλον ἢ θυμούμενος
πρὸς κέντρα λακτίζοιμι θνητὸς ὢν θεῷ.

I would sacrifice to him [Dionysus] rather than rage and
kick against the goads, a mortal against a god.

---

[33] Rhoda is a common enough name in antiquity, so perhaps we should not read too much into the fact that a Rhoda is named as one of the nurses of Dionysus in Nonnus's *Dionysiaca* (14.223).

Luke and Euripides—Part Two

In response to the raging Paul's persecution and imprisonment of the followers of Jesus, even into the outer cities and as far away as Damascus, Jesus himself appears to him in a bright light from heaven and warns him that he should not "kick against the goads" (Acts 26:14):

πάντων τε καταπεσόντων ἡμῶν εἰς τὴν γῆν ἤκουσα φωνὴν λέγουσαν πρός με τῇ Ἑβραΐδι διαλέκτῳ, Σαοὺλ Σαούλ, τί με διώκεις; σκληρόν σοι πρὸς κέντρα λακτίζειν.

And all of us fell to the ground, and I heard a voice saying to me in the Hebrew dialect, "Saul, Saul, why do you persecute me? It is difficult for you to kick against the goads."

This expression appears nowhere else in the New Testament or the Septuagint. While it is the sort of aphorism that would be at home in any agricultural society, there do not in fact appear to be any surviving attestations in Jewish literature.[34] However, the aphorism is very common in Archaic and Classical Greek poetry, most famously in Euripides' *Bacchae*, and it appears in later, secular (non-Christian and non-Jewish) prose as well.

In order to appreciate the full resonance of Luke's use of this aphorism within its context in Acts 26 it is worthwhile to consider its surviving attestations in Greek literature from before the time of Luke: Pindar's *Pythian* 2.94–5; Aeschylus's *Agamemnon* 1624 and *Prometheus Bound* 323 (in a slight variation of the expression); Euripides' *Bacchae* 795, fr. 604 (*Peliades?*), and an unidentified iambic fragment (Diehl fr. 13). The literary context of the expression, where discernible, is commonly of a recalcitrant human resisting divine will (Pindar, *Pyth.* 2.94–5: ποτὶ κέντρον δέ τοι λακτιζέμεν τελέθει ὀλισθηρὸς οἶμος "kicking against the goad is surely a slippery path") or divine retribution (Aeschylus, *Ag.* 1624: πρὸς κέντρα μὴ λάκτιζε "don't kick against the goads"). A variation on the expression (Aeschylus, *Prom.* 323: πρὸς κέντρα κῶλον ἐκτενεῖς "you will stretch out your leg against the goads") is used, very much as in the *Bacchae* and in Acts, to describe the Titan Prometheus's resistance to the new god Zeus.

The aphorism is also attested in other, more fragmentary, sources from antiquity: in the scholia to Pindar and Aeschylus, in the writings of Hellenistic grammarians and lexicographers, in some later quotations of lines of dramatic poetry, and among collections of aphorisms on inscriptions from Asia Minor. The aphorism appears to have been known in at least two different forms:

---

[34] A. Vögeli, "Lukas und Euripides," 416–17, claims that there is no equivalent aphorism in Hebrew literature. M. Dibelius, "Literary Allusions," 188, observes that the proverb is not found in any Semitic form. L. Schmid, "κέντρον," in *Theological Dictionary of the New Testament*, eds. G. Kittel and G. Friedrich (Grand Rapids: Eerdmans, 1966), 3:663–8, notes the absence of the aphorism in all of surviving Jewish literature: "The fact remains that the common Greek and Roman saying πρὸς κέντρα λακτίζειν does not occur at all in the Jewish sphere (666)."

204   *The Formal Education of the Author of Luke-Acts*

ὁ γὰρ πρὸς κέντρα λακτίζων τοὺς ἰδίους πόδας αἱμάσσει. [largely iambics]

"For he who kicks against the goads bloodies up his own feet."

λακτίζεις πρὸς κέντρα, πρὸς ἀντία κύματα μοχθεῖς [a dactylic hexameter]

"You are kicking against the goads, you are toiling against contrary waves."

But since these are just isolated fragments, lacking any larger literary context, it is impossible to appreciate their resonance.

The resonance of the expression in Euripides' *Bacchae*, however, for which we do know the larger literary context, is very close to its resonance in Acts. Pentheus, a strong and stubborn mortal and a θεομάχος, is resisting the will of the newly arrived divinity Dionysus, who, disguised as a "stranger," directly warns the recalcitrant θεομάχος not to resist angrily the will of the newly arrived god and not to "kick against the goads" (795: πρὸς κέντρα λακτίζοιμι) but rather to sacrifice to him, a mortal to a god. Likewise in Acts, Saul, a strong and stubborn mortal and a θεομάχος, is persecuting the adherents of the new Christian God Jesus, who speaks to him directly in a voice from heaven warning him that he should not "kick against the goads" (26:14: πρὸς κέντρα λακτίζειν).

While the contexts of the Pindaric and Aeschylian passages are similar to that of Acts, the context of the Euripidean passage is by far the closest. Moreover, Euripides' *Bacchae*, as we have observed, would have been the most accessible to someone like Luke and his audience; neither Pindar nor Aeschylus was as well known in Luke's time, in school texts, in private reading, or in public performance, while Euripides remained a mainstay in all three media. Moreover, I think it can be said with some confidence that Luke is not simply inserting here a trite aphorism drawn from the well of common sayings; rather, he is recalling both the larger context and the very words of Euripides' *Bacchae*. He has this specific drama in mind, and he wants his audience to recall it as well.

This is a controversial stance, of course, for as in the cases of the other thematic and verbal parallels that have been proposed between Euripides' *Bacchae* and Luke's Acts of the Apostles—the varied responses to a new and strange cult from Asia, the opposition by some to the new god as a form of *theomachia*, the many details in the accounts of the miraculous prison escapes—the response of scholars to the shared expression "to kick against the goad" has taken two tracks. Some see in Luke's use of the expression a direct borrowing from Euripides' *Bacchae*; others reject any genetic relationship and regard the attestation of the proverb in both Euripides and Luke as independent uses of a common expression.[35]

---

[35] Among the former are W. Nestle, "Anklänge an Euripides," 46–57; F. Smend, "Untersuchungen zu den Acta-Darstellungen von der Bekehrung des Paulus," *Angelos* 1 (1925): 34–45; O. Weinreich, "Gebet und Wunder," 326–41; H. Windisch, "Die Christusepiphanie vor Damaskus (Act 9, 22 und 26) und ihre religionsgeschichtlichen Parallelen," *Zeitschrift für die neutestamentliche Wissenschaft* 31 (1932): 1–23; E. R. Dodds, *Euripides: Bacchae*, 164; J. L. Moles, "Jesus and Dionysus," 65–104; R. I. Pervo, *Acts: A Commentary*, 631–2; D. R. MacDonald, *Luke and Vergil*, 11–65; C. J. P. Friesen, *Reading Dionysus*, 207–35. Among the latter are A. Vögeli, "Lukas und Euripides," 415–38; M. Dibelius, "Literary Allusions," 188–91; J. Hackett, "Echoes of Euripides in Acts of the Apostles?" *Irish Theological Quarterly* 23 (1956): 218–27; J. Hackett, "Echoes of the *Bacchae*," 350–66; E. Haenchen, *The Acts of the Apostles*, 685; H. Conzelmann, *Acts of the Apostles*, 210–11.

We can now consider in more depth the context of Paul's account of his conversion in Acts 26 in order truly to appreciate the powerful resonance of the aphorism. Paul's experience on the road to Damascus was so vital to the evolution of his spiritual life that he alludes to it several times in his letters (Gal. 1:1, 11-17; 1 Cor. 9:1, 15:8; 2 Cor. 11:32-3); and it was also so central to the message of Acts that Luke presents three accounts of the event spaced out over the course of his narrative: 9:1-19; 21:40–22:21; 25:23–26:32. It is worthwhile, for our purposes, to compare the three accounts in some detail and to consider why the aphorism found in Euripides' *Bacchae* 795 is included only in the last of the three (Acts 26:14).

The fundamental elements of the three accounts are similar: at the instruction of the Chief Priest(s) Saul and his companions set out for Damascus to bind and bring back to Jerusalem some of the early Christians; on the way to Damascus a light flashes down from heaven that causes Saul, at least, to fall to the ground; a voice from heaven asks, "Saul, Saul, why do you persecute me?"; Saul replies, "Who are you, Lord?" and the voice answers "I am Jesus whom you persecute"; the voice then instructs Saul to stand up and continue on to Damascus. Amidst these similarities, however, there are some interesting differences that are largely due, I believe, to the various narratological settings of the three accounts. The first account is presented in the third person by the external narrator (author of Acts) to the external narratee (Theophilus). The second account is presented in the first person by an internal narrator (the just-arrested Paul) to some internal narratees (a crowd of hostile Jews at the temple in Jerusalem). The third account is presented in the first person by an internal narrator (the captive Paul) to some internal narratees (an assembly of mostly gentile dignitaries at the auditorium in Caesarea).

There are several notable differences, both small and large, among the three accounts. It has often been observed, for example, that in the first account, Saul's companions hear a voice but do not see anyone (9:7); in the second, they see a light but do not hear the voice of the speaker (22:9); and in the third, they again appear only to see the light (26:13-14). It has also been observed that in the first account Saul's companions remain standing while he falls to the ground (9:4-7); in the second only Saul is described falling to the ground (22:7); and in the third the entire group falls to the ground (26:14). I am more concerned here, though, with some of the more substantial differences that seem to result from the narratological settings of the three accounts. Therefore, I have extended the text under consideration to those passages that both precede and follow the short accounts of the specific events that occurred on the road to Damascus.

The most numerous and remarkable differences are between the first two accounts and the third: in the first two accounts the early Christians are called followers of "The Way," while in the third account they are called "Saints"; in the first two accounts Saul and his companions are approaching Damascus when they see the light, while in the third they are simply described as somewhere on their way to Damascus; in the first two accounts the voice from heaven asks only, "Saul, Saul, why do you persecute me?" while the third account appends the aphorism "it is difficult for you to kick against the goads"; in the first two accounts Saul is instructed to rise and proceed to Damascus, where he will be told what to do, while in the third he is simply told to rise and stand

206 *The Formal Education of the Author of Luke-Acts*

on his feet; consequently, in the first two accounts Ananias plays a major role as the one who instructs Saul in Damascus, while in the third Ananias plays no part, but rather the voice of Jesus himself instructs Saul while still on the road; in the first two accounts Saul is blinded by the light and needs to be led by the hand to Damascus by his companions, while in the third this detail is not included; in the first two accounts Saul is baptized as a sign of his conversion, while in the third this detail is absent.

For our purposes it is especially critical to explain why, while all three accounts have the voice from heaven say, "Saul, Saul, why do you persecute me?" (Σαοὺλ Σαούλ, τί με διώκεις 9:4; 22:7; 26:14), only the third account appends the aphorism "it is difficult for you to kick against the goads" (σκληρόν σοι πρὸς κέντρα λακτίζειν 26:14).[36] I believe that the explanation lies in the narratological situations of the three accounts.

The first account, narrated in the third-person by the author of Acts, is the most straightforward and bare-bones. It emphasizes Saul's individual experience of the sight and sound of the risen Jesus (his companions mostly hover in the background), his blinding by the bright light, and his subsequent healing by the hand of Ananias. It is, in fact, primarily a story about a miraculous healing of Saul's blindness (both physically and metaphorically). It is perhaps the form of the story that Luke inherited from his source, while the second and third accounts have undergone some Lucan refashioning.[37]

The second account is placed by the author of Acts in the mouth of Paul himself, who is defending himself before an angry Jewish crowd in the Jerusalem temple. Paul ingratiates himself to his Jewish audience by speaking "in the Hebrew dialect" (i.e., Aramaic) (21:40; 22:2), which has the desired effect of calming his audience down (22:2). He introduces himself as a zealous Jew, like his audience, born in Tarsus but raised in Jerusalem, and strictly educated in their ancestral law at the feet of the great Rabbi Gamaliel (22:3). He reminds his audience that he had persecuted the followers of "the Way," with the blessing of the Chief Priest and the Sanhedrin, shackling, imprisoning, and even executing them; in fact it was in such pursuit that he was going to Damascus when his conversion experience occurred (22:4-5). Paul's account of his experience on the road to Damascus is, with minor variations, the same as Luke's first account (cf. 9:3-9 and 22:6-11), but subsequently places much greater emphasis on the reputation of Ananias as a law-abiding Jew, highly regarded by all the Jews in Damascus (22:12), and he presents Ananias's role in the narrative not so much as a healer of his blindness, which is downplayed here in comparison with the first account, but rather as a commissioner of his divinely inspired ministry to all men (22:13-16). Paul perspicaciously leaves out the details, so central in Luke's first account, of Jesus's instructions to Ananias in a dream (9:10-16)—why risk antagonizing his Jewish audience by asserting the role of the figure of Jesus? Instead Paul appends an account of a second vision that he experienced while praying in the very temple in Jerusalem at which he is now speaking (22:17-21): the voice of the Lord, the God of the Jews,

---

[36] The aphorism appears in the second account in some Western witnesses (after 9:4) and in the Vulgate (after 9:5), but these are classic cases of harmonization.

[37] So M. Dibelius, "The Speeches in Acts and Ancient Historiography," 158–161, C. W. Hedrick, "Paul's Conversion/Call: A Comparative Analysis of the Three Reports in Acts," *Journal of Biblical Literature* 100 (1981): 427–8.

Luke and Euripides—Part Two   207

worshipped in this very temple, had spoken to him while he was praying in the temple, instructing him, much to his chagrin, to extend his ministry outside of Jerusalem to the very people whom he had been persecuting. In short, in this second account of Paul's conversion, Luke has refashioned the account that he had inherited in order to mold it to its narratological setting.

The third account, like the second, is placed by the author of Acts in the mouth of Paul himself, who is, this time, defending himself before an entirely different audience: an assembly of powerful and highly educated gentiles in the audience hall of the Roman town of Caesarea, including King Agrippa and his sister Bernice, the Roman procurator Festus, some Roman tribunes, and the most prominent men of the city. The group is assembled with all pomp and circumstance, and when King Agrippa announces formally that Paul is permitted to address the audience, presumably in Greek, Paul musters all the rhetorical devices at his disposal. He gestures with his hand to signal the beginning of his formal defense. He begins his speech with a formal *captatio benevolentiae* (26:2-3): "I am most fortunate to be offering my defense in your presence today, King Agrippa, since you are knowledgeable of Jewish customs and controversies. Therefore, I request that you listen to me patiently." He elevates his language with Classical vocabulary (26:11 ἐμμαίνομαι, 26:22 ἐπικουρία), forms (26:4 ἴσασι, 26:5 ἀκριβεστάτην, 26:13 poetic οὐρανόθεν (contrast colloquial ἐκ τοῦ οὐρανοῦ in the first two accounts)), constructions (26:21 ἕνεκα + genitive, 26:29 the potential optative εὐξαίμην ἄν), and expressions (26:14 σκληρόν σοι πρὸς κέντρα λακτίζειν, 26:26 οὐ γάρ ἐστιν ἐν γωνίᾳ πεπραγμένον τοῦτο).

The core of Paul's account of his experience on the road to Damascus is, with some variations, quite similar to the first and second accounts (cf. 9:3-9; 22:6-11; and 26:12-18), except that the motif of blindness and miraculous healing is dispensed with altogether in favor of a narrative about his divine commission (26:16-23). Moreover, the commission is put in the mouth of the divine voice itself, and so there is no need for the figure of Ananias (the pious, Jewish healer and mouthpiece of God would not be a sympathetic figure for Paul's largely gentile audience here anyway). In a revealing twist, it is not Paul's eyes that have to be opened through a miraculous healing; rather, Paul himself is commissioned to "open the eyes" of those to whom he is being sent. He describes the objects of his divine commission first as the Jews in Damascus and Jerusalem, and then as those in all Judaea, and finally as the gentiles. The subjects of God's commission to Paul, then, would include his current audience of gentile dignitaries and indeed King Agrippa himself.

Now back to the main point in comparing these three accounts so closely. In the third account, Luke is imagining Paul taking into consideration his narratological setting, and part of this involves alluding at various levels of specificity to a work that would have been well known to Paul's gentile audience in Caesarea: Euripides' *Bacchae.* As in the second account of his conversion, Paul introduces his narrative by burnishing his Jewish credentials and asserting that he was persecuting "the Saints" with the blessing of the Chief Priest(s) (26:4-11). But just as he is about to launch into his account of the events on the road to Damascus he adds an extraordinary description of his personal feelings toward the Christians: "being exceedingly mad at them, I pursued them even into the outer cities" περισσῶς τε ἐμμαινόμενος αὐτοῖς ἐδίωκον ἕως καὶ εἰς τὰς ἔξω πόλεις (26:11). The compound verb ἐμμαίνομαι is used only here in the New Testament. It appears to be an allusion to a famous and memorable description in Euripides' *Bacchae*, where an adjectival form of this compound occurs describing the frenzied maenads, running through the woods and the mountains, hunting and then stoning their human prey, "maddened by the inspiration of their god" θεοῦ πνοαῖσιν ἐμμανεῖς (*Bacch.* 1094). The motif of madness is picked up at the end of Paul's defense as well, creating a literary frame for Paul's speech, when Festus interrupts Paul with the accusation "You are mad (μαίνῃ), Paul; your excessive learning leads you to madness (μανίαν) (26:24)." To this Paul responds "I am not mad" (οὐ μαίνομαι), most excellent Festus, but I am proclaiming words of truth and "moderation" (σωφροσύνης) (26:25). Like the verb ἐμμαίνομαι, the noun μανία is used only here in the New Testament. This passage also accounts for two of the three uses of the simplex form of the verb μαίνομαι in Acts, the other referring to Rhoda, as discussed above. But, as rare as they are in the New Testament, both the verb and noun forms, and the notion of madness generally, are ubiquitous in Euripides' *Bacchae*, where, as we have seen, words for the divine "madness" provoked by Dionysus prevail. The rarity of this word root in Acts, and in the New Testament generally, combined with its ubiquity in Euripides' *Bacchae*, suggests that here Paul is being implicitly associated with Pentheus in the *Bacchae*, who like Paul had "kicked against the goad" of the new god and had "gone mad" (*Bacch.* 326, 359, 999). Unlike Pentheus, however, who suffers a savage death because of the madness inflicted upon him by Dionysus, Paul is allowed by the Christian God to "see the light," and the mania that has filled Paul before his conversion (26:11) has been replaced, as he claims, by moderation (σωφροσύνη) (26:25). Once again, it appears, the Christian God has proven himself superior to Dionysus.

10

Luke and Plato

The Study of Plato's *Apology of Socrates* in the Ancient Educational Curriculum

Here in our final chapter, as throughout this work, we shall assume that the author of the Gospel of Luke and the Acts of the Apostles was a πεπαιδευμένος/*pepaideumenos* "educated man" who had completed at least the first two stages of the ἐγκύκλιος παιδεία/*enkyklios paideia* "curricular education" regularly experienced by children of the upper social classes throughout the eastern Mediterranean during the Hellenistic and Roman Imperial periods. And we can assume a similar educational background for at least some of Luke's audience, beginning with the "most excellent Theophilus" of Luke 1:3 and Acts 1:1.[1]

As we have seen, the "curricular education" began with the basics of reading and writing (letters, syllables, words, and, finally, full sentences), followed by a carefully graded series of exercises called προγυμνάσματα/*progymnasmata*. These exercises included the reading, writing, and studying of maxims, fables, and short stories about the lives of famous historical and mythical figures. One of the most prominent of these figures was the Athenian philosopher Socrates, the story of whose life and death had reached mythic proportions by the first century CE. Education at the secondary level also included a wide range of Classical and Hellenistic literature, chiefly the poetry of Homer, Hesiod, Euripides, and Menander but also some prose texts, such as the fables of Aesop and Babrius and the gnomic works of Isocrates.[2] Prose readings at the secondary level would

---

[1] A. J. Malherbe, *Social Aspects*, 29–59, imagines the early Christian audiences of both Paul and Luke's writings comprising urban intellectuals, politicians, and people of noble birth, as well as a socially pretentious class of people made up of artisans and tradesmiths. This is a sharp contrast to A. Deissmann's influential proposal—*Light from the Ancient East*, 4th ed. (New York: Harper & Brothers, 1922), 466—that early Christianity attracted adherents from only the least privileged social classes: "a movement among the weary and heavy-laden, men without power or position, 'babes,' as Jesus Himself calls them, the poor, the base, the foolish, as St. Paul with a prophet's sympathy describes them."

[2] On the emphasis of poetry over prose at the primary and secondary level, see R. Cribiore, *Gymnastics of the Mind*, 137–43, 192–201. But prose texts were not excluded: Sextus Empiricus, late second-century CE physician and philosopher, records in the first book of his *Adversus Mathematicos*, which is a criticism of grammarians in particular, that the γραμματικός/*grammatikos* (a "grammarian" who taught at the secondary level of the educational curriculum) interprets such works as Homer, Hesiod, Pindar, Euripides, Menander, and others, among the poets, and Herodotus, Thucydides, and Plato, among the prose writers (1.57–60). In support of the inclusion of prose Sextus quotes the famous second-century BCE grammarian Dionysius Thrax's treatise on grammar. γραμματική ἐστιν ἐμπειρία ὡς ἐπὶ τὸ πλεῖστον τῶν παρὰ ποιηταῖς τε καὶ συγγραφεῦσι λεγομένων "Grammar is for the most part the study of the language of both poets and prose-writers."

210   *The Formal Education of the Author of Luke-Acts*

likely have included at least some indirect, if not direct, exposure to Plato's most famous work, the *Apology of Socrates*. The study of Plato's philosophical dialogues was a mainstay only in the advanced (tertiary) level of the educational curriculum, in which formal grammar, rhetoric, and philosophy were introduced, partly through the study of the Attic orators (especially Demosthenes), the historians Herodotus, Thucydides, and Xenophon, and the philosopher Plato. I am not inclined to think that Luke attained so advanced a level of education that he was required to undergo in-depth study of Plato's dialogues. But that does not mean that he would have been unacquainted with Plato and with the very famous *Apology of Socrates* in particular, which, as mentioned, he probably would have encountered in some form at the primary and secondary levels of his education, and which would have been available in libraries and bookshops throughout the Mediterranean world for him to encounter as an adult as well, whether he chose to borrow or to buy the text or even to commission a scribe to make a private copy.[3]

Socrates' life, teaching, trial, and execution spawned an industry of literature by his epigoni. There are ancient references to at least eight "Apologies of Socrates" composed during the fourth century BCE: by the orator Lysias, the philosopher Aeschines of Sphettus, the philosopher Plato, the philosopher Crito, the historian Xenophon, the tragic poet and orator Theodectes, the statesman and orator Demetrius of Phaleron, and the Stoic philosopher Zeno (not the famous Zeno of Citium). Two of these *Apologies*—those of Plato and Xenophon—have survived to our time. The practice of composing "Apologies of Socrates" continued to be widespread throughout later antiquity as well, even as far afield as the Levant, as attested by the efforts of the first-century BCE Stoic philosopher Theon of Antioch, the second-century CE philosophical orator Maximus of Tyre, and the fourth-century CE Sophist Libanius of Antioch (whose *Apology of Socrates* has survived). This practice resulted in the stories about Socrates, who over time became increasingly idealized and even mythologized, becoming well known throughout antiquity, even in the most remote recesses of the Mediterranean world.

The life and character of Socrates, first as a historical person, then as a mythical idea, also became increasingly integrated into the educational curriculum. Aelius Theon, the first-century CE (?) rhetorician from Alexandria in Egypt, who offers the earliest surviving specimen of *progymnasmata*, refers to the formulation of "anecdotes" (χρεῖαι/*khreiai*) and "encomia" (ἐγκώμια/*enkomia*) about Socrates (*Progymnasmata* 98, 111). Additional references to progymnastic exercises about Socrates can be found in the later educational treatises attributed to Hermogenes, the second-century CE (?) rhetorician from Tarsus (*Progymnasmata* 7.1–12 mentions encomia of Socrates), and Nicolaus, the fifth-century CE rhetorician who taught in Constantinople (*Progymnasmata* 58 mentions encomia of Socrates).

---

[3]   On the availability and circulation of literary texts in the ancient world, see R. J. Starr, "The Circulation of Literary Texts in the Roman World," *Classical Quarterly* 37 (1987): 213–23; T. Kleberg, "Commercio librario ed editoria nel mondo antico," in *Libri, editori e pubblico nel mondo antico: guida storica e critica*, 3rd ed., ed. G. Cavallo (Bari: Laterza, 1984): 27–80.

Familiarity with Plato's *Apology of Socrates* among Luke's Contemporaries

Familiarity with stories about Socrates, including Plato's account of his trial, is poignantly illustrated in the ancient Greek papyri. Among the papyri that date to around the time of Luke (100 BCE–200 CE), Plato is by far the most widely attested philosopher: 74 different papyri cite or quote Plato's works, followed by Aristotle with 25, and then Theophrastus with 7. Two papyri from the extreme ends of the Mediterranean world illustrate well the popularity of Plato's *Apology* during this period: a first-century BCE papyrus roll from Herculaneum in Italy (*P.Herc.* 467) includes a reference by the philosopher Philodemus to Plato's *Apology* (fr. 8 appears to reference *Apol.* 38c);[4] a mid-first- to mid-second-century CE papyrus roll from Arsinoites in Egypt (BKT 9.114) preserves quotations from Plato's *Apology* 25b–c, 28b, and 40b–41c and appears to be a part of what was once an entire text of the work.[5] That Philodemus would refer to Plato's *Apology* in a philosophical treatise housed in the private library of an aristocrat's villa in Italy is not very remarkable, but that an entire text of Plato's *Apology* was circulating in so extreme an outpost as Arsinoites in Middle Egypt shows just how popular this work must have been throughout the Mediterranean world precisely during Luke's own lifetime.

Platonic dialogues were highly recommended by rhetoricians of the time as a course of study. The first-century BCE historian and rhetorician Dionysius of Halicarnassus includes Plato among the philosophers who must be studied by young people who aspire to be orators, and he speaks in some detail about the nature of Plato's *Apology* (*Ars rhet.* 8.8; 9.11, etc.). The first-century CE philosopher and rhetorician Dio Chrysostom of Bithynia recommends the study of the Socratics (i.e., Plato and Xenophon) as indispensable for an older person who has failed to get a proper education as a youth and now wants to assume a larger role in public life, and Chrysostom himself demonstrates his familiarity with the text of Plato's *Apology* specifically (*Or.* 43.9–15).

Such recommendations were taken seriously. Writers of various backgrounds from all over the Mediterranean in the first and second century CE frequently reference Plato's dialogues in their works. As we would expect, these include highly educated grammarians like Didymus, Apollonius Dyscolus, and Herodian, rhetoricians like Aelius Aristides, Maximus of Tyre, and Julius Pollux, and philosophers like Epictetus, Sextus Empiricus, and Athenaeus, all of whom demonstrate in their works that they knew Plato's dialogues well. But they also include writers of other genres of literature: the biographer Plutarch, who cites, quotes, paraphrases, or otherwise references Plato

---

[4] The papyrus was first edited by S. Sudhaus, *Philodemi Volumina Rhetorica* II (Leipzig: Teubner, 1896), 2:286; the fragment is described by T. Dorandi, "Per una ricomposizione dello scritto di Filodemo sulla Retorica," *Zeitschrift für Papyrologie und Epigraphik* 82 (1990): 80.

[5] This papyrus was published in W. Schubart, "Ein Platon-Papyrus," *Journal of Juristic Papyrology* 4 (1950): 83–7. A third, somewhat earlier, papyrus from Egypt demonstrates Socrates' popularity more generally: a third-century BCE papyrus roll (*P.Hibeh* 182) from Ankyropolis that contains a collection of anecdotes about Socrates along with some doxography (published in I. Gallo, *Frammenti Biografici da Papiri Volume 2* (Rome: Edizioni dell'Ateneo & Bizzarri, 1980): 177–218).

212   *The Formal Education of the Author of Luke-Acts*

915 times in his surviving works (ten of which are of Plato's *Apology*); the geographer Strabo, who refers several times to specific dialogues of Plato in his *Geography*; the satyrist Lucian, who knew Plato so well that he wrote comic dialogues that were parodies of Platonic dialogues; the physician Galen, who was heavily influenced by Platonism and regularly references Platonic dialogues throughout his works.

Familiarity with Plato generally, and with his *Apology of Socrates* specifically, extended to Jewish writers. The authors of Second Maccabees and *Fourth Maccabees* demonstrate their familiarity with Socrates in their use of the literary topos of the "noble death" in their descriptions of the executions of Eleazar (2 Macc. 6:18-31 and *4 Macc.* 5–7) and of the seven brothers and their mother (2 Macc. 7:1-42 and *4 Macc.* 8–18). In both cases the authors assume that their audiences are knowledgeable of the events around the trial and death of Socrates that served as a background to their own narratives (more on this below). Closer to Luke's own time and cultural milieu is Josephus, the first-century CE Jewish historian from Jerusalem, who implies that he has perused the dialogues of Plato and who claims that Plato's notion of god was very similar to that of Moses (*Apion* 2.167–8). Josephus shows familiarity with intimate details of Plato's *Republic*—e.g., the banishment of Homer and other poets from the ideal city-state (*Apion* 2.256–8)—and he summarizes the proceedings of Plato's *Apology* specifically: he blames the Athenians for killing Socrates, noting that his accusers complained that he corrupted the youth (*Apion* 2.263–4). The echoes of vocabulary and phrases from Plato's *Apology* in Josephus's summary suggest that he has actually read the work. Also close to Luke's own time and cultural milieu is Philo, the first-century CE Jewish philosopher from Alexandria, who, like Luke, was steeped in the Hebrew Scripture, which he knew through the Greek Septuagint, but was also educated in secular Greek literature and philosophy, a course of instruction that he describes in detail and refers to as ἐγκύκλιος παιδεία/*enkyklios paideia* (*De congressu eruditionis gratiae* 71–80). It is germane to our topic that Philo recommends this typical Greek education even for the Jewish boys of Alexandria (*Spec. Leg.* 2.229–30).[6] Philo illustrates the fruits of his own secular Greek education throughout his works, mentioning such Greek literary figures as Homer, Hesiod, Pindar, Aeschylus, Sophocles, and Euripides, and an entire range of philosophers, including many of the pre-Socratics, Socrates, Plato, and Zeno of Citium.[7] Philo quotes several of Plato's dialogues and is notably familiar with Plato's *Timaeus*. The depth of his acculturation to Plato is well illustrated by his understanding of his own Jewish faith in Platonic terms, as he attempts through allegorical exegesis to reconcile God's revelation to Moses with Platonic philosophy (e.g., *Op. Mund.* and the second book of *Vit. Mos.*).

Philo's Platonism may have even influenced some of the writers of the New Testament, though perhaps indirectly, for example in some of the theological conceptions, such as the flesh/spirit dichotomy, expressed in the letters of Paul and in

---

[6] On Philo's position on the proper usage of the ἐγκύκλιος παιδεία/*enkyklios paideia*, see A. Mendelson, *Secular Education*.

[7] On Philo's references to secular Greek literature, see M. Alexandre, "La culture profane chez Philon," 105–29; also D. Lincicum, "A Preliminary Index," 139–67, and D. Lincicum, "Philo's Library," 99–114.

Luke and Plato 213

the doctrine of the Divine Logos in the Gospel of John.[8] It is much more certain that Philo's Platonism influenced the early Christian apologists, who also knew Plato well. Platonic influence, some of it at least filtered through Philo, is evident in Clement of Alexandria, Theophilus of Antioch, and Origen of Alexandria, whose Christian theologies were greatly influenced by Platonism, and who cite Plato's dialogues regularly.[9] The second-century CE Christian apologist Justin Martyr, who claimed to have delighted in the teachings of Plato (*2 Apol.* 12) since he believed that Plato drew his knowledge from Moses (*1 Apol.* 44, 59–60), appears to know the actual texts of Plato's *Republic* (*1 Apol.* 3, 8, 44; *2 Apol.* 3, 10), *Timaeus* (*1 Apol.* 60; *2 Apol.* 10), and *Apology* (*1 Apol.* 5; *2 Apol.* 10). The myth of Socrates would have been particularly appealing to early Christians, who saw in Socrates a prefigurement of Christ: a simple and morally upright man who questioned the religious and political establishment and was unjustly condemned and executed by his fellow citizens. Justin suggests that Socrates, by virtue of his reason, knew the one god of creation and even had some prescience of Christ (*2 Apol.* 10).[10]

Finally, closest of all to Luke's time and cultural milieu is his putative mentor and traveling companion Paul, who, as I shall propose below, is portrayed by Luke as a second Socrates in Acts, and who may himself have been familiar with some of the works of Plato. If, as Luke implies, Paul grew up in the Hellenized city of Tarsus, he would likely have received an education not unlike that of Luke, including some study of Plato, and especially the *Apology*.[11] Hence, it should not surprise us to find some echoes of Plato in Paul's letters. Those who suppose that they have found such Platonic

---

[8] On Philo's possible influence on the New Testament generally, see F. Siegert, "Philo and the New Testament," in *The Cambridge Companion to Philo*, ed. A. Kamesar (Cambridge: Cambridge University Press, 2009), 175–209.

[9] On Philo's influence on the early Patristics, see D. T. Runia, "Philo and the Early Christian Fathers," in *The Cambridge Companion to Philo*, ed. A. Kamesar (Cambridge: Cambridge University Press, 2009), 210–30.

[10] On the use of the Socratic tradition in the early church see A. Harnack, "Sokrates und die alte Kirche," *Reden und Aufsätze* (Gieben: Töpelmann, 1903), 1:29–48; J. M. Pfättisch, "Christus und Sokrates bei Justin," *Theologische Quartalschrift* 90 (1908): 503–23; E. Benz, "Christus und Sokrates in der alten Kirche (ein Beitrag zum altkirchlichen Verständnis des Märtyrers und des Martyriums)," *Zeitschrift für die neutestamentliche Wissenschaft* 43 (1951): 195–224; E. Fascher, "Sokrates und Christus: Eine Studie'zur aktuellen Aufgabe der Religionsphänomenologie' dem Andenken Heinrich Fricks," *Zeitschrift für die neutestamentliche Wissenschaft* 45 (1954): 1–41; K. Döring, *Exemplum Socratis: Studien zur Sokratesnachwirkung in der kynisch-stoischen Popularphilosophie der frühen Kaiserzeit und im frühen Christentum* (Wiesbaden: Steiner, 1979), 143–61.

[11] T. Vegge, *Paulus und das antike Schulwesen: Schule und Bildung des Paulus* (Berlin: Walter de Gruyter, 2006), 343–520, has recently offered a lengthy treatment on the formal education of Paul, surmising, for example, from 1 Corinthians 7 (Paul's use of the *progymnasmata* thesis and hypothesis) and 2 Corinthians 10–13 (Paul's use of diatribe, enthymemic argumentation, and irony) that Paul must have had at least a literary education, if not a rhetorical and philosophical one. In my opinion Vegge has overestimated the Hellenistic influence on Paul, ascribing to him too high a level of education in Greek rhetoric and philosophy, while at the same time he has underestimated the Jewish influence, even going so far as to claim that the following are all inventions of the author of Acts: 1) Paul's defense, in Aramaic, before his fellow Jews in the temple, in which he claims to have been educated at the feet of the Rabbi Gamaliel (Acts 22:3); 2) Paul's defense before the Sanhedrin, in which he claims to be a Pharisee and a son of a Pharisee (Acts 23:6); 3) Paul's defense before King Agrippa, in which he claims to be accused for his hope in the promise made by God to his Jewish ancestors (Acts 26:3-6).

214   *The Formal Education of the Author of Luke-Acts*

echoes usually point to broad conceptual similarities. For example, Paul's flesh/spirit dichotomy is thought by some to be influenced by Plato's body/soul dichotomy. Paul's well-known analogy of the ideal Christian community as a human body with many parts, each cooperating with the other (1 Cor. 12:12-31; Rom. 12:4-8; cf. Eph. 4:11-16), is supposed to be derived, directly or indirectly, from Plato's analogy of the ideal political state as a harmoniously functioning human body (*Resp.* 462a–464e; cf. *Prot.* 329d). Paul's assertions that we currently see darkly, as though through a mirror (1 Cor. 13:12), that we look not at the things that are seen, which are temporal, but at the things that are unseen, which are eternal (2 Cor. 4:18, and 4:16–5:10 generally), and that we should contemplate the things above, not the things on the earth (Col. 3:1-2; cf. Phil. 3:19) are thought to align well with Plato's sharp distinction between opinions about the visible objects of human sense-perception and true knowledge about the invisible objects of human reason, as illustrated, for example, in the allegory of the cave in the *Republic* 514a–521b and in the story of the ladder of love in the *Symposium* 210a–212a.[12] But these broad conceptual parallels often turn out to be commonplaces in antiquity, appearing in a host of unrelated authors; their universality and lack of distinctiveness prevent us from attributing these Pauline concepts directly to Plato with any measure of confidence. Indeed, some of these concepts were surely as at home in Rabbinic preaching as in Platonic dialogues. The same can be said about almost all the parallels that have been drawn between Plato and Paul in both the old and new *Wettstein*. One need only page through the 1,000 pages or so on the Pauline epistles in Band II/1-2 of the *Neuer Wettstein* to discover nearly 100 proposed parallels between Paul's letters and Plato's dialogues.[13] But almost all of these are conceptual parallels of a general, even universal, nature: "the power of god," "the uselessness of human wisdom," "the preference of death over life," and so forth. Almost none of the parallels is at the same time similar enough and distinctive enough to warrant drawing a direct line of influence from Plato to Paul.

---

[12] Some representative studies on the supposed influence of Plato on Paul (of a broad, conceptual nature): R. I. Hicks, "The Body Political and the Body Ecclesiastical," *Journal of Bible and Religion* 31 (1963): 29–35; E. B. Howell, "St. Paul and the Greek World," 7–29; H. D. Betz, *Der Apostel Paulus und die sokratische Tradition* (Tübingen: Mohr Siebeck, 1972); H. D. Betz, "Humanisierung des Menschen: Delphi, Plato, Paulus," in *Hellenismus und Urchristentum*, ed. H. D. Betz (Tübingen: Mohr Siebeck, 1990), 120–34; M. M. Mitchell, *Paul and the Rhetoric of Reconciliation* (Louisville: Westminster/John Knox Press, 1992), 157–64; W. Burkert, "Towards Plato and Paul: The 'Inner' Human Being," in *Ancient and Modern Perspectives on the Bible and Culture: Essays in Honor of Hans Dieter Betz*, ed. A. Y. Collins (Atlanta: Scholars Press, 1998), 59–82; J. K. McVay, "The Human Body as Social and Political Metaphor in Stoic Literature and Early Christian Writers," *Bulletin of the American Society of Papyrologists* 37 (2000): 135–47; M. Gawlina, "Paulus und Plato: *prosopon* gegen *idea*," *Theologie und Philosophie* 80 (2005): 17–30; J. Strijdom, "On Social Justice: Comparing Paul with Plato, Aristotle and the Stoics," *Hervormde Teologiese Studies* 63 (2007): 19–48; C. A. Evans, "Paul and the Pagans," in *Paul: Jew, Greek, and Roman*, ed. S. E. Porter (Leiden: Brill, 2008), 117–39; C. S. Keener, "'Fleshly' versus Spirit Perspectives in Romans 8:5-8," in *Paul: Jew, Greek, and Roman*, ed. S. E. Porter (Leiden: Brill, 2008), 211–29; J. W. Jipp, "Educating the Divided Soul in Paul and Plato: Reading Romans 7:7-25 and Plato's *Republic*," in *Paul: Jew, Greek, and Roman*, ed. S. E. Porter (Leiden: Brill, 2008), 231–57.

[13] G. Strecker, U. Schnelle, and G. Seelig, eds., *Neuer Wettstein* II/1-2, 1–1073.

Luke and Plato 215

There is one possible exception, mentioned briefly in an earlier chapter, that deserves consideration: an apparent quotation of Plato's *Apology* in Paul's letter to the Galatians. As Paul winds down his letter to his Galatian audience and begins to express his farewells, he offers several pieces of advice to the recipients of his letter (Gal. 6:1-10), among which is this warning (6:3): "for if someone thinks that he is something, being nothing, he deceives himself." Similarly, as Socrates winds down his speech to his Athenian jurors, according to Plato's *Apology*, and begins to express his farewells, he offers several pieces of advice to his audience (38c–42a), and then he makes a request regarding his own sons (*Apol.* 41e): "and if they think that they are something, being nothing, rebuke them as I have rebuked you." Paul's final warning is very close verbally and syntactically to Socrates' famous last words:

εἰ γὰρ δοκεῖ τις εἶναί τι μηδὲν ὤν

"for if someone thinks that he is something, being nothing"

καὶ ἐὰν δοκῶσί τι εἶναι μηδὲν ὄντες

"and if they think that they are something, being nothing"

The similarities in diction, word order, and overall construction as a conditional clause are remarkable. The main differences are the use of the singular rather than the plural and the use of εἰ plus indicative rather than ἐάν plus subjunctive in the protasis of the condition. As we have observed, Plato's *Apology* would have been well known, even in the Hellenistic East, and particularly this memorable passage right at the end of Socrates' final speech to the Athenian jurors.[14]

Having determined, then, that authors so well educated as Luke and, possibly, Paul would, like many of their contemporaries, have been familiar with some of Plato's dialogues, and, in particular, would have known Plato's most famous work, the *Apology of Socrates*, we proceed to examine how Luke may have used Plato's *Apology* as a literary backdrop in his narration of three episodes describing innocent people on trial in Luke-Acts: Jesus, Peter, and Paul.

[14] Several commentators have noticed this parallel but have ventured no explanation of the relationship between the passages: e.g., J. B. Lightfoot, *St. Paul's Epistle to the Galatians* (London: Macmillan, 1865) 207; M.-J. Lagrange, *Saint Paul Épître aux Galates* (Paris: J. Gabalda, 1918) 157; H. Schlier, *Der Brief an die Galater*, 10th ed. (Göttingen: Vandenhoeck & Ruprecht, 1949) 201; H. D. Betz, *Galatians: A Commentary on Paul's Letter to the Churches in Galatia* (Philadelphia: Fortress, 1979) 301; F. Vouga, *An die Galater* (Tübingen: Mohr Siebeck, 1998), 147. The *Neuer Wettstein* observes the parallel in Plato's *Apology*, along with seventeen other ancient parallels, of which only Epictetus's *Dissertations* 2.24.19 is verbally similar (G. Strecker, U. Schnelle, and G. Seelig, eds., *Neuer Wettstein* II/1-2, 581–588). R. Renehan, "Classical Greek Quotations in the New Testament," 23-4, who is usually very cautious in his acknowledgment of Classical parallels to the New Testament, compares these two passages, among others, calls it a "clear echo" of Plato's *Apology*, and remarks that there is no reason why Paul could not have read Plato's *Apology* in school or elsewhere since it had an early and constant fame. He concludes that Paul's inspiration here, one way or another, can safely be traced back to Plato.

Luke's Portrayal of Jesus as a Socratic Figure in the Gospel of Luke

The figure of Socrates functioned as a moral exemplar in late antiquity for the lives and deaths of other men and especially other philosophers.[15] The depiction of Socrates, especially in Plato's *Apology*, *Crito*, and *Phaedo*, is of a pious and completely just man (δικαιότατος *Phaed.* 118), unjustly accused and sentenced, who remains calm and fearless, indeed cheerful, in the face of persecution and death, and who accepts his divinely determined fate and dies courageously and nobly. Instead of lamenting himself, he comforts his close friends and followers who surround him and lament for him; he spends the last hours of his life dining with his followers and using his impending execution as an opportunity to teach them about the meaning of life and death; even as he maintains his own composure, he tries to prevent expressions of grief among his followers, and he even sends away his wife and the other women who cannot seem to stop grieving.

This Platonic depiction of Socrates wielded great influence, for example, on the accounts of three of Luke's Greco-Roman contemporaries: Plutarch's depiction of the death of the orator and Stoic philosopher Cato the Younger (*Cat. Min.* 66–72); Dio Chrysostom's depiction of the death of the young religious philosopher Charidemus (*Or.* 30); Tacitus's depiction of the death of the Stoic philosopher Seneca (*Ann.* 15.60–4).[16] The literary topos of the "noble death," and of Socrates' death specifically, appears to have been used in describing Jewish (and, later, Christian) martyrs as well, as in the description of the execution of Eleazar in Second Maccabees 6:18-31 and *Fourth Maccabees* 5–7 and in the execution of the seven Jewish brothers and their mother in Second Maccabees 7:1-42 and *Fourth Maccabees* 8–18.[17]

Some have proposed that this literary topos of the "noble death" has even influenced Luke's account of Jesus's Passion in his gospel: that is, Luke has refashioned the material that he inherited from his sources in order to present a Jesus who, like Plato's Socrates, faces his death calmly and fearlessly, comforting those around him who are lamenting his impending doom. This proposal is most strongly advocated in two recent articles by

---

[15] Much of the following appeared in an earlier version in S. Reece, "Echoes of Plato's *Apology of Socrates* in Luke-Acts," *Novum Testamentum* 63 (2021): 177–97.

[16] One can readily add more: Plutarch's accounts of Pericles, Phocion, Pompey, Anthony, Otho, and many others; Diogenes Laertius's accounts of Zeno of Elea, Anaxarchus of Abdera, and Epicurus; Tacitus's account of P. Clodius Thrasea Paetus. See F. A. Marx, "Tacitus und die Literatur der Exitus Illustrium Virorum," *Philologus* 92 (1937): 83–103; A. Ronconi, "Exitus Illustrium Virorum," in *Reallexikon fur Antike und Christentum*, vol. 6, ed. T. Klauser (Stuttgart: Hiersemann, 1966), 1258–68.

[17] M. Hadas, *The Third and Fourth Books of Maccabees* (New York: Harper and Bros., 1953), 101: "Eleazar is like Socrates at too many points for the resemblance to be accidental." J. A. Goldstein, *II Maccabees* (Garden City: Doubleday, 1983), 285: "No educated Greek could miss the resemblance of Eleazar to Socrates." On the literary topos in the ancient descriptions of Jewish and Christian martyrs more generally, see: H. A. Musurillo, *The Acts of the Pagan Martyrs: Acta Alexandrinorum* (Oxford: Oxford University Press, 1954); D. Seeley, *The Noble Death: Graeco-Roman Martyrology and Paul's Concept of Salvation* (Sheffield: JSOT Press, 1990); J. Droge and J. D. Tabor, *A Noble Death: Suicide and Martyrdom among Christians and Jews in Antiquity* (San Francisco: Harper, 1992); J. W. van Henten, *Martyrdom and Noble Death: Selected Texts from Graeco-Roman, Jewish and Christian Antiquity* (London and New York: Routledge, 2002).

Luke and Plato   217

J. S. Kloppenborg and G. E. Sterling and in a short monograph by P. J. Scaer.[18] Kloppenborg proposes that Luke's apologetic purpose, unlike that of the other gospels, was to avoid anything that would risk offending Greco-Roman sensibilities and especially anything that might be taken as subversive or base or impious. Hence, Luke blames Jesus's death on the high priestly authorities rather than on the Roman officials. For the same reason, Luke presents Jesus's death as a typical Greco-Roman *exitus clari viri*, the demise of a noble man, in which the noble man dies fearlessly and nobly, even heroically, after offering last words of wisdom and advice to his followers. Jesus shows no signs of fear or regret, no grief or cry of dereliction—like Socrates, he dies well and nobly. Sterling has expanded somewhat on Kloppenborg's proposal, noting that Luke eliminates Mark's references to Jesus's anxiety and struggle in the face of death and makes Jesus more like the calm, fearless Socrates. Luke also stresses that Jesus, like Socrates, was innocent of the charges against him. Like later Christians, i.e., the Church Fathers, Luke makes selective use of Socratic traditions to transform an embarrassment—the doubtful, fearful, anguished, crucified Jesus—into an exemplum—the calm, fearless, noble, Socratic Jesus. Scaer concurs that Luke's redactions of his sources have been inspired by the topos of the "noble death," the primary exemplar of which was Socrates. Luke's redactional changes include an emphasis on Jesus's piety, courage, and willingness to die, as well as on his overall control over his situation, his generosity in comforting others, and, finally, his honorable burial. Scaer concludes that Luke knew the story of Socrates and consciously drew on its features in order to present Jesus as a wise philosopher and an innocent man unjustly put to death.

Indeed, a comparison of the details of Luke's account of the Passion of Jesus with those of Mark and Matthew reveals a very different Jesus: one who looks and acts quite a lot like Socrates. Luke's unique features include the following:

1. *Jesus is portrayed as equanimous throughout Luke's narrative, with the expressions of sorrow, anxiety, and fear related in Mark and Matthew transferred instead to Jesus's followers.* Mark and Matthew note that Jesus begins to be greatly distressed and troubled (sorrowful and troubled) in the garden of Gethsemane, and they include a speech by Jesus to three of his disciples in which Jesus says that his soul is deeply grieved, even to death (Mk 14:33-4; Mt. 26:37-8). Luke does not include these descriptions of Jesus. Instead he seems to transfer Jesus's sorrow to his disciples (Lk. 22:45). Then, according to Mark and Matthew, Jesus proceeds through the garden by himself, falls to the ground (falls on his face), and prays to God to "remove this cup" from him (Mk 14:35-6; Mt. 26:39). Both Mark and Matthew have Jesus utter this prayer a second and third time. Luke's version has Jesus kneel rather than fall to the ground, and while he prays the same prayer, he does so only once (Lk. 22:41-2).[19]

---

[18] J. S. Kloppenborg, "'Exitus clari viri': The Death of Jesus in Luke," *Toronto Journal of Theology* 8 (1992): 106–20; G. E. Sterling, "Mors Philosophi: The Death of Jesus in Luke," *The Harvard Theological Review* 94 (2001): 383–402; P. J. Scaer, *The Lukan Passion and the Praiseworthy Death* (Sheffield: Sheffield Phoenix Press, 2005).

[19] Along with most textual critics, I regard what follows in some manuscripts (Lk. 22:43-4) as a later addition to the text: the interpolated passage describes an angel appearing to Jesus as he prays in order to strengthen him, and it then describes Jesus's agony and his sweat falling like drops of blood to the ground. See B. D. Ehrman and M. A. Plunkett, "The Angel and the Agony: The Textual Problem of Luke 22:43-44," *Catholic Biblical Quarterly* 45 (1983): 401–16.

218   *The Formal Education of the Author of Luke-Acts*

Only Luke includes a description of a multitude of people, including women, lamenting for him during his procession to Golgotha. Jesus, on the other hand, shows no emotion and addresses the crowd, telling them not to weep for him but for themselves and their children (Lk. 23:27-31). Whereas Mark and Matthew report that at the ninth hour Jesus cried out with a loud voice, "My God, my God, why have you forsaken me" (Mk 15:34; Mt. 27:46), Luke does not include this lament, instead reporting that Jesus cries out, "Father, into your hands I commit my spirit" (Lk. 23:46). Luke again seems to transfer the lamentation of Jesus to his followers, as he describes the dismay of the crowds following Jesus, who beat their breasts at the sight of his death (Lk. 23:48).[20]

2. *Jesus does not suffer so many degrading abuses in Luke's account.* Mark and Matthew include accounts of various degrading abuses committed against Jesus: the Jewish leaders spitting on Jesus (in his face) (Mk 14:65; Mt. 26:67); Pilate scourging Jesus (Mk 15:15; Mt. 27:26); the Roman soldiers mocking Jesus by clothing him in royal purple and placing a crown of thorns on his head, and then striking him on the head and spitting on him (Mk 15:17-20; Mt. 27:28-31). These details are absent in Luke.

3. *Jesus's innocence is stressed in Luke's account.* Of the Synoptics, only Luke has Pilate say (three times!), "I find no crime in this man" (Lk. 23:4, 13-14, 22). And only Luke has Herod too exonerate Jesus (Lk. 23:15). In Mark and Matthew both criminals who are crucified with Jesus mock him (Mk 15:32; Mt. 27:44). In Luke, on the other hand, one of the criminals reprimands the other for mocking Jesus and attests to Jesus's innocence (Lk. 23:39-41). The Roman centurion who witnesses Jesus's death says in Mark and Matthew, "Truly this man was the Son of God" (Mk 15:39; Mt. 27:54). But Luke reports that the centurion says, "Truly this man was just (δίκαιος)" (Lk. 23:47).

4. *Jesus is in greater control of matters in Luke's account.* Of the Synoptics only Luke includes the detail that Jesus heals the severed ear of the high priest's slave (Lk. 22:51); only Luke introduces Jesus into the scene of Peter's denial, describing him poignantly turning and looking at him (Lk. 22:61); only Luke has Jesus assure the criminal on the cross that he will be with him in Paradise (Lk. 23:43). Even in death, Luke's Jesus seems to maintain control, saying in a loud voice as he dies, "Father, into your hands I commit my spirit" (Lk. 23:46).

5. *Jesus's followers are seen in a better light in Luke's account.* Mark and Matthew mention that all of Jesus's disciples abandon him in the Garden of Gethsemane (Mk 14:50; Mt. 26:56). Luke does not include this detail. In Mark and Matthew both the common people and the Jewish leaders mock Jesus on the cross (Mk 15:29-32; Mt. 27:39-43). In Luke the common people simply stand by and watch, while the Jewish leaders and Roman soldiers mock him (Lk. 23:35-7).

In sum, these Lucan redactions are numerous and remarkable, and one yearns for a comprehensive explanation. As Kloppenborg, Sterling, and Scaer have suggested, an explanation that makes relatively good sense is that Luke is attempting in his version of the Passion to present Jesus as a Socratic figure: an innocent man, unjustly accused and

---

[20] On Luke's general downplaying of Jesus's emotions, see J. H. Neyrey, "The Absence of Jesus' Emotions—the Lucan Redaction of Lk 22,39-46," *Biblica* 61 (1980): 153–71; J. H. Neyrey, *The Passion According to Luke: A Redaction Study of Luke's Soteriology* (New York: Paulist, 1985), 49–68, 108–55.

Luke and Plato 219

sentenced, who remains calm, fearless, and dignified in the face of persecution, even comforting his loyal followers, and in the end dying courageously and nobly.

Admittedly, there are some potential objections to this explanation. First, Luke has left no obvious signal in his narrative that he is making a conscious association between the trials and deaths of Jesus and Socrates, as Plutarch has, for example, in the case of Cato the Younger's death, when he relates that Cato read through Plato's *Phaedo* twice on the night of his execution (*Cat. Min.* 68.2; 70.1). The only possible intertextual reference that I detect in Luke's Passion story is the unique expression that he places in the mouth of the Roman centurion who has just witnessed Jesus's death (Lk. 23:47): "Truly this man was just (δίκαιος)." For this is exactly the adjective that Plato, in the very memorable last sentence of his *Phaedo* (118), places in the mouth of someone who has just witnessed Socrates' death: "This was the end, O Echecrates, of our companion, a man, as we may say, who was, of those of that time whom we knew, the best and also the wisest and the most just (δικαιότατος)." Of course it may very well be the case that Luke is simply being more subtle than Plutarch by having the Socrates figure hover rather more nebulously behind his figure of Jesus. Other writers of the time used the literary topos of the Socratic figure in such a manner: Tacitus, for example, in his depiction of the death of the Stoic philosopher Seneca (*Ann.* 15.60–4) and of the Stoic Roman Senator P. Clodius Thrasea Paetus (*Ann.* 16.34–5).[21]

A second potential objection is that Socrates is not the only wise philosopher/teacher of antiquity who died a "noble death." Perhaps Luke is simply embracing a traditional literary topos here, without having the figure of Socrates specifically in mind. Perhaps Luke is even drawing from a Jewish rather than Greco-Roman literary tradition, for there also exist Jewish models for noble deaths. The Hebrew Bible includes stories of the prophets of God dying at the hands of the people: e.g., Zechariah (2 Chron. 24:20-2). The Septuagint narrates the noble deaths of several Jews: Eleazar (2 Macc. 6:18-31; *4 Macc.* 5:1–7:23); the seven brothers and their mother (2 Macc. 7:1-42; *4 Macc.* 8:1–18:24). And both Philo and Josephus relate accounts of Jews dying gladly and courageously for their religion: e.g., Philo, *Omn. Prob. Lib.* 27, 88–91; Josephus, *Apion* 1.42-4, 2.232-5. The Jewish "martyrologies" in Second Maccabees and *Fourth Maccabees*, for example, could have been the immediate inspiration for Luke's account of Jesus's Passion.[22] Yet it should be acknowledged that these Jewish "martyrologies," like the accounts of the deaths of various Greco-Roman heroes in Plutarch, Lucian, and Tacitus, may themselves have drawn from the literary topos of the death of Socrates.[23] This raises the possibility that Luke's Passion narrative was influenced most directly by Jewish stories of martyrdom, as in Second Maccabees and *Fourth Maccabees*, and thereby only indirectly by Plato's accounts of Socrates.

---

[21] On Tacitus's use of this literary topos see F. A. Marx, "Tacitus und die Literatur," 83–103.
[22] H. W. Surkau, *Martyrien in jüdischer und frühchristlicher Zeit* (Göttingen: Vandenhoeck & Ruprecht, 1938), 90–100, traces the influence of Jewish martyrologies on Luke's Passion, and he does not mention Plato or Socrates at all.
[23] So M. Hadas *The Third and Fourth Books of Maccabees*, 101; J. A. Goldstein, *II Maccabees*, 285: G. E. Sterling, "Mors Philosophi," 392–3.

220   *The Formal Education of the Author of Luke-Acts*

A third potential objection, or rather precaution, in the context of my own attempt to identify some echoes of Plato's *Apology* specifically in Luke-Acts is that Kloppenborg, Sterling, Scaer, and others have traced Socratic influence on Luke's Passion story not from any specific Platonic dialogue but from several of Plato's dialogues, as well as from Xenophon's *Apology* and *Memorabilia*, and even from later biographers who elevated the figure of Socrates to the level of myth, such as Plutarch and Diogenes Laertius, with the result that they are dealing not with the historical Socrates, or even with the purportedly historical one from Plato's *Apology*, but with a mythic exemplum. In contrast, I hope to show in what follows that Luke's portrayals of Peter, to some extent, and Paul, to a much greater extent, as Socratic figures manifest themselves in the specific language of his presentations as well as in general themes. That is to say, Luke appears to be echoing the actual text of Plato's *Apology*.

Luke's Portrayal of Peter (and Other Apostles) as a Socratic Figure in Acts 4 and 5

It is widely acknowledged that Luke's description of Jesus's response to persecution and death in his gospel served as a model for his descriptions of the fates of Jesus's followers in Acts: Stephen's last words at his execution echo the last words of Jesus on the cross (Acts 7:59 and Lk. 23:46); Peter and John, like Jesus, answer boldly when they are brought before the Sanhedrin to be questioned (Acts 4:5-31; 5:17-42; and Lk. 22:54-71); despite signs of impending doom, Paul, like Jesus, insists on proceeding to Jerusalem, where he will be arrested and eventually put on trial (Acts 20:22-5, 37-8; 21:4, 7-14; and Lk. 9:22; 13:31-5; 17:25; 18:31-4).[24] It is much less widely acknowledged that Plato's description in his *Apology* of Socrates' trial appears to be echoed in Luke's description of Peter and John's questioning in Acts 4 and 5, just as it appears to have been echoed in his description of Jesus's trial in his gospel (see above), and just as it would be echoed in his description of Paul's trial later in Acts (see below).

In the fourth chapter of Acts, Luke describes the Jewish authorities becoming so annoyed at Peter and John for teaching in the Jerusalem temple about Jesus and the resurrection of the dead that they arrest them and place them in custody. The following day they bring the two apostles before the council for questioning and warn them to speak no more to anyone in Jesus's name. But Peter and John reply (4:19):

Εἰ δίκαιόν ἐστιν ἐνώπιον τοῦ θεοῦ ὑμῶν ἀκούειν μᾶλλον ἢ τοῦ θεοῦ κρίνατε.

You must judge if it is just in God's sight to listen to you rather than God.

---

[24] For a summary of the long tradition of scholarship on this topic, see D. P. Moessner, "'The Christ Must Suffer': New Light on the Jesus, Stephen, Paul Parallels in Luke-Acts," *Novum Testamentum* 28 (1986): 220–56.

Luke and Plato 221

The apostles then proceed to disregard utterly the warning of the Jewish authorities, teaching and performing miracles of healing in public, even in the temple area. Filled with jealousy the high priest and the Sadducees arrest the apostles again and put them in the public prison, but an angel of the Lord opens the prison doors during the night and frees them. Perplexed and annoyed to find the apostles once again teaching in the temple the following morning, they send the temple police to fetch them and bring them before the council, where the chief priest admonishes them for disregarding their earlier warning. But Peter and the apostles again reply, this time more strongly and succinctly (5:29):

Πειθαρχεῖν δεῖ θεῷ μᾶλλον ἢ ἀνθρώποις.

It is necessary to obey god rather than men.

The Jewish authorities are enraged and wish to kill the apostles, but, advised by the Pharisee Gamaliel to leave them alone lest they be found to be "wagers of war against god" (θεομάχοι 5:39—an echo, as we have earlier observed, of a leitmotif in Euripides' *Bacchae*), they have the apostles flogged, order them not to speak anymore in the name of Jesus, and allow them to go.

The entire scene occurs in a Jewish context, in the Jerusalem temple, and before the Jewish authorities. And Peter and John's first reply to the Jewish council in Acts 4:19 is expressed in common, prosaic, Septuagintal and New Testament Greek: especially the construction ἐνώπιον τοῦ θεοῦ, κρίνατε in the imperative plural, and ἀκούειν meaning "to obey." In their second reply to the Jewish council in Acts 5:29, however, their expression is more eloquent and poetic, and its vocabulary and syntax are entirely Classical. In fact Luke appears to be echoing a passage from Plato's *Apology* describing Socrates on trial before the Athenian authorities for violating the religious sensibilities of the Athenians. To their (hypothetical) offer that they will let him go if he agrees to speak no longer publicly of these matters, Socrates replies (*Apol.* 29d):

Πείσομαι δὲ μᾶλλον τῷ θεῷ ἢ ὑμῖν.

I shall obey god rather than you.

Acts 5:29 and Plato's *Apology* 29d present remarkably similar circumstances. Both Peter (and other apostles) and Socrates are defending themselves before the authorities for following their divine calling and teaching publicly about theological matters. Both have been/will be imprisoned by the authorities for spreading these teachings among the people. Both are offered the opportunity by the authorities to go free if only they agree to stop speaking publicly about their religious convictions. Both refuse, declaring that they are obliged to obey God rather than men and expressing their refusals in succinct, powerful phrases that are verbally and syntactically similar.

Admittedly, anyone who wishes to maintain that there is a genetic relationship between the two passages will have to acknowledge that the sentiments expressed are general, widespread, even universal, and that sentiments like this must have been expressed throughout history by many fervent advocates of a religion in the face of

222   *The Formal Education of the Author of Luke-Acts*

persecution.[25] Yet the similarities between Acts 5:29 and the *Apology* 29d go beyond general sentiments to include verbal and syntactical parallels: a form of the verb πείθω plus the dative case of θεός, a comparison using the construction μᾶλλον ἤ plus, again, the dative case of the word for the humans with whom god is being compared. Moreover, as already observed, the two passages are embedded in very similar circumstances: a formal defense of religious views in a public arena before authorities who are persecuting them.[26]

Hence, it does not seem inconceivable that the ancient readers/hearers of the text of Acts would have perceived Plato's description of Socrates' defense at his trial before the Athenian jurors hovering in the background of Luke's presentation of Peter's arrest and defense before the Jewish council. Luke and his audience knew the memorable, indeed famous, passage from the *Apology*, which presented a paradigmatic figure of Socrates that offered them the possibility of fitting Peter's story, as, earlier in Luke's gospel, Jesus's story, and, later in Acts, Paul's story, into an ancient tradition that they already knew. In short, while these two passages on their own do not provide sufficient evidence for positing a direct line of influence from Plato's *Apology* to Luke's Acts, a genetic connection is given some plausibility, at least, by the similarities of their contexts and, further, by the similarities in the contexts of what precedes in the Gospel of Luke and what follows in Acts.

Luke's Portrayal of Paul as a Socratic Figure in Acts

In his account of Paul's visit to Athens in Acts 17:16-34, Luke portrays Paul as a Socratic figure, engaging in dialogue with whomever he chances upon in the Athenian Agora, introducing newfangled ideas and foreign divinities into Athens, and being judged by the Athenians for doing so.[27] We shall examine this particular narrative in Acts 17 in detail below, but it is worthwhile first to remind ourselves of the context by tracing

---

[25] In ancient Greek literature, similar circumstances and sentiments, though not similar vocabulary and syntax, occur in Sophocles' *Antigone* 450-70, where Antigone defends her pious actions before the authoritarian Creon, and in Herodotus 5.63.2, where the historian states aphoristically that among the Spartans the will of the god (at Delphi) takes precedence over the will of men. Closer to the time and/or milieu of Luke, similar sentiments are expressed in Second Maccabees 7:1-42; *Fourth Maccabees* 5:14-6:30; Dio Chrysostom, *Orationes* 80.5-6; Epictetus, *Dissertations* 1.30.1-2; and Josephus, *Antiquities* 17.158-9.

[26] Several commentators have observed the similarity in sentiment between both Acts 4:19 and 5:29 and Plato's *Apology* but do not offer any further comment or explication: e.g., F. J. Foakes Jackson and K. Lake, eds., *The Beginnings of Christianity*, 4:45; H. Conzelmann, *Acts of the Apostles*, 33, 42; F. F. Bruce, *The Acts of the Apostles*, 155, 172. But some commentators have entertained the possibility of an actual line of influence from Plato's *Apology* to Luke's *Acts*: E. Haenchen, *The Acts of the Apostles*, 219, 251; C. K. Barrett, *A Critical and Exegetical Commentary on the Acts of the Apostles*, 1:237, 289; C. S. Keener, *Acts: An Exegetical Commentary*, 2:1161, 1217-18.

[27] It has long been suspected that the figure of Socrates informs Luke's description of Paul's visit to Athens in Acts 17. Most of the standard commentaries comment, at least in passing, on the parallels. Recent detailed treatments of the parallels include: K. O. Sandnes, "Paul and Socrates: The Aim of Paul's Areopagus Speech," *Journal for the Study of the New Testament* 50 (1993): 13-26; L. C. A. Alexander, "Acts and Ancient Intellectual Biography," in *The Book of Acts in Its Ancient Literary*

Luke's presentation of Paul as a Socratic figure more generally throughout the narrative of Acts, for this motif is not unique to the "trial" scene before the Athenians in Acts 17; it simply reaches a culmination in that critical scene. In contrast to my treatment of Jesus as a Socratic figure above, I hope to show in what follows that Luke's portrayal of Paul as a Socratic figure manifests itself in the specific language of his presentation as well as in its general themes and that Luke was in fact echoing the actual text of Plato's *Apology*. If, as appears likely, Luke studied Plato's *Apology* as a schoolboy or read the popular work later in life, the depiction of Socrates specifically in the *Apology* may very well have influenced his depiction of Paul in Acts, including in his use of specific words and phrases.

Both Socrates and Paul receive divine calls that set into motion their primary missions for the rest of their lives: to pursue a life of philosophy, examining himself and others, in the case of Socrates (*Apol.* 28e–29a); to know God's will and to be God's witness to all humankind, in the case of Paul (Acts 22:14-15). Socrates receives his divine call from a comrade's consultation of the oracle at Delphi, which plays a central role in Plato's *Apology* as the motivation for Socrates' life's pursuit (20e–23b). Socrates has a distinctive relationship with the gods, and he claims that he has heard a divine voice frequently throughout his life (31d, 40a–c). Paul receives his divine call from a vision on his way to Damascus, which is so central to his mission that the experience is narrated three times throughout Acts (9:1-9; 22:6-11; 26:12-18). It is emphasized in Acts that Paul has been handpicked by God to know God's will and to hear God's voice (9:15; 22:14-15; 26:16-18): hence, as the narrative unfolds, we are not surprised to witness God appearing frequently to Paul in dreams and visions (16:9; 18:9-10; 22:17-21; 23:11; 27:23-5).

Both Socrates and Paul relate their memories of their divine calls in the first person when they are on trial for pursuing the very mission to which they were called. The entirety of Socrates' defense in Plato's *Apology* is in the first person and is referred to as an ἀπολογία, including by Socrates himself (24b, 28a). Paul is virtually on trial throughout the last quarter of the narrative of Acts (from chapter 21 to the end), and his four formal defenses are, like Socrates', narrated in the first person: before the Roman and Jewish authorities in the Jerusalem temple (21:40–22:24), before the Roman governors Felix and then Festus in Caesarea (24:10-21; 25:6-12), and before King Agrippa in Caesarea (26:1-29). All four of these formal defenses are referred to as ἀπολογίαι in Acts (22:1; 24:10; 25:8; 26:1-2, 24). It should not escape our notice that in every case Paul, like Socrates, is defending himself against charges of impiety.

Both Socrates and Paul endure severe hardships in pursuit of their divine missions. Socrates claims in his ἀπολογία that he has endured enmity, anger, prejudice, slander, hatred, and violence at the hands of his fellow citizens, that he has suffered false accusations, and that he has been forced to lead a life of severe poverty, all on account

Setting, eds. B. W. Winter and A. D. Clarke (Grand Rapids: Eerdmans, 1993), 31–63, esp. 57–63; D. M. Reis, "The Areopagus as Echo Chamber: *Mimesis* and Intertextuality in Acts," *Journal of Higher Criticism* 9 (2002): 259–77; J. W. Jipp, "Paul's Areopagus Speech of Acts 17:16-34 as *Both* Critique *and* Propaganda," *Journal of Biblical Literature* 131 (2012): 567–88; C. S. Keener, *Acts: An Exegetical Commentary*, 3:2600-607; D. R. MacDonald, *Luke and Vergil*, 76–81; S. Reece, "Jesus as Healer," 195–200; S. Reece, "Echoes of Plato's *Apology*," 177–97.

224   *The Formal Education of the Author of Luke-Acts*

of his service to the god (*Apol.* 23a–34b). Paul's suffering in God's name (9:16) is a leitmotif throughout the narrative of Acts: he constantly encounters hostile audiences and false accusations (13:45, 50; 14:2; 16:22; 17:5-9, 13, 18-19, 32; 18:5-6; 19:9, 30; 22:22-3; 23:1-2); he is subjected to physical abuse, suffering beatings (16:23; 21:32; 23:2), stoning (14:19), and arrest and imprisonment (16:23-34; 20:23; 21:33-23:30; 23:35-26:32; 28:16-31); there are even several attempts on his life (9:23-5, 29; 14:5, 19; 20:3, 19; 21:4, 10-14, 27-36; 23:12-30; 25:2-3; 27:42-4). Although neither Plato's *Apology* nor Luke's Acts records the actual deaths of Socrates and Paul, their executions are thoroughly anticipated: at the end of their respective narratives both Socrates and Paul are virtually dead.[28]

The motif of Paul as a Socratic figure reaches a culmination in the critical "trial" scene in Athens (Acts 17:16-34), where there appear not just conceptual parallels but actual verbal allusions to Plato's account of Socrates' trial in his *Apology*.[29] Given the setting (Athens) and circumstances (a "trial" scene), it should not be surprising to find Luke echoing Plato's *Apology* in his account of Paul's visit to Athens. As we have earlier observed, the setting and circumstances have led Luke to attribute to Paul in his defense before the Athenians two other quotations of ancient Greek authors associated with Athens as well. Acts 17:28b Τοῦ γὰρ καὶ γένος ἐσμέν "For we too are his offspring" is the beginning of a dactylic hexameter verse (- - / - ˘ ˘ / - ˘), and it has long been recognized as the fifth verse of the third-century BCE Cilician poet Aratus's astronomic poem *Phaenomena*. Aratus spent some of his adult life in Athens, where he studied with Peripatetic and Stoic philosophers, including Zeno, the founder of Stoicism, who taught in the Stoa Poikile, just a stone's throw from the Areopagus. Acts 17:28a Ἐν αὐτῷ γὰρ ζῶμεν καὶ κινούμεθα καὶ ἐσμέν "For in him (God) we live and move and are" is probably a quotation associated with the ancient Cretan seer Epimenides, possibly from a work titled *On Minos and Rhadamanthus*. According to tradition, Epimenides had effected the purification of Athens from a plague after the sacrilege of the Alcmaeonidae (late seventh century BCE), who had murdered the followers of Cylon while they sat as suppliants at the altars on the Acropolis (Herodotus 5.71; Thucydides 1.126; Diogenes Laertius, *Lives* 1.110). At that time Epimenides was said to have placed altars to various local divinities all around the Areopagus. These included "anonymous altars" (Diogenes Laertius, *Lives* 1.110).

---

[28] L. C. A. Alexander, "Acts and Ancient Intellectual Biography," 57–63, detects a few additional similarities between Socrates and Paul: both are physically beaten by crowds; both sing hymns while in prison; both remain unmoved by women who weep for them in the face of their death. But Alexander is drawing the figure of Socrates not just from Plato's *Apology*, where these details are absent, but from a potpourri of both early and late literary traditions about Socrates: early Platonic dialogues, such as the *Crito* and *Phaedo*; much later biographical traditions such as those recorded in Seneca, Dio Chrysostom, Plutarch, Epictetus and, especially, Diogenes Laertius. In other words, Alexander—like Kloppenborg, Sterling, and Scaer (above)—is thinking in terms of a mythic paradigm of Socrates that was familiar to Luke and his readers and that offered them a traditional context within which to understand the story of Paul.

[29] Some of the following appeared as part of a more extensive treatment of this topic in S. Reece, "Jesus as Healer," 195–200, and S. Reece, "Echoes of Plato's *Apology*," 177–97.

Luke and Plato

In our earlier chapter on Luke and Epimenides we considered a possible reconstruction of the Epimenidean verse that appeared to contain a popular folk etymological connection between the name "Zeus" (Ζεύς) and the verb "to live" (ζάω):

Ἐν σοὶ [Ζεύς] γὰρ ζῶμεν καὶ κινεόμεσθα καὶ εἰμέν.

For in you [Zeus] we live and move and are.

One could even go a step further with the reconstruction to create a double etymological wordplay on Zeus's name:

ὅν [Ζεύς] τε διὰ ζῶμεν καὶ κινεόμεσθα καὶ εἰμέν.

Because of him [Zeus] we live and move and are.

The first, and most obvious, wordplay is the (false) association of Ζεύς and ζάω ("to live"), which became a common folk etymology in antiquity: Plato's *Cratylus* 395e–396b; Pseudo-Aristotle's *De mundo* 401a; Diogenes Laertius's *Lives of the Philosophers* 7.147. The second, and rather more outlandish, etymological wordplay is the association of Ζεύς and the preposition διά "because of." That is to say, the alternative form of Zeus's name, seen in the oblique cases, as in the accusative Δία, is associated with the preposition διά "because of," since Zeus is the one "because of whom" or "on account of whom" we live. Allusions to this etymology appear in poetry as early as Homer (*Od.* 8.82), Hesiod (*Op.*1–4, 122; *Theog.* 465), and Aeschylus (*Ag.* 1485–6), and the etymology is spelled out explicitly in Plato's *Cratylus* 395e–396b; Pseudo-Aristotle's *De mundo* 401a; Chrysippus's fr. 1062; Diogenes Laertius's *Lives of the Philosophers* 7.147.[30] Most pertinent for our purposes here is Plato's detailed and influential etymologizing of Zeus's name in the *Cratylus*, a work with which Luke, who is very fond of etymologies, may have been familiar (*Crat.* 395e–396b):

φαίνεται δὲ καὶ τῷ πατρὶ αὐτοῦ λεγομένῳ τῷ Διὶ παγκάλως τὸ ὄνομα κεῖσθαι· ἔστι δὲ οὐ ῥᾴδιον κατανοῆσαι. ἀτεχνῶς γάρ ἐστιν οἷον λόγος τὸ τοῦ Διὸς ὄνομα, διελόντες δὲ αὐτὸ διχῇ οἱ μὲν τῷ ἑτέρῳ μέρει, οἱ δὲ τῷ ἑτέρῳ χρώμεθα—οἱ μὲν γὰρ "Ζῆνα," οἱ δὲ "Δία" καλοῦσιν—συντιθέμενα δ᾽ εἰς ἓν δηλοῖ τὴν φύσιν τοῦ θεοῦ, ὅ δὴ προσήκειν φαμὲν ὀνόματι οἵῳ τε εἶναι ἀπεργάζεσθαι. οὐ γὰρ ἔστιν ἡμῖν καὶ τοῖς ἄλλοις πᾶσιν ὅστις ἐστὶν αἴτιος μᾶλλον τοῦ ζῆν ἢ ὁ ἄρχων τε καὶ βασιλεὺς τῶν πάντων. συμβαίνει οὖν ὀρθῶς ὀνομάζεσθαι οὗτος ὁ θεὸς εἶναι, δι᾽ ὃν ζῆν ἀεὶ πᾶσι τοῖς ζῶσιν ὑπάρχει· διείληπται δὲ δίχα, ὥσπερ λέγω, ἓν ὂν τὸ ὄνομα, τῷ "Διὶ" καὶ τῷ "Ζηνί."

And it appears that his father too, who is called Dii [dative of Zeus], has a very excellent name. But it is not easy to understand, for the name of Zeus is exactly like

---

[30] On this folk etymology of Zeus, see L. P. Rank, *Etymologiseering en verwante verschijnselen bij Homerus* (Assen: van Gorcum, 1951), 43–4; M. L. West, *Hesiod: Works and Days* (Oxford: Clarendon, 1978), 138–9; C. Watkins, *How to Kill a Dragon: Aspects of Indo-European Poetics* (Oxford: Oxford University Press, 1995), 98–9.

226   *The Formal Education of the Author of Luke-Acts*

a statement, and having divided it into two parts, some of us use one part, and others the other part. For some call him Zena [an accusative form of Zeus], and others call him Dia [another accusative form of Zeus]. But the two in combination reveal the nature of the god, which is what we say a name should be able to do. For certainly no one is more the cause of "life" [Zen] for us and for all others than the ruler and king of all. Therefore this god happens to be correctly named, "because of" [Dia] whom there is "life" [Zen] for all living things. But, as I say, though the name is one, it has been divided into the two parts: Dii [a dative form of Zeus] and Zeni [another dative form of Zeus].

It is possible that Luke was familiar with Plato's etymologizing of Zeus's name in the *Cratylus*, and that this influenced his description of the relationship between the human and divine in Acts 17:28a Ἐν αὐτῷ γὰρ ζῶμεν καὶ κινούμεθα καὶ ἐσμέν. Some have even suggested that Luke's description here was inspired not by a work of Epimenides but by similar concepts and expressions in Plato's dialogues. H. Hommel, for example, argues that the triad in 17:28a (live, move, be) can be traced back to Plato (e.g., *Tim.* 37c; *Resp.* 369d; *Soph.* 248e–249a; *Symp.* 206b–c), likely through the Stoic Posidonius as an intermediary (or, more precisely, he argues that Luke was familiar with a text of Posidonius that had already been altered by a well-educated, Hellenistic Jew).[31] I am not convinced that Luke's formulation in Acts 17:28a is a direct borrowing from Posidonius or any of the Platonic dialogues, but it seems plausible that his choice to use this Epimenidean expression may owe something to his familiarity with Plato's etymologizing of Zeus's name in the *Cratylus*. In any case, if, as I propose, Luke is referencing Plato's *Apology* in Acts 17, it finds itself in the good company of Aratus's *Phaenomena*, probably Epimenides' *On Minos and Rhadamanthus*, and possibly even Plato's *Cratylus*.

The influence of Plato's *Apology* can be seen right away in Luke's initial portrayal of Paul in Athens: like Socrates, he spends his time "dialoguing" (διελέγετο) every day in the "Agora" (ἀγορᾷ) with those "happening by" (παρατυγχάνοντας), including the Athenian philosophers (Acts 17:17-18). Plato regularly used this same verb διαλέγομαι to describe Socrates' method of teaching (8 times in the *Apology*, and an additional 255 times elsewhere in Plato's dialogues). The Agora was Socrates' favorite place to teach too: in the first words of his defense in the *Apology*, Socrates asks his audience's patience "if he speaks in the same manner in which he has been accustomed to speak 'in the Agora' (ἐν ἀγορᾷ)." And Socrates' audience was often composed of those whom he just "happens upon" (ἐντυγχάνω in *Apol.* 29d and 30a), including other Athenian philosophers.[32]

---

[31] H. Hommel, "Neue Forschungen," 145–78 (esp. 165–9), and H. Hommel, "Platonisches bei Lukas: Zu Act 17:28a (Leben-Bewegung-Sein)," *Zeitschrift für die neutestamentliche Wissenschaft* 48 (1957): 193–200.

[32] The general description of Socrates' daily routine in Xenophon's *Memorabilia* is similar, but it does not share the specific diction (1.1.10): Ἀλλὰ μὴν ἐκεῖνός γε ἀεὶ μὲν ἦν ἐν τῷ φανερῷ· πρῴ τε γὰρ εἰς τοὺς περιπάτους καὶ τὰ γυμνάσια ᾔει καὶ πληθούσης ἀγορᾶς ἐκεῖ φανερὸς ἦν, καὶ τὸ λοιπὸν ἀεὶ τῆς ἡμέρας ἦν ὅπου πλείστοις μέλλοι συνέσεσθαι· καὶ ἔλεγε μὲν ὡς τὸ πολύ, τοῖς δὲ βουλομένοις ἐξῆν ἀκούειν. "Moreover, he (Socrates) was always in public; for early in the morning he went to the Peripatoi and the Gymnasia, and when the Agora was full of people he was in public there, and for the remainder of the day he was always wherever he might meet the most people; and he talked as much as possible, and anyone who wanted to could listen."

Luke and Plato 227

Among those with whom Paul "dialogues" are some Epicurean and Stoic philosophers whom Luke portrays as puzzled about the nature of Paul's teaching and concerned that he is introducing into Athens two foreign, and perhaps related, divinities—Iesous/Ἰησοῦς and Anastasis/Ἀνάστασις (17:18):

τινὲς δὲ καὶ τῶν Ἐπικουρείων καὶ Στοϊκῶν φιλοσόφων συνέβαλλον αὐτῷ, καί τινες ἔλεγον, Τί ἂν θέλοι ὁ σπερμολόγος οὗτος λέγειν; οἱ δέ, Ξένων δαιμονίων δοκεῖ καταγγελεὺς εἶναι· ὅτι τὸν Ἰησοῦν καὶ τὴν Ἀνάστασιν εὐηγγελίζετο.

And some of the Epicurean and Stoic philosophers debated with him, and some said, "What does this seed-picker purport to say?" And others replied: "He seems to be a proclaimer of foreign divinities" (since he was preaching *Iesous* and *Anastasis*).

Luke appears to be dabbling sardonically in some subtle wordplay here at the expense of the Athenian philosophers. Paul has presumably been teaching, as usual, about the bodily resurrection (ἀνάστασις) of Jesus (Ἰησοῦς), as he will explicitly in his speech that follows (17:31-2). But in what looks like an authorial aside at the end of 17:18— and Luke offers another aside shortly in 17:21—Luke appears to portray the Athenian philosophers naively misunderstanding Paul's teaching about the resurrection (ἀνάστασις) of Jesus (Ἰησοῦς) as an attempt to introduce two foreign divinities into the city: Ἰασώ (Ἰησώ in Ionic) "Healing" and Ἀνάστασις "Resurrection." The plural δαιμονίων "divinities" and the definite articles attached to both Ἰησοῦν and Ἀνάστασιν support this understanding of the text.[33]

Ἰασώ/Ἰησώ was, in fact, an obscure, minor divinity among the ancient Greeks. According to the more common tradition, she was a daughter of the healing god Asclepius, having received her name from the abstract noun ἴασις (ἴησις in Ionic) "healing" because she was able to effect recuperation from illness. The healing cult of Asclepius involved incubation of the patient: after a ritual cleansing, the patient would fall asleep in the innermost sanctum of the shrine in order to receive a dream from the

---

[33] John Chrysostom, already in the fourth century, proposed that the Athenians misunderstood Paul's preaching about bodily resurrection (ἀνάστασις) (Homily 38 on the Acts of the Apostles): "For they considered even resurrection (ἀνάστασις) to be a God, since they were accustomed to worship females too." Many medieval and modern commentators have embraced this view. An etymological connection between Jesus's name and the verb "to heal" (ἰῆσθαι) or the noun "healing" (ἴασις) was entertained by the author of the Gospel of Bartholomew (4:65) and by some of the Church Fathers, such as Athanasius (*De sancta trinitate* (Migne 28.1260) and *In caecum a nativitate* (Migne 28.1012)), Eusebius (*Dem. ev.* 4.10.19), and Cyril of Jerusalem (*Catecheses ad illuminandos* 10.4, 13), but no ancient or medieval commentator on this passage in Acts 17 has raised the possibility that the Athenian philosophers may have conflated the name Ἰησοῦς, which would have been unintelligible to them, with the word ἴασις/ἴησις (healing) and the name Ἰασώ/Ἰησώ (goddess of healing). The first modern commentator to do so is F. H. Chase, *The Credibility of the Book of the Acts of the Apostles* (London: Macmillan, 1902), 205: "Others [of the Athenian philosophers] started the half-mocking theory that he was a Socrates redivivus, introducing strange or foreign deities, a new god of healing, Ἰησοῦς, and a new companion goddess, Ἀνάστασις." Also 205–6, note 3: "The name Ἰησοῦς, otherwise unintelligible, would be naturally connected by the Athenians with ἴασις (Ionic ἴησις) and Ἰασώ (Ἰησώ), the goddess of healing and health (e.g., Ar. *Plut.* 701)." On this wordplay on the name "Jesus," here and elsewhere in Luke-Acts, see, S. Reece, "Jesus as Healer," 186–201.

228   *The Formal Education of the Author of Luke-Acts*

gods that might reveal a path to healing (Aristophanes, *Plut.* 653–747; Pausanias 1.34.5). This is perhaps pertinent to our understanding of the response of the Epicurean and Stoic philosophers to Paul's preaching in Acts 17, for the ritual of incubation served as a symbolic death from which the patient would hopefully receive "resurrection" and "healing."

Why then would Luke have the Athenian philosophers suspect that Paul's Iesous/Ἰησοῦς and Anastasis/Ἀνάστασις are "foreign" divinities? Partly, perhaps, it was because Iaso/Ieso Ἰασώ/Ἰησώ was not a Panhellenic Olympian divinity but rather an obscure and provincial figure. Mostly, though, it was because of the second of Paul's "foreign" divinities: Ἀνάστασις "Resurrection." The Classical and Hellenistic Greeks very rarely use the term ἀνάστασις to denote a rising/return/resurrection of the physical body from death, as in the Septuagint and New Testament, and when they do, it is only to deny (or condemn) the possibility (Aeschylus, *Eum.* 647–8; Sophocles, *El.* 138–9). Though they speculated philosophically about the reincarnation of the soul, the ancient Greeks did not embrace a physical resurrection: "all-receiving" Hades did not relinquish his dead easily, and only the most eminent of the mythic heroes— Heracles, Orpheus, Theseus, Odysseus—were able to overcome Hades' clutches. Asclepius had some success in bringing some other heroes back from Hades— Capaneus, Lycurgus, Hippolytus—but he was killed by Zeus for violating this boundary (Apollonius, *Bibliotheca* 3.121–2).

It is notable that at this very place where Paul is preaching to the Athenians in Acts 17, the Athenian Areopagus, Apollo had once, in his defense of Orestes before Athena and the Athenian jurors, argued against the possibility of any return from death (Aeschylus, *Eum.* 647–8): "When the dust has drawn up the blood of a man, once he is dead, there is no resurrection (ἀνάστασις)." This mythical trial of Orestes had provided the aetiology for the existence of the court of the Areopagus in Athens, so the story would have been well known to Athenian citizens, and especially to Areopagites, even centuries later. Paul's concept of ἀνάστασις would have struck them as something foreign, even inimical, to their fundamental beliefs. Its personification as a deity would have posed a major stumbling block for many of the Athenians. It is heavy in irony, then, that it is Dionysius the Areopagite who is named as the first Athenian convert to Christianity (17:34)—and, presumably, to Christianity's central belief in bodily resurrection (ἀνάστασις).

Luke's depiction of the Athenian philosophers as naively misunderstanding Paul's teaching about the resurrection (ἀνάστασις) of Jesus (Ἰησοῦς) as an effort to introduce the two foreign divinities Ἰασώ "Healing" and Ἀνάστασις "Resurrection" into the city is not simply an entertaining and isolated detail. Rather, it is part of Luke's larger portrayal of Paul as a Socratic figure who introduces new gods into Athens and is judged by the Athenians for doing so. The Athenian philosophers accuse Paul of being a "messenger of foreign divinities" (ξένων δαιμονίων δοκεῖ καταγγελεὺς εἶναι), of promoting a "new teaching" (ἡ καινὴ . . . διδαχή), and of "introducing foreign matters" (ξενίζοντα γάρ τινα εἰσφέρεις) to their ears (Acts 17:19-20). These were precisely the accusations leveled against Socrates and in almost exactly the same terms. One of the two formal charges brought before the court against Socrates in the *Apology* was that "he does not regard the gods that the city regards but rather other new divinities" (θεοὺς οὓς ἡ πόλις νομίζει οὐ νομίζοντα, ἕτερα δὲ δαιμόνια καινά) (*Apol.* 24b–c).[34] Socrates had supposedly introduced a panoply of "new gods" into Athens that were non-anthropomorphic, non-traditional, non-Olympian divinities (i.e., ones without an established cult). Aristophanes offers some clues about the identity of these "new gods" in his parody of the philosopher in his comedy *Clouds* (264–6, 423–4). They are personifications of abstract concepts like Air, Aether, Clouds, Chaos, and Speech. Would it not have been clear to Luke's audience that he was drawing a caricature of the Athenians by having them mistake Paul's teaching as an attempt to introduce two new gods of a similar type into the city—namely, Healing and Resurrection?

Two more similarities between Luke's account of Paul and Plato's account of Socrates deserve recognition: First, in Acts 17:19 the Athenians "take hold of Paul and lead him to the Areopagus" (ἐπιλαβόμενοί τε αὐτοῦ ἐπὶ τὸν Ἄρειον Πάγον ἤγαγον). Elsewhere in Acts the verb ἐπιλαμβάνω is used of formal arrest (cf. Acts 16:19; 18:17; 21:30, 33), and, of course, the Areopagus, whether denoting the hill or the court itself, was well known as a formal judicial body. It would not have escaped the notice of Luke's audience that the law court where Socrates was tried and condemned—as well as the jail where he was confined and eventually executed—lay in the shadow of the Areopagus.[35] Second, in Acts 17:22, Paul stands up in the middle of the Areopagus and begins his address to the Athenians with the words "Athenian men" (ἄνδρες Ἀθηναῖοι). Again, it would not have escaped the notice of Luke's audience that this is exactly the form of address, ὦ ἄνδρες Ἀθηναῖοι, with which Socrates begins his famous defense before the same audience (*Apol.* 17a, and an additional 44 times elsewhere in the *Apology*).

For anyone in Luke's audience who was aware of the momentous trial and execution of Socrates through later traditions about him, or who, more specifically, had studied Plato's *Apology* in school or read it later in life—and I assume that this would include the author of Luke-Acts as well as much of his audience—Paul's situation as described by Luke would have seemed both momentous and ominous. By casting Paul as a Socratic figure Luke was elevating Paul's status to that of the most distinguished philosopher of the ancient world. But by positioning Plato's *Apology* in the background of his own narrative, Luke was also ringing an ominous note: Paul might end up suffering the same fate as Socrates. In a subtle but powerful way this scene in Acts 17 anticipates Paul's eventual execution and death, which, though never actually narrated in Acts, is foreshadowed numerous times.

---

[34] This accusation is repeated almost verbatim in Xenophon's *Memorabilia* 1.1.1 ἀδικεῖ Σωκράτης οὓς μὲν ἡ πόλις νομίζει θεοὺς οὐ νομίζων, ἕτερα δὲ καινὰ δαιμόνια εἰσφέρων (cf. Xenophon, *Apol.* 10–12). Xenophon's accounts of Socrates' activities are in one respect even closer than Plato's to Luke's account of Paul's activities: Xenophon and Luke both use the verb "to introduce" (εἰσφέρω).

[35] On Paul's experience as a legal action: F. J. Foakes Jackson and K. Lake, eds., *The Beginnings of Christianity*, 4:212–13 on Acts 17:19; T. D. Barnes, "An Apostle on Trial," *Journal of Theological Studies* 20 (1969): 407–19; D. L. Balch, "The Areopagus Speech," 52–79; R. I. Pervo, *Profit with Delight*, 44–55.

Appendix I: Earliest Known Manuscript of the Gospel of Luke

Figure 12 Earliest known manuscript of the Gospel of Luke (P75 = *P.Bodmer* XIV (Luke)–XV (John) = *Hanna Papyrus* 1). Courtesy of the Biblioteca Apostolica Vaticana.

P75 (= *P.Bodmer* XIV (Luke)–XV (John) = *Hanna Papyrus* 1) is a single-quire papyrus codex containing the Gospels of Luke and John, dated by its first editors between 175–225 CE and, if this dating is correct, the earliest known copy of Luke. This section of the manuscript contains the end of the Gospel of Luke and the beginning of the Gospel of John and includes the titles for both gospels.

232 *The Formal Education of the Author of Luke-Acts*

According to the practice of the time, the text is written *scriptio continua* (there are no spaces between words except, rarely, at major breaks in the narrative) but not *scriptio plena* (vowels elided in pronunciation are not spelled out). There are only sporadic punctuation marks and no accents, breathing marks, elision marks, or iota subscripts or adscripts. Several contractions and abbreviations occur, which are indicated by superlinear lines, a diaeresis is occasionally marked, especially on non-Greek names, and there are some paragraph marks (spaces and/or lines), but the general lack of lectional aids must have resulted in difficult reading for all but the very experienced reader.

Other than the addition of some of the contractions and abbreviations, especially of divine names and titles, the handwriting, style, and format of this text, the earliest surviving manuscript of Luke's gospel, offers us a fairly close picture of what Luke's autograph—the original text of his gospel—would have looked like. Luke's autograph would have been written only on one side of a papyrus roll rather than on both sides of the folios of a papyrus codex, and, of course, it would not have been attached to the Gospel of John. Luke's gospel and his Acts of the Apostles would have been written on separate rolls.

Appendix II: Latin Literary Texts Preserved on Documents Contemporary with Luke

Egypt

The following is the sum total of Latin literary texts on documents roughly contemporary with Luke (100 BCE–200 CE) that have been preserved on papyri, parchment, and ostraca discovered in various places in the sands of Egypt:

- Nine lines of elegiac verse from the first-century BCE poet Gaius Cornelius Gallus on a first-century BCE papyrus discovered in 1978 in the Roman fortress town of Qaṣr Ibrîm, Egypt (*P.Qaṣr Ibrîm* inv. 78-3-11/1 (L1/2) (case 7, item 84)). It was likely brought to the garrison from abroad by a Roman officer. It is written in a book hand (i.e., it is not a school text).
- Portions of eight lines of Cicero's *In Verrem* 2.2.3–4 on a first-century CE papyrus of unknown origin in Egypt (*P.Iand.* 5.90, inv. 210). The style of writing indicates that this is a manuscript of Cicero's entire speech, not a passage used as an exercise in a school text.
- Portions of seven lines of Sallust's *Bellum Iugurthinum* 31.7 on a first-century CE papyrus from an unknown place in Egypt (*P.Ryl.* 1.42). The style of writing indicates that this is a full manuscript of Sallust's history, not simply a quotation, and not a passage in a school text.
- Portions of sixteen lines of Sallust's *Historiae* on a first-century CE papyrus found at Oxyrhynchus (*P.Ryl.* 3.473). The expert Rustic Capital script and generous margins indicate that this is part of a full manuscript of Sallust's history and, moreover, that the volume was likely imported from elsewhere.
- Portions of twenty lines of a history about Rome's Macedonian wars, possibly from Trogus Pompeius's nonextant work, on a parchment codex from Oxyrhynchus (*P.Oxy.* 1.30). The date could be as late as the third century CE.

All the remaining documents are passages from Vergil's *Georgics*, *Eclogues*, and, predominately, *Aeneid*. Most come from a Roman military context: e.g., soldiers writing out a line or two of poetry from memory; school children of veteran colonists learning their letters by writing verses repeatedly.

234   *The Formal Education of the Author of Luke-Acts*

- Vergil's *Georgics* 4.1–2 written six times as a writing exercise on a discarded financial account found in the town of Tebtunis (*P.Tebt.* 2.686, second to third century CE).
- Vergil's *Eclogues* 8.53–62 written on a papyrus fragment found in a house in the village of Narmouthis (*P.Narm.* inv. 66.362, late first century CE). This is not a writing exercise but rather a text of this entire *Eclogue*, and perhaps even of several of them. If so, it is the oldest surviving "book" of a work of Vergil.
- Vergil's *Aeneid* 1.1–3 written on an ostracon found in Mons Claudianus, a quarry administered by the Roman army (*O.Claud.* 1.190, early second century CE).
- The first lines of books one and two of Vergil's *Aeneid* appended to the bottom of a letter of recommendation written in Latin, of unknown origin, but from somewhere in Egypt (*P.Hamb.* 2.167, late first century CE).
- Vergil's *Aeneid* 1.1–9, 11–14, 17, 19–20, 66–7, 71; 2.1–2; 9.367–8, written haphazardly on an ostracon that has broken into thirteen surviving pieces, discovered in a cistern at the Roman fort Xeron Pelagos halfway between Coptos and Berenice (*O.Xeron* inv. 871, late second to early third century CE). Although writing errors are numerous, this does not appear to be a school exercise; rather, the verses appear to have been written from memory, probably by a soldier who had as a student committed to memory some of the *Aeneid* but had since forgotten much of what he had memorized.
- Vergil's *Aeneid* 2.601 written seven times as a writing exercise on a papyrus originally from Arsinoites (*P.Haw.* 24, late first century CE) and on the reverse possibly *Aeneid* 4.174 and Horace's *Ars Poetica* 78, both verses likewise written several times. The quality of the writing suggests that a fairly experienced scribe was practicing calligraphy.
- Vergil's *Aeneid* 11.371–2 written six or seven times as a writing exercise, on the back of a Greek document, on a papyrus from Oxyrhynchus (*P.Oxy.* 50.3554, late first century CE).

Judaea (Masada)

At least nineteen first-century CE Latin papyri (plus one bilingual papyrus) have been discovered at the Roman fortress of Masada on the southwestern shore of the Dead Sea. The Roman origin of these papyri is indicated primarily by their use of Latin but also, of course, by the contents of the documents. All nineteen Latin papyri, three of which can be dated on internal grounds to between 70 and 75 CE, were found together in locus 1039, one of the casements in the northwestern section of the wall of the fortress. These papyri include documents that one would expect to find in a Roman military camp—lists of names of soldiers of the Tenth Legion stationed at Masada, letters from abroad sent to these soldiers, records of legionary pay—but one document includes a quotation of Vergil's *Aeneid* 4.9: *P.Masada* 721 from around 73 CE. A Roman soldier who was stationed far from home at the fortress at Masada was apparently trying to preserve some of his calligraphic skills by writing down a memorable verse of Dido's speech to her sister Anna.

Appendix II   235

Britain (Vindolanda)

Excavations at the Roman fort of Vindolanda near Hadrian's Wall have revealed the oldest handwritten documents ever discovered in Britain: several hundred wooden "leaf tablets," dating from 90–120 CE, written in ink with split-nibbed reed or quill pens on very thin shavings of alder and birch wood about the size of modern postcards. Most of the tablets contain personal letters, but there are also military documents, accounts, and even a few passages of Vergil composed as writing exercises: *Aeneid* 9.473 on Vindolanda 118; *Aeneid* 1.1 on Vindolanda 452; *Georgics* 1.125 on Vindolanda 854; possibly *Aeneid* 10.860–1 on Vindolanda 855; possibly *Aeneid* 7.373 on Vindolanda 856.

Italy (Herculaneum and Pompeii)

Italy was, of course, another story, and a wide spectrum of Latin literary texts would have been readily available to the general public there in the time of Luke. The evidence preserved by the eruption of Mt. Vesuvius in 79 CE both among the charred papyrus rolls of the library of the Villa of the Papyri at Herculaneum and among the graffiti written on the walls at Pompeii is illustrative.

Although the Latin papyri from the Villa of the Papyri at Herculaneum are far fewer and generally in much worse condition than the Greek, fragments of several Latin literary texts have been identified: e.g., the historian Ennius's *Annales* (*P.Herc.* 21), the comic poet Caecilius Statius's *Obolostates sive Faenerator* (*P.Herc.* 78), the epic poet Lucretius's *De Rerum Natura* (*P.Herc.* 395, 1829, 1830, 1831), a hexameter poem about Octavian's campaign in Egypt (*P.Herc.* 817), a juridical speech by Lucius Manlius Torquatus (*P.Herc.* 1475). There likely exists a much more extensive collection of Latin literary texts in the still unexcavated sections of the villa's library. On the Latin literary papyri from Herculaneum, see D. Sider, *The Library of the Villa dei Papiri at Herculaneum* (Los Angeles: J. Paul Getty Museum, 2005) 66–72.

The popularity of Vergil is colorfully illustrated by the numerous Vergilian graffiti in Pompeii. Full lines, or parts of lines, of Vergil's *Aeneid* appear fifty-two times on the Pompeiian graffiti, along with thirteen lines of the *Eclogues* and two of the *Georgics*, all dating, necessarily, to a period before 79 CE. Sixteen of the fifty-two graffiti from the *Aeneid* contain the first line of the first book of the epic; another fourteen contain the first line of the second book of the epic. The most recent edition of Vergilian papyri generally is M. C. Scappaticcio, *Papyri Vergilianae: l'apporto della Papirologia alla Storia della Tradizionee virgiliana (I-VI d.C.). Papyrologica Leodiensia, 1* (Liège: Presses Universitaires de Liège, 2013), who catalogues thirty-five examples from between the first and the sixth centuries CE of Vergilian verses on papyri, wooden tablets, ostraca, and parchment. For a convenient catalogue of the Pompeiian grafitti, see K. Milnor, "Literary Literacy in Roman Pompeii: the Case of Vergil's *Aeneid*," in *Ancient Literacies: The Culture of Reading in Greece and Rome*, eds. W. A. Johnson and H. N. Parker (Oxford: Oxford University Press, 2009), 288–319.

Bibliography

Adrados, F. R. *History of the Graeco-Latin Fable: Volume One: Introduction and From the Origins to the Hellenistic Age.* Leiden: Brill, 1999.

Adrados, F. R. *History of the Graeco-Latin Fable: Volume Two: The Fable during the Roman Empire and in the Middle Ages.* Leiden: Brill, 2000.

Adrados, F. R. "The 'Life of Aesop' and the Origins of the Novel in Antiquity." *Quaderni Urbinati di Cultura Classica*, n.s. 1, 30 (1979): 93–112.

Aland, K. *Synopsis Quattuor Evangeliorum.* 15th ed. Stuttgart: Deutsche Bibelgesellschaft, 1996.

Alexander, L. C. A. "Acts and Ancient Intellectual Biography." In *The Book of Acts in Its Ancient Literary Setting*, edited by B. W. Winter and A. D. Clarke, 31–63. Grand Rapids: Eerdmans, 1993.

Alexander, L. C. A. *The Preface to Luke's Gospel.* Cambridge: Cambridge University Press, 1993.

Alexander, L. C. A. "The Preface to Acts and the Historians." In *History, Literature and Society*, edited by B. Witherington III, 73–103. Cambridge: Cambridge University Press, 1999.

Alexander, L. C. A. "Septuaginta, Fachprosa, Imitatio: Albert Wifstrand and the Language of Luke-Acts." In *Die Apostelgeschichte und die hellenistische Geschichtsschreibung: Festschrift fur Eckhard Plümacher zu seinem 65. Geburtstag*, edited by C. Breytenbach and J. Schroter, 1–26. Leiden: Brill, 2004.

Alexander, L. C. A. *Acts in Its Ancient Literary Context: A Classicist Looks at the Acts of the Apostles.* London: T&T Clark, 2005.

Alexandre, M. "La culture profane chez Philon." In *Philon d'Alexandrie, Lyon Colloque*, edited by R. Arnaldez, C. Mondésert, and J. Poillous, 105–29. Paris: Cerf, 1967.

Alexandre, M., Jr., "Philo of Alexandria and Hellenic *Paideia*." *Euphrosyne* 37 (2009): 121–30.

Alviar, J. José. "Recent Advances in Computational Linguistics and their Application to Biblical Studies." *New Testament Studies* 54 (2008): 139–59.

Andreassi, M. "The *Life of Aesop* and the Gospels: Literary Motifs and Narrative Mechanisms." In *Holy Men and Charlatans in the Ancient Novel*, edited by S. Panayotakis, G. L. Schmeling, and M. Paschalis, 151–66. Eelde: Barkhuis Publishing, 2015.

Arend, W. *Die typischen Scenen bei Homer.* Berlin: Weidmann, 1933.

Argyle, A. W. "The Greek of Luke and Acts." *New Testament Studies* 20 (1974): 441–5.

Austin, C., and G. Bastianini, *Posidippi Pellaei quae supersunt omnia.* Milan: Edizioni Universitarie di Lettere Economia Diritto, 2002.

Balch, D. L. "The Areopagus Speech: An Appeal to the Stoic Historian Posidonius against Later Stoics and the Epicureans." In *Greeks, Romans, and Christians*, edited by D. L. Balch et al., 52–79. Minneapolis: Fortress, 1990.

Barnes, T. D. "An Apostle on Trial." *Journal of Theological Studies* 20 (1969): 407–19.

Barrett, C. K. *A Critical and Exegetical Commentary on the Acts of the Apostles.* Vols. 1–2. London: T&T Clark, 1994–98.

238 Bibliography

Bartelink, G. J. M. "Homer." *Reallexikon für Antike und Christentum* 121 (1991): 116–47.

Bastianini, G., C. Gallazzi, and C. Austin, eds. *Posidippo di Pella Epigrammi (P. Mil. Vogl. VIII 309)*. Milan: Edizioni Universitarie di Lettere Economia Diritto, 2001.

Bauckham, R., ed. *The Book of Acts in Its Palestinian Setting*. Grand Rapids: Eerdmans, 1995.

Bauernfeind, O. "θεομαχέω." In *Theological Dictionary of the New Testament*, vol. 4, edited by G. Kittel and G. Friedrich. Grand Rapids: Eerdmans, 1967.

Bauernfeind, O. *Kommentar und Studien zur Apostelgeschichte*. Tübingen: Mohr Siebeck, 1980.

Baur, F. C. *Paulus, der Apostel Jesu Christi: sein Leben und Wirken, seine Briefe und seine Lehre*. Stuttgart: Becher & Müller, 1845.

Bazant, J., and G. Berger-Doer. "Pentheus." In *Lexicon Iconographicum Mythologiae Classicae*, vol. 7.1, edited by H. Christoph Ackerman and Jean-Robert Gisler, 306–17. Zurich: Artemis, 1994.

Beare W. *The Roman Stage: A Short History of Latin Drama in the Time of the Republic*. 3rd ed. London: Methuen, 1964.

Beavis, M. A. "Parable and Fable." *Catholic Biblical Quarterly* 52 (1990): 473–98.

Bellinati, C. "Peregrinazioni del corpo di San Luca nel primo millennio." In *San Luca evangelista testimone della fede che unisce. Atti del Congresso internazionale, Padova, 16–21 ottobre 2000*, vol. 2, edited by V. T. W. Marin and F. G. B. Trolese, 173–99. Padua: Istituto per la storia ecclesiastica Padovana, 2003.

Benz, E. "Christus und Sokrates in der alten Kirche (ein Beitrag zum altkirchlichen Verständnis des Märtyrers und des Martyriums)." *Zeitschrift für die neutestamentliche Wissenschaft* 43 (1951): 195–224.

Berger, K. "Hellenistische Gattungen im Neuen Testament." *Aufstieg und Niedergang der römischen Welt* II 25, no. 2 (1984): 1031–432.

Betz, H. D. *Der Apostel Paulus und die sokratische Tradition*. Tübingen: Mohr Siebeck, 1972.

Betz, H. D. *Galatians: A Commentary on Paul's Letter to the Churches in Galatia*. Philadelphia: Fortress, 1979.

Betz, H. D. "Humanisierung des Menschen: Delphi, Plato, Paulus." In *Hellenismus und Urchristentum*, edited by H. D. Betz, 120–34. Tübingen: Mohr Siebeck, 1990.

Beudel, P., *Qua ratione Graeci liberos docuerint, papyris, ostracis, tabulis in Aegypto inventis illustratur*. Monasterii Guestfalorum: Aschendorffiana, 1911.

Bidez, J. *L'empereur Julien*. Paris: Les Belles Lettres, 1932.

Bieber, M. *The History of the Greek and Roman Theater*. 2nd ed. Princeton: Princeton University Press, 1961.

Birt, Th. "'Αγνωστοι θεοί und die Areopagrede des Apostels Paulus." *Rheinisches Museum für Philologie* 69 (1914): 380.

Black, M. *An Aramaic Approach to the Gospels and Acts*. 3rd ed. Oxford: Clarendon, 1967.

Blass, F. *Acta apostolorum sive Lucae ad Theophilum liber alter: editio philologica*. Göttingen: Vandenhoeck & Ruprecht, 1895.

Blass, F. *Philology of the Gospels*. London: Macmillan and Company, 1898.

Blass, F., A. Debrunner, and R. W. Funk. *A Greek Grammar of the New Testament and Other Early Christian Literature*. Chicago: University of Chicago Press, 1961.

Bloedow, E. F. "Evidence for an Early Date for the Cult of Cretan Zeus." *Kernos: Revue Internationale et Pluridisciplinaire de Religion Grecque Antique* 4 (1991): 139–77.

Boccaccini G., and C. A. Segovia, eds. *Paul the Jew: Rereading the Apostle as a Figure of Second Temple Judaism*. Minneapolis: Fortress, 2016.

Böhlig, H. *Die Geisteskultur von Tarsos im augusteischen Zeitalter mit Berücksichtigung der paulinischen Schriften*. Göttingen: Vandenhoeck and Ruprecht, 1913.

Bonhöffer, A. *Epiktet und das Neue Testament*. Giessen: Töpelmann, 1911.

Bonner, S. F. *Education in Ancient Rome: From the Elder Cato to the Younger Pliny*. Berkeley: University of California Press, 1977.

Bonz, M. *The Past as Legacy: Luke-Acts and Ancient Epic*. Minneapolis: Fortress, 2000.

Booth, A. D. "Elementary and Secondary Education in the Roman Empire." *Florilegium* 1 (1979): 1–14.

Bouquiaux-Simon, O., and P. Mertens. "Les papyrus de Thucydide." *Chronique d'Égypte* 66 (1991): 198–210.

Bouquiaux-Simon, O., and P. Mertens. "Les témoignages papyrologiques d' Euripide: Liste sommaire arrêtée au 1/6/1990." In *Papiri letterari greci e latini*, edited by M. Capasso, 97–107. Lecce: Congredo, 1992.

Brant, J-A. A. *Dialogue and Drama: Elements of Greek Tragedy in the Fourth Gospel*. Peabody: Hendrickson, 2004.

Brashear, W. "A Trifle." *Zeitschrift für Papyrologie und Epigraphik* 86 (1991): 231–2.

Brawley, R. L. *Luke-Acts and the Jews: Conflict, Apology, and Conciliation*. Atlanta: Scholars Press, 1987.

Bremer, J. M. "The Popularity of Euripides' *Phoenissae* in Late Antiquity." In *Actes du VIIe Congrès de la Fédération Internationale des Associations d'Études classiques*, vol. 1, edited by J. Harmatta, 281–8. Budapest: Akadémiai Kiadó, 1984.

Bremmer, J. "Scapegoat Rituals in Ancient Greece." *Harvard Studies in Classical Philology* 87 (1983): 299–320.

Bruce, F. F. *The Speeches in the Acts of the Apostles*. London: The Tyndale Press, 1944.

Bruce, F. F. *The Acts of the Apostles*. London: The Tyndale Press, 1951.

Bruce, F. F. "The Speeches in Acts—Thirty Years After." In *Reconciliation and Hope*, edited by R. Banks, 53–68. Grand Rapids: Eerdmans, 1974.

Bultmann, R. *Der Stil der paulinischen Predigt und die kynisch-stoische Diatribe*. Göttingen: E. A. Huth, 1910.

Bultmann, R. *Das Urchristentum im Rahmen der antiken Religionen*. Zurich: Artemis, 1949.

Burkert, W. *Structure and History in Greek Mythology and Ritual*. Berkeley: University of California Press, 1979.

Burkert, W. "Towards Plato and Paul: The 'Inner' Human Being." In *Ancient and Modern Perspectives on the Bible and Culture: Essays in Honor of Hans Dieter Betz*, edited by A. Y. Collins, 59–82. Atlanta: Scholars Press, 1998.

Burridge, R. A. *What are the Gospels? A Comparison with Graeco-Roman Biography*. 3rd ed. Waco: Baylor University Press, 2018.

Cadbury, H. J. *The Style and Literary Method of Luke*. Cambridge: Harvard University Press, 1919.

Cadbury, H. J. "Commentary on the Preface of Luke." In *The Beginnings of Christianity: The Acts of the Apostles*, edited by F. J. Foakes Jackson and K. Lake, 2:489–510. London: Macmillan, 1922.

Cadbury, H. J. "Speeches in Acts." In *The Beginnings of Christianity: The Acts of the Apostles*, edited by F. J. Foakes Jackson and K. Lake, 5:402–27. London: Macmillan, 1933.

Casey, M. *An Aramaic Approach to Q*. Cambridge: Cambridge University Press, 2002.

Cauderlier, P. "Cinq tablettes en bois au Musée du Louvre." *Revue archéologique* 2 (1983): 259–80.

240 *Bibliography*

Chadwick, H. "Some Ancient Anthologies and Florilegia, Pagan and Christian." In *Studies on Ancient Christianity*, edited by H. Chadwick, 1–10. Aldershot: Ashgate Publishing, 2006.

Chambry, E. *Aesopi Fabulae*. Vols. 1–2. Paris: Société d'Édition 'Les Belles Lettres,' 1925–1926.

Charitonidis, S., L. Kahil, and R. Ginouvès. *Les mosaïques de la maison du Ménandre à Mytilène*. Bern: Francke, 1970.

Chase, F. H. *The Credibility of the Book of the Acts of the Apostles*. London: Macmillan, 1902.

Clark, A. C. *The Acts of the Apostles: A Critical Edition with Introduction and Notes on Selected Passages*. Oxford: Clarendon, 1933.

Clarke, M. L. *Higher Education in the Ancient World*. London: Routledge & K. Paul, 1971.

Clarke, W. K. L. "The Use of the Septuagint in Acts." In *The Beginnings of Christianity: The Acts of the Apostles*, edited by F. J. Foakes Jackson and K. Lake, 2:66–105. London: Macmillan, 1922.

Clarysse, W., and A. Wouters. "A Schoolboy's Exercise in the Chester Beatty Library." *Ancient Society* 1 (1970): 201–35.

Colaclides, P. "Acts 17,28A and Bacchae 506." *Vigiliae Christianae* 27 (1973): 161–4.

Collart, P. *Les Papyrus Bouriant*. Paris: H. Champion, 1926.

Collart, P. "A l'école avec les petits Grecs d'Égypte." *Chronique d'Égypte* 11 (1936): 489–507.

Collart, P. "Les papyrus scolaires." In *Mélanges offerts à A. M. Desrousseaux*, edited by "*ses amis et ses élèves*," 69–80. Paris: Hachette, 1937.

Collins, A. Y. "Finding Meaning in the Death of Jesus." *The Journal of Religion* 78 (1998): 175–96.

Collins, J. J. *Between Athens and Jerusalem: Jewish Identity in the Hellenistic Diaspora*. New York: Crossroad, 1983.

Collins, J. J., and G. E. Sterling, eds. *Hellenism in the Land of Israel*. Notre Dame: University of Notre Dame Press, 2001.

Compton, T. "The Trial of the Satirist: Poetic *Vitae* (Aesop, Archilochus, Homer) as Background for Plato's *Apology*." *American Journal of Philology* 111 (1990): 330–47.

Compton, T. *Victim of the Muses: Poet as Scapegoat, Warrior and Hero in Greco-Roman And Indo-European Myth and History*. Washington, DC: Center for Hellenic Studies, 2006.

Conybeare, C. "The Commentary of Ephrem on Acts." In *The Beginnings of Christianity: The Acts of the Apostles*, edited by F. J. Foakes Jackson and K. Lake, 3:373–453. London: MacMillan, 1926.

Conzelmann, H. *Acts of the Apostles: A Commentary on the Acts of the Apostles*. Philadelphia: Fortress, 1987.

Cook, A. B. *Zeus: A Study in Ancient Religion*. Vol. 1. Cambridge: Cambridge University Press, 1914.

Cook, J. G. "1 Cor 15:33: The Status Quaestionis." *Novum Testamentum* 62 (2020): 375–91.

Courcelle, P. "Un vers d'Épiménide dans le 'discours sur l'Aréopage.'" *Revue des Études Grecques* 76 (1963): 404–13.

Cramer, J. A. *Anecdota Graeca e Codd. Manuscriptis Bibliothecarum Oxoniensium*. Vol. 2. Oxford: Typographeus Academicus, 1835.

Cramer, J. A. *Anecdota Graeca e Codd. Manuscriptis Bibliothecae Regiae Parisiensis*. Vol. 4. Oxford: Typographeus Academicus, 1891.

Cribiore, R. *Writing, Teachers, and Students in Graeco-Roman Egypt*. Atlanta: Scholars Press, 1996.

Bibliography   241

Cribiore, R. "The Grammarian's Choice: The Popularity of Euripides' *Phoenissae* in Hellenistic and Roman Education." In *Education in Greek and Roman Antiquity*, edited by Y. L. Too, 241–59. Leiden, Brill, 2001.

Cribiore, R. *Gymnastics of the Mind: Greek Education in Hellenistic and Roman Egypt.* Princeton: Princeton University Press, 2001.

Cribiore, R. "Education in the Papyri." In *The Oxford Handbook of Papyrology*, edited by R. S. Bagnall, 328–32. Oxford: Oxford University Press, 2009.

Cribiore, R., and P. Davoli. "New Literary Texts from Amheida, Ancient Trimithis (Dakhla Oasis, Egypt)." *Zeitschrift für Papyrologie und Epigraphik* 187 (2013): 1–14.

Cribiore, R., P. Davoli, and D. M. Ratzan. "A Teacher's Dipinto from Trimithis (Dakhleh Oasis)." *Journal of Roman Archaeology* 21 (2008): 170–91.

Crusius, O. *Babrii Fabulae Aesopeae.* Leipzig: Teubner, 1897.

Csapo, E., and W. J. Slater. *The Context of Ancient Drama.* Ann Arbor: University of Michigan Press, 1994.

Csapo, E. "Performance and Iconographic Tradition in the Illustrations of Menander." *Syllecta Classica* 10 (1999): 154–88.

Cukrowski, K. L. "Paul as Odysseus: An Exegetical Note on Luke's Depiction of Paul in Acts 27:1–28:10." *Restoration Quarterly* 55 (2013): 24–34.

Cumont, F. *Les religions orientales dans le paganisme romain.* Paris: E. Leroux, 1906.

Davies, W. D., and D. C. Allison, *A Critical and Exegetical Commentary on the Gospel According to Saint Matthew.* Vol. 2. Edinburgh: T&T Clark, 1991.

Debut, J. "Les documents scolaires." *Zeitschrift für Papyrologie und Epigraphik* 63 (1986): 251–78.

Deissmann, A. *St. Paul: A Study in Social and Religious History.* London: Hodder and Stoughton, 1912.

Deissmann, A. *Light from the Ancient East.* 4th ed. New York: Harper & Brothers, 1922.

de Lacy, P. "Biography and Tragedy in Plutarch." *American Journal of Philology* 73 (1952): 159–71.

DeMaris, R. E. *The New Testament in its Ritual World.* London: Routledge, 2008.

de Montfaucon, B. *Bibliotheca Coisliniana Olim Segueriana.* Paris: Ludovicum Guérin et Carolum Robustel, 1715.

Devreesse, R. *Essai sur Théodore de Mopsueste.* Città del Vaticano: Biblioteca Apostolica Vaticana, 1948.

De Zwaan, J. "The Use of the Greek Language in Acts." In *The Beginnings of Christianity: The Acts of the Apostles*, edited by F. J. Foakes Jackson and K. Lake, 2:30–65. London: Macmillan, 1922.

Dibelius, M. "Literary Allusions in the Speeches in the Acts." In *Studies in the Acts of the Apostles*, edited by H. Greeven, 186–91. New York: Charles Scribner's Sons, 1956.

Dibelius, M. "Paul on the Areopagus." In *Studies in the Acts of the Apostles*, edited by H. Greeven, 26–77. New York: Charles Scribner's Sons, 1956.

Dibelius, M. "The Speeches in Acts and Ancient Historiography." In *Studies in the Acts of the Apostles*, edited by H. Greeven, 138–91. New York: Charles Scribner's Sons, 1956.

Dibelius, M. *Studies in the Acts of the Apostles.* New York: Charles Scribner's Sons, 1956.

Dickey, E. *The Colloquia of the Hermeneumata Pseudodositheana, Vol. I: Colloquia Monacensia-Einsidlensia, Leidense-Stephani, and Stephani.* Cambridge: Cambridge University Press, 2012.

Dickey, E. *The Colloquia of the Hermeneumata Pseudodositheana, Vol. II: Colloquium Harleianum, Colloquium Montepessulanum, Colloquium Celtis, and Fragments.* Cambridge: Cambridge University Press, 2015.

Dickey, E. "Teaching Latin to Greek Speakers in Antiquity." In *Learning Latin and Greek from Antiquity to the Present*, edited by E. P. Archibald, W. Brockliss, and J. Gnoza, 30–51. Cambridge: Cambridge University Press, 2015.

Diels, H. *Die Fragmente der Vorsokratiker*. Vol. 2. 2nd ed. Berlin: Weidmann, 1907.

Dihle, A. *Der Prolog der "Bacchen" und die antike Überlieferungsphase des Euripides-Textes*. Heidelberg: Carl Winter, 1981.

Dithmar, R., ed. *Fabeln, Parabeln und Gleichnisse: Beispiele didaktischer Literatur*. Munich: Deutscher Taschenbuch-Verlag, 1970.

Dodds, E. R. *Euripides: Bacchae*. Oxford: Clarendon, 1944.

Dodson, J. R., and A. W. Pitts, eds. *Paul and the Greco-Roman Philosophical Tradition*. London: Bloomsbury T&T Clark, 2017.

Dorandi, T. "Per una ricomposizione dello scritto di Filodemo sulla Retorica." *Zeitschrift für Papyrologie und Epigraphik* 82 (1990): 59–87.

Döring, K. *Exemplum Socratis: Studien zur Sokratesnachwirkung in der kynisch-stoischen Popularphilosophie der frühen Kaiserzeit und im frühen Christentum*. Wiesbaden: Steiner, 1979.

Doutreleau, L., and P. Nautin, *Didyme l'Aveugle. Sur la Genèse*. Vol. 1. Paris: Éditions du Cerf, 1976.

Droge, J., and J. D. Tabor. *A Noble Death: Suicide and Martyrdom among Christians and Jews in Antiquity*. San Francisco: Harper, 1992.

Dunbabin, K. M. D. *Theater and Spectacle in the Art of the Roman Empire*. Ithaca: Cornell University Press, 2016.

Dupont, J. *The Sources of the Acts*. New York: Herder and Herder, 1964.

Earp, J. W. "Indices to Volumes I–X." In *Philo*, vol. 10, edited by F. H. Colson, 269–486. Cambridge: Harvard University Press, 1962.

Easterling, P. E. "Menander: Loss and Survival." In *Stage Directions. Essays in Ancient Drama in Honour of E. W. Handley*, edited by A. Griffiths, 153–60. London: University of London Institute of Classical Studies, 1995.

Easterling, P. E., and B. M. W. Knox, eds. *The Cambridge History of Classical Literature*. Vol. 1. Cambridge: Cambridge University Press, 1985.

Eddy, P. R., and G. A. Boyd. *The Jesus Legend: A Case for the Historical Reliability of the Synoptic Jesus Tradition*. Grand Rapids: Baker Academic, 2007.

Edmonds, J. M. *The Fragments of Attic Comedy after Meineke, Bergk, and Kock*. Vol. 3. Leiden: Brill, 1961.

Edwards, M. J. "Quoting Aratus: Acts 17:28." *Zeitschrift für die neutestamentliche Wissenschaft* 83 (1992): 266–9.

Ehrhardt, A. A. T. "Greek Proverbs in the Gospel." *Harvard Theological Review* 46 (1953): 59–77.

Ehrman, B. D., and M. A. Plunkett. "The Angel and the Agony: The Textual Problem of Luke 22:43-44." *Catholic Biblical Quarterly* 45 (1983): 401–41.

Eichhorn, J. G. *Einleitung in das Neue Testament*. Leipzig: Weidmann, 1810.

Elliott, S. S. "Witless in your Own Cause: Divine Plots and Fractured Characters in the *Life of Aesop* and the Gospel of Mark." *Religion & Theology* 12 (2005): 397–418.

Estienne, H. *Comicorum Graecorum Sententiae*. Geneva: Henricus Stephanus, 1569.

Evans, C. A. "Paul and the Pagans." In *Paul: Jew, Greek, and Roman*, edited by S. E. Porter, 117–39. Leiden: Brill, 2008.

Farnell, L. R. *The Cults of the Greek State*. Vol. 4. Oxford: Clarendon, 1907.

Farrar, F. W. *The Life and Work of St. Paul*. Vol. 1. New York: E. P. Dutton & Company, 1879.

Bibliography

Fascher, E. "Sokrates und Christus: Eine Studie 'zur aktuellen Aufgabe der Religionsphänomenologie' dem Andenken Heinrich Fricks." *Zeitschrift für die neutestamentliche Wissenschaft* 45 (1954): 1–41.

Feldman, L. H. *Josephus: Jewish Antiquities Book XX and General Index.* Cambridge: Harvard University Press, 1965.

Feldman, L. H. *Josephus's Interpretation of the Bible.* Berkeley: University of California Press, 1998.

Feldman, L. H. *Studies in Josephus' Rewritten Bible.* Leiden: Brill, 1998.

Fischel, H. A. *Rabbinic Literature and Greco-Roman Philosophy.* Leiden: Brill, 1973.

Fisher, B. F. *A History of the Use of Aesop's Fables as a School Text from the Classical Era through the Nineteenth Century.* Bloomington: Indiana University Dissertation, 1987.

Fitzmyer, J. A. *The Gospel According to Luke I–IX.* New York: Doubleday, 1981.

Fitzmyer, J. A. *The Semitic Background of the New Testament.* Grand Rapids: Eerdmans, 1997.

Flusser, D. "Aesop's Miser and the Parable of the Talents." In *Parable and Story in Judaism and Christianity,* edited by C. Thoma and M. Wychogrod, 9–25. Mahwah: Paulist Press, 1989.

Flusser, D. *Die rabbinischen Gleichnisse und der Gleichniserzähler Jesus.* Bern: Peter Lang, 1981.

Foakes Jackson, F. J., and K. Lake, eds. *The Beginnings of Christianity: The Acts of the Apostles Volumes 1–5.* London: Macmillan, 1920–1933.

Fraser, P. M. *Ptolemaic Alexandria.* Vols. 1–3. Oxford: Clarendon, 1972.

Frazer, J. G. *The Golden Bough: A Study in Comparative Religion.* Vol. 2. London: Macmillan, 1890.

Frazer, J. G. *The Golden Bough: A Study in Magic and Religion.* Vol. 3. 2nd ed. London: Macmillan, 1900.

Friedländer, L. *Darstellungen aus der Sittengeschichte Roms.* Vols. 1–2. 6th ed. Leipzig: S. Hirzel, 1888–1890.

Friesen, C. J. P. *Reading Dionysus: Euripides' Bacchae and the Cultural Contestations of Greeks, Jews, Romans, and Christians.* Tübingen: Mohr Siebeck, 2015.

Friesen, C. J. P. "Hannah's 'Hard Day' and Hesiod's 'Two Roads': Poetic Wisdom in Philo's De ebrietate." *Journal for the Study of Judaism* 46 (2015): 44–64.

Froelich, M., and T. E. Phillips. "Throw the Blasphemer off a Cliff: Luke 4:16-30 in Light of the *Life of Aesop.*" *New Testament Studies* 65 (2019): 21–32.

Galé, J. M. *Las escuelas del antiguo Egipto a través de los papiros griegos.* Madrid: Publicaciones de la Fundación Universitaria Española, 1961.

Gallo, I. *Frammenti Biografici da Papiri Volume 2.* Rome: Edizioni dell'Ateneo & Bizzarri, 1980.

Gathercole, S. J. *The Gospel of Thomas: Introduction and Commentary.* Leiden: Brill, 2014.

Gawlina, M. "Paulus und Plato: *prosopon gegen idea.*" *Theologie und Philosophie* 80 (2005): 17–30.

Gempf, C. "Public Speaking and Published Accounts." In *The Book of Acts in its Ancient Literary Setting,* edited by B. W. Winter and A. D. Clarke, 259–303. Grand Rapids: Eerdmans, 1993.

Gentili, B. *Theatrical Performances in the Ancient World: Hellenistic and Early Roman Theatre.* Amsterdam: Gieben, 1979.

Gibbs, L. *Aesop's Fables.* Oxford: Oxford University Press, 2002.

Gibson, C. A. *Libanius's Progymnasmata: Model Exercises in Greek Prose Composition and Rhetoric.* Atlanta: Society of Biblical Literature, 2008.

244   *Bibliography*

Gibson, M. D. *The Commentaries of Isho'dad of Merv: Volume IV: Acts of the Apostles and Three Catholic Epistles.* Cambridge: Cambridge University Press, 1913.

Gibson, M. D. *The Commentaries of Isho'dad of Merv: Volume V: The Epistles of Paul,* Cambridge: Cambridge University Press, 1916.

Girard, R. *Violence and the Sacred.* Baltimore: Johns Hopkins, 1977.

Girard, R. *The Scapegoat.* Baltimore: Johns Hopkins, 1986.

Girard, R. *Things Hidden Since the Foundation of the World.* London: Athlone Press, 1987.

Glockmann, G. *Homer in der frühchristlichen Literatur bis Justinus.* Berlin: Akademie Verlag, 1968.

Goldstein, J. A. *II Maccabees.* Garden City: Doubleday, 1983.

Goodenough, E. R. *Jewish Symbols in the Greco-Roman Periods.* Vols. 1–13. New York: Pantheon Books, 1953–1968.

Grammatiki, K. *Vita Aesopi: Überlieferung, Sprache und Edition einer frühbyzantinischen Fassung des Äsopromans.* Wiesbaden: Reichert, 2001.

Green, J. R. *Theatre in Ancient Greek Society.* London and New York: Routledge, 1994.

Grenfell, B. P., and A. S. Hunt. "Excavations at Oxyrhynchus." In *Archaeological Report of the Egypt Exploration Fund,* edited by F. Griffith, 8–16. London: Gilbert and Rivington, 1905–06.

Grenfell, B. P., and A. S. Hunt. *The Hibeh Papyri: Part I.* London: Egypt Exploration Society, 1906.

Gressmann, H. "Review of M. D. Gibson, *The Commentaries of Isho'dad of Merv.*" *Berliner Philologische Wochenschrift* 30 (1913): 935–9.

Gruen, E. S. "Jewish Perspectives on Greek Culture." In *Hellenism in the Land of Israel,* edited by J. J. Collins and G. E. Sterling, 62–93. Notre Dame: University of Notre Dame Press, 2001.

Guaglianone, A. *Phaedri Augusti Liberti Liber Fabularum.* Turin: Paravia, 1969.

Guéraud, O., and P. Jouguet. *Un livre d'écolier du IIIe siècle avant J.-C.* Cairo: Institut français d'Archéologie orientale, 1938.

Gutzwiller, K., and Ö. Çelik, "New Menander Mosaics from Antioch." *American Journal of Archaeology* 116 (2012): 573–623.

Hackett, J. "Echoes of Euripides in Acts of the Apostles?" *Irish Theological Quarterly* 23 (1956): 218–27.

Hackett, J. "Echoes of the *Bacchae* in the Acts of the Apostles." *Irish Theological Quarterly* 23 (1956): 350–66.

Hadas, M. *The Third and Fourth Books of Maccabees.* New York: Harper and Bros., 1953.

Haenchen, E. *The Acts of the Apostles.* Philadelphia: Westminster, 1971.

Halm, K. *Fabulae Aesopicae Collectae.* Leipzig: Teubner, 1852.

Hamerton-Kelly, R. G. *The Gospel and the Sacred: Poetics of Violence in Mark.* Minneapolis: Fortress, 1994.

Harnack, A. "Sokrates und die alte Kirche." *Reden und Aufsätze.* Vol. 1. Gieben: Töpelmann, 1903.

Harris, J. R. "The Cretans Always Liars." *The Expositor* 7, no. 2 (1906): 305–17.

Harris, J. R. "A Further Note on the Cretans." *The Expositor* 7, no. 3 (1907): 332–7.

Harris, J. R. "St. Paul and Epimenides." *The Expositor* 8, no. 4 (1912): 348–53.

Harris, J. R. "Once More the Cretans." *The Expositor* 8, no. 9 (1915): 29–35.

Harris, J. R. *St. Paul and Greek Literature.* Cambridge: W. Heffer & Sons, 1927.

Harris, W. V. *Ancient Literacy.* Cambridge: Harvard University Press, 1989.

Harrison, J. E. *Prolegomena to the Study of Greek Religion.* Cambridge: Cambridge University Press, 1903.

Bibliography 245

Hausrath, A. *Corpus Fabularum Aesopicarum*. Leipzig: Teubner, 1940.

Hays, R. B. *The Conversion of the Imagination: Paul as Interpreter of Israel's Scripture*. Grand Rapids: Eerdmans, 2005.

Hedrick, C. W. "Paul's Conversion/Call: A Comparative Analysis of the Three Reports in Acts." *Journal of Biblical Literature* 100 (1981): 415–32.

Heinemann, I. *Philons griechische und jüdische Bildung*. Breslau: Marcus, 1932.

Helmbold, W. C., and E. N. O'Neil. *Plutarch's Quotations*. Baltimore: American Philological Association, 1959.

Hemer, C. *The Book of Acts in the Setting of Hellenistic History*. Tübingen: Mohr Siebeck, 1989.

Hemer, C. "The Speeches of Acts: I. The Ephesian Elders at Miletus." *Tyndale Bulletin* 40 (1989): 77–85.

Hemer, C. "The Speeches in Acts: II. The Areopagus Address." *Tyndale Bulletin* 40 (1989): 239–59.

Hengel, M. *Judaism and Hellenism: Studies in their Encounter in Palestine during the Early Hellenistic Period Volume I*. Minneapolis: Fortress, 1974.

Hengel, M. *Jews, Greeks, and Barbarians: Aspects of Hellenization of Judaism in the Pre-Christian Period*. Philadelphia: Fortress, 1980.

Hengel, M. *Between Jesus and Paul*. London: SCM Press, 1983.

Hengel, M. *The Hellenization of Judaea in the First Century after Christ*. London: SCM Press, 1989.

Hense, O., and C. Wachsmuth. *Ioannis Stobaei anthologium*. Vol. 1. 1884. Reprint, Berlin: Weidmann, 1958.

Hepding, H. "Die Arbeiten zu Pergamon 1908–1909, II: Die Inschriften." *Mitteilungen des kaiserlich deutschen archäologischen Instituts, Athenische Abteilung* 35 (1910): 401–93.

Hervieux, L. *Les fabulistes latins depuis le siècle d'Auguste jusqu'à la fin du moyen âge*. Vol. 4. Paris: Firmin-Didot, 1896.

Hesseling, D. C. "On Waxen Tablets with Fables of Babrius (Tabulae Ceratae Assendelftianae)." *Journal of Hellenic Studies* 13 (1893): 293–314.

Hezser, C. *Jewish Literacy in Roman Palestine*. Tübingen: Mohr Siebeck, 2001.

Hicks, R. I. "The Body Political and the Body Ecclesiastical." *Journal of Bible and Religion* 31 (1963): 29–35.

Hock, R. F. "Homer in Greco-Roman Education." In *Mimesis and Intertextuality in Antiquity and Christianity*, edited by D. R. MacDonald, 56–77. Harrisburg, Trinity Press International, 2001.

Hock, R. F. "The Educational Curriculum in Chariton's *Callirhoe*." In *Ancient Fiction: The Matrix of Early Christian and Jewish Narrative*, edited by J-A. A. Brant, C. W. Hedrick, and C. Shea, 15–36. Atlanta: Society of Biblical Literature, 2005.

Hogeterp, A., and A. Denaux. *Semitisms in Luke's Greek: A Descriptive Analysis of Lexical and Syntactical Domains of Semitic Language Influence in Luke's Gospel*. Tübingen: Mohr Siebeck, 2018.

Holl, K. *Ancoratus und Panarion*. Vol. 2. Leipzig: Hinrichs, 1922.

Holzberg, N. *The Ancient Fable*. Bloomington: Indiana University Press, 2002.

Hommel, H. "Neue Forschungen zur Areopagrede Acta 17." *Zeitschrift für die neutestamentliche Wissenschaft* 46 (1955): 145–78.

Hommel, H. "Platonisches bei Lukas: Zu Act 17:28a (Leben-Bewegung-Sein)." *Zeitschrift für die neutestamentliche Wissenschaft* 48 (1957): 193–200.

Houston, G. "Grenfell, Hunt, Breccia, and the Book Collections of Oxyrhynchus." *Greek, Roman, and Byzantine Studies* 47 (2007): 327–59.

246 *Bibliography*

Houston, G. *Inside Roman Libraries: Book Collections and Their Management in Antiquity.* Chapel Hill: University of North Carolina Press, 2014.

How, W. W., and J. Wells. *A Commentary on Herodotus.* Oxford: Clarendon, 1912.

Howell, E. B. "St. Paul and the Greek World." *Greece & Rome* 11 (1964): 7–29.

Hughes, D. D. *Human Sacrifice in Ancient Greece.* London: Routledge, 1991.

Humphrey, J. H. "'Amphitheatrical' Hippo-Stadia." In *Caesarea Maritima—Retrospective after Two Millennia,* edited by A. Raban and K. G. Holum, 121–9. Leiden: Brill, 1996.

Huskinson, J. "Theatre, Performance and Theatricality in Some Mosaic Pavements from Antioch." *Bulletin of the Institute of Classical Studies* 46 (2002): 131–65.

Jacobs, J. C. *The Fables of Odo of Cheriton.* Syracuse: Syracuse University Press, 1985.

Jacquier, E. *Les Actes des apôtres.* Paris: J. Gabalda, 1926.

Jay, J. "The Problem of the Theater in Early Judaism." *Journal for the Study of Judaism in the Persian, Hellenistic, and Roman Periods* 44 (2013): 218–53.

Jenkins, C. "Documents: Origen on I Corinthians. III." *The Journal of Theological Studies* 9 (1908): 500–514.

Jeremias, J. *New Testament Theology.* New York: Charles Scribner's Sons, 1971.

Jervell, J. *Luke and the People of God: A New Look at Luke-Acts.* Minneapolis: Augsburg, 1984.

Jipp, J. W. "Educating the Divided Soul in Paul and Plato: Reading Romans 7:7–25 and Plato's *Republic.*" In *Paul: Jew, Greek, and Roman,* edited by S. E. Porter, 231–57. Leiden: Brill, 2008.

Jipp, J. W. "Paul's Areopagus Speech of Acts 17:16-34 as *Both* Critique *and* Propaganda." *Journal of Biblical Literature* 131 (2012): 567–88.

Johnson, L. T. *The Acts of the Apostles.* Collegeville, Minnesota: Liturgical Press, 1992.

Johnson, L. T. "Review of *Does the New Testament Imitate Homer? Four Cases from the Acts of the Apostles.*" *Christianity and Literature* 54, no. 2 (2005): 285–7.

Jones, C. P. "Greek Drama in the Roman Empire." In *Theater and Society in the Classical World,* edited by R. Scodel, 39–52. Ann Arbor: University of Michigan Press, 1993.

Jouguet, P., and P. Perdrizet. "Le Papyrus Bouriant no. 1: Un cahier d'écolier grec d'Egypte." *Studien zur Palaeographie und Papyruskunde* 6 (1906): 148–61.

Jülicher, A. *Die Gleichnisreden Jesu.* Vol. 1. 2nd ed. Tübingen: Mohr Siebeck, 1899.

Kaibel, G. "Aufführungen in Rhodos." *Hermes* 23 (1888): 268–78.

Kamerbeek, J. C. "On the Conception of ΘΕΟΜΑΧΟΣ in Relation with Greek Tragedy." *Mnemosyne* 1 (1948): 271–83.

Kasher, A. *Jews and Hellenistic Cities in Eretz Israel.* Tübingen: Mohr Siebeck, 1990.

Kaster, R. A. "Notes on 'Primary' and 'Secondary' Schools in Late Antiquity." *Transactions of the American Philological Association* 113 (1983): 323–46.

Kauppi, L. A. *Foreign but Familiar Gods: Greco-Romans Read Religion in Acts.* London: T&T Clark, 2006.

Keener, C. S. "'Fleshly' versus Spirit Perspectives in Romans 8:5-8." In *Paul: Jew, Greek, and Roman,* edited by S. E. Porter, 211–29. Leiden: Brill, 2008.

Keener, C. S. *Acts: An Exegetical Commentary Volumes 1–4.* Grand Rapids: Baker Academic, 2012–2015.

Kellenberger, E. "Once Again: the Fable of Jotham (Judg 9) and Aesop." *Semitica* 60 (2018): 131–7.

Kennedy, G. A. *New Testament Interpretation through Rhetorical Criticism.* Chapel Hill: University of North Carolina Press, 1984.

Kennedy, G. A. *Progymnasmata: Greek Textbook of Prose Composition and Rhetoric.* Atlanta: Society of Biblical Literature, 2003.

Kenyon, F. G. "Two Greek School-Tablets." *Journal of Hellenic Studies* 29 (1909): 29–40.

Kidd, D. *Aratus: Phaenomena*. Cambridge: Cambridge University Press, 1997.

Kindstrand, J. F. *Homer in der Zweiten Sophistik. Studien zu der Homerlektüre und dem Homerbild bei Dion von Prusa, Maximos von Tyros und Ailios Aristeides.* Uppsala: Almqvist & Wiksell, 1973.

Klauck, H.-J. *Ancient Letters and the New Testament: A Guide to Context and Exegesis.* Waco: Baylor University Press, 2006.

Kleberg, T. "Commercio librario ed editoria nel mondo antico." In *Libri, editori e pubblico nel mondo antico: guida storica e critica*, 3rd ed., edited by G. Cavallo, 27–80. Bari: Laterza, 1984.

Klinghardt, M. *Das lukanische Verstandnis des Gesetzes nach Herkunft, Funktion und seinem Ort in der Geschichte der Urchristentums.* Tübingen: Mohr Siebeck, 1988.

Kloppenborg, J. S. "'Exitus clari viri': The Death of Jesus in Luke." *Toronto Journal of Theology* 8 (1992): 106–20.

Knopf, R. *Paulus.* Leipzig: Quelle & Meyer, 1909.

Knopf, R. "Paul and Hellenism." *American Journal of Theology* 18 (1914): 497–520.

Kock, T. *Comicorum Atticorum Fragmenta.* Vol. 3. Leipzig: Teubner, 1888.

Kokolakis, M. "Zeus' Tomb. An Object of Pride and Reproach." *Kernos: Revue Internationale et Pluridisciplinaire de Religion Grecque Antique* 8 (1995): 123–38.

Königsmann, B. L. "*De fontibus commentariorum sacrorum, qui Lucae nomen praeferunt deque eorum consilio et aetate.*" In *Sylloge Commentationum Theologicarum*, vol. 3, edited by D. J. Pott, 215–39. Helmstadt: Fleckeisen, [1798] 1802.

Koskenniemi, E. "Philo and Classical Drama." In *Ancient Israel, Judaism and Christianity in Contemporary Perspective: Essays in Memory of Karl-Johan Illman*, edited by J. Neusner et al., 137–52. Lanham: University Press of America, 2006.

Koskenniemi, E. "Philo and Greek Poets." *Journal for the Study of Judaism* 41 (2010): 301–22.

Koskenniemi, E. "Philo and Classical Education." In *Reading Philo: A Handbook to Philo of Alexandria*, edited by T. Seland, 93–113. Grand Rapids: Eerdmans, 2014.

Koskenniemi, E. *Greek Writers and Philosophers in Philo and Josephus: A Study of their Secular Education and Educational Ideals.* Leiden: Brill, 2019.

Kramer, J. *Glossaria Bilinguia in Papyris et Membranis Reperta (C. Gloss. Biling. I).* Bonn: R. Habelt, 1983.

Kramer, J. *Glossaria Bilinguia Altera (C. Gloss. Biling. II).* Munich: K. G. Saur, 2001.

Kratz, R. *Rettungswunder: Motiv-, traditions- und formkritische Aufarbeitung einer biblischen Gattung.* Frankfurt: Lang, 1979.

Krenkel, M. *Josephus und Lucas: Der schriftstellerische Einfluss des jüdischen Geschichtschreibers auf den christlichen nachgewiesen.* Leipzig: H. Haessel, 1894.

Krüger, J. *Oxyrhynchos in der Kaiserzeit: Studien zur Topographie und Literaturrezeption.* Frankfurt: Peter Lang, 1990.

Lagrange, M.-J. *Saint Paul Épître aux Galates.* Paris: J. Gabalda, 1918.

Lagrange, M.-J. *Évangile selon Saint Luc.* Paris: J. Gabalda, 1921.

Larsson, K. "Intertextual Density, Quantifying Imitation." *Journal of Biblical Literature* 133 (2014): 309–31.

Lauxtermann, M. D. *The Spring of Rhythm. An Essay on the Political Verse and Other Byzantine Metres.* Vienna: Österreichische Akademie der Wissenschaften, 1999.

Lawlor, H. J. "St. Paul's Quotations from Epimenides." *Irish Church Quarterly* 9, no. 35 (1916): 180–93.

Lenaerts, J., and P. Mertens. "Les papyrus d'Isocrate." *Chronique d'Égypte* 64 (1989): 216–30.

248 *Bibliography*

Leonardi, G. "*Comunità Destinatarie dell' Opera di Luca e Identità dell' Autore.*" In *San Luca evangelista testimone della fede che unisce. Atti del Congresso internazionale, Padova, 16–21 ottobre 2000*, vol. 1, edited by G. Leonardi and F. G. B. Trolese, 187–215. Padua: Istituto per la storia ecclesiastica Padovana, 2002.

Levi, D. *Antioch Mosaic Pavements Volumes 1 and 2.* Princeton: Princeton University Press, 1947.

Leyerle, B. *Theatrical Shows and Ascetic Lives: John Chrysostom's Attack on Spiritual Marriage.* Berkeley: University of California Press, 2001.

Lichtenberger, A. "Jesus and the Theater in Jerusalem." In *Jesus and Archaeology*, edited by J. H. Charlesworth, 283–99. Grand Rapids: Eerdmans, 2006.

Lieberman, S. *Greek in Jewish Palestine.* New York: Jewish Theological Seminary, 1942.

Lieberman, S. *Greek in Jewish Palestine.* 2nd ed. New York: Jewish Theological Seminary, 1962.

Lieberman, S. *Hellenism in Jewish Palestine.* New York: Jewish Theological Seminary, 1962.

Lightfoot, J. B. *St. Paul's Epistle to the Galatians.* London: Macmillan, 1865.

Lightfoot, J. B. *Biblical Essays.* London: Macmillan, 1893.

Lincicum, D. "A Preliminary Index to Philo's Non-Biblical Citations and Allusions." *The Studia Philonica Annual* 25 (2013): 139–67.

Lincicum, D. "Philo's Library." *The Studia Philonica Annual* 26 (2014): 99–114.

Ling, P. H. "A Quotation from Euripides." *The Classical Quarterly* 19 (1925): 22–7.

Luz, U. *Matthew 8–20: A Commentary.* Minneapolis: Augsburg Fortress, 2001.

Luzzatto, M. J., and A. La Penna. *Babrii Mythiambi Aesopei.* Leipzig: Teubner, 1986.

Maas, P. "Der byzantinische Zwölfsilber." *Byzantinische Zeitschrift* 12 (1903): 278–323.

Maccoby, H. *Paul and Hellenism.* London: SCM Press, 1991.

MacDonald, D. R. "Luke's Eutychus and Homer's Elpenor: Acts 20:7-12 and *Odyssey* 10–12." *Journal of Higher Criticism* 1 (1994): 5–24.

MacDonald, D. R. "Secrecy and Recognitions in the *Odyssey* and Mark: Where Wrede Went Wrong." In *Ancient Fiction and Early Christian Narrative*, edited by R. F. Hock, J. B. Chance, and J. Perkins, 139–53. Atlanta: Scholars Press, 1998.

MacDonald, D. R. "The Shipwrecks of Odysseus and Paul." *New Testament Studies* 45 (1999): 88–107.

MacDonald, D. R. "The Soporific Angel in Acts 12:1-17 and Hermes' Visit to Priam in *Iliad* 24: Luke's Emulation of the Epic." *Forum* 2, no. 2 (1999): 179–87.

MacDonald, D. R. "The Ending of Luke and the Ending of the *Odyssey*." In *For a Later Generation: The Transformation of Tradition in Israel, Early Judaism and Early Christianity*, edited by R. A. Argall, B. A. Bow, and R. A. Werline, 161–8. Harrisburg: Trinity Press International, 2000.

MacDonald, D. R. *The Homeric Epics and the Gospel of Mark.* New Haven: Yale University Press, 2000.

MacDonald, D. R. "Renowned Far and Wide: The Women Who Anointed Odysseus and Jesus." In *A Feminist Companion to Mark*, edited by A. J. Levine and M. Blickenstaff, 128–35. Sheffield: Sheffield Academic Press, 2001.

MacDonald, D. R. *Does the New Testament Imitate Homer? Four Cases from the Acts of the Apostles.* New Haven: Yale University Press, 2003.

MacDonald, D. R. "Paul's Farewell to the Ephesian Elders and Hector's Farewell to Andromache: A Strategic Imitation of Homer's *Iliad*." In *Contextualizing Acts: Lukan Narrative and Greco-Roman Discourse*, edited by T. Penner and C. V. Stichele, 189–203. Atlanta: Society of Biblical Literature, 2003.

Bibliography 249

MacDonald, D. R. "The Breasts of Hecuba and those of the Daughters of Jerusalem: Luke's Transvaluation of a famous Iliadic Scene." In *Ancient Fiction: The Matrix of Early Christian and Jewish Narrative*, edited by J.-A. A. Brant, C. W. Hedrick, and C. Shea, 239–54. Atlanta: Society of Biblical Literature, 2005.

MacDonald, D. R. "Imitations of Greek Epic in the Gospels." In *The Historical Jesus in Context*, edited by A-J. Levine, D. C. Allison, and J. D. Crossan, 372–84. Princeton: Princeton University Press, 2006.

MacDonald, D. R. *The Gospels and Homer: Imitations of Greek Epic in Mark and Luke-Acts.* Lanham: Rowman & Littlefield, 2015.

MacDonald, D. R. *Luke and Vergil: Imitations of Classical Greek Literature.* Lanham: Rowman & Littlefield, 2015.

MacDonald, D. R. *Luke and the Politics of Homeric Imitation: Luke-Acts as Rival to the Aeneid.* Lanham: Lexington Books/Fortress Academic, 2019.

Maehler, M. "Der 'wertlose' Aratkodex P. Berol. Inv. 5865." *Archiv für Papyrusforschung und verwandte Begiete* 27 (1980): 19–32.

Malherbe, A. J. *Social Aspects of Early Christianity.* 2nd ed. Philadelphia: Fortress, 1983.

Maltomini, F., and C. Römer. "Noch einmal 'Ad Demonicum' auf einer Schultafel." *Zeitschrift für Papyrologie und Epigraphik* 75 (1988): 297–300.

Marcotte, D., and P. Mertens. "Les papyrus de Callimaque." *Papyrologica Florentina* 19 (1990): 409–27.

Marcotte, D., and P. Mertens. "Catalogue des Femmes et Grandes Éoées d' Hésiode." In *Storia, poesia e pensiero nel mondo antico: studi in onore di Marcello Gigante*, edited by F. del Franco, 407–23. Naples, Bibliopolis, 1994.

Marguerat, D. *Les Actes des Apôtres (1–12).* Genève: Labor et Fides, 2007.

Margulies, Z. "Aesop and Jotham's Parable of the Trees (Judges 9:8-15)." *Vetus Testamentum* 69 (2019): 81–94.

Marin, V. T. W., and F. G. B. Trolese, eds., *San Luca evangelista testimone della fede che unisce. Atti del Congresso internazionale, Padova, 16–21 ottobre 2000 Volume 2.* Padua: Istituto per la storia ecclesiastica Padovana, 2003.

Marrou, H.-I. *Histoire de l'éducation dans l'antiquité.* Paris: Éditions du Seuil, 1948.

Marrou, H.-I. *A History of Education in Antiquity.* London and New York: Sheed and Ward, 1956.

Marshall, C. W. "*Alcestis* and the Ancient Rehearsal Process (*P.Oxy.* 4546)." *Arion* 11, no. 3 (2004): 27–45.

Martin, M. W. "Progymnastic Topic Lists: A Compositional Template for Luke and other Bioi?" *New Testament Studies* 54 (2008): 18–41.

Marx, F. A. "Tacitus und die Literatur der Exitus Illustrium Virorum." *Philologus* 92 (1937): 83–103.

Mason, S. *Josephus and the New Testament.* Peabody: Hendrickson, 1992.

Matějka, J. "La donazione del capo di San Luca all'Imperatore Carlo IV di Lussemburgo nel 1354." In *San Luca evangelista testimone della fede che unisce. Atti del Congresso internazionale, Padova, 16–21 ottobre 2000*, vol. 3, edited by F. G. B. Trolese, 331–51. Padua: Istituto per la storia ecclesiastica Padovana, 2004.

Mattill, A. J., Jr. "The Jesus-Paul Parallels and the Purpose of Luke-Acts: H. H. Evans Reconsidered." *Novum Testamentum* 17 (1975): 15–46.

McMahan, C. T. "More than Meets the 'I': Recognition Scenes in *The Odyssey* and Luke 24." *Perspectives in Religious Studies* 35 (2008): 87–107.

250   *Bibliography*

McVay, J. K. "The Human Body as Social and Political Metaphor in Stoic Literature and Early Christian Writers." *Bulletin of the American Society of Papyrologists* 37 (2000): 135–47.

Mendelson, A. *Secular Education in Philo of Alexandria.* Cincinnati: Hebrew Union College Press, 1982.

Mertens, P. "Vingt années de papyrologie odysséenne." *Chronique d'Égypte* 60 (1985): 191–203.

Mertens, P. "Les témoins papyrologiques de Ménandre: Essai de classement rationnel et esquisse d' étude bibliologique." In *Serta Leodiensia secunda: mélanges publiés par les Classiques de Liège à l'occasion du 175 anniversaire de l'université,* edited by A. Bodson, P. Wathelet, and M. Dubuisson, 331–56. Liège: Université de Liège, 1992.

Mertens, P., and J. A. Straus. "Les papyrus d'Hérodote." *Annali della Scuola Normale Superiore di Pisa, Classe di Lettere e Filosofia* 3, no. 22 (1992): 969–78.

Mertens, P. "Les papyrus d'Aristophane. Actualisation des données bibliologiques et bibliographiques." In *Hodoi Dizesios: studi in onore di Francesco Adorno,* edited by M. S. Funghi, 335–43. Firenze: Olschki, 1996.

Metzger, B. M. *A Textual Commentary on the Greek New Testament.* 2nd ed. Stuttgart: Deutsche Bibelgesellschaft, 1994.

Meyer, R. *Hellenistisches in der rabbinischen Anthropologie.* Stuttgart: W. Kohlhammer, 1937.

Millis, B. W., and S. D. Olson. *Inscriptional Records for the Dramatic Festivals in Athens.* Leiden: Brill, 2012.

Milne, H. J. M., D. Cockerell, and T. C. Skeat. *Scribes and Correctors of the Codex Sinaiticus.* London: British Museum, 1938.

Milne, J. G. "Relics of Graeco-Egyptian Schools." *Journal of Hellenic Studies* 28 (1908): 121–32.

Milne, J. G. "More Relics of Graeco-Egyptian Schools." *Journal of Hellenic Studies* 43 (1923): 40–3.

Milnor, K. "Literary Literacy in Roman Pompeii: the Case of Vergil's *Aeneid.*" In *Ancient Literacies: The Culture of Reading in Greece and Rome,* edited by W. A. Johnson and H. N. Parker, 288–319. Oxford: Oxford University Press, 2009.

Minn, H. R. "Classical Reminiscence in St. Paul." *Prudentia* 6 (1974): 93–8.

Mitchell, M. M. "Homer in the New Testament." *Journal of Religion* 83 (2003): 244–60.

Mitchell, M. M. *Paul and the Rhetoric of Reconciliation.* Louisville: Westminster/John Knox Press, 1992.

Mitchell, S. "Festivals, Games, and Civic Life in Roman Asia Minor." *Journal of Roman Studies* 80 (1990): 183–93.

Moessner, D. P. "'The Christ Must Suffer': New Light on the Jesus, Stephen, Paul Parallels in Luke-Acts." *Novum Testamentum* 28 (1986): 220–56.

Moles, J. L. "Jesus and Dionysus in *The Acts of the Apostles* and Early Christianity." *Hermathena* 180 (2006): 65–104.

Moles, J. L. "Jesus the Healer in the Gospels, the *Acts of the Apostles,* and Early Christianity." *Histos* 5 (2011): 117–82.

Molin, G., G. Salviulo, and P. Guerriero, "Indagini sulle reliquie attribuite a 'San Luca Evangelista,' Basilica di Santa Giustina in Padova: Studi cristallochimici, isotopici e datazione mediante ^{14}C dei reperti ossei." In *San Luca evangelista testimone della fede che unisce. Atti del Congresso internazionale, Padova, 16–21 ottobre 2000,* edited by V. T. W. Marin and F. G. B. Trolese, 2:173–99. Padua: Istituto per la storia ecclesiastica Padovana, 2003.

Molinié, G. *Chariton: Le roman de Chairéas et Callirhoë*. Paris: Budé, 1979.

Morgan, T. *Literate Education in the Hellenistic and Roman Worlds*. Cambridge: Cambridge University Press, 1998.

Moulton, J. H., and W. F. Howard, *A Grammar of New Testament Greek*. Vol. 2. Edinburgh: T&T Clark, 1929.

Murray, G. *The Rise of the Greek Epic*. Oxford: Clarendon, 1907.

Musurillo, H. A. *The Acts of the Pagan Martyrs: Acta Alexandrinorum*. Oxford: Oxford University Press, 1954.

Nervegna, S. "Staging Scenes or Plays? Theatrical Revivals of 'Old' Greek Drama in Antiquity." *Zeitschrift für Papyrologie und Epigraphik* 162 (2007): 14–42.

Nervegna, S. "Menander's *Theophoroumene* between Greece and Rome." *American Journal of Philology* 131 (2010): 23–68.

Nervegna, S. *Menander in Antiquity: The Contexts of Reception*. Cambridge: Cambridge University Press, 2013.

Nestle, W. "Anklänge an Euripides in der Apostelgeschichte." *Philologus* 59 (1900): 46–57.

Neyrey, J. H. "The Absence of Jesus' Emotions—the Lucan Redaction of Lk 22:39-46." *Biblica* 61 (1980): 153–71.

Neyrey, J. H. *The Passion According to Luke: A Redaction Study of Luke's Soteriology*. New York: Paulist, 1985.

Nicklin, T. "Epimenides' *Minos*." *Classical Review* 30 (1916): 33–7.

Norden, E. *Die antike Kunstprosa vom VI. Jahrhundert v. Chr. bis in die Zeit der Renaissance*. Vol. 2. Leipzig: Teubner, 1898.

Norden, E. *Agnostos Theos: Untersuchungen zur Formengeschichte religiöser Rede*. Leipzig: Teubner, 1913.

Otranto, R. *Antiche liste di libri su papiro*. Rome: Edizioni di Storia e Letteratura, 2000.

Pack, R. A. *The Greek and Latin Literary Texts from Greco-Roman Egypt*. Ann Arbor: University of Michigan Press, 1952.

Pack, R. A. *The Greek and Latin Literary Texts from Greco-Roman Egypt*. 2nd ed. Ann Arbor: University of Michigan Press, 1965.

Papathomopoulos, M., ed. Ὁ βίος τοῦ Αἰσώπου: ἡ παραλλαγή W: *Editio Princeps*. Athens: Papadimas, 1999.

Parker R. *Miasma: Pollution and Purification in Early Greek Religion*. Oxford Clarendon, 1983.

Parsons, M. C. "Luke and the *Progymnasmata*: A Preliminary Investigation into the Preliminary Exercises." In *Contextualizing Acts: Lukan Narrative and Greco-Roman Discourse*, edited by T. Penner and C. Vander Stichele, 43–63. Atlanta: Society of Biblical Literature, 2003.

Parsons, M. C., and R. I. Pervo. *Rethinking the Unity of Luke and Acts*. Minneapolis: Fortress, 1993.

Parsons, P. J. "A School-Book from the Sayce Collection." *Zeitschrift für Papyrologie und Epigraphik* 6 (1970): 133–49.

Patrich, J. "Herod's Theatre in Jerusalem: A New Proposal." *Israel Exploration Journal* 53 (2002): 231–9.

Perry, B. E. *Aesopica*. Urbana: University of Illinois Press, 1952.

Perry, B. E. "Demetrius of Phalerum and the Aesopic Fables." *Transactions and Proceedings of the American Philological Association* 93 (1962): 287–346.

Perry, B. E. *Babrius and Phaedrus*. Cambridge: Harvard University Press, 1965.

Pervo, R. I. *Profit with Delight: The Literary Genre of the Acts of the Apostles*. Philadelphia: Fortress, 1987.

252   *Bibliography*

Pervo, R. I. "A Nihilist Fabula: Introducing the *Life of Aesop*." In *Ancient Fiction and Early Christian Narrative*, edited by R. F. Hock, J. B. Chance, and J. Perkins, 77–120. Atlanta: Scholars Press, 1998.

Pervo, R. I. *Dating Acts: Between the Evangelists and the Apologists*. Santa Rosa: Polebridge Press, 2006.

Pervo, R. I. *Acts: A Commentary*. Minneapolis: Fortress, 2009.

Pesch, R. *Die Apostelgeschichte II*. Zurich: Benziger, 1986.

Peterson, W. M. *Fabi Quintiliani Institutionis Oratoriae Liber Decimus*. Oxford: Clarendon, 1891.

Pfättisch, J. M. "Christus und Sokrates bei Justin." *Theologische Quartalschrift* 90 (1908): 503–23.

Pfeiffer, R. *Callimachus*. Vol. 2, Oxford: Clarendon, 1953.

Pfeiffer, R. *History of Classical Scholarship from the Beginnings to the End of the Hellenistic Age*. Oxford: Clarendon, 1968.

Plepelits, K. *Chariton von Aphrodisias: Kallirhoe*. Stuttgart: Hiersemann, 1976.

Plümacher, E. *Lukas als hellenistischer Schriftsteller: Studien zur Apostelgeschichte*. Göttingen: Vandenhoeck & Ruprecht, 1972.

Plümacher, E. "Die Missionsreden der Apostelgeschichte und Dionys von Halikarnass." *New Testament Studies* 39 (1993): 161–77.

Pohlenz, M. "Paulus und die Stoa." *Zeitschrift für die neutestamentliche Wissenschaft* 42 (1949): 69–104.

Porath, Y. "Why Did Josephus Name the Chariot-Racing Facility at Caesarea 'Amphitheatre'?" *Scripta Classica Israelica* 24 (2004): 63–7.

Porter, S. E. "The 'We' Passages." In *The Book of Acts in its Graeco-Roman Setting*, edited by D. W. J. Gill and C. Gempf, 545–74. Grand Rapids: Eerdmans, 1994.

Postlethwaite, N. "The Death of Zeus Kretagenes." *Kernos: Revue Internationale et Pluridisciplinaire de Religion Grecque Antique* 12 (1999): 85–98.

Powell, J. U. *Collectanea Alexandrina*. Oxford: Clarendon, [1925] 1970.

Praeder, S. M. "Acts 27:1–28:16: Sea Voyages in Ancient Literature and the Theology of Luke-Acts." *Catholic Biblical Quarterly* 46 (1984): 683–706.

Priest, J. F. "The Dog in the Manger: In Quest of a Fable." *Classical Journal* 81 (1985): 49–58.

Pruneti, P. "L'*Ad Demonicum* nella scuola antica: esempi di utilizzazione." In *Munus Amicitiae: Scritti in memoria di Alessandro Ronconi*, edited by G. Pasquali, 211–19. Firenze: Le Monnier, 1986.

Ramsay, W. M. "A Cretan Prophet." *Quarterly Review* 231, no. 459 (1919): 378–95.

Rank, L. P. *Etymologiseering en verwante verschijnselen bij Homerus*. Assen: van Gorcum, 1951.

Reardon, B. P. "Chariton." In *The Novel in the Ancient World*, edited by G. Schmeling, 309–35. Leiden: Brill, 1996.

Reece, S. *The Stranger's Welcome: Oral Theory and the Aesthetics of the Homeric Hospitality Scene*. Ann Arbor: University of Michigan Press, 1993.

Reece, S. "Homer's *Iliad* and *Odyssey*: From Oral Performance to Written Text." In *New Directions in Oral Theory*, edited by M. Amodio, 43–89. Tempe: Center for Medieval and Renaissance Studies, 2005.

Reece, S. *Homer's Winged Words: The Evolution of Early Greek Epic Diction in the Light of Oral Theory*. Leiden: Brill, 2009.

Reece, S. "Aesop, Q, and Luke." *New Testament Studies* 62 (2016): 357–77.

Reece, S. "Jesus as Healer: Etymologizing of Proper Names in Luke-Acts." *Zeitschrift für die neutestamentliche Wissenschaft* 110 (2019): 186–201.

Bibliography 253

Reece, S. "Passover as 'Passion': A Folk Etymology in Luke 22:15." *Biblica* 100 (2019): 601–10.

Reece, S. "Echoes of Plato's *Apology of Socrates* in Luke-Acts." *Novum Testamentum* 63 (2021): 177–97.

Reich, R., and Y. Billig. "A Group of Theater Seats Discovered Near the South-Western Corner of the Temple Mount." *Israel Exploration Journal* 50 (2000): 175–84.

Reis, D. M. "The Areopagus as Echo Chamber: *Mimesis* and Intertextuality in Acts." *Journal of Higher Criticism* 9 (2002): 259–77.

Reitzenstein, R. *Die hellenistischen Mysterienreligionen: Ihre Grundgedanken und Wirkungen.* Leipzig: Teubner, 1910.

Renan, E. *Saint Paul.* Paris: Michel Lévy Frères, 1869.

Renehan, R. "The Collectanea Alexandrina Selected Passages." *Harvard Studies in Classical Philology* 68 (1964): 375–88.

Renehan, R. "Classical Greek Quotations in the New Testament." In *The Heritage of the Early Church: Essays in Honor of Georges Vasilievich Florovsky on the Occasion of his Eightieth Birthday,* edited by D. Neiman and M. Schatkin, 17–45. Rome: Pontificium Institutum Studiorum Orientalium, 1973.

Renehan, R. "Acts 17:28." *Greek, Roman, and Byzantine Studies* (1979): 347–53.

Rigato, M. L. "Luca originario giudeo, forse di stirpe levitica, seguace dei 'testimoni oculari' (Lc 1.2–3)." In *San Luca evangelista testimone della fede che unisce. Atti del Congresso internazionale, Padova, 16–21 ottobre 2000,* vol. 1, edited by G. Leonardi and F. G. B. Trolese, 391–422. Padua: Istituto per la storia ecclesiastica Padovana, 2002.

Robbins, V. K. "By Land and By Sea: The We-Passages and Ancient Sea Voyages." In *Perspectives on Luke-Acts,* edited by C. H. Talbert, 215–42. Edinburgh: T&T Clark, 1978.

Robbins, V. K. "The Social Location of the Implied Author of Luke-Acts." In *The Social World of Luke-Acts,* edited by J. Neyrey, 305–32. Peabody: Hendrickson, 1991.

Rochette, B. *Le Latin dans le Monde Grec: Recherches sur la Diffusion de la Langue et des Lettres Latines dans les Provinces Hellénophones de l'Empire Romain.* Brussels: Latomus, 1997.

Roetzel, C. J. "Paul and the Law: Whence and Whither?" *Currents in Research: Biblical Studies* 3 (1995): 249–75.

Ronconi, A. "Exitus Illustrium Virorum." In *Reallexikon fur Antike und Christentum,* vol. 6, edited by T. Klauser, 1258–68. Stuttgart: Hiersemann, 1966.

Ross, W. "Ὦ ἀνόητοι καὶ βραδεῖς τῇ καρδίᾳ': Luke, Aesop, and Reading Scripture." *Novum Testamentum* 58 (2016): 369–79.

Rothschild, C. K. *Paul in Athens: The Popular Religious Context of Acts 17.* Tübingen: Mohr Siebeck, 2014.

Runia, D. T. *Philo of Alexandria and the* Timaeus *of Plato.* Leiden: Brill, 1986.

Runia, D. T. "Philo and the Early Christian Fathers." In *The Cambridge Companion to Philo,* edited by A. Kamesar, 210–30. Cambridge: Cambridge University Press, 2009.

Rusam, D. *Das Alte Testament bei Lukas.* Berlin: Walter de Gruyter, 2003.

Rydbeck, L. *Fachprosa, vermeintliche Volkssprache und Neues Testament.* Stockholm: Almquist & Wiksell, 1967.

Sala, B. "I resti di microvertebrati della tomba di San Luca Evangelista." In *San Luca evangelista testimone della fede che unisce. Atti del Congresso internazionale, Padova, 16–21 ottobre 2000,* vol. 2, edited by V. T. W. Marin and F. G. B. Trolese, 373–88. Padua: Istituto per la storia ecclesiastica Padovana, 2003.

Salomone, S. "Esopo 'Capro espiatorio.'" In *Il Capro espiatorio: Mito, Religione, Storia,* edited by S. Isetta, 49–64. Genova: Tilgher, 2007.

254   Bibliography

Sanders, E. P. *Paul and Palestinian Judaism: A Comparison of Patterns of Religion.* Philadelphia: Fortress, 1977.

Sandnes, K. O. "Paul and Socrates: The Aim of Paul's Areopagus Speech." *Journal for the Study of the New Testament* 50 (1993): 13–26.

Sandnes, K. O. "Imitatio Homeri? An Appraisal of Dennis R. MacDonald's 'Mimesis Criticism.'" *Journal of Biblical Literature* 124 (2005): 715–32.

Sandnes, K. O. *The Challenge of Homer: School, Pagan Poets and Early Christianity.* London: Bloomsbury T&T Clark, 2009.

Sandys, J. E. *History of Classical Scholarship: From the Sixth Century B.C. to the End of the Middle Ages.* Cambridge: Cambridge University Press, 1903.

Saudelli, L. *Eraclito ad Alessandria: studi e ricerche intorno alla testimonianza di Filone.* Turnhout: Brepols, 2012.

Scaer, P. J. *The Lukan Passion and the Praiseworthy Death.* Sheffield: Sheffield Phoenix Press, 2005.

Scappaticcio, M. C. *Papyri Vergilianae: l'apporto della Papirologia alla Storia della Tradizionee virgiliana (I-VI d.C.). Papyrologica Leodiensia, 1.* Liège: Presses Universitaires de Liège, 2013.

Schierling, M. J., and S. Schierling. "The Influence of the Ancient Romances on the Acts of the Apostles." *The Classical Bulletin* 54 (1978): 81–8.

Schlier, H. *Der Brief an die Galater.* 10th ed. Göttingen: Vandenhoeck & Ruprecht, 1949.

Schmid, L. "κέντρον." In *Theological Dictionary of the New Testament*, vol. 3, edited by G. Kittel and G. Friedrich, 663–8. Grand Rapids: Eerdmans, 1966.

Schnabel, E. J. "Contextualising Paul in Athens: The Proclamation of the Gospel Before Pagan Audiences in the Graeco-Roman World." *Religion and Theology* 2 (2005): 172–90.

Schneider, F. E. *Mark Challenges the Aeneid.* Eugene: Wipf & Stock, 2019.

Schnelle, U., M. Labahn, and M. Lang, eds. *Neuer Wettstein: Texte zum Neuen Testament aus Griechentum und Hellenismus (I/2: Texte zum Johannesevangelium).* Berlin: Walter de Gruyter, 2001.

Schnelle, U., M. Lang, and M. Labahn, eds. *Neuer Wettstein: Texte zum Neuen Testament aus Griechentum und Hellenismus (I/1.1: Texte zum Markusevangelium).* Berlin: Walter de Gruyter, 2008.

Schnelle, U., and M. Lang, eds. *Neuer Wettstein: Texte zum Neuen Testament aus Griechentum und Hellenismus (I/1.2 (1): Texte zum Matthäusevangelium: Matthäus 1–10).* Berlin: Walter de Gruyter, 2013.

Scholten, J. H. *Das Paulinische Evangelium: kritische Untersuchung des Evangeliums nach Lucas und seines Verhältnisses zu Marcus, Matthäus und der Apostelgeschichte.* Elberfeld: R. L. Friderichs, 1881.

Schubart, W. "Ein Platon-Papyrus." *Journal of Juristic Papyrology* 4 (1950): 83–7.

Schwager, R. *Must there be Scapegoats? Violence and Redemption in the Bible.* San Francisco: Harper and Row, 1987.

Schwarzbaum, H. "Talmudic-Midrashic Affinities of Some Aesopic Fables." *Laographia* 22 (1965): 466–83.

Seaford, R. "Thunder, Lightning, and Earthquakes in the *Bacchae* and the Acts of the Apostles. In *What is God? Studies in the Nature of Greek Divinity*, edited by A. B. Lloyd, 139–51. London: Duckworth, 1997.

Seeley, D. *The Noble Death: Graeco-Roman Martyrology and Paul's Concept of Salvation.* Sheffield: JSOT Press, 1990.

Segal, A. *Theatres in Roman Palestine and Provincia Arabia.* Leiden: Brill, 1995.

Segal, A. "Theatre." In *Oxford Encyclopedia of Archaeology of the Near East*, vol. 5, edited by E. M. Meyers, 199–202. Oxford: Oxford University Press, 1997.

Sherwin-White, A. N. *Roman Society and Roman Law in the New Testament*. Oxford: Clarendon, 1963.

Shiner, W. "Creating Plot in Episodic Narratives: The Life of Aesop and the Gospel of Mark." In *Ancient Fiction and Early Christian Narrative*, edited by R. F. Hock, J. B. Chance, and J. Perkins, 155–76. Atlanta: Scholars Press, 1998.

Sider, D. *The Library of the Villa dei Papiri at Herculaneum*. Los Angeles: J. Paul Getty Museum, 2005.

Siegert, F. "Philo and the New Testament." In *The Cambridge Companion to Philo*, edited by A. Kamesar, 175–209. Cambridge: Cambridge University Press, 2009.

Smend, F. "Untersuchungen zu den Acta-Darstellungen von der Bekehrung des Paulus." *Angelos* 1 (1925): 34–45.

Smith, M. "Palestinian Judaism in the First Century." In *Israel: Its Role in Civilization*, edited by M. Davis, 67–81. New York: Jewish Theological Seminary, 1956.

Snell, B., ed. *Griechische Papyri der Hamburger Staats- und Universitäts-Bibliothek*. Hamburg: J. J. Augustin, 1954.

Soards, M. L. "The Historical and Cultural Setting of Luke and Acts." In *New Views on Luke-Acts*, edited by E. Richard, 33–47. Collegeville: The Liturgical Press, 1990.

Soards, M. L. *The Speeches in Acts: Their Content, Context, and Concerns*. Louisville: Westminster/John Knox Press, 1994.

Sparks, H. F. D. "The Semitisms of St. Luke's Gospel." *The Journal of Theological Studies* 44 (1943): 129–38.

Sparks, H. F. D. "The Semitisms of the Acts." *The Journal of Theological Studies*, n.s., 1 (1950): 16–28.

Spengel, L. *Rhetores Graeci*. Vol. 2. Leipzig: Teubner, 1854.

Stambaugh, J. E., and D. L. Balch. *The New Testament in Its Social Environment*. Philadelphia: Westminster, 1986.

Starr, R. J. "The Circulation of Literary Texts in the Roman World." *Classical Quarterly* 37 (1987): 213–23.

Steffen, G. *De canone qui dicitur Aristophanis et Aristarchi*. Leipzig: Typis Reuschi, 1876.

Stendahl, K. *Paul Among Jews and Gentiles*. Philadelphia: Fortress, 1976.

Sterling, G. E. "Mors Philosophi: The Death of Jesus in Luke." *The Harvard Theological Review* 94 (2001): 383–402.

Stökl, D. J. "The Christian Exegesis of the Scapegoat between Jews and Pagans." In *Sacrifice in Religious Experience*, edited by A. I. Baumgarten, 207–32. Leiden: Brill, 2002.

Strecker, G., U. Schnelle, and G. Seelig, eds. *Neuer Wettstein: Texte zum Neuen Testament aus Griechentum und Hellenismus* (II/1–2: *Texte zur Briefliteratur und zur Johannesapokalypse*). Berlin: Walter de Gruyter, 1996.

Strijdom, J. "On Social Justice: Comparing Paul with Plato, Aristotle and the Stoics." *Hervormde Teologiese Studies* 63 (2007): 19–48.

Strocka, V. M. *Die Wandmalerei der Hanghäuser in Ephesos*. Vienna: Österreichische Akademie der Wissenschaften, 1977.

Sudhaus, S. *Philodemi Volumina Rhetorica*. Vol. 2. Leipzig: Teubner, 1896.

Surkau, H. W. *Martyrien in jüdischer und frühchristlicher Zeit*. Göttingen: Vandenhoeck & Ruprecht, 1938.

Symeonoglou, S. *The Topography of Thebes from the Bronze Age to Modern Times*. Princeton: Princeton University Press, 1985.

256 *Bibliography*

Talbert, C. H. *Literary Patterns, Theological Themes, and the Genre of Luke-Acts*. Missoula: Scholars Press, 1974.

Tcherikover, V. *Hellenistic Civilization and the Jews*. Philadelphia: Jewish Publication Society of America, 1959.

Thom, J. C. *Cleanthes' Hymn to Zeus*. Tübingen: Mohr Siebeck, 2005.

Turner, E. G. "Dramatic Representations in Graeco-Roman Egypt: How Long Do They Continue?" *L'Antiquité Classique* 32 (1963): 120–8.

Turner, E. G. "P.Oxy. L 3533: Menander's *Epitrepontes*." *The Oxyrhynchus Papyri* 50 (1983): 36–48.

Ursing, U. *Studien zur griechischen Fabel*. Lund: H. Ohlsson, 1930.

Usener, H. *Dionysii Halicarnassensis Librorum de Imitatione Reliquiae Epistulaeque Criticae Duae*. Bonn: M. Cohen, 1889.

Uziel, J., T. Lieberman, and A. Solomon. "The Excavations beneath Wilson's Arch: New Light on Roman Period Jerusalem." *Tel Aviv: Journal of the Institute of Archaeology of Tel Aviv University* 46 (2019): 237–66.

van der Horst, P. "The Altar of the 'Unknown God' in Athens (Acts 17:23) and the Cults of 'Unknown Gods' in the Hellenistic and Roman Periods." *Aufstieg und Niedergang der römischen Welt* II 18, no. 2 (1989): 1426–56.

van Dijk, G.-J. *AINOI, ΛOΓOI, MYΘOI: Fables in Archaic, Classical, and Hellenistic Greek Literature*. Leiden: Brill, 1997.

van Henten, J. W. *Martyrdom and Noble Death: Selected Texts from Graeco-Roman, Jewish and Christian Antiquity*. London and New York: Routledge, 2002.

Vegge, T. *Paulus und das antike Schulwesen: Schule und Bildung des Paulus*. Berlin: Walter de Gruyter, 2006.

Vernant, J.-P., and P. Vidal-Naquet. *Tragedy and Myth in Ancient Greece*. Brighton: Harvester Press, 1981.

Vernesi, C. et al. "Genetic Characterization of the Body Attributed to the Evangelist Luke." *Proceedings of the National Academy of Sciences* 98, no. 23 (2001): 13, 460–3.

Vernesi, C., et al. "Caratterizzazione genetica del corpo attribuito a San Luca." In *San Luca evangelista testimone della fede che unisce. Atti del Congresso internazionale, Padova, 16–21 ottobre 2000*, vol. 2, edited by V. T. W. Marin and F. G. B. Trolese, 337–53. Padua: Istituto per la storia ecclesiastica Padovana, 2003.

Vlček, E. "Studio antropologico del cranio attribuito a San Luca della Cattedrale di San Vito di Praga." In *San Luca evangelista testimone della fede che unisce. Atti del Congresso internazionale, Padova, 16–21 ottobre 2000*, vol. 2, edited by V. T. W. Marin and F. G. B. Trolese, 201–54. Padua: Istituto per la storia ecclesiastica Padovana, 2003.

Vögeli, A. "Lukas und Euripides." *Theologische Zeitschrift* 9 (1953): 415–38.

von Arnim, J. *Stoicorum veterum fragmenta*. Vol. 1. Leipzig: Teubner, 1905.

von Wilamowitz-Moellendorff, U. *Die Griechische Literatur des Altertums*. Leipzig: Teubner, 1907.

Vössing, K. "Augustins Schullaufbahn und das sog. dreistufige Bildungssystem." In *L'Africa Romana*, vol. 2, edited by A. Mastino, 881–900. Sassari: Gallizzi, 1992.

Vouga, F. *An die Galater*. Tübingen: Mohr Siebeck, 1998.

Vouga, F. "Die Parabeln Jesu und die Fabeln Äsops: Ein Beitrag zur Gleichnisforschung und zur Problematik der Literarisierung der Erzählungen der Jesus-Tradition." *Wort und Dienst* 26 (2001): 149–64.

Wallace, D. R. *The Gospel of God: Romans as Paul's Aeneid*. Eugene: Pickwick, 2008.

Walters, P. *The Assumed Authorial Unity of Luke and Acts: A Reassessment of the Evidence*. Cambridge: Cambridge University Press, 2009.

Bibliography 257

Watkins, C. *How to Kill a Dragon: Aspects of Indo-European Poetics.* Oxford: Oxford University Press, 1995.

Watson, D. F. "The *Life of Aesop* and the Gospel of Mark: Two Ancient Approaches to Elite Values." *Journal of Biblical Literature* 129 (2010): 699–716.

Weaver, J. B. *Plots of Epiphany: Prison-Escape in Acts of the Apostles.* Berlin: Walter de Gruyter, 2004.

Webster, T. B. L. *Monuments Illustrating Tragedy and Satyr Play.* London: University of London Institute of Classical Studies, 1967.

Webster, T. B. L., J. R. Green, and A. Seeberg. *Monuments Illustrating New Comedy.* Vol. 1. 3rd ed. London: University of London Institute of Classical Studies, 1995.

Weinreich, O. "Gebet und Wunder." In *Genethliakon Wilhelm Schmid,* edited by F. Focke et al., 280–341. Stuttgart: W. Kohlhammer, 1929.

Weiss, J. "Beiträge zur Paulinischen Rhetorik." In *Theologische Studien: Festschrift für Bernard Weiss,* edited by C. R. Gregory et al., 165–247. Göttingen: Vandenhoeck and Ruprecht, 1897.

Weiss, J. *Der erste Korintherbrief.* Göttingen: Vandenhoeck and Ruprecht, 1910.

Weiss, Z. "Buildings for Mass Entertainment: Tradition and Innovation in Herodian Construction." *Near Eastern Archaeology* 77 (2014): 98–107.

Weitzmann, K. "Illustrations of Euripides and Homer in the Mosaics of Antioch." In *Antioch-on-the-Orontes III The Excavations of 1937–1939,* edited by R. Stillwell, 233–47. Princeton: Princeton University Press, 1941.

Wellhausen, J. *Der syrische Evangelienpalimpsest vom Sinai.* Göttingen: Dieterichschen Verlagsbuchhandlung, 1895.

Wellhausen, J. "Review of A. Meyer's Jesu Muttersprache." *Göttingische gelehrte Anzeigen* 158 (1896): 265–8.

Wendland, P. "Jesus als Saturnalien Koenig." *Hermes* 33 (1898): 175–9.

Wendland, P. *Die urchristlichen Literaturformen.* Tübingen: Mohr Siebeck, 1912.

West, M. L. "The Dictaean Hymn to the Kouros." *Journal of Hellenic Studies* 85 (1965): 149–59.

West, M. L. *Hesiod: Works and Days.* Oxford: Clarendon, 1978.

West, M. L. *The Orphic Poems.* Oxford: Clarendon, 1983.

Wettstein, J. J. *H ΚΑΙΝΗ ΔΙΑΘΗΚΗ, Novum Testamentum Graecum editionis receptae cum lectionibus variantibus codicum MSS., editionum aliarum, versionum et Patrum, nec non commentario pleniore ex scriptoribus veteribus Hebraeis, Graecis et Latinis Historiam et vim verborum illustrante opera et studio Joannis Jacobi Wetstenii.* Vols. 1–2. Amsterdam: Dommeriana, 1751–1752.

Wick, P. "Jesus gegen Dionysos? Ein Beitrag zur Kontextualisierung des Johannesevangeliums." *Biblica* 85 (2004): 179–98.

Wiechers, A. *Aesop in Delphi.* Meisenheim am Glan: Hain, 1961.

Wifstrand, A. "Lukas och den grekiska klassicismen." *Svensk Exegetisk Årsbok* 5 (1940): 139–51.

Wifstrand, A. "Lukas och Septuaginta." *Svensk Teologisk Kvartalskrift* 16 (1940): 243–62.

Wilckens, U. *Die Missionsreden der Apostelgeschichte.* Neukirchen-Vluyn: Neukirchener Verlag, 1961.

Wilcox, M. *The Semitisms of Acts.* Oxford: Clarendon, 1965.

Willis, W. H. "A Census of the Literary Papyri from Egypt." *Greek, Roman, and Byzantine Studies* 9 (1968): 205–41.

Wills, L. M. *The Quest of the Historical Gospel: Mark, John, and the Origins of the Gospel Genre.* London: Routledge, 1997.

Bibliography

Wills, L. M. "The Aesop Tradition." In *The Historical Jesus in Context*, edited by A.-J. Levine, D. C. Allison, and J. D. Crossan, 222–37. Princeton: Princeton University Press, 2006.

Windisch, H. "Die Christusepiphanie vor Damaskus (Act 9, 22 und 26) und ihre religionsgeschichtlichen Parallelen." *Zeitschrift für die neutestamentliche Wissenschaft* 31 (1932): 1–23.

Wittkowsky, V. "'Pagane' Zitate im Neuen Testament." *Novum Testamentum* 51 (2009): 107–26.

Wojciechowski, M. "Aesopic Tradition in the New Testament." *Journal of Greco-Roman Christianity and Judaism* 5 (2008): 99–109.

Zahn, Th. *Das Evangelium des Matthäus*. Leipzig: G. Böhme, 1903.

Zahn, Th. *Introduction to the New Testament*. Vol. 1. New York: Charles Scribner's Sons, 1909.

Zahn, Th. *Die Apostelgeschichte des Lucas*. Vol. 2. Leipzig: A. Deichert, 1921.

Zalateo, G. "Papiri scolastici." *Aegyptus* 41 (1961): 160–235.

Zeller, D. "Die Bildlogik des Gleichnisses Mt 11:16/Lk 7:31." *Zeitschrift für die neutestamentliche Wissenschaft* 68 (1977): 252–7.

Zeller, E. *Die Apostelgeschichte nach ihrem Inhalt und Ursprung kritisch untersucht*. Stuttgart: Carl Mäcken, 1854.

Ziebarth, E. *Aus der antiken Schule: Sammlung griechischer Texte auf Papyrus, Holtztafeln, Ostraka*. Bonn: A. Marcus & E. Weber, 1910.

Zuntz, G. *An Inquiry into the Transmission of the Plays of Euripides*. Cambridge: Cambridge University Press, 1965.

Index of Modern Authors

Adrados, F. R. 119, 124, 135, 139
Aland, K. 17
Alexander, L. C. A. 25–6, 93, 222, 224
Alexandre, M. 78, 212
Allison, D. C. 92, 121, 133
Alviar, J. J. 22
Andreassi, M. 121
Arend, W. 102
Argyle, A. W. 23
Austin, C. 7

Balch, D. L. 152–3, 229
Barnes, T. D. 229
Barrett, C. K. 95–6, 110, 153, 196, 222
Bartelink, G. J. M. 89
Bastianini, G. 7
Bauckham, R. 2
Bauernfeind, O. 195, 200
Baur, F. C. 23
Bazant, J. 191
Beare, W. 178
Beavis, M. A. 121
Bellinati, C. 18
Benz, E. 213
Berger, K. 152
Berger-Doer, G. 191
Betz, H. D. 214–15
Beudel, P. 34
Bieber, M. 181–2
Billig, Y. 176
Birt, Th. 106
Black, M. 107
Blass, F. 46, 91, 96, 109–10
Bloedow, E. F. 166
Boccaccini, G. 2
Böhlig, H. 2, 189
Bonhöffer, A. 2
Bonner, S. F. 33
Bonz, M. 45, 93
Booth, A. D. 34
Bouquiaux-Simon, O. 59
Boyd, G. A. 97

Brant, J-A. A. 1, 83, 92
Brashear, W. 37
Brawley, R. L. 24
Bremer, J. M. 39, 66
Bremmer, J. 124
Bruce, F. F. 91, 96, 110, 148, 164, 222
Bultmann, R. 2, 189
Burkert, W. 124, 214

Cadbury, H. J. 22, 25–6, 108, 148
Cauderlier, P. 35
Çelik, Ö. 175, 179, 181–2
Chadwick, H. 152
Chambry, E. 121–45
Charitonidis, S. 181
Chase, F. H. 227
Clark, A. C. 23
Clarke, W. K. L. 25
Clarysse, W. 34
Cockerel, D. 22
Colaclides, P. 198
Collart, P. 34
Collins, A. Y. 124, 214
Collins, J. J. 3, 24, 150
Compton, T. 124
Conybeare, C. 16
Conzelmann, H. 95, 148, 196, 201, 204, 222
Cook, A. B. 163
Cook, J. G. 5
Courcelle, P. 164
Cramer, J. A. 11, 53
Cribiore, R. 33–5, 39, 45, 58–60, 66–7, 88, 120, 150, 209
Crusius, O. 135–6
Csapo, E. 179, 182
Cukrowski, K. L. 91–2, 110
Cumont, F. 189

Davies, W. D. 133
Davoli, P. 45
Debrunner, A. 46
Debut, J. 34, 59

Deissmann, A. 157, 209
DeMaris, R. E. 124
Denaux, A. 25
Devreesse, R. 22
De Zwaan, J. 22
Dibelius, M. 12, 108, 147–8, 153, 155, 164, 195, 203–4, 206
Dickey, E. 49
Diels, H. 161
Dihle, A. 178
Dithmar, R. 121
Dodds, E. R. 195, 200, 204
Dodson, J. R. 1
Dorandi, T. 211
Döring, K. 213
Doutreleau, L. 148, 157
Droge, J. 216
Dunbabin, K. M. D. 179, 182
Dupont, J. 21

Earp, J. W. 76
Easterling, P. E. 34, 179
Eddy, P. R. 97
Edmonds, J. M. 11
Edwards, M. J. 150
Ehrhardt, A. A. T. 133
Ehrman, B. D. 217
Eichhorn, J. G. 12
Elliott, S. S. 121
Estienne, H. 5
Evans, C. A. 214

Farnell, L. R. 124
Farrar, F. W. 152
Fascher, E. 213
Feldman, L. H. 80
Fischel, H. A. 24
Fisher, B. F. 119
Fitzmyer, J. A. 2, 133
Flusser, D. 128, 133–4
Foakes Jackson, F. J. 16, 22, 25, 91, 95–6, 108, 110, 153, 157, 164, 222, 229
Fraser, P. M. 52
Frazer, J. G. 124
Friedländer, L. 178
Friesen, C. J. P. 78, 188, 199, 204
Froelich, M. 127
Funk, R. W. 46

Galé, J. M. 34
Gallazzi, C. 7
Gallo, I. 211
Gathercole, S. J. 129, 144
Gawlina, M. 214
Gempf, C. 21, 148
Gentili, B. 177
Gibbs, L. 121
Gibson, C. A. 33
Gibson, M. D. 148, 161–4
Ginouvès, R. 181
Girard, R. 124
Glockmann, G. 89, 91
Goldstein, J. A. 216, 219
Goodenough, E. R. 24
Grammatiki, K. 125
Green, J. R. 179, 181–2
Grenfell, B. P. 5, 68–9
Gressmann, H. 164
Gruen, E. S. 150
Guaglianone, A. 119
Guéraud, O. 34, 37–42
Guerriero, P. 20
Gutzwiller, K. 175, 179–82

Hackett, J. 201, 204
Hadas, M. 216, 219
Haenchen, E. 91, 96, 103, 110, 148, 196, 201, 204, 222
Halm, K. 121, 129, 132–40, 145
Hamerton-Kelly, R. G. 124
Harnack, A. 213
Harris, J. R. 16, 160–4
Harris, W. V. 31
Harrison, J. E. 124
Hausrath, A. 121, 126, 129, 132–3, 135, 139–40, 145
Hays, R. B. 2
Hedrick, C. W. 83, 92, 206
Heinemann, I. 78
Helmbold, W. C. 72
Hemer, C. 148
Hengel, M. 3, 23, 24, 80, 88, 187
Hense, O. 154
Hepding, H. 156
Hervieux, L. 139
Hesseling, D. C. 58, 120
Hezser, C. 80
Hicks, R. I. 214

Index of Modern Authors

Hock, R. F. 66, 83–4, 88, 92, 121
Hogeterp, A. 25
Holl, K. 157
Holzberg, N. 119
Hommel, H. 153, 226
Houston, G. 69
How, W. W. 133
Howard, W. F. 25
Howell, E. B. 164, 214
Hughes, D. D. 124
Humphrey, J. H. 175
Hunt, A. S. 5, 68, 69
Huskinson, J. 175, 182

Jacobs, J. C. 139
Jacquier, E. 26
Jay, J. 184
Jenkins, C. 150
Jervell, J. 24
Jipp, J. W. 214, 223
Johnson, L. T. 97, 164
Jones, C. P. 179, 182
Jouguet, P. 34, 37–44
Jülicher, A. 121, 133

Kahil, L. 181
Kaibel, G. 180
Kamerbeek, J. C. 194–5
Kasher, A. 24
Kaster, R. A. 34
Kauppi, L. A. 24
Keener, C. S. 95–8, 148, 152, 195, 200,
  214, 222–3
Kellenberger, E. 139
Kennedy, G. A. 33, 148
Kenyon, F. G. 34, 36, 42
Kidd, D. 153
Kindstrand, J. F. 88
Klauck, H.-J. 1
Kleberg, T. 210
Klinghardt, M. 24
Kloppenborg, J. S. 217–20, 224
Knopf, R. 2
Knox, B. M. W. 34
Kock, T. 11
Kokolakis, M. 166
Königsmann, B. L. 21
Koskenniemi, E. 78, 80, 89, 184
Kramer, J. 34, 49

Kratz, R. 200
Krenkel, M. 79
Krüger, J. 66

La Penna, A. 119
Labahn, M. 9, 128
Lagrange, M.-J. 26, 215
Lake, K. 16, 22, 25, 91, 95–6, 108, 110, 153,
  157, 164, 222, 229
Lang, M. 9, 128
Larsson, K. 97
Lauxtermann, M. D. 138
Lawlor, H. J. 164
Lenaerts, J. 59
Leonardi, G. 24
Levi, D. 175, 182
Leyerle, B. 178
Lichtenberger, A. 176
Lieberman, S. 24
Lieberman, T. 176
Lightfoot, J. B. 153, 215
Lincicum, D. 76, 212
Ling, P. H. 153
Luz, U. 131
Luzzatto, M. J. 119

Maas, P. 139
Maccoby, H. 189
MacDonald, D. R. 1, 45, 66, 89–98, 110,
  195, 204, 223
McMahan, C. T. 89
McVay, J. K. 214
Maehler, M. 150
Malherbe, A. J. 152, 209
Maltomini, F. 66
Marcotte, D. 59
Marguerat, D. 196
Margulies, Z. 139
Marin, V. T. W. 18–20
Marrou, H.-I. 33–4, 88, 120, 150
Marshall, C. W. 180
Martin, M. W. 32
Marx, F. A. 216, 219
Mason, S. 79
Matějka, J. 19
Mattill, A. J., Jr. 105
Mendelson, A. 78, 212
Mertens, P. 8, 36, 59
Metzger, B. M. 101

Index of Modern Authors

Meyer, R. 24
Millis, B. W. 190
Milne, H. J. M. 22
Milne, J. G. 34
Milnor, K. 235
Minn, H. R. 153
Mitchell, M. M. 97, 214
Mitchell, S. 179
Moessner, D. P. 220
Moles, J. L. 164, 193, 200, 204
Molin, G. 20
Molinié, G. 83
Morgan, T. 33–4, 59–60, 66–7, 88, 120
Moulton, J. H. 25
Murray, G. 124
Musurillo, H. A. 216

Nautin, P. 148, 157
Nervegna, S. 67, 178–81
Nestle, W. 194–6, 204
Neyrey, J. H. 24, 218
Nicklin, T. 163
Norden, E. 2, 26, 147–8, 153, 164

Olson, S. D. 190
O'Neil, E. N. 72
Otranto, R. 69

Pack, R. A. 34, 58–9
Papathomopoulos, M. 125
Parker, R. 124
Parsons, M. C. 23, 32
Parsons, P. J. 42
Patrich, J. 176
Perdrize, P. 44
Perry, B. E. 119, 121, 125, 144
Pervo, R. I. 23, 79, 83, 98, 105, 110, 121, 195, 201, 204, 229
Pesch, R. 153
Peterson, W. M. 53
Pfättisch, J. M. 213
Pfeiffer, R. 52, 191
Phillips, T. E. 127
Pitts, A. W. 1
Plepelits, K. 83
Plümacher, E. 25, 148
Plunkett, M. A. 217
Pohlenz, M. 153, 164
Porath, Y. 175

Porter, S. E. 21, 214
Postlethwaite, N. 166
Powell, J. U. 154
Praeder, S. M. 92, 96, 103, 110
Priest, J. F. 144
Pruneti, P. 68

Ramsay, W. M. 164
Rank, L. P. 225
Ratzan, D. M. 45
Reardon, B. P. 83
Reece, S. 89–90, 134, 165, 216, 223–4, 227
Reich, R. 176
Reis, D. M. 223
Reitzenstein, R. 189
Renan, E. 193
Renehan, R. 153–5, 164, 200, 215
Rigato, M. L. 24
Robbins, V. K. 24, 91, 94
Rochette, B. 50
Roetzel, C. J. 2
Römer, C. 66
Ronconi, A. 216
Ross, W. 134, 138
Rothschild, C. K. 164–6
Runia, D. T. 77, 213
Rusam, D. 2
Rydbeck, L. 26

Sala, B. 18
Salomone, S. 121
Salviulo, G. 20
Sanders, E. P. 2
Sandnes, K. O. 78, 89, 97, 222
Sandys, J. E. 52
Saudelli, L. 78
Scaer, P. J. 217–18, 220, 224
Scappaticcio, M. C. 235
Schierling, M. J. 83
Schierling, S. 83
Schlier, H. 215
Schmid, L. 203
Schnabel, E. J. 153
Schneider, F. E. 45
Schnelle, U. 9, 128, 214–15
Scholten, J. H. 23
Schubart, W. 211
Schwager, R. 124
Schwarzbaum, H. 145

Index of Modern Authors

Seaford, R. 201
Seeberg, A. 179–82
Seeley, D. 216
Seelig, G. 9, 214–15
Segal, A. 176–8
Segovia, C. A. 2
Sherwin-White, A. N.
Shiner, W. 24
Sider, D. 235
Siegert, F. 213
Skeat, T. C. 22
Slater, W. J. 179
Smend, F. 204
Smith, M. 3
Snell, B. 150
Soards, M. L. 12, 24
Solomon, A. 176
Sparks, H. F. D. 25
Spengel, L. 132
Stambaugh, J. E. 152
Starr, R. J. 210
Steffen, G. 52
Stendahl, K. 2
Sterling, G. E. 150, 217
Stökl, D. J. 124
Straus, J. A. 59
Strecker, G. 9, 214–15
Strijdom, J. 214
Strocka, V. M. 182
Sudhaus, S. 211
Surkau, H. W. 219
Symeonoglou, S. 177

Tabor, J. D. 216
Talbert, C. H. 22, 91
Tcherikover, V. 24
Thom, J. C. 153–4
Trolese, F. G. B. 18–20, 24
Turner, E. G. 180

Ursing, U. 139
Usener, H. 53
Uziel, J. 176

van der Horst, P. 157
van Dijk, G.-J. 119

van Henten, J. W. 216
Vegge, T. 213
Vernant, J.-P. 124
Vernesi, C. 20
Vidal-Naquet, P. 124
Vlček, E. 19
Vögeli, A. 196, 201–4
von Arnim, J. 154
von Wilamowitz-Moellendorff, U. 147
Vössing, K. 34
Vouga, F. 121, 215

Wachsmuth, C. 154
Wallace, D. R. 45
Walters, P. 23
Watkins, C. 225
Watson, D. F. 121
Weaver, J. B. 97, 196, 199–200
Webster, T. B. L. 179, 181–2
Weinreich, O. 199–200, 204
Weiss, J. 2
Weiss, Z. 176
Weitzmann, K. 175, 182
Wellhausen, J. 131
Wells, J. 133
Wendland, P. 2, 124
West, M. L. 157, 166, 225
Wettstein, J. J. 8–9, 193
Wick, P. 187–8
Wiechers, A. 124
Wifstrand, A. 25–6
Wilckens, U. 148
Wilcox, M. 24–5
Willis, W. H. 59
Wills, L. M. 121, 124
Windisch, H. 204
Wittkowsky, V. 150
Wojciechowski, M. 128, 133
Wouters, A. 34

Zahn, Th. 133, 153, 164
Zalateo, G. 34
Zeller, D. 131
Zeller, E. 105
Ziebarth, E. 34
Zuntz, G. 172

Index of Ancient Passages

Old Testament

Genesis
9:27 — 2

Judges
9:8-15 — 139

1 Samuel
14:45 — 107

2 Samuel
14:11 — 107

1 Kings
1:52 — 107

2 Chronicles
24:20-2 — 219

Isaiah
61:1-2 — 122

Deuterocanonical Works

2 Maccabees
6:7 — 187
6:18-31 — 212, 216, 219
7:1-42 — 212, 216, 219
7:19 — 195
14:33 — 187

3 Maccabees
2:28-30 — 187

4 Maccabees
5:1–7:23 — 212, 216, 219
8:1–18:24 — 212, 216, 219

Sirach
13:2 — 120–1, 143
39:1-4 — 143

New Testament

Matthew
8:28-34 — 3
10:30 — 107
11:7-8 — 128–30
11:17-19 — 130–4
13:6-9 — 128
13:47-8 — 128
13:53-8 — 122
23:13 — 144
25:14-30 — 128
26:37-9 — 217
26:56 — 218
26:67 — 218
27:26-31 — 218
27:39-46 — 218
27:54 — 218

Mark
4:24 — 140
6:1-6 — 122
13:14 — 22
14:33-6 — 217
14:50 — 218
14:65 — 218
15:15-20 — 218
15:29-34 — 218
15:39 — 218

Luke
1:1-4 — 17, 25, 142
1:3 — 21–14, 209
4:14-30 — 122–7
7:24-5 — 128–30, 142–3
7:32-4 — 130–4, 143
11:5-8 — 128
11:52 — 144
12:7 — 107
21:18 — 11, 107
22:41-2 — 217
22:45 — 217

266 Index of Ancient Passages

22:51	218
22:61	218
23:4	218
23:13-15	218
23:22	218
23:27-31	218
23:35-7	218
23:39-48	218
23:47	219
24:13-35	89
24:25	134–43

John

20:30-1	22
21:24-5	22

Acts

1:1	21–22, 209
1:1-2	25
1:4	21–22
1:15-26	24
4:19	220–2
5:17-42	194, 197–202
5:29	221–2
5:39	194–7, 221
8:4-25	24
9:1-19	205–8, 223
9:16	224
11:28	16
12:1-19	197–202
12:7	198
12:10	198
12:20-3	24
13:4-12	24
14:8-18	24
14:11-13	24
16:6-8	21
16:10-17	16, 95
16:12-40	21
16:16-18	24
16:16-24	201
16:16-40	197–202
16:26	198
17:16-34	24, 192, 222–9
17:18	227
17:18-21	192
17:19	229
17:19-20	228
17:22	229

17:23	147–69
17:24-6	165–6, 193
17:28	4–6, 142, 147–69, 192, 224–6
17:31-2	153, 193, 227
17:34	11, 193, 228
18:1-17	21
18:23	21
19:1	21
19:9	147
19:17-20	24
19:23-8	24
19:23-41	24
19:28-40	174
19:35	24
20:5-15	16, 95
20:7-9	147
21:1-18	16, 95
21:39	142
21:40–22:21	205–8, 223, 223
22:14-15	223
24:10-21	223
25:6-12	223
25:23–26:32	205–8, 223
26:1-29	223
26:14	142, 202–8
26:24	202
27:1–28:16	16, 21, 92, 93–112
27:7-20	99–101
27:15	101–2
27:21-6	102–5
27:29	105–6, 111
27:34	106–8
27:39	108, 111
27:41	91, 96–7, 108–12
28:4	24
28:11	24

Romans

12:4-8	214

1 Corinthians

12:12-31	214
13:12	214
15:33	5–6, 67, 158, 173

2 Corinthians

4:18	214
10:10-11	115

11:6	115		*Stromata*	
11:23-7	116		1.14.59	5, 158
			1.19.91	5, 151, 158
Galatians			1.21.145	17
6:3	10–11, 215		4.25.162	188, 191
			5.12.82	17
Ephesians			5.14.101	151
4:11-16	214		6.2.14	191
			7.6.33	121, 144
Colossians				
3:1-2	214		Didymus Caecus	
4:10-14	15–17, 23		*In Genesim*	
			227	157
2 Timothy				
4:6	10		Epiphanius	
4:11	15		*Index apostolorum*	
			116–17	18
Titus				
1.12	5–6, 12, 157, 160–4		Eusebius	
			Historia ecclesiastica	
Philemon			3.4	18
23-25	16		6.25.6	17
24	15, 17		6.25.14	17
[Gospel of Thomas			*Praeparatio evangelica*	
78	129		13.12.6	150
102	121, 144]			
			Gregory of Nazianzus	
Early Christian Authors			*Orationes*	
			33	18
Athanasius				
Contra gentes			Irenaeus	
16.33	159		*Adversus haereses*	
17.11	159		3.1.1	17
			3.14.1–4	16–17, 21
De incarnatione				
41-2	159		Isho'dad of Merv	
			Commentarium in acta	
Augustine			*apostolorum*	148, 161–4
Confessionum libri XIII				
1.14	87		Jerome	
7.9.15	159		*Commentariorum in evangelium*	
			Matthaei prologus	18
De civitate Dei				
16.23	159		*De viris illustribus*	
			7	18
Clement of Alexandria				
Protrepticus			*Epistulae*	
7.73	151		70.2	5
12.118-23	188, 191		22.29.7	1

Epistula ad Damasum	
20.4	13, 25

Commentarium ad Esaiam	
3.6.9	13, 25

Justin Martyr
1 Apologia	
3	213
5	213
8	213
21	188
25	188
39	159–60
44	213
54	188
59–60	213

2 Apologia	
3	213
10	213
12	213

Origen
Commentarium in epistulam I ad Corinthios	
XLIII	150

Contra Celsum	
2.33–5	188–9, 191, 199
8.42	188–9, 191

Procopius
De aedificiis	
1.4.9–24	18

Socrates Scholasticus
Historia ecclesiastica	
3.16.24–6	5

Tertullian
Ad nationes	
2.9	156

Adversus Marcionem	
1.9	156
4.2	17

Apologeticus pro Christianis	
47	1

De praescriptione haereticorum	
7	1

Theodore of Mopsuestia
Commentarium in acta apostolorum	160–1

Theophilus of Antioch
Ad Autolycum	
2.8	150–1

Rabbinic Literature
b. B. Qam. 60b	121, 144–5
b. Meg. 9b	2
b. Shab. 66b	174
y. Meg. 1:11, 71b	2
y. Shab. 6:8, 8c	174
y. Taʾan. 1:4, 64b	174
Gen. Rab. 36:8	2

Greek Authors

Aeschylus
Agamemnon	
1624	142, 203

Eumenides	
647–8	228

Prometheus Bound	
323	203

Aesop
Fables	
Chambry 24	132–3
Chambry 25	128
Chambry 40	134–43
Chambry 52	121, 145
Chambry 85	128
Chambry 101	129–30, 133
Chambry 128	137
Chambry 155	126
Chambry 191	126
Chambry 253	139
Chambry 286	128
Chambry 345	127–8

Index of Ancient Passages

Chambry 355	121, 143
Hausrath 192	126
Perry 74	121
Perry 114	140
Life	124–7
Aphthonius	
Progymnasmata	56–7
Apollonius	
(paradoxographer)	
Historiae mirabiles	
1.1–4	156
Aratus	
Phaenomena	
1–18	149–53
5	142
Aristophanes	
Clouds	
264–6	229
423–4	229
Plutus	
653–747	228
Wasps	
1446–9	125
Aristotle	
Constitution of Athens	
1	156
Nicomachean Ethics	
1128a	31
Poetics	
1456a	184
Rhetoric	
1418a	156
Athenaeus	
Deipnosophist	
9.29	41

Callimachus	
Epigrams	
48	191
Hymn to Zeus	
4–9	167
8–9	162–3
Chariton	
Callirhoe	83–4
6.1.6.3	105
Cleanthes	
Hymn to Zeus	
1–6	153–5
Dio Chrysostom	
Orations	
10.27	184
11.7–9	183
18.6–17	54, 67
19.5	183
30.1–46	216
32.94	184
43.9–15	211
53.6	87–8
Diodorus Siculus	
Bibliotheca historica	
33.7.7	31
Diogenes Laertius	
Lives of the Philosophers	
1.109–15	156
1.110	156, 165, 224
1.112	160–1
7.147	225
Dionysius of Halicarnassus	
On Arrangement of Words	54
On Imitation	53–4, 67
Rhetoric	
8.8	211
9.11	211

Index of Ancient Passages

Epimenides
"On Minos and
   Rhadamanthus" 155–69, 224, 226

Euripides
Alcestis
344–82 180

Bacchae
23–42 194
43–46 194
45 194
226–7 194, 197–202
284 10
325 194
352–7 197–202
443–50 194, 197–202
488–9 198
494 191
497–514 197–202
506 193
576–659 197–202
635–6 194
794–5 142, 202–8
1255–66 194

Ino
fr. 420 39–40

Ion
8 142

Phoenissae
529–34 39–40

Heraclitus the Grammarian
Homeric Questions
1.5–7 87

Herodotus
Histories
1.141 132
2.134 125
5.71 224

"Hermogenes"
Progymnasmata 56–7
7.1–12 210

Josephus
Jewish Antiquities
15.268 176
15.272 176
15.341 176

Against Apion
1.42–4 219
2.167–8 212
2.232–5 219
2.256–8 212
2.263–4 212

Jewish War
1.415 176

Varia 79–82

Homer
Hymn to Demeter
120–44 101

Iliad
9.240 105

Odyssey
1.1–5 116
3.276–302 100
4.351–586 100
5.116–24 40–41
5.278–493 104
5.299–312 103
5.333–50 103
9.76–192 105
9.138 110
9.146–51 111
9.148–9 110–11
9.151 106, 111–12
9.546 111–12
10.511 111
12.5–7 112
12.7 106
13.113–14 110
13.113–16 111
13.187–90 108, 111
14.192–359 101
14.379–85 101
19.172–7 100
19.172–348 101

Index of Ancient Passages

"Libanius"
Progymnasmata 56–7

Longus
Dapnis and Chloe
2.8.2.5 105
2.23.4.3 105

Lucian
De saltatione
76 175

Philopseudes
3 168

Menander
Thais 5, 67, 158, 173

Nicolaus
Progymnasmata 56–7
58 210

Pausanias
Description of Greece
1.1.4 156
1.34.5 228
9.16.6 177

Philo
De congressu eruditionis gratiae
71–8 212

De ebrietate
177 174

De specialibus legibus
2.229–30 212

Quod omnis probus liber sit
27 219
88–91 219
141 174, 180, 184

Varia 75–8

Philostratus
Life of Apollonius
5.14–15 120
6.3.5 156

Lives of the Sophists
569 167–8

Pindar
Pythian Odes
2.94–5 203
2.172–3 142
10.51–2 105

Plato
Apology 209–15
17a 229
17a–18a 115
20e–23b 223
23a–34b 223–4
24b 223
24b–c 229
25b–c 211
28a 223
28b 211
28e–29a 223
29d 221–2
31d 223
38c 211
40a–c 223
40b–41c 211
41e 10, 215

Cratylus
395e–396b 165, 225–6

Laws
642d–e 156
654d 31
677d–e 156

Phaedo
118 216, 219

Republic
376e–398b 87
462a–464e 214
514a–521b 214

Symposium
210a–212a 214

Plutarch
Alexander
53.4 191

272 *Index of Ancient Passages*

Cato Minor
66–72   216, 219

Crassus
33   191

De fortuna
328d   191

Demosthenes
2.2–3   46

Solon
12.7–12   156

Moralia
323c   46
326a   46
556a   184, 191
611d   187
786e   46
797d   46
854a–b   67
998e   184, 191

Quaestionum convivialium libri IX
4:6   187

Varia   72–4

Stobaeus
Anthology
1.1.12   5, 154

Strabo
Geography
16.2.29   3

Strato
Phoenicides   41

Theon
Progymnasmata   55–56, 132
94–6   167
98   210
101–5   32
111   210

Thucydides
Peloponnesian War
1.126   224

Xenophon
Memorabilia
1.1.10   226
4.7.2   31

Latin Authors
Livy
Ab urbe condita
39.13   188

Quintilian
Institutio oratoria
1.4   55
1.8   55
1.9   32, 120
1.11   67
2.1   32
2.4   32
10.1   55, 67, 149

Suetonius
De rhetoribus
1   32

Tacitus
Annales
15.44   188
15.60–4   216, 219
16.34–5   219

Historiae
5.5   187–8

Vergil
Aeneid
1.81–101   103

Papyri, Ostraca, Tablets, and Inscriptions
Papyri
BKT 9.114   211
Egyptian Museum in Cairo
     no. 65445   37–43

P.Berol. inv. 5865	150	Ostraca		
P.Bodm. XIV	16, 231–2	O.Claud. 1.190	234	
P.Bour. 1	43–5	O.Xer. inv. 871	234	
P.Hamb. 2.121	150			
P.Hamb. 2.167	234	**Tablets**		
P.Haw. 24	234	British Library Manuscripts accession		
P.Herc. 21	235	number Add MS 34186	36–7	
P.Herc. 78	235	T.Bodl.Gk.Inscr. 3019	42	
P.Herc. 395	235	T.Louvre inv. AF 1195	35	
P.Herc. 467	211	T.Vind. 118	235	
P.Herc. 817	235	T.Vind. 452	235	
P.Herc. 1475	235	T.Vind. 854	235	
P.Herc. 1829–31	235	T.Vind. 855	235	
P.Hib. 1.7	5, 173	T.Vind. 856	235	
P.Hib. 182	211	Tabulae ceratae graecae		
P.Iand. 5.90, inv. 210	233	Assendelftianae	58, 120	
P.Mas. 721	234			
P.Narm. inv. 66.362	234	**Inscriptions**		
P.Oxy. 1.30	233	CIG 2759	179	
P.Oxy. 27.2458	180	CIJ II 748–9	174	
P.Oxy. 33.2659	70	IG II² 2318	190	
P.Oxy. 50.3533	67, 180	IG II² 2320	190	
P.Oxy. 50.3554	234	IG V,1 594	157	
P.Oxy. 53.3705	67	IG VII 1760	179	
P.Oxy. 67.4546	180	IG VII 1773	179	
P.Oxy. 78.5162	49	IG XII,4 2:845	179	
P.QaṣrIbrîm inv.		IGUR I 223	180	
78-3-11/1 (L1/2)	233	IThesp 168	179	
P.Ryl. 1.42	233	IThesp 177–9	179	
P.Ryl. 3.473	233	SEG 3.334	179	
P.Sorb. inv. 826	43–5	SEG 16.931	174	
P.Tebt. 2.686	234	SEG 19.335	179	
P.Vindob.Gr. inv.		SEG 25.501	179	
39966	69	SEG 38.1462B	179	
PSI Laur. inv. 19662	70	SIG3 1080	180, 190	